CLASSIC	ROMANTIC	MODERN	
wide variety of instrumental and vocal sonorities; brilliant sound, transparent; much contrast between light and full; wide dynamic range; exploration of higher registers	increase in fullness, richness, and denseness of sound; concern with special color effects; striking contrasts; widened range of pitch and dynamics	extremes of and density in new sonority effects; sharp contrasts of color; tendency to reduce the "sweetness" of sound	QUALITIES OF SOUND
2, 3 to many parts; emphasis on principal melody, with some polyphony, some give-and-take	tendency toward amplification of lines by doublings; active part-writing, often with rich ornamentation; 3, 4 to many parts	1, 2 to many parts; prominent polyphonic action, also give-and-take; also use of baroque, classic, romantic textural layouts	TEXTURE
same consonance values as preceding eras	same consonance values as before; lesser proportion of consonance than previously	consonance no longer a synonym for stability, although traditional ideas of consonance and dissonance still have considerable force	CONSONANCE
dissonance used for harmonic tension, for dramatic emphasis, often without preparation; many "tritone" dissonances	greater saturation of dissonance, often without intervening consonance; dissonances make rich sounds, and represent instability; tritone, 7ths, 9ths, altered intervals	as a rule, considerable saturation of dissonance, with dissonances frequently at points of arrival; functional distinction between consonance and dissonance disappears frequently	DISSONANCE
saturation of cadential action; long-range definition, long-range contrast of key; very strong harmonic drive	retention of classic cadence feeling with tendency toward deceptive and elided resolutions; rapid elusive shifts of tonal center; harmonic color an objective; weakened harmonic drives	partial abandonment of older chord types; substitutes for older cadences; rapid shifts of tonal areas; modal, atonal, polytonal, tone-row, microtonal systems; little harmonic drive	HARMONIC ACTION
wide range of pace and manner; strongly influenced by typical song and dance manners; steady, active pace, with strong accentuation	wide range of pace and manner; appearance of imbalanced, unsteady qualities of movement; preference for slower pace, less vigorous accent	emphasis on active, percussively accented pace, with cross-rhythms and imbalances, often in rapidly paced music; wide range of pace and manner; uncertain, shifting pace often found	MOVEMENT
clear, frequent, strong points of arrival; momentum often carries beyond, aiming for emphatic cadential points	obscured cadences, disguised points of arrival more frequent	in neo-classic and folkloric music well-defined points of arrival; in expressionistic music, uncertain sense of arrival	ARRIVAL
well-defined period structure in all forms and types; extension of periods	in small pieces, clear periodization in symmetrical structure; in larger works, tendency toward asymmetrical phrase structure	as a rule, asymmetrical phrase structure; some use of baroque continuous expansion and classic periodization	PHRASE STRUCTURE

Dominic J. Keller, O. S. B.

McGRAW-HILL SERIES IN MUSIC
Douglas Moore, *Consulting Editor*

Music ∾ The Listener's Art

McGRAW-HILL SERIES IN MUSIC
Douglas Moore, *Consulting Editor*

AtKisson: Basic Counterpoint

Chase: America's Music

Ratner: Music: The Listener's Art

Wagner: Orchestration: A Practical Handbook

Other titles in preparation

Music ~ THE LISTENER'S ART

Leonard G. Ratner
STANFORD UNIVERSITY

McGRAW-HILL BOOK CO., INC.

1957 ⋎ New York ⋎ Toronto ⋎ London

MUSIC—THE LISTENER'S ART

Library of Congress Catalog Card Number 56-11724

Preface

M USIC is an art of listening. This book, therefore, is intended for the listener who wants to increase his understanding of music. It aims to provide him with tools, with means by which he can better analyze, evaluate, and appreciate the music he hears.

We start with the listener's reaction to music. First, we listen. What are the immediate impressions? Sound itself, its strength, its color, then the movement of sound, how it is set in motion, its pace, its regularity, how it reaches a point of arrival. These effects carry expressive values; they become our first criteria. Thus, at the very outset, the listener can interpret his impressions in nontechnical terms.

Afterwards, we discover how specific musical elements and processes—melody, rhythm, texture, harmony, phrase structure—help to create musical impressions. In this way we begin to see the relationship between musical techniques and expressive values in music. In order to show how fundamental musical procedures underlie various types of expression, we have drawn the material for the first section (Chapters 1 and 2) from a wide range of sources, from medieval to modern music, from folk song to symphony. This will enable the listener to make his way more confidently and quickly within the various areas of musical style and expression. The criteria established in the first chapters are used throughout the entire book to guide us in our listening.

The approach described above invites comparison for fuller understanding and greater satisfaction. For this reason, the historical framework is used. It enables us to illustrate systematically different kinds of music; it helps us to visualize the growth which, during history, has given rise to many and various musical styles. A perspective is developed and a sympathy awakened for perhaps unfamiliar modes of musical expression. At no time, however, does historical data take precedence over the actual experience of listening to the music itself. Throughout the second section of this book (Chapters 3 to 8) there is constant reference to the ideas explained in the first section—sound, movement, departure, arrival.

When the layman comes to a music-appreciation class or takes up a book on music, he wants to retain his musical experience, to have it illuminated; he wants the instruction to be organized around what he can hear, what he can grasp by listening. Psychologically this is justified. This need of the listener has been the guiding principle in organizing the entire presentation of this book. It has resulted in establishing the nontechnical criteria of the first chapter, and, throughout the book, in offering the music first, and then discussing it. It is an approach that is sympathetic to the listener's already strong motivations for wanting to know music better.

The greatest organized demand for a book of this kind is in the courses offered in colleges and universities for the general student, courses which usually have such titles as "Music Appreciation," "Survey of Music," or "Introduction to Music." It is hoped that this book will help serve the needs of such instruction. But the musical needs and curiosities of students in such courses are no different from those of the layman who listens to music at home or at a concert. From the public at large there is perhaps an even greater demand for help in musical understanding. The approach adopted in this book—from impression to evaluation, and thence to some insight into the qualities and structures of music—will, we hope, appeal to the listener.

LEONARD G. RATNER

Contents

Chapter *1. The Musical Experience*

WHY DO you listen to music? If you should put this question to a number of people, you might receive answers like these: "I like the beat of music," "I like music for dancing," "I look for attractive tunefulness," "I am moved by the sound of choral singing," "I listen to music for many reasons but I could not begin to describe them to you clearly." Answers to this question would be many and diverse, yet almost no one would reply, "Music means nothing to me." To most of us, music means something; it evokes some response. We obtain some satisfaction in listening to music.

For many, the enjoyment of music does not remain at a standstill. We feel that we can get more satisfaction from the musical experience. We want to make closer contact with music in order to learn more of its nature; thus we can range more broadly and freely in the areas of musical style, form, and expression. This book explores ways of achieving these objectives. It deals, of course, with the techniques of music, but only in order to show how technique is directed toward expressive aims in music and toward the listener's musical experience. In this way, we may get an idea of the composer's intentions, for indeed, the composer uses every musical device for its power to communicate and for its contribution to the musical experience.

Although everyone hears music differently, there is a common ground from which all musical experiences grow. That source is *sound* itself. Sound is the raw material of music. It makes up the body and substance of all musical activity. It is the *point of departure* in the musical experience.

The kinds of sound that can be used for musical purposes are amazingly varied. Throughout the cultures of the world, East and West, a virtually limitless array of sounds has been employed in the service of musical expression. Listen to Oriental theater music, then to an excerpt from a Wagner work; these two are worlds apart in their qualities of sound as well

1

as in almost every other feature, yet each says something of importance to some listeners. Each can stir a listener and evoke a response in him. All music, whether it be the pulsation of primitive tribal drums or the complex coordination of voices and instruments in an opera, has this feature: *it is based upon the power of sound to stir our senses and feelings.*

Yet sound alone is not music. Something has to happen to the sound. *It must move forward in time.* Everything that takes place musically involves the movement of sound. If we hear a series of drumbeats, we receive an impression of movement from one stroke to the next. When sounds follow each other in a pattern of melody, we receive an impression of movement from one tone to the next. All music moves; and because it moves, it is associated with a fundamental truth of existence and experience. We are stirred by impressions of movement because our very lives are constantly in movement. Breathing, the action of the pulse, growth, decay, the change of day and night, as well as the constant flow of physical action—these all testify to the fundamental role that movement plays in our lives. Music appeals to our desire and our need for movement.

Still, we find it difficult to appreciate movement unless it has relation to some goal, *some point of arrival.* Movement that gives a random impression, going on without purpose, control, or stop, leaves us somewhat baffled. In our way of thinking, feeling, and acting, movement must have an aim, a reason. For example, when we move our feet in walking, we expect each step to arrive at a point of contact with the earth; each breath reaches its point of arrival at the instant of maximum intake; every motion is made with the anticipation of arrival at a point of rest. Motion is not continuous; *it is marked off in phases or cycles by points of arrival.* Likewise, the movement of musical sound proceeds in phases directed to points of arrival. Listen to a series of drumbeats. You can feel that each stroke is like the touching of the foot to the ground; it is a point of arrival. Then, the intervals of time between the drum strokes become phases of movement. Similarly, in a melody, each successive tone is a point of arrival and departure, and the progression from one tone to the next represents a very small phase of melodic movement. Thus, the flow of music, although it pauses at each tone, gives us an impression of being continuous in time, very much like the spot of light that seems to move in space when successive lamps are lit in an electrical display.

Music is made up of sound moving in time to points of arrival; yet not all kinds of moving sound have made acceptable music. Composers and listeners pick and choose; certain procedures have been more effective than others. Some have been accepted universally for centuries; others have been used at different times in the history of music to create special styles and forms. In this book, we shall first consider the basic elements of the musical experience. Then we shall proceed to discover how each age created its own music and how various techniques were applied to achieve goals of musical expression at different times in history.

THE FIRST CRITERIA OF ANALYSIS

We shall first listen for the basic constituents of the musical experience, the perceptions which underlie all musical processes. These are: (1) quality of sound; (2) nature of movement; (3) effect of arrival. We shall see how these factors can interact; also, we shall relate them to expressive values in music.

At this point nontechnical vocabulary is in order, for two reasons:

1. A nontechnical vocabulary has direct meaning to the layman who is sympathetic to music, sensitive and alert to its effects, but unschooled in its professional language.

2. We can relate musical impressions, perceptions, and feelings to other aspects of experience if we use general, nonspecialized ideas that have widespread acceptance and are understood by all persons.

In music, as in all communication and expression, each technical and descriptive term represents a meaningful process or concept; if we have such concepts in mind when our discussion later turns to a technical matter, we shall realize the point of our study and interest.

The musical illustrations to follow in this chapter are clear-cut representations of specific points. They will give a kind of black-and-white picture. We shall use these first examples as points of departure and reference, but we should not take them to represent rigid categories that cover all instances. Actually, most music represents shadings and blendings of the types of values we are setting up as first criteria.

The Point of Departure

All music must make a beginning. The composer has an idea, an image which moves him to set tones together so that they will suggest meaning to the listener. The solemnity of the Mass, the pathos of a tragic opera heroine, the gaiety of a country-dance, the vigor of a bold instrumental flight, the wonderfully intricate, yet beautiful interweaving of a motet, the sweet lyricism of a song—these may be the composer's points of departure. The very first tones he assigns to the piece begin to shape his image.

For the listener the point of departure may be a sound quality or a specific gesture. Once this is projected, the music is set in motion and the image gradually becomes fuller and richer in import. Thus, the first impact, the point of departure, is a critical factor in the cycle of the musical experience. In our work we shall take account of the effect of departure especially when we deal with qualities of sound.

Qualities of Sound

We have established that music depends upon the power of sound to stir our senses and feelings. There are many kinds of sound and we react differently to different qualities. Hence, one of the first concerns of the composer is to control the quality of sound in his music. Indeed, in some pieces a certain effect of sound appears to be the most important single value; it can tell us more about the expressive intention than perhaps any other element. We hear a certain kind of sound at first contact with a piece; this provides a significant clue to the nature of the composition. It is the first *point of departure* in the cycle of experience which the entire composition provides.

Musical sound is qualified by its *level,* its *amount,* its *strength,* and its *color.* We shall listen for these in turn.

Pitch or level of sound. A musical passage may be high, medium, or low in range; it may fluctuate between several levels; at any given time the total sound may cover a wide range. The Scherzo from Mendelssohn's *A Midsummer Night's Dream* begins high, suggesting lightness and agility, to convey an atmospheric, fairylike effect. Liszt's *Les Préludes* opens with a very low sound, giving an impression of weight, deliberate manner; therefore, it is suggestive of the introspective, metaphysical ideas bound up in the piece. The opening of Brahms' First Symphony covers the entire range of sound from low to high. The effect is massive, grandiose, and full; it is proper for a piece in a heroic vein.

Amount of sound. There is no difficulty in determining the amount of sound. We can detect immediately whether few or many notes are being sounded at the same time. Yet consider the effect of large mass that is created by a full, rich sound, then contrast this effect with the thinness and transparency of a small amount of sound. The examples mentioned above (the Mendelssohn and the Brahms pieces) will do very well to illustrate the different effects that various amounts of sound can create. The first, of course, begins with a small body of sound; the second, with a very large amount. Later we shall see how the amount of sound affects the quality of movement.

Strength of sound. This simply means, "How loud or soft is the music?" As with the level and the amount of sound, we have a very obvious feature, but one that has great power to convey expressive values. Loud music affects us with direct impact; soft music moves us with persuasion. The examples we have given from Mendelssohn and Brahms apply as well to strength. Gradual increase in the strength of sound can give an impression of growing tension; gradual decrease is often associated with relaxation. One of the most celebrated examples of a growing increase in amount and strength of sound is Ravel's *Bolero.* The entire piece is built upon the idea of an ever-growing excitement, finally reaching the point of frenzy. On the other hand, the mood of utter despair and total resignation at the end of Tchaikovsky's Sixth Symphony is enhanced by the gradual decrease in the strength and amount of sound.

Color of sound. The *kinds* of sound that have been used effectively for musical purposes are limitless in number. Color of sound, or *tone color,* is one of the principal concerns of the composer and constitutes one of the chief criteria by which a musical composition is judged. Very often we recognize a composition or a specific musical style by the special color of its sound. Some types of tone color have had distinctive connotations. For example, the brilliant, clear, sharp-edged tone of trumpets has an air of command, authority, and decision. Nowhere is this effect more dramatically projected than in Beethoven's *Leonore* Overture, No. 3. At the height of a stormy, rushing, heavy passage, there is a sudden break in movement and the clear, penetrating tone of the trumpet is heard, signaling the rescue of the hero and heroine. Horns have been used in hunting and in music suggesting the hunt because of their rich, faraway color of sound that reverberates and carries great distances.

Listen to the beginning of Weber's *Oberon* Overture. The opening notes of the single horn immediately transfer us in imagination to the enchanted forest of Oberon and Titania. The heavy, somewhat lean sound of trombones has been traditionally associated with solemn ceremonies, often religious in nature. Throughout the history of music, and particularly in the last two centuries, there has been a constant search to discover fresh nuances of tone color and to expand the variety of available sound. Special qualities of tone color can also be set against each other with telling effect, so that each value is highlighted and dramatized by contrast. Listen to the opening of Mozart's *Prague* Symphony for a kaleidoscopic variety of tone color passing in a very short time. Small musical fragments passed back and forth among many instruments create striking shifts of tone color.

Qualities of Movement

Sound, no matter how evocative it may be, must progress forward in time in order to make a musical point. The progression of sound in time, its *movement,* has much in common with physical movement in time and space. This similarity has been used to advantage by composers from the times of antiquity to the present day. Music has accompanied dances, ceremonies, dramatic performances, and many other kinds of presentation where its qualities of movement could enhance other kinds of action. In addition, musical movement has relation to a more subtle and elusive kind of experience, the *emotional experience.* Just as musical movement can awake in us impressions of physical action, so can it suggest moods and emotional states. The attributes of musical movement, underlying both physical and emotional connotations, are its *pace,* its *regularity,* and its *articulation.* In aiming for points of arrival, it has direction, but this we shall consider a bit later.

Pace of movement. We are sensitive to pace and to rates of speed. Quick movement can exhilarate, excite, or alarm us; slow movement can relax and calm us. Musical pace also affects us strongly. Quick musical movement has generally been associated with vigorous physical action, excitement, or agitation; it rouses feelings quickly and leaves little time for reflection. Slow musical movement can give the impression of concentration, of reflection, of feelings stirred deeply and deliberately; it can also convey a relaxed quality. There are many nuances and shades of musical effect that can be projected by degrees of quick or slow movement. For the present it is enough to realize that when we listen to music, we can learn something about its expressive qualities by being alert to its pace.

The Scherzo from Mendelssohn's *A Midsummer Night's Dream* has a very quick pace. This, together with the light, high, airy quality of sound, conveys a picture of disembodied magical spirits moving about capriciously with complete freedom. The slow pace of the second movement in Beethoven's Third Symphony is combined with a very low level of sound, making use of the darkest tones of the string instruments. Such effects enhance the expressive aim of the piece, which is to convey the idea of the deliberate, measured step of a funeral march.

Regularity of movement. When music begins at a given pace, quick, slow, or moderate, we may expect it to continue at that pace, and thereby to give an impression of regularity. We accept that pace and adjust ourselves to it, very much as we accommodate ourselves to the flow of traffic while driving or as we keep step while marching. If the pace is changed, however, or the flow of the music is interrupted in a noticeable manner, we are surprised and perhaps even shocked. While this may be quite irritating in physical movement, it can increase interest and present a challenge in musical movement if handled properly. Disturbances in pace can build up a sense of excitement and importance in music.

Two highly contrasted examples will illustrate regularity and irregularity in musical movement. The first movement of Bach's *Brandenburg* Concerto, No. 5 has a quick, regular pace that gives an impression of vigorous and exuberant activity. Moreover, the quality of sound is brilliant and full with concentration on a rather high level. We hear many changes of pace in Liszt's Sonata for Piano in B minor. At the beginning of this work the pace is slow and uncertain; then it becomes quick and strenuous; both the quality and level of sound change quickly. A mood of dark, brooding introspection, broken by outbursts of passionate feeling, is created by these values of sound and movement.

Articulation of movement. Articulation of movement in music is comparable to types of physical gesture. The flow of music may be *continuous,* without marked breaks in the sound. Conversely, there may be regular, well-marked breaks in the flow of sound, creating an *incisive, sharply defined* effect. Very frequently there may be changes in the manner of movement from one passage to another. This represents a different level of organization, in which the composer creates contrast in the quality of movement over a larger part of his piece. The Nocturne from Mendelssohn's *A Midsummer Night's Dream* moves along quite smoothly and continuously, although we can detect certain instants where the movement relaxes a bit. On the other hand, the familiar melody of the *Blue Danube Waltz* has many regular and well-defined breaks in the melodic line, and these certainly contribute to the buoyancy and brilliance of the music. At the beginning of the last movement of Beethoven's Third Symphony, we hear rapid changes in the manner of movement, from a headlong rush to an extremely deliberate manner which gradually smoothens out to a rather flowing style. Such changes suggest that the piece is going to be rather searching and profound, and that it will be worked out on a grand scale.

In the articulation of movement, we should include intensity of action.

Intensity of movement refers to the amount of energy or effort involved, rather than to pace or regularity. We ask, "Is the music relaxed and easy in its movement, or does it seem to be reaching for some point, developing a quality of tension as it progresses?" For example, the *Blue Danube Waltz* moves along at about the same pace as the first movement of Beethoven's Third Symphony. Yet the waltz seems to swing along easily in a pleasant manner, inviting free and open physical movement. The Beethoven piece, very different from the waltz, seems to be building up emotional crises constantly. Later we shall see how this is brought about; but for the present it is enough to recognize the contrast in the manner of movement when we hear the two pieces.

Points of Arrival

As we have said before, movement cannot be appreciated unless it is observed or felt in relation to points of arrival. When you heard the first illustrations of sound and movement, you were no doubt aware of certain moments or instants in the music that gave the impression of resting, stopping, or ending. These are *points of arrival* in music. Likewise, they are points of departure for new phases of movement. They help create ideas of pace, regularity, and manner in music, since they control, shape, and organize the flow of sound. We can assess the particular effects that arrival creates according to its degree of *emphasis, clarity,* and *finality.*

Emphasis of arrival. After the headlong downward rush at the beginning of the last movement of Beethoven's Third Symphony, the music puts on its brakes, so to speak, and slows down to a complete stop. Hardly any effect of arrival could be more *emphatic.* In contrast, the points of arrival at the beginning of the Scherzo in *A Midsummer Night's Dream* represent little more than touching points and turns in an easy, capricious flight; here, emphasis is at a minimum. Naturally, emphasis with respect to arrival will vary according to the nature of the idea being expressed. A calm, flowing piece with gentle and steady movement cannot absorb emphatic points of arrival; a piece that has an intense quality of movement, vigorous, agitated, or heavy, would very likely require more emphatic points of arrival, particularly at critical moments.

Clarity of arrival. While clarity and emphasis depend upon each other to a great extent, they are not synonymous. For example, in our Mendelssohn Scherzo, we can hear quite clearly when each phase of movement comes to an end, although the flow of music continues without interruption. There is a clear articulation between sections, both small and large. Yet, as we have seen, there is very little emphasis in the arrival effect. Listening to the motet by Orlandus Lassus, *Tristis est anima mea* (Sad Is My Soul), we should find it very difficult, within the piece, to identify clear points of arrival, points where the music stops or rests for an instant, or where it seems to reach a goal. Arrival, in this piece, is not clear, except at the end.

Certain kinds of music, such as dance music, tend to have a number of very clear points of arrival; yet, these will vary but little in the degree of emphasis, as in the principal strain of the *Blue Danube Waltz*. In more highly developed types of music, there has been a tendency to disguise some points of arrival, and then to compensate by making others more emphatic and clear. Such is the case at the beginning of Beethoven's Third Symphony. The music flows along with little marked articulation; yet we feel that it is progressing unmistakably to a grandiose and important point of arrival which will eventually appear.

The degree of clarity of various points of arrival in a piece is not only indicative of the style of the piece, but, as we shall see later, will help us to understand the structure of the work.

Finality of arrival. Most of us have had the experience of not being certain that a piece had come to its end. Perhaps all movement ceased for a moment, leading us to assume an ending; then the music picked up its movement again. Or perhaps we heard a grand, final-sounding flourish, and were about to clap, and then the music went on. Perhaps the piece simply ended up in the air, so to speak, without any strong effect of arrival. Johann Strauss amused himself and his audience greatly in his *Perpetuum Mobile* by playing upon these expectations but refusing to fulfill them. For the listener, the need for arrival, especially when long phases of movement are involved, is very strong, and is a fact which the skillful composer can well turn to his advantage.

Relatively few points of arrival, however, need give an absolute sense of finality or completion. If we use an analogy of speech, this becomes quite clear. Certain sentences come to a full close with a period; yet the train of thought has not been completed and some continuation is necessary. Other sentences finish off a series of ideas and give an impression of complete finality; the subject has been covered. In a similar manner, musical points of arrival will be so arranged that only the last in a composition is intended to be the thoroughly final one. All others will have an effect of ending, but only partially so, and will invite continuation. Almost any composition you listen to will give you some idea of the degree of finality of its points of arrival simply by the position of these points in the larger scheme. For example, the song, *Drink to Me Only with Thine Eyes,* has four clear points of arrival. We hear that the first, second, and fourth points are identical, and that each might be acceptable for final arrival. Only the third demands continuation. Yet only the last point of arrival seems like a satisfactory ending for the entire piece. The first and second, although they *sound* final, appear *too soon* in the piece for us to accept the idea that the music can end at those points.

Interaction of Movement and Arrival

So far we have considered qualities of sound, types of movement, and effects of arrival. When sound moves to a point of arrival, a *phase of musical movement* is created. Such phases of movement are the units of musical structure and they differ greatly in length as well as in their internal qualities. We can learn something of these basic structural units by observing how they are formed by the interaction of movement and arrival. This interaction involves the *length* of the phase of movement and the *approach* to the point of arrival.

Length of phases of movement. There is no absolute length for a phase of musical movement. Like speech, which is built up by phrases and clauses into sentences and paragraphs, musical structure is created by combining smaller phases of movement into larger ones. Possibly the smallest appreciable phase of musical movement would be two tones sounded in succession. This would be comparable to a very short statement, such as, "I go." At the other end of the scale, an entire composition represents an elaborate, extended single phase of movement built up from shorter units.

The manner in which small phases are joined to build up larger structures provides one of the most important clues regarding the nature of a musical composition. Let us compare, for example, the song, *Drink to Me Only with Thine Eyes,* with the first large phase of movement at the beginning of Beethoven's Quartet in F major, Op. 59, no. 1. These are equal to each other in length. The song is composed of four rather short phases of movement, each with a clearly defined, rather emphatic point of arrival. In the Quartet the smaller phases of movement are run together, merged, and their points of arrival covered; momentum continues unbroken until a very emphatic, climactic point of arrival is reached. The style of the song is sweet, sentimental, and touching. The style of the Quartet is broad, bold, and soaring. Each has the form, with relation to phases of movement, that best suits the musical values to be expressed.

Approach to the point of arrival. There is often a close correlation between the approach to the point of arrival and the length of a phase of movement. In certain types of music, the point of arrival is a resting place, a breathing point. It is an incidental moment of relaxation or articulation. We are likely to find that phases of movement are not extended greatly in such music. Early Christian plain song has many examples of this kind of structure. In other music movement develops increasing intensity and excitement as it approaches the point of arrival. We have the idea of a *drive* toward a goal. Often such a drive will extend the phase of movement, imparting a broad and sweeping quality. The points of arrival in such music have a dramatic and momentous effect. Music of the eighteenth and nineteenth centuries frequently shows this kind of structure. The song, *Drink to Me Only with Thine Eyes,* has a gentle, easy manner of reaching its points of arrival; the Quartet of Beethoven we heard reaches its first point of arrival with a tremendous climax.

Summary

In this first chapter we presented the idea that music provides a meaningful experience based upon the power of sound to stir the feelings and senses. In nontechnical terms we established certain criteria dealing with the movement of sound in time to points of arrival. We made certain evaluations of music on the basis of these first criteria. We found that each piece represents a special interaction of general qualities and to that extent must be judged on its own terms. By way of summing up, we shall listen to two complete pieces, using the criteria established in this chapter. The compositions are the Ostinato from Book Six of Béla Bartók's *Mikrokosmos* and the second movement of Beethoven's Fifth Symphony.

BARTÓK

1. Quality of Sound

a. Level of sound. Middle to high; occasional sections on low level for contrast; now and then abrupt shifts from high to low and vice versa, crossing over a steady middle-level flow.

b. Amount of sound. Relatively small at beginning, increasing gradually and dropping off several times; section of considerable fullness toward end serving as kind of climax.

c. Strength of sound. Contrasts between loud and soft, sometimes sharp, sometimes gradual; some soft, full-sounding places contrasted with thin, loud passages.

d. Color of sound. Wide range from dark to brilliant; sharp contrasts in color; use of many different special effects drawing upon the flexibility and the numerous resources of the piano.

2. Quality of Movement

a. Pace. Quick; one section in middle somewhat slower.

b. Regularity. Strict regularity within sections, except for one or two places that seem to be held back momentarily.

c. Articulation. Basically, a driving energetic manner, with emphatic articulation, occasional contrasting lyric manner; sometimes a sense of easy, regular, somewhat relaxed movement; at other times a more intense, strained effect, generally when color is most brilliant and sound is at its strongest.

3. Effects of Arrival

a. Emphasis. Generally quite strong due to separation of passages; some intermediate points very light; final points of arrival extremely strong; effect of ending very emphatic due to repetition of passages denoting arrival.

b. Clarity. Clarity tied up with emphasis in this piece.

4. Interaction of Movement and Arrival

a. Length of phases of movement. Rather short phases at beginning; longer toward the end; no regular relationships of length; grouping into larger phases of movement very clearly defined.

b. Approach to points of arrival. Simple articulations at beginning of piece; toward the end a strong sense of drive to points of arrival.

The quick, energetic pace and the driving quality of movement in this piece suggest some kind of vigorous, well-patterned physical movement, probably a dance. Working against this steady basic flow, we find certain striking contrasts of color and pace that increase interest and intensify movement. Toward the end a climax to the dance is suggested by strong and repeated effects of arrival.

BEETHOVEN

1. Quality of Sound

a. Level of sound. Wide range through the entire piece. Each section on a given level. Occasional sharp contrasts between sections. Very few sudden or rapid changes of level within a section. Low level at beginning to set the lyric, thoughtful mood of the piece.

b. Amount of sound. Wide variation in amount of sound. Often only a few instruments playing; occasionally full orchestra for substantial period of time. Consistent alternation between full and thin sound.

c. Strength of sound. Almost completely identified with amount of sound. Soft for few instruments, loud for many.

d. Color of sound. Wide range, from mellow to brilliant, from dark to light. Use of many different instrumental colors in salient passages. Sharp contrast of trumpet fanfares with all the rest of the orchestra.

2. Quality of Movement

a. Pace. Slow, but with a swinging sense of movement.

b. Regularity. Regular, except for occasional moments of pause.

c. Articulation. Continuously flowing, lyric, even. Deviations from this manner in sections which contrast a sense of the suspension of movement with bold, driving trumpet fanfares. Occasional broadening into a rather grand manner, particularly when fullness of sound is involved.

3. Effects of Arrival

a. Emphasis. Rather large number of emphatic points of arrival. Final section of piece apparently concerned with giving a very strong impression of final arrival.

b. Clarity. Almost all points of arrival, gentle or emphatic, quite clear in this piece. Repetitions of passages denoting arrival to add emphasis and clarity to arrival effect.

4. Interaction of Movement and Arrival

a. Length of phases of movement. Well-defined, rather short phases of movement, marked by clear points of arrival. Some phases spun out to greater length.

b. Approach to points of arrival. Simple articulations and gentle rounding off contrasted with occasional strong and dramatic drives to important goals.

The slow yet easily moving pace of this composition, together with its rich, varied, and luminous qualities of tone color, suggest at first some kind of deliberate dance or song. The new element introduced by the fanfare, however, combined with the moments in which a suspension of movement seems to occur, raise the expressive level of this piece far above that of a dance or song. In this piece there is a long-range feeling of growth and expansion. It seems to include a great many different ideas and values.

MUSICAL EXPRESSION

Our study thus far has served two purposes: (1) the listener has been provided with a means for making first contact with a composition in order to evaluate it; (2) standards of reference have been established to which the listener can refer technical, historical, and aesthetic data. Throughout this chapter we suggested or indicated the expressive quality of a given passage or composition by means of the criteria of sound, movement, and arrival. In considering the expressive values of music we were pursuing a line of thought followed by many great writers on music from the times of antiquity to the present day. The ability of music to convey ideas of emotion and feeling has been recognized for centuries.

Plato, in the third book of his *Republic,* made distinctions between music which provokes violence and that which promotes tranquillity. Gioseffe Zarlino, the most influential music theorist of the Renaissance, devoted the final sections of his *Istituzioni armoniche* to a careful consideration of the expressive effects of all the tone systems or scales available to the composers of his time. Writers of the seventeenth and eighteenth centuries constantly discussed the emotional effects of various kinds of movement, qualities of sound, and tone systems. The entire aesthetic philosophy of these two centuries was centered upon a system called the *doctrine of the affections* in which the methods by which music could stir the feelings were thoroughly investigated and described. Alfred Einstein, the modern writer on Mozart, devoted an entire chapter to "Mozart's Choice of Keys," in which he showed how Mozart chose keys for their affective quality, in order to stir the listener's emotions in one way or another. Paul Hindemith, the contemporary composer, assigned, in his song cycle, *Das Marienleben,* emotional values of very specific nature to various tones.

In all these cases music seems to have been neither an intricate pattern of tones nor an exact description of emotions or objects. Rather these writers and composers have dealt with the power of music to suggest and imply. We have adopted this approach, and in this chapter have offered some criteria that may provide a way of making entry into the world of musical value and meaning.

Chapter 2. Musical Elements
and Their Relationships

U NTIL NOW in our listening we have been seeking general impressions. Music was loud or
soft; it moved quickly, slowly, vigorously, or gently; it had brilliant or
dark color; it arrived with a flourish, or perhaps it did not seem to arrive
at all. Through these impressions we were stirred to various kinds of emotional reaction; this testified to the expressive power of the music. Now we
ask how these effects and impressions were evoked by the music. Such
questions as the following arise: "Why does this passage move smoothly
while another progresses with much effort?"; "Why is one piece easy to
follow while another seems to lead into strange bypaths?"; "How are
various qualities of sound created?"; "In what ways does music move?"
These questions, and many others like them, deal with the structure of
music. To find the answers, we must look at the musical resources which
the composer has at his command. This we shall begin to do.

THE PHRASE

We all know that musical effects take place in relation to each other,
that they must be coordinated and combined in order to create a satisfactory
musical impression. In this respect music is similar to language. Words
must be gathered into clauses, phrases, and sentences in order to convey
ideas; and musical sounds, too, need each other in order to make sense.

When tones follow each other in time they create patterns of various
kinds and lengths. These patterns range in size from very small to very
large. However, we cannot at first cope with extremes. The layman is
equipped neither with musical microscope nor telescope. His attention first
settles upon fairly short sections with clearly defined points of arrival. In

music such sections are called *phrases*. Phrases in music are analogous to phrases or clauses in language. Both in music and in language, phrases contain clearly formed ideas, yet lack something in form or sense to be complete. The feeling of completion comes only when another phrase or more finishes the thought.

Musical phrases have no prescribed length. Here are some examples:

Ex. 2–1.

a. Mozart: *Jupiter* Symphony, second movement.
(quite short)

Andante cantabile

b. Brahms: Variations on a Theme of Joseph Haydn.
(rather long)

Andante

We judge the length of a phrase according to the musical idea it expresses; we are carried along by a sense of progression to a point of arrival. In language a single phrase can sometimes carry a complete thought; it will be a short sentence and will end with a full stop at its point of arrival, as, "I go." At other times a series of phrases may go on for some time without a conclusive ending. The thought is more complex and highly developed; it needs the ample room which a structure of many clauses and phrases provides. In music, as in literature, we are not likely to find full stops occurring regularly and frequently. Rather, there will be many partial stops which help us to get our bearings but at the same time invite us to continue. This we heard when listening for the finality of points of arrival.

Whenever a full or conclusive point of arrival is reached, after one or more phrases, such a section becomes a *period*. A period in music is comparable to a complete sentence in language. Thus, in the *Star-Spangled*

Banner, the first musical period as well as the first poetic period ends with the words, "twilight's last gleaming." Whether the point of arrival at the end of a phrase or period be light or strong, conclusive or inconclusive, it serves the purpose of creating a resting point or a point of division. Thus it is called a *caesura,* which may be likened to the comma, semicolon, or period of a sentence. To be sure, we do not always encounter complete thoughts in literature. Today especially, some schools of writing have an aversion to carrying out a fully rounded idea. Theirs is a cryptic manner. Likewise in music, some music written today seems obscure in the sense of progression that its phrases give. All this can be perfectly valid artistic procedure, *if* it does not disguise an inability to make a well-built phrase.

The phrase, as a rule, has the following characteristics:

1. It is readily understood as a unit.
2. It contains a distinctive and well-formed musical idea.
3. It carries a sense of progression to a point of arrival.

The phrase is a convenient and proper framework for the study of basic musical elements and relationships.

Within a phrase, the listener will most likely fix his attention first upon its *melody*; later, the less salient, although no less important elements, *rhythm, texture,* and *harmony,* will come into focus. Following the listener's path, we shall explore these elements in the order given above.

MELODY

Melodic Line

Apart from the general impression that a piece creates, if you were asked what you recall most clearly about a familiar composition such as the *Blue Danube Waltz,* Tchaikovsky's Piano Concerto No. 1, Gershwin's *Rhapsody in Blue,* or *America,* you would no doubt answer, "Its melody, its tune." In music the memorable moments, the highlights are often furnished by melody. Quite frequently the themes, melodies, or tunes in a piece are its most salient features. They can give in concentrated form an impression of the general style of a piece, in addition to being valuable in their own right. Composers have constantly used striking melodies to point up important moments in their compositions. Often we recognize or recall a work by its principal themes. Listed below are some notable melodies to be found in familiar concert literature:

Bach: Aria from Suite in D major, No. 3
Dvorak: Theme from second movement of *From the New World* Symphony
   (Goin' Home)
Mozart: Non più andrai from *The Marriage of Figaro*
Ravel: *Pavane pour une infante défunte*

The ways in which melody functions are designated by terms such as *subject, theme,* or *tune.* The distinction between these terms is not entirely clear; they are sometimes used interchangeably. Still, when the term *subject* is used, it generally refers to some substantial and distinctive melodic statement which will be the subject for further treatment later on. The term *theme* has much the same meaning, without necessarily implying further treatment. A *tune* is generally thought of as a complete, rounded melody that can stand independently. *America, Swanee River,* or *The St. Louis Blues* are tunes.

The opening measures of a fugue present its *subject*; and the most important *theme* of a symphony is usually heard at the beginning.

It is difficult to say what is distinctive about a melody, what it is that gives it personality. This can be answered only partially. Melody deals with the nature of musical imagination and inspiration. Like emotion, the melodic gift is something that can be observed, its results described, its effect upon the listener suggested, but its secret never thoroughly explored. Some composers, such as Mozart and Tchaikovsky, seem to overflow with melodic riches. Others address themselves to different, though no less important, musical values. Nevertheless, all music has to deal with melody, whether it be frankly songlike or complex and involved.

These characteristics can be noted regarding melody:

1. A melody has distinctive shapes.
2. A melody has a distinctive manner or style.
3. A melody seems to be built of well-defined phrases, rounded off by clear points of arrival.

Melody gives us an impression of shape. When we listen to a melody, it is as if we were observing an artist sketching a figure. The path of his pencil gradually delineates a meaningful pattern. Similarly, the line of tones in a melody gradually forms and completes a meaningful musical shape.

The distinctive shapes and patterns of melodic phrases come to life in the process of time; thus, we would have to take time values of music into consideration, were we to make an intensive study of melody. Yet we can understand much about a melody if we direct our attention at first exclusively to its shape, which can suggest expressive value. Thus when a melody rises steadily, it may connote increasing tension or greater energy of movement. Conversely, a melody which drops steadily may convey a sense of relaxation or settling. Melody that is more or less level or works around a given tone may suggest steadiness and evenness of movement. Abrupt rise or fall, involving widely different levels, indicates a bold, emphatic, and perhaps strenuous quality of movement. The song, *Drink to Me Only with Thine Eyes,* has an even, level quality of melodic movement, with somewhat more expansiveness in the third phrase. On the other hand, the first strain of the *Blue Danube Waltz* owes much of its sense of exuberant physical movement to the bold upward drive of its melodic phrases.

The melodic line of a phrase gives us the clearest sense of progression; it tells much concerning the way in which the music is moving. The following examples illustrate various patterns of melodic movement; note that their shapes come into being as *forward* movement in time!

Ex. 2–2. Melodic movement.

a. Rising.

b. Falling. Beethoven: Sonata in F minor, Op. 2, no. 1, first movement.

c. Remaining on a level. Beethoven: Fifth Symphony, third movement.

d. Turning around one or two points. Schubert: Symphony in B minor, first movement.

Allegro moderato

e. Connected or *conjunct.* Beethoven: Ninth Symphony, Hymn to Joy.

Allegro assai

f. Disconnected or *disjunct.* Bach: Concerto for Two Violins in D minor, first movement.

Vivace

g. Directly to a point. Beethoven: Sonata in F minor, Op. 2, no. 1, first movement.

Allegro

h. Rounded. Mozart: Symphony in G minor, Menuetto.

Allegretto

i. Ornamented. Mozart: Sonata in A major, K. 331, Alla Turca.

Allegretto

Composers have sometimes linked distinctive melodic figures to specific literary ideas, taking advantage of music's strong powers of suggestion. This is called *pictorialism,* and here is an example:

Ex. 2–3. Musical pictorialism. Handel: *The Messiah,* Why do the nations rage?

(Rage here is expressed by a grand melodic flourish)

Richard Strauss went so far as to imitate a baby crying in his bath in his *Sinfonia Domestica.* We may concede his expertness in musical realism; we may also reserve our admiration for other works of his.

Melody can also be humorous. Saint-Saëns managed to imitate "personages with long ears" very effectively in *The Carnival of the Animals.* We receive a most realistic picture of the hee-haws of their conversation in the extremely abrupt and wide skips in the violins.

When the composer tells us to make such specific connections by associating the text with the music, we are on safe ground. But we must guard against reading exact meanings into music which has no direct literary counterpart. In any case, it is better to keep such stories to ourselves. Pictorialism is simply a demonstration of music's ability to adapt itself to other media of expression.

Melodic Motives

The melodic phrases we have heard were made up from smaller melodic figures. These smaller figures, called *motives,* might be compared to word groups which contain fragments of sentences or phrases, such as "my country," "with thine eyes," "far away," etc.

Like the musical phrase, the length of a motive is not fixed. Two notes may sometimes be sufficient to create a motive which the composer will find satisfactory for manipulation. At other times we may find that the pattern of a motive includes as many as six or seven tones. The length of a motive is generally indicated by a light caesura or point of articulation. Motives are linked together to build themes, tunes, and subjects.

Listen to the first four notes of the opening movement of Beethoven's Fifth Symphony. These four notes constitute a motive which Beethoven uses constantly throughout the piece. This motive offers a challenging signal which sets the stormy manner of the entire piece. Here it is:

Ex. 2–4. Beethoven: Fifth Symphony, beginning.

What does Beethoven do with this motive? First, he repeats it at a lower pitch, then he restates it eleven times in varied forms to build a broadly scaled period which rises steadily to a point of climax. Thus, a single four-note motive has been used to give a sense of progression, of going somewhere in a specific manner. Below is a melodic sketch of the entire period:

Ex. 2–5. Beethoven: Fifth Symphony.

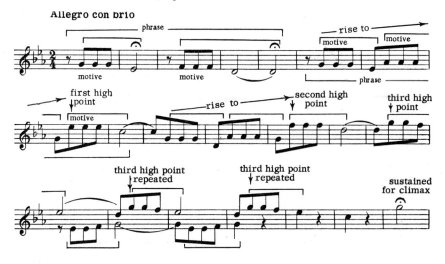

Not only does a series of motives give a broader shape to the melody, but the motives themselves display various mutual relationships. Thus, every bit of motivic material in the Beethoven example was taken from the first four notes. This figure was *repeated* and *varied*. There was an idea of strong single-minded purpose given, due to the intensive working over or *development* of the one figure.

Here is the beginning of another broadly scaled work, the *Jupiter* Symphony by Mozart.

Ex. 2–6. Mozart: *Jupiter* Symphony, beginning.

Allegro vivace

bold flourish   lyric contrast

The whole orchestra begins with a flourish of three bold strokes; this is followed immediately by a reply, which offers, in *contrast,* the merest fragment of a soft lyric melody. Listen further. Once again you hear the alternation of bold and lyric motives, this time at a different pitch. Mozart continues the piece in the bold manner with fresh motives to reach the point of arrival of his first large period. In this example, Mozart has made effective use of *contrast* of motives in a very striking manner.

Repetition, variation, and *contrast* of motives convey different ideas of musical movement. Repetition and variation spin out or extend a single idea; therefore, they will tend to suggest a steadiness or unbroken continuity of musical thought. Contrast, particularly when it is sharp, introduces a fresh element, often a conflicting one. While it may interrupt the continuity of musical thought, the impact of contrasting motives may intensify the quality of movement.

When you listen to any composition, pay attention to its salient motives. Within a very few seconds after the piece has begun, you will find that you have made solid contact with the piece, having recognized its first important motives. Also, direct your attention to the number and variety of motives which make up the melodic content. For example, in the first movement of Beethoven's Third Symphony, you will hear a tremendous number of highly contrasted motives working against each other. This contributes significantly to the sense of breadth and of dramatic conflict which characterizes this piece. In Orlandus Lassus' motet, *Tristis est anima mea,* no. 23 in *Masterpieces of Music before 1750,* we hear motives which are similar to each other, or, at most, represent a very gentle sort of contrast. This helps to maintain the sense of unified and continuous flow established at the very beginning of the piece by the smoothly rounded initial motive.

The motive in music does not represent a fully developed musical idea, yet its very brevity, coupled with its distinct manner, enables it to serve a very powerful role in carrying forward musical movement. Each time we hear a familiar motive restated or a new motive enter, we sense that the music has gained fresh melodic momentum.

One special way of organizing motives that has been very useful for centuries is by the *sequence*. In a sequence, a single motive is restated several times in succession at a higher or lower pitch. This is one of the most valuable techniques for broadening and extending a musical phrase. The effect of the sequence is to carry the entire level of the music gradually upward or downward; it creates a longer line of melodic movement, and governs and guides the play of intervals and motives.

Ex. 2–7. Bach: Two-part Invention in G major.

Melodic motives can act as binding factors in a piece of music. We hear a melody with its distinctive motives. Later on this melody returns. We connect and relate the various appearances; the melody thus becomes a point of reference, a landmark in the flow of the music. As a matter of fact, melodies can retain their identities even when they are altered or broken up in different ways. Certain parts or features of a theme are immediately recognizable, although they may undergo a number of changes. These changes are aspects of *development* and occur extensively in all styles of Western music. Here is an example from a contemporary work.

Ex. 2–8. Bartók: Sixth String Quartet, first movement.

a. Original motive group—nine notes.

b. Shortened—seven notes, four notes.

c. Extended.

Development represents an evolution in the life of the melody itself; therefore it is another way in which movement in music is made manifest.

Our interest in melodic motives has been twofold:

1. We were interested in the style or manner suggested by a motive, because this gave us a clue to the style of perhaps the whole piece.

2. We were interested in the way motives were linked to form phrases and periods.

Melodic Intervals

The smallest patterns in melody, two tones heard in succession, are called *melodic intervals*. Intervals and motives should be distinguished from each other, as follows: (1) when we speak of a *motive,* we refer to something which has a musical life of its own, which is created by the composer; (2) when we speak of an *interval,* we refer to the distance in pitch between two tones, or to a quality of sound created by these two tones. Yet an interval or a series of intervals can become a motive when endowed with musical vitality.

Intervals differ in size; therefore, they differ in the impression of movement which they can give in a motive. For example, listen to the beginning of Mozart's *Haffner* Symphony:

Ex. 2–9. Mozart: *Haffner* Symphony.

The bold and arresting effect of this music is created by extremely large intervals in the melody. Certainly this is a most striking way of calling attention to the brilliant and festive piece to follow.

Quite different is the effect at the beginning of *Drink to Me,* where there is actually no melodic movement up or down at first, and then, only a gentle rise and fall. The melodic intervals here are proper to an elegant, persuasive, and fanciful love song.

In order to get acquainted with the more common intervals, we can make use of the keyboard. At the piano, play the note C as indicated on the diagram below. The white note immediately to the right of C is D; the interval connecting these two tones is called a *second.* Each interval is named according to the number of degrees on the musical staff which it includes.

Ex. 2–10. Common musical intervals.

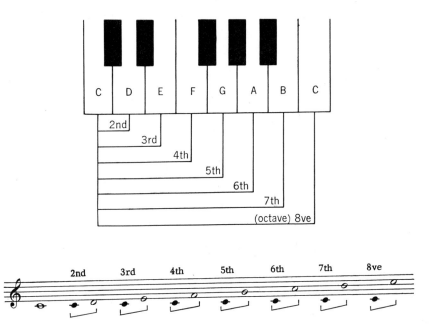

Listen carefully to each interval: you will notice that each has a characteristic quality of sound. Thirds and sixths tend to be full and rich; fourths and fifths have a rather open feeling; sevenths and ninths seem unsteady and tense; seconds are rather smooth and neutral in effect. These values will affect the nature of the melodies of which they are part. Here are some examples of melodies built with concentrations of a certain kind of interval:

Ex. 2–11.

a. Thirds and sixths.

b. Fourths and fifths.

c. Sevenths.

d. Seconds. Mozart: *Jupiter* Symphony, Menuetto.

As an example of the importance which every interval has within a melody, let us try the first phrase of *Drink to Me* with a slight alteration. Starting on the tone C, instead of the proper note E, play the melody through using white keys. The small change in the position of the first tone with relation to the rest of the melody destroys the effect of the passage, causing it to lose its sweetness and charm.

Of all the intervals you have heard above, only one kind gives the impression of gradual melodic movement, of conjunct movement. This is the *second*. All others are disjunct, and give the impression of taking a leap. The bold, arresting melodic manner of the *Star-Spangled Banner* is due to the disjunct intervals which separate the first six notes. See Example 2–2, *f*, *g*.

Summarizing: in order to evaluate the melodic content of a piece, we listen for the following features:

1. The general contour of the melody and its effect of movement.

2. The salient motives, their distribution according to position, repetition, variation, and contrast.

3. When, and how frequently do important melodies appear?

More than any other aspect of music, melody and its treatment are the clues to the personality of music, its style, its manner of speaking to the listener. Most of us have entered the realm of music by way of melody, by way of tunes that have delighted us and won our affection. As we listen to an important piece of music, however, we become increasingly aware that melody does not tell the whole story, that the movement of music cannot be borne by melody alone. Many striking gestures seem to have relatively small melodic content or interest; they deal with other effects. Moreover, in order to come alive, melody needs to work with the other elements of music, rhythm, harmony, and to a lesser extent, with texture. So, in our study, we move on to these other factors, the first of which is *rhythm*.

RHYTHM

Everyone has found himself at one time or another tapping his foot to music. The beat of a march or a dance is most persuasive. When you keep time with music by tapping your foot, by dancing, by walking, or marching, you are responding to the *rhythm* of the music.

Rhythm deals with the control of musical time. In controlling musical time, we not only *measure* it, we also *generate movement*; that is, we get musical time started. Also, in controlling musical movement in time, we give it a style, a manner which has expressive value.

We have already measured some musical time. This we did when we decided that the phrase was long enough to contain a fairly well-developed musical idea, and yet short enough for us to grasp immediately as a unit of musical structure. Rhythmic measurement of this kind marks off sections and binds them together by various kinds of musical relationship; it helps make musical movement intelligible.

Another kind of rhythmic measurement is necessary in the process of generating musical movement. This is demonstrated very simply. Tap your foot for a short time at a given rate. Each tap marks off a brief period of time. As the taps go on, our minds leap across the silence between taps; thus, we sense movement, movement that would not take place except for the series of measured taps. Also, and equally important, the measurement of the taps determines the pace and regularity of the impression of movement. Try an irregular series of taps. Notice then how the regular series and the irregular each suggest a different kind of musical expression, as if the rhythmic patterns were the barest outlines of a picture that was being sketched and yet were indicative of what the finished portrait would be. Rhythm in music, then, deals with the following functions:

1. It *generates* movement.
2. It gives a *characteristic manner* to musical movement.
3. It *controls* movement, marking off units of musical time.

Beat—Pace—Tempo

In tapping your foot, you have created a *beat* or a pulse. Musical movement in time arises from a basic beat, pulse, or stroke that is felt continuously throughout a piece. In music the beat is a sign of life; it not only gives evidence of vitality, but also provides a clue as to the kind of life there is in the music. Pulse or beat establishes the fundamental quality of movement, its *pace* and its emphasis or *accent*. For example, in *Drink to Me,* we hear a steady, moderately slow beat, with little emphasis; this creates a gently flowing quality of movement. In the Scherzo from Mendelssohn's *A Midsummer Night's Dream,* we hear a rather quick, light, but crisp beat which contributes to the gay, buoyant sense of movement. The majestic quality of the *Star-Spangled Banner* owes much to its vigorous, rather quick, and heavily accented beat.

Although we are sensitive to the presence of a beat in music, we cannot always define or determine the extent of the beat in exact terms. The beat sometimes appears to fluctuate in pace, quickening or slowing down. Perhaps it may be subdivided into smaller beats; perhaps it may, at times, coalesce into longer beats. Sometimes it may not be present at all, or it may be so irregular that we have difficulty in finding it. Listen to the opening of Richard Wagner's Prelude to *Tristan und Isolde.* Can you detect a beat easily? The answer is negative. Only when the piece is well under way does the beat come forward sufficiently to be recognized in its pace, its emphasis, and its groupings.

The listener tends to associate physical or emotional states with various qualities of beat. If the pulse is strong, regular, and active, as in a dance or march, the connotation is physical action. If the pulse is doubtful, irregular, gentle, or changing, we tend to associate the music with emotional states or moods. Compare *The Stars and Stripes Forever* with the Prelude to

Tristan. One strikes the earth with each beat; the other seems to glide forward uncertainly.

The *pace* at which a series of beats moves along is called the *tempo* of a piece. Tempo has generally been indicated by terms which describe the general rate of speed, and which may also give some idea of the quality of movement. Here are some examples of tempo indications, along with compositions which bear them:

presto — very quickly	Beethoven: Symphony No. 7, third movement
vivace — lively	Beethoven: Symphony No. 7, first movement
allegro con brio — quick, with vivacity or spirit	Beethoven: Symphony No. 3, first movement
andante — moderately slow and moving	Mozart: *Don Giovanni* Overture, opening
adagio — slowly	Berlioz: *Symphonie fantastique,* third movement
largo — broad and slow	Berlioz: *Symphonie fantastique,* opening of first movement

Some terms that qualify the manner of pace and give some indication of the expressive value are:

con anima — with life	maestoso — majestically
con spirito — with spirit	dolce — softly or sweetly
grazioso — gracefully	con fuoco — with fire

There is no fixed value for tempo terms. The performer has the task of determining the exact pace of the music for himself. Within the general limits set by the composer, the performer must find a pace that will project the musical movement effectively and yet allow the nuances and details to speak forth. This is not easy, and there is possibly no single correct answer. In two recorded performances of the same work by eminent artists, there may be several minutes difference in the duration of the two readings. One may appeal to one listener but not to another. If nothing else, this makes for a great deal of critical commentary.

Meter and Measure

Listening for beats, we find ourselves organizing their steady flow into small groups. Sometimes this is very easy to do, as in the *Blue Danube Waltz.* We find ourselves counting 1, 2, 3—1, 2, 3—1, 2, 3, etc. In other music, such as the Prelude to *Tristan,* the grouping seems uncertain and difficult to hear. In any case, there seems to be a strong tendency to listen for groups of beats as music moves along.

Groups of beats appear to us as small phases of movement. The beat that we hear at the beginning of one group is at the same time the point of arrival for a preceding group. Each first beat in a group generates fresh movement, while serving at the same time as a goal for the previous phase of movement. A link is thus established between groups. *This link by which groups are joined is one of the bases of musical structure.* Such links serve dual roles: they are simultaneously points of arrival and departure.

Ex. 2–12. Linking groups of beats.

The simplest of all such groups are those that contain *two* or *three* beats. *These simple groups combine into larger groups in multiples of two or three.*

Ex. 2–13. Groups of beats.

a. Simple duple. Beethoven: Quartet in G major, Op. 18, no. 2, finale.

b. Simple triple. Mozart: *Marriage of Figaro,* Se vuol ballare.

c. Compound duple in multiples of three. Mendelssohn: Symphony No. 3 in A minor (*Scotch*), first movement.

In this case, we often feel a stronger beat at the beginning of each group; and thus we might find ourselves tapping the *Blue Danube* as:

Ex. 2–14. Strauss: the *Blue Danube Waltz.*

Meter is the term used to refer to grouping of beats. We designate special types as duple, triple, simple, or compound meter, as illustrated in Example 2–13.

Each grouping, together with a given pace, has a characteristic quality of movement. For example, a simple grouping in quick tempo, in duple meter, has a vigorous, straightforward quality of movement, as in the final movement of the First Symphony by Beethoven. A compound group, in slow tempo, built up from triple meter, has a deliberate and somewhat swinging motion. Both are illustrated in Example 2–15, as well as a fairly quick simple triple meter:

Ex. 2–15. Types of meter.

a. Beethoven: First Symphony, final movement.

b. Drink to Me.

c. Star-Spangled Banner.

Musical metric groups were first based on dance patterns and on poetic rhythms, to which the music had to accommodate. As we all know, traditional dances and poetry moved in a series of equal time groups known as *feet*. The more familiar poetic rhythms are illustrated below:

Ex. 2–16. Poetic meters.

Iambic

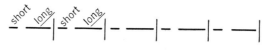

Trochaic

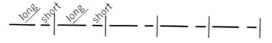

Anapest

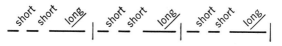

Dactylic

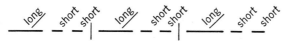

Music borrowed this type of organization and applied the term *measure* to its metrical time groups, particularly from the seventeenth century to the present time.

Much can be learned about a musical style from examination of the relationship between its metric groups and the tempo and emphasis of its beat. In early Christian church song there was a characteristic beat of moderate tempo that did not change appreciably. The size of metric groups varied freely, however. In this music, the beat was not emphasized strongly. The result was a poised, smoothly flowing quality of movement, as illustrated in the antiphon *Laus Deo Patri* (Praise Be to God, the Father), *Masterpieces of Music before 1750, no. 1*. The metrical procedures of early Christian church song apply also to sacred music of the late Renaissance period (the sixteenth century).

Music written in the seventeenth and eighteenth centuries often had a vigorous, regular quality of movement based on equal metric groups and well-emphasized beats in a rather quick tempo. The listener can easily make out, in the first movement of the Third Symphony of Beethoven, a metric group of three quick and light beats. This goes on so regularly that we begin to feel that the first beat in each group of three is the important one, and that these stronger, more widely spaced beats themselves form groups of two and four. We feel thus, an *accent,* or stress, returning periodically to help organize the flow of steady quick beats. This sort of accent has come to serious music from dance music and from simpler types of poetry, in which a marked stress was made regularly either by the foot, as in dancing, or by a strong syllable, as in poetry.

In twentieth-century music, we find passages with changes in the tempo and the length of the beat, as well as in the size of the metric group. Such procedure creates a subtle, somewhat imbalanced, often uneasy quality of movement. Properly handled, it can intensify movement effectively and make a very strong impact upon the emotions. A striking example is the Dance of the Adolescents from Igor Stravinsky's work *Le Sacre du printemps*. Part of the curious, fantastic, primitive effect of this music is due to its metric unevenness.

Gradual change in tempo, either by going faster or slower, has a marked effect upon the expressive quality of the music. We have all heard performances in which greater excitement and brilliance were sought by a quickening of tempo; conversely, many an artist hopes to make a greater expressive impact upon his audience by slowing down at critical points. Composers will write such indications into their music: *accelerando* and *ritardando*. They will also compose the music so that it seems to lose or gain speed of tempo. Listen to the slowdown after the grand avalanche at the beginning of the finale of Beethoven's Third Symphony. These rapid changes of tempo certainly provide an effective foil for the precise, regular dance music to follow.

Ex. 2–17. Beethoven: Third Symphony, last movement.

Note Values

You have heard that notes have different lengths, or *values* in time. In the written examples, these values corresponded to certain written symbols. Note values are not fixed in length. They take their length according to a proportional scale of values. Thus, a half note, ♩, is twice the length of a quarter note, ♩; a sixteenth note, ♬, is half as long as an eighth note, ♪. The composer decides how long a certain type of note will be; the others then are played in a fixed ratio, as we have indicated above. Since about 1820, instructions for note lengths have been communicated by indicating how many notes of a given value should occupy a minute of time.

We not only receive impressions of length or quantity from note values; we also sense a difference in the *weight* or accent of short or long notes. Short notes move quickly; they give an impression of buoyancy. Long notes move slowly; they give a sense of greater weight; they carry accent. Therefore, when long and short notes are combined in a passage, we assign the effect of arrival to long notes, the effect of movement to short notes. This can take place within the smallest rhythmic unit, the measure or the *foot*. Probably the most convincing effect takes place when the second of two notes is the longer. This is a universally familiar pattern; it corresponds to the iambic or the trochaic feet, the two most widely employed of poetic meters. Carried out regularly it produces an easy, balanced, and virtually automatic quality of movement. A line from the song, *The Jolly Miller,* illustrates iambic meter in the poetry and trochaic in the music.

Ex. 2–18. *The Jolly Miller.*

The short notes in *The Jolly Miller* are called *upbeats*; the long notes are *downbeats*. Ordinarily, upbeats precede a strong accent; they carry a sense of movement. Downbeats coincide with accent; they represent arrival, as well as new points of departure.

When a long note is the first tone in a passage, it becomes a point of departure. Frequently, the last sound in a composition will seem to continue beyond its actual duration, taking on added power of length; and hence, it will give a stronger impression of arrival.

We tend to expect a long note at the beginning of a measure, reckoning simply on the basis of weight, accent, and arrival. Suppose we shift the long note out of its normal position. The point of arrival in the measure changes momentarily, the metric groups around that note shift their positions, and a conflict arises in the flow of the music. This is called *syncopation*. See for yourself what effect syncopation has. In the example given below, count four equal beats to each measure; tap each note out. In the third measure, the displacement of the long note throws the music momentarily off balance, but in the fourth measure things are once again set to rights. In this example, as well as in many passages which use syncopation, the imbalance creates a stronger push toward the point of arrival at the end of the phrase than if the rhythm were completely regular. Syncopation can thus be used to build musical climaxes. Try this example at different speeds.

Ex. 2–19. Syncopation.

In the following example, from the opening movement of Beethoven's Third Symphony, a series of syncopations and changes in metric groups builds up a tremendous accumulation of rhythmic momentum. These imbalances finally discharge their energy at a climactic point of arrival. It is typical of eighteenth- and nineteenth-century composers to build a growing sense of rhythmic urgency as a phrase or period moves toward its climax and completion. Rhythmic balance and imbalance played against each other comprise the chief resource in such rhythmic progression.

Ex. 2–20. Beethoven: Third Symphony, first movement.

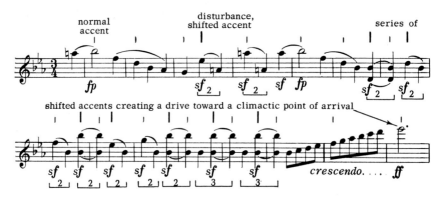

Syncopation can also create a buoyant, jazzy effect of movement. It is the very trade-mark of jazz itself, and is the only way that this kind of music can escape from the perfectly regular rhythm which dance music requires.

Ex. 2–21. Syncopation.

a. Melody in even quarter notes.

b. Same melody with syncopations creating a jazzy bounce.

There is one more question about note values. How much of its allotted time does a note actually sound?

1. When each tone sounds its full value and moves without break into the next tone, the manner of performance is *legato,* meaning connected, tied, and the effect of movement is slurred and smooth. The church song, *Laus Deo Patri,* is performed in legato manner.

2. If a tiny separation is made between successive tones, so that each tone is heard slightly less than its full value and the remainder taken up by the break, the manner is *détaché,* meaning separated. The first movement of the Fifth Symphony of Beethoven is played *détaché,* with the exception of certain passages.

3. When the notes are very short, and there is marked separation between them, more so than in *détaché,* the manner is *staccato.* The second movement of Joseph Haydn's *Surprise* Symphony illustrates the light, bouncing effect that staccato can project.

Rhythmic Motives

The measurement of musical time does more than set a pace, organize beats into groups, and create types of movement. It forms distinctive patterns, called *rhythmic motives.* The rhythmic motive at the beginning of Beethoven's Fifth Symphony is a very famous one. These four notes comprise the main rhythmic pattern of the entire first movement; we hear them hundreds of times. Characteristic dances, such as the rhumba, the tango, the mazurka, the gavotte, and the minuet, all have their special rhythmic patterns or motives that set the quality of movement which distinguishes each dance. Here are some:

Ex. 2–22. Characteristic rhythmic patterns of dances.

a. Tango—rather slow.

syncopation after first beat

b. Gavotte—moderate tempo.

rhythmic groups begin in middle of measure

c. Polonaise—moderate.

characteristic groups of short notes

d. Mazurka—fairly quick.

rhythmic emphasis on second beat

e. Minuet (late eighteenth century)—rather fast.

vigorous upbeat

Some minuets are performed in slower tempo and begin immediately with a downbeat. The Minuet from Mozart's *Don Giovanni* is a familiar example of this type.

Rhythmic motives combine with salient melodic shapes to provide the basic structural materials of musical composition. As an illustration of the way in which rhythmic patterns can affect musical expression, listen to the five examples given below. In each the same melodic shape is used. A different tempo and rhythmic pattern, however, are imposed in each case and the expressive quality is therefore different. The changes in rhythmic pattern, using the same melodic material, would be comparable to a sculptor creating five figures, each human, but each different in posture, proportion, and expression.

Ex. 2–23. Changes in rhythmic pattern, using same melody.

As you listen for the rhythmic quality of a phrase, note whether it maintains a sense of even flow, whether it seems to settle or relax as it approaches the caesura, or whether it gathers strength and intensity as it drives toward its point of arrival. Each phrase has a sense of *rhythmic progression,* as illustrated in the example given below:

Ex. 2–24. Tchaikovsky: *Nutcracker Suite,* Russian Dance.

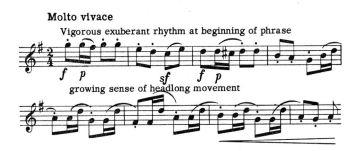

Rhythmic action ebbs and flows within a piece. We can sense a growing excitement as motives become shorter and more densely packed. When motives are sharply contrasted, a feeling of conflict may develop. The sense of rhythmic action in a phrase, period, or an entire composition is a clue to the very life of the music. Like the general rise and fall of melody, rhythmic action, as it increases and decreases, can organize extended phases of musical movement.

Beat, tempo, meter, measure, motive, and phrase constitute the basic rhythmic categories of music. As we listen for rhythmic values, the following points will serve as guides:

1. Clarity and strength of caesuras
2. Quality of beat or pulse with respect to regularity, strength, and clarity
3. Approximate tempo
4. Approximate metric groupings
5. Correlation of beat, tempo, and meter. For example, a light, steady beat, in simple triple meter in a quick tempo, giving a sense of buoyant movement, as in a waltz
6. Salient rhythmic motives and their distribution
7. Manner of performance: legato, *détaché*, or staccato
8. Sense of rhythmic progression within the phrase
9. Relation of above criteria to the style and expressive qualities of the piece

Applying these criteria to the first movement of Beethoven's Third Symphony, we discover the following general rhythmic qualities:

1. Generally clear and very strong caesuras, with new phases of movement tending to begin at caesura point; coincidence of arrival and departure.
2. A clear and definite beat or pulse, sometimes emphatic, sometimes gentle; regular beat throughout the piece.
3. Quick tempo but with a deliberate, almost heavy effect.
4. Triple meter, with metric groups of two and four measures as the usual patterns; frequent syncopation.
5. A firm, steady beat in triple time, moving quickly, with sudden interruptions and displacements of the regular movement; a sense of vigorous, purposeful movement, intensified by the characteristic use of syncopation preceding important points of arrival.
6. A great variety of rhythmic motives handled so that they contrast effectively with each other.
7. Legato, *détaché*, and staccato manner intermingled throughout.
8. Most phrases and periods built so that rhythmic intensity grows toward points of arrival.

9. The steady vigorous pulse sets the piece going with great assurance. Rhythmic displacements and contrasts set up striking conflicts which are settled with grand flourishes at widely spaced and emphatic points of arrival. Rhythmic interest is maintained and intensified by rhythmic contrasts. All these factors combine to create a tremendously broad and powerful rhythmic structure.

Rhythm serves a number of purposes in music. Most obviously it creates the basic quality of movement by the delineation of small time units, such as tones, measures, and motives. It sets our foot tapping; it quickens our spirit. Rhythm also has a long-range action, one which is felt strongly but not so easily recognized or described. This long-range action suggests what should be done and when. It guides the composer in shaping periods and phrase groups; it tells him when to make caesuras, how long he can go on doing one sort of thing, and when some contrast or fresh gesture is necessary. We, as listeners and critics, are also governed by this long-range time sense in music, which is like the mental time clock that tells us when to eat, to work, to arise in the morning. With every composer, and indeed, with every piece, its action results in a long-range plan of action. Thus, rhythm, in the broadest sense, is a basic factor in the over-all structure of music, even though we cannot set specific rules for its operation on this large scale.

TEXTURE

When we studied melody and rhythm, we were principally concerned with a single line of music. Still, we must have been aware that the total effect of movement in a musical passage is the result of a number of voices or instruments working together. If we turn our attention to the manner in which these parts move with or against each other, we can learn more about how a piece of music moves. This aspect of music is called *texture,* and it refers particularly to the *action of the component parts.*

When there is (1) *one part* playing, or (2) *one principal part* taking a featured melody, or (3) *one procedure* governing the entire texture, the texture is called *homophonic.* The examples below illustrate two kinds of homophonic texture. The first example comprises a melody and its *accompaniment.* The accompaniment furnishes a steady rhythmic background by means of a simple ornamental figure. This creates a light and flowing sense of movement.

Ex. 2–25. Mozart: Sonata in C major, K. 545, second movement.

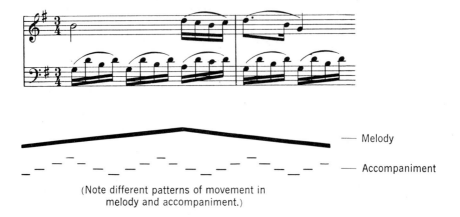

— Melody

— Accompaniment

(Note different patterns of movement in
melody and accompaniment.)

In the second kind of homophonic texture, Example 2–26, one procedure dominates, although the melody is carried by the uppermost part. There is a massive, forthright, and vigorous quality to the movement.

Ex. 2–26. Beethoven: Fifth Symphony, last movement.

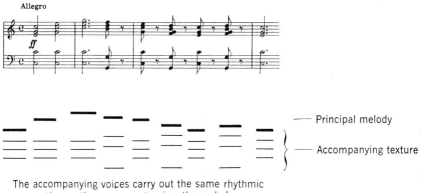

— Principal melody

— Accompanying texture

The accompanying voices carry out the same rhythmic
action as the uppermost voice, the melody.

When several voices play clearly separate and independent lines, with all appearing to be equal in importance, the texture is called *polyphonic*. The terms *counterpoint* and *contrapuntal* also describe this kind of texture. In Example 2–27, polyphonic texture creates a tightly knit and intense kind of movement; many musical events seem to take place in a short time.

Ex. 2–27. Bach: Sinfonia in D minor.

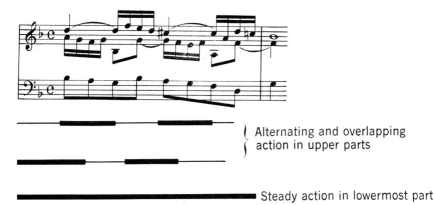

} Alternating and overlapping
} action in upper parts

Steady action in lowermost part

If the voices take up the same melody or *subject* in turn, the procedure is called *imitation*. The use of the same subject binds the voices together even more tightly than in nonimitative counterpoint. Example 2–28 illustrates imitation, which is a form of polyphony.

Ex. 2–28. Bach: Prelude in E♭ major, *Well-Tempered Clavier, Book I.*

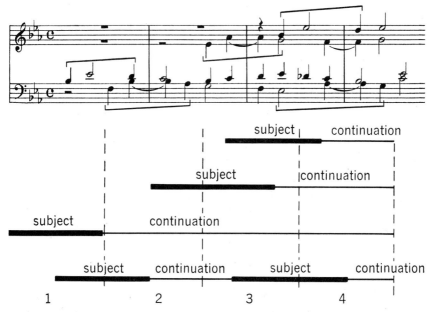

A familiar, simple type of imitative polyphony is the *round,* such as *Row, Row Your Boat.* In singing such a piece, each performer feels that his part works against the others in a neatly fitted texture; he thus gains a vivid satisfaction in musical participation. Indeed, much polyphonic music was written originally with this purpose in mind; in such music, the values are sensed most keenly from the inside out, rather than by the nonpartici-pating listener.

With regard to *phrase structure,* homophonic and polyphonic textures tell completely different stories. When there is but one salient idea, the progress of the music is relatively easy to follow and points of arrival tend to be clear. The line pauses, and we have a caesura. In polyphonic music, especially imitation, different phases of movement overlap each other. The caesura of one part is covered by the movement of another. Polyphonic music, for this reason, tends to flow along continuously for long periods of time, and frequently to give an impressive effect of accumulation. The diagram below illustrates the two different procedures in relation to phrase structure:

Ex. 2–29.

a. Phrase structure of melody and accompaniment.

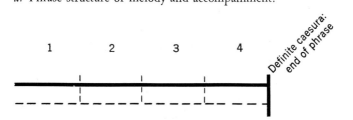

b. Phrase structure of continuous polyphonic texture.

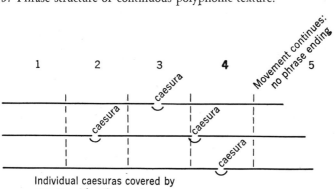

A great deal of music that is basically homophonic in texture shows elements of contrapuntal treatment. Perhaps the accompaniment will take on some personality of its own by means of a distinctive melodic figure; perhaps the principal melody will be shared by different voices; sometimes incidental and short-lived imitations will appear to give a bit more interest and momentum to the music. In Example 2–30, this kind of texture, designated as *give-and-take* in this book, is illustrated. The principal melody is in the uppermost part, yet the bass voice is quite active and important and at one point suggests an imitation of the melody.

Ex. 2–30. Beethoven: Sonata for Piano in B♭ major, Op. 22, second movement.

Throughout the first movement of the Third Symphony of Beethoven, we hear a wide variety of textures, covering the categories we have described above. This, of course, corresponds to the rich melodic content and the wide range of rhythmic procedures we have found in this piece. Here is a list of the textural layouts in the first eighty-two measures of this piece:

- 1–2: full orchestra, full chords
- 3–15: *melody* in cello, *accompaniment,* melody taken over by violins, light texture
- 15–23: *melody and accompaniment,* handled in give-and-take fashion, light texture
- 23–37: a moment of *counterpoint* at beginning, superseded by *one procedure* dominating the entire texture, heavier sound
- 38–45: *melody and accompaniment* in full orchestra
- 45–57: *give-and-take* with some *contrapuntal* action, light texture; heavy texture, full orchestra, *one procedure* at end of period
- 58–65: *melody* with *contrapuntal* line in basses, light texture increasing in heaviness
- 65–80: *melody and accompaniment,* heavy texture

As we listen for textural values, it becomes apparent that we must take into account the relationship of tone qualities within the texture. Tones will be blended when the instruments are similar in quality; tones will be set off sharply from each other if the instruments are contrasted in tone quality. In some kinds of music, such as the Lassus motet, *Tristis est anima mea,* or a composition for string quartet, all the voices and instruments have similar qualities of tone. In other music, sharp contrasts in tone color will cause even a melody-and-accompaniment texture to sound contrapuntal. This we heard from time to time in the Beethoven Third Symphony.

Hector Berlioz elevated this principle of contrast between instrumental qualities of sound to a very important position in his scheme of composition, and it is the basis of much of his contrapuntal writing. His *Symphonie fantastique* is typical in this respect. To use an analogy of painting, the boldness of contrast in line can be intensified frequently by sharp contrasts in color or shade. On the other hand, when many colors are run together, the result may be a rich blend in which no single value dominates. This would be comparable to a massive effect for the full orchestra, in which all instruments blend but partially cancel each other's specific qualities of sound.

Each conscientious performer or conductor makes a special study of the textural values in a piece. He must have a clear idea of the action of the component voices and the degree of blend or separation. This is necessary so that what the composer has to say remains clear and undistorted. How often in a performance do we miss an important figure or voice because of a poorly projected texture, and thereby lose the thread of movement and the meaning of the music itself for a time.

The two most important voices or parts in a musical texture have traditionally been the outer, that is, the lowermost and uppermost parts. This is simply because we can hear better what goes on in these parts than we can hear inner parts. Example 2–31 on the facing page shows how the outer parts assume textural leadership. At various times, the lowermost part has been called a *bass, pedal, tenor,* or *basso continuo.* The uppermost voice, which sang the most important melodic part, was called a *discant, superius, soprano, duplum,* or *treble,* at different times. To this day, outer voices form the skeleton of most musical textures, with other voices adding or filling in for richer sound.

As we might expect, textural values provide important clues in the analysis of different musical styles. We shall find perhaps the greatest con-

Ex. 2–31. Haydn: Quartet in D major, Op. 64, no. 5, first movement.

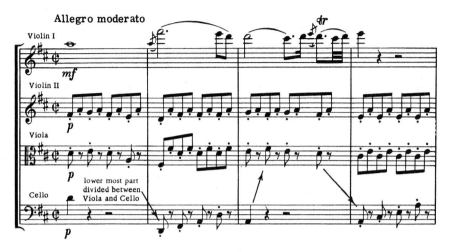

trasts in comparing a vocal piece of the Renaissance period, such as the Lassus motet, with a modern work for a small group of instruments, such as Igor Stravinsky's *L'Histoire du soldat*. The Renaissance piece would have the following textural features:

1. A blending of voices; homogeneity of sound
2. Limited range of sound
3. Much contrapuntal activity, but because of factors 1 and 2, not a very strong impression of the independence of voices

The texture of the modern piece would show:

1. Sharp contrasts of sound; heterogeneity of sound
2. Wide range of sound; wide separation in the pitches of different instruments
3. Strong impression of contrapuntal activity, even when a melodic line with accompaniment is used, due to the extreme independence of the voices, their lack of blend in sonority

To summarize:

1. Note the action of the component voices.
2. Judge the effect of this action upon phrase structure and caesuras.
3. Take note of the varieties of texture used.
4. Consider the effect of tone color upon texture.

It is easy to see that textural values add much color and interest to music. Not only are they arresting in their own right, but they give sharp relief and fresh nuance to the play of melodic motives and they support and carry forward rhythmic action.

DYNAMICS

Much of the general expressive quality we perceive in a musical passage is created by the sheer strength and amount of sound being produced. This aspect of music is called *dynamics*. The vehemence of many passages in Beethoven's music arises directly from the fact that he is making the orchestra play in full numbers and at maximum strength. On the other hand, the disembodied, airy quality of much of Debussy's music is dependent principally upon the fact that a minimum of sound is required.

The dynamic range of musical sound is indicated by certain conventional signs and terms, as given below:

ppp	pianississimo	extremely soft
pp	pianissimo	very soft
p	piano	soft
mp	mezzo piano	moderately soft
mf	mezzo forte	moderately full or loud
f	forte	strong or loud
ff	fortissimo	very loud
fff	fortississimo	extremely loud

Sometimes, to dramatize their point, composers have written ppppp or fffff to indicate the utter extremes of soft or loud in their music.

One extremely important aspect of dynamics in music is the gradual increase or decrease of loudness and strength. These changes, called *crescendo* or *decrescendo,* are directed to the ebb and flow of emotional tension and excitement in music. This is particularly the case when the dynamic range is great and the amount of time occupied in the rise or fall is considerable. Ravel's *Bolero,* which we mentioned in Chapter 1, is built on a huge crescendo.

Dynamic changes can be minute and subtle, and thus add expressive nuances to musical performance. Very often the difference between a moving performance and a dull one is the degree of shading which the master artist uses to shape the phrase, the slight swellings and taperings of sound which place the phrase in clear and meaningful perspective. This also can be overdone; nevertheless, when projected with subtlety and taste, it is one of the delights of the musical experience.

Dynamic strength can also vary sharply between sections of a piece. This was frequently the case in music of Bach's time and earlier. When you listen to an organist change registration from a full to a light quality, as if he were ascending or descending the levels of a terrace, you are hearing what is called *terrace dynamics*. This is also associated with the alternation of a single or a few instruments with a full body of performers. The amount of sound here changes the dynamic quality.

Dynamic strength also has a great bearing on textural values. Consider how effectively a heavy, single-action texture, such as that in Example 2–26, is projected when its dynamic level is high in strength. On the other hand, an actively contrapuntal texture could not make its point effectively if all voices were performing at either maximum or minimum strength. A medium level of dynamics would suit such a texture best.

If we can coordinate and evaluate these four basic elements of music, melody, rhythm, texture, and dynamics, we shall be able to look far into the substance and quality of a musical composition.

HARMONY

As you were listening for melodic shapes, rhythmic movement, and the interaction of voices moving along together, you may have observed that the tones themselves created combinations of various kinds, that they had the power to arrange themselves in a number of relationships. *Harmony* has to deal with the ways in which groups of tones can be related to each other, apart from melodic, rhythmic, or textural considerations.

When tones are sounded together or in succession, there seems to be a tendency for *one tone to assert itself* in our hearing more strongly than others, to establish itself as a point of reference. This can be illustrated quite simply. Hum to yourself a familiar song such as *My Old Kentucky Home* or *America*. Stop humming just before the last note. In this case the song is incomplete. No matter what you do rhythmically or melodically, the sense of arrival necessary to round off the piece is missing unless you sing the last note; this tone, thus, is a point of reference for the whole piece. It has established itself as a *tonal center*.

Listen now to *Laus Deo Patri* (*Masterpieces,* no. 1). In this piece, can you hear one tone, or one pitch that seems more prominent than any other? The answer is *yes*; the tone is E. Its prominence arises from four factors:

1. It is the first tone we hear, a point of departure.
2. We hear the tone more frequently.
3. In a number of its appearances, it has greater length than its neighboring tones.
4. It is the last tone we hear, in almost every phrase, and at the end of the piece.

Four conditions, *first impression, frequency, length,* and *finality,* satisfy the requirements for prominence in this piece. We would probably all agree that the most important of these conditions is the last, *finality*—particularly if it agrees with the first. It is the last sound we hear in each of a number of substantial phases of movement; therefore, we assign to this tone a position of reference with regard to the other tones. It occupies a central position in the constellation of tones which make up this piece; it is, therefore, a *tonal center,* a *tonic,* to use specific musical terms.

Harmonically, a tonal center is an extremely important factor. It sets a position according to which all tones adjust themselves in our hearing. It is analogous to a geographical point or center of gravity by which we can measure and evaluate distances and positions. Once we receive the impression that a tonal center has been established, we can appreciate movement to and from it; we have another way to gauge movement and arrival. A shift of tonal center will then give us the impression of a change of position, and hence, of relationship, between the tones involved.

Any tone heard often enough will take on something of the role of a tonal center, provided nothing is done to erase or contradict its effect. This is definition of a tonal center by *prominence.* Prominence is a mechanical and quantitative method for defining a tonal center.

Harmony also has to do with the effects which tones create when they sound together. Try this for yourself. Go to the keyboard and select one tone. Play different tones in turn together with the tone you have selected. You will notice that each interval, each combination has a different sound. These qualities and distinctions represent another important aspect of harmony.

Tones in their harmonic relationships are like chemical substances which have affinities for each other. When elements come near each other they can combine to form new, distinctive compounds; similarly when tones come together they form distinctive intervals and combinations.

In the combinations you played, you must have hit upon some that sounded like the harmony of familiar music; other combinations may have sounded strange and provocative. Some were sweet-sounding, others harsh and edgy. Each sound, however, might conceivably find a proper place in some kind of musical action; it might participate in some phase of movement or it might underscore some point of arrival.

Stability and Instability

Not only do harmonic sounds have special qualities; they also give impressions of being *stable* or *unstable*. You can discover this for yourself. The diagram below represents a section of a piano keyboard. Indicated upon this diagram, you will find two harmonic intervals, one *stable,* the other highly *unstable*. In addition to playing these, you can experiment with other combinations, listening for their degree of stability or instability.

Ex. 2–32. Stability and instability.

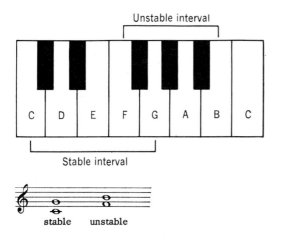

For further illustration, let us contrast the first few measures of the Prelude to *Tristan* with the song *Drink to Me*. The combinations of tones, the chords in the song, give much firmer impressions of stability than those in the Prelude. Indeed, the very first chords of each piece provide a clue to the harmony of the entire composition. In the song, the first chord seems stable; it poses no harmonic problem, and could act just as well for arrival as it does for departure. In the Prelude, the first chord is markedly unstable; it suggests restlessness and movement; by itself it would call for some kind of answer. Throughout the song we hear the first chord a number of times, and this strengthens the impression of stability. In the Prelude, each new chord seems to suggest a rather marked shift of position, and each new sound adds to the general impression of instability. If you will refer back to Example 2–26, you will hear an alternation of stable and unstable chords, beginning with the third chord.

We may reasonably expect to find effects of harmonic stability at important points of arrival, at the ends of phrases and periods. Conversely, harmonic effects of lesser stability are suitable for maintaining musical movement. We have only to listen once more to our song, *Drink to Me,* in order to see how this relationship of stability and instability operates in the phrase structure of familiar music. At the end of the first, second, and fourth phrases a satisfying effect of harmonic stability has been created. Although the entire song does not venture far into harmonic problem areas, the final chords, relatively speaking, are considerably more stable than those within the phrases. You may have noticed that in order to secure an effect of harmonic stability, it is necessary to reach a strong rhythmic point of arrival, a marked caesura. Thus, rhythm and harmony work together to build the outlines of phrase structure.

Ex. 2–33. Rhythm and harmony in phrase structure.

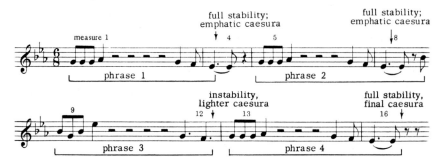

Wagner, in his Prelude, seems to have tried deliberately to counteract this feeling for harmonic arrival. There is hardly one chord in the entire piece that would satisfy a need for arrival. The listener has to depend partly on texture, partly on the rhythmic caesuras to tell him that a point of arrival has been reached.

In the first period of the opening movement of Beethoven's Quartet in F major, Op. 59, no. 1, we can hear a tremendously strong point of rhythmic and harmonic arrival, settling the problem of harmonic instability which the preceding measures have created.

The fact that some tonal relationships carry movement forward and others tell us that we have arrived indicates that order and system can be made out of the wide variety of sounds and tone relationships. We have heard octaves and unisons signaling arrival, lending their stability to points of rest. Aside from the unison and octave, when two voices are performing together, by far the most important stable interval they can sound is the *perfect fifth*. This is the stable interval given in Example 2–32. The ear accepts this interval as the embodiment of a universally stable condition of sound. Of the two tones comprising this interval, *the lower* is felt as being the more stable, the better representative of arrival. Test this for yourself. At the piano, using the chart of Example 2–32, play first C, then G; immediately following, play G, then C. The first figure will pose a question; the second provides the fitting answer. The ending on C, the lower note of the perfect fifth, gives a complete sense of arrival. This relationship between the two notes of the perfect fifth is so strong and pervasive that it has been used effectively to organize phrases, periods, and, indeed, entire

compositions harmonically. The $\begin{Bmatrix} \text{tonal centers} \\ \text{C–G; G–C} \\ \text{1–5; 5–1} \end{Bmatrix}$ scheme has often represented points of departure and arrival which mark off the two halves of a large piece. The note G represents the *dominant* to the *tonic* C.

We can hear how the perfect fifth is used for stability, position, and arrival in the dance from medieval times which is reproduced in no. 12 of *Masterpieces,* the estampie. Listen for the perfect fifth which ends most of the phrases. Others end with a single prominent tone, doubled in the octave. Both effects give a sense of arrival within the phrase. In Bartók's *Ostinato,* we are oriented harmonically at the very beginning by a perfect fifth which is repeated many times in the lower register of the piano. The first part of this piece takes this perfect fifth as the indication of its tonal center. Listen for the change of perfect fifth in the left hand of the piano; at that point, you have a change of tonal center. Such a change can have a strong kinesthetic effect, as if we had moved a floor up or down in an elevator.

In the three pieces we have just heard, the *Laus Deo,* the estampie, and the *Ostinato,* we had little difficulty hearing harmonic effects of stability and arrival. The prominent tones and the perfect fifths enabled us to get our harmonic bearings very comfortably. However, if we should try to discover these effects in the Prelude to *Tristan,* we should be at quite a loss. Hardly a single tone throughout the entire piece acts as a stabilizing factor. The prominence of any tone in this piece does nothing to create a sense of tonal center, because each prominent tone seems to cancel the impression of previous tones. *Tristan*'s harmony is like a kaleidoscopic shifting of colored lights that merge, blend, and separate in ever new combinations without allowing any hue or tint to dominate for long. As for perfect fifths, when they appear, they are disguised or combined with other tones which erase, which destroy the effect of stability. All the harmony moves and shifts in this piece, never once settling for any appreciable period.

What creates harmonic instability? How did Wagner manage to create such a consistent and systematic impression of harmonic tension? At this point, we shall certainly not go into all the subtleties of Wagner's harmonic language, but we can point to some basic harmonic relationships which lie at the root of his style, and which pervade the harmonic techniques of five centuries, from 1400 to 1900.

Once again play the unstable interval diagramed in Example 2–32. You will not only hear that it is unstable, but that it seems to have something of a pull in a specific direction, as if its instability could be resolved by playing another specific interval. We have here harmonic *tension*; an important harmonic *question* is being asked. To *answer* this question, proceed as in the following diagram:

Ex. 2–34. Harmonic question and answer.

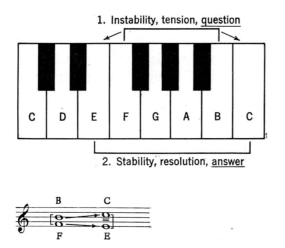

This progression binds these four tones together in a formula of harmonic *tension* and *resolution,* creating a harmonic question and its answer. Test

each of these four tones in order to determine which gives the most satisfactory impression of arrival, of tonal center. Without question, you should
decide on the note C.

If you take the first member of this progression, the interval of tension,
you will find that one tone resolves upward, the other downward. Experiment further with this first interval; this time place F on top, B at the
bottom. F will move down; B will move up. No matter what position this
combination assumes, the tones will resolve in opposite directions if their
natural tendency is realized. This tendency governs this interval very
strongly. F–B, or any other interval of the same size, is called the *tritone,*
meaning an interval of three whole tones or steps. B–F, which creates the
same effect, is called the *false fifth* or diminished fifth.

We usually designate the rising member of the tritone or the false fifth
as the *leading tone,* since it leads to the *tonic* note. By extension, harmonies
which contain the leading tone, and which thereby contain an element of
tension, are called *leading-tone harmonies.* The importance of leading-tone
harmonies becomes clear to us if we realize that they are the strongest
embodiments of movement in harmony, and occupy a vital position in the
movement-arrival formulas which govern music.

We now have three ways in which a tonal center may be defined: (1) by
prominence; (2) by the lower note of the perfect fifth; (3) by its position
in a *tension-resolution* formula. Putting these all together, we create an
extremely powerful definition of tonal center. In the following example:

1. C is prominent by virtue of its being in the outer voices and at the end
of the progression.
2. C is the resolution of the tension created by B.
3. C is the lower note of the perfect fifth.

Ex. 2–35. Tonal center defined by tension and resolution.

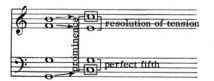

You will hear this particular kind of progression at almost every important
point of arrival in music of the eighteenth and nineteenth centuries. The
tonal relationships it embodies form the basis of the harmonic system used
in Western music from the Renaissance to the present day. This progression

can be varied infinitely in color and weight, with rhythmic, melodic, and textural values, but when it is present in a harmonic passage, its action is felt strongly. It provides the clearest kind of focus to harmonic movement. We can see now that Wagner used only tension factors; instead of resolving his chords of tension, he simply replaced the resolutions with other problem chords with leading-tone harmonies.

Intervals other than the perfect fifth and tritone are stable or unstable in varying degrees. Octaves and unisons are stable, but they lack the anchorage in musical space which characterizes the perfect fifth. As a group, thirds and sixths are relatively stable; fourths, seconds, sevenths, and ninths are unstable. Generally speaking, relatively stable intervals are described as being *consonant*; relatively unstable intervals are described as being *dissonant*.

Consonance and dissonance values have not been fixed during the history of Western music. There have been different ideas about harmonic stability and instability through the past one thousand years. Until around the year 1300, only fourths, fifths, and octaves were considered fully consonant, as our two examples from the medieval period clearly illustrate. All other intervals were considered dissonant and were accepted only when the music was moving past them quickly within a phrase. From about 1400 to 1900, thirds and sixths were added to the list of consonant intervals, and the fourth was taken as a dissonance on account of its instability. Today, traditionally dissonant or unstable intervals have been treated frequently as though they were consonant, so that a phrase or period could well arrive upon a chord of extremely harsh dissonant quality. Standards of consonance and dissonance provide important clues to the nature of a musical style. Thus, Wagner's and Schönberg's music has a high concentration of dissonance and their music seems restless and searching. *Drink to Me* is almost entirely consonant; to this characteristic it owes much of its calm sweetness. As we might expect, consonance will generally be associated with arrival, dissonance with movement.

Briefly summarizing the above, we have:

Movement	Arrival
Harmonic Instability	Harmonic Stability
Subordinate tones	Prominent tone
Tension	Resolution
Tritone	Perfect fifth
Dissonance	Consonance
Subsidiary tones	Tonic or tonal center

The stability and consonance values of intervals have been linked with their position in the *harmonic series*. The harmonic series is a combination of tones that accompany, faintly but appreciably, a tone that is sounded on a string, pipe, tube, membrane, or any other medium that gives out a relatively fixed pitch. The sounding body vibrates in its entire length, giving out the tone we hear. The body also vibrates in a series of fractions: one-half, one-third, one-fourth, one-fifth, one-sixth, etc., presumably to infinity. The first six, including the principal or fundamental, give us a widely spaced combination, the notes of which create a most agreeable consonance. Very likely, through millenia of adaptation to this *chord of nature,* we have come to accept it as a pleasant and thoroughly stable sound. Therefore, the intervals comprising this chord (octaves, fifths, fourths, and thirds, also sixths) seem to embody consonance more convincingly than any other intervals. Here is the harmonic series of C.

Ex. 2–36.

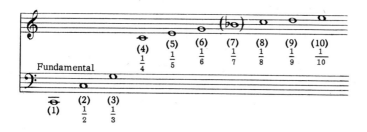

Chords

The harmonic procedures we have been describing are generally embodied in combinations of tones sounded together called *chords.* If we listen for the kind of chords that are used in a piece of music, we can tell much about when it was written. The open, even sparse sound of medieval music comes from the consistent use of chords that contain only fifths, fourths, and octaves. The continuous sweetness of Renaissance music comes from the blend of thirds and sixths added to fifths or octaves. The strong harmonic gestures of seventeenth-, eighteenth-, and nineteenth-century music arise from the judicious use of dissonances, particularly those that contain the tritone, intermingled with the harmony inherited from Renaissance music. Greater and greater use of dissonance in the late nineteenth century leads to a dense, colorful, and rich sound, often disturbing in its effect of instability. While modern music has drawn from all of these procedures, and sometimes sounds like earlier music, its specific contribution has been fresh and experimental combinations, often involving seconds, sevenths, and ninths. The effect is often that of a hypercharged tension. Chords in a composition are like a fabric which has a distinctive feel and look.

The most familiar chord of all is the *major triad*. It is called *triad* because it contains three notes; it is called *major* because the middle note is a *major*, or large third above the lowermost note. The two outer notes form a perfect fifth. The diagram in Example 2–37 shows you how to obtain triads.

Ex. 2–37. Triads.

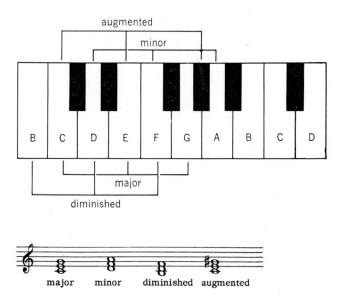

The major triad presents a compact, well-blended, sonorous, and sweet sound, the most perfect embodiment of harmonic balance, coherence, and fullness. Indeed, this combination was called the *armonia perfetta,* the perfect harmony, by musicians of the seventeenth and eighteenth centuries.

Other kinds of triads are built in a manner similar to the major, but have slightly different intervals. The *minor* triad has a small or *minor* third above its lowermost note.

Try D, F, and A on the piano, using our diagram as a guide. The sound of the minor triad is not as bold and bright as that of the major triad; it is somewhat darker and rather clouded in effect. The second movement of Beethoven's Third Symphony has a great concentration of minor-triad sounds; in this piece, as in many others, the minor triad lends itself to tragic qualities of expression.

Both the major and minor triads, since they are consonant sounds and contain the perfect fifth, can stand as harmonic points of arrival; they can represent the tonic note providing they are approached by the tritone.

The tritone itself is embodied in the *diminished* triad, B–D–F. This is called *diminished* because its fifth is smaller than the perfect fifth. The diminished triad has a hard, compact kind of dissonant quality. Since it contains the tritone, it is a most useful harmonic device to carry movement forward. We can hear it frequently, either by itself or in combination with one or two other tones, in the harmonic progressions of eighteenth- and nineteenth-century music.

A much less familiar kind of triad is the *augmented* triad; here the fifth is larger than the perfect fifth. Try C, E, and the middle black key next to G. The sound is rich, perhaps a bit oversweet, suggesting nostalgia or a poignant turn of feeling. The sound is also unstable, but not strongly dissonant. Much late nineteenth-century music uses the augmented triad for special emotional effects.

Chords that contain more than three different tones are named according to their distinguishing interval. Thus, if we place the note B above the triad C–E–G, we obtain a four-note chord in which there is an interval of a *seventh*. So, such a chord is called a *seventh* chord. In traditional harmony, additions are generally made by piling thirds on top of each other. So we can go on to *ninth* chords, *eleventh* chords, and *thirteenth* chords. By the time we arrive at the *fifteenth,* we find ourselves duplicating the root, or first note of the chord, and so we have reached a limit. For practical purposes, the sevenths are useful; the others appear but occasionally. All these chords are dissonant in sound, and will, therefore, serve specifically for musical movement.

The sound combinations we are likely to hear in modern music do not fit into the picture we have given above. There seems to be little agreement about chord types; each combination has a special, perhaps unique sound. Most of the chords in modern music are unstable, yet not many of them give a clear indication of leading somewhere. Sometimes the vertical combinations appear to be the accidental meeting of tones within several energetic contrapuntal lines; at other times, a very special evocative effect is projected by a freshly devised mélange of tones and textures. In listening for chordal values, we should not judge these works by what we expect from earlier music. Likewise, the modern age should not underrate the power and the logic of key-centered harmony.

Triads are identified according to the position which their lowermost tones, called *roots*, take in relation to a given tonal center. The following diagram illustrates the positions of the triads that have relation to the tonal center, C.

Ex. 2–38. Triad relationships.

Cadences

In Example 2–35 we heard a chord progression that had a most familiar ring. We can find it at the end of a great many compositions, as well as at the points of arrival in periods. This progression, in which the tritone resolves to the tonic chord, is called a *cadence*. It is the harmonic equivalent of a strong rhythmic caesura, and serves as a very emphatic gesture of arrival. Phrase structure in music, like that of language, has need of several types of arrival and articulation. This has given rise to a number of different kinds of cadence, the most important of which are described below.

Authentic cadence. This is the progression heard in Example 2–35. It has the effect of a period in a sentence, giving a positive impression of completion. It ends many periods in music and is the preferred harmonic ending for an entire movement or composition. The first, second, and fourth phrases of *Drink to Me* end with authentic cadences. On a grandiose scale the last twelve measures of the first movement of Beethoven's Third Symphony make an authentic cadence.

Half cadence. This is a partial ending, a point of rest within a musical period, like the comma or semicolon in language. It leaves a harmonic question to be answered; this question is generally put by the chord built up from the fifth degree of the key, the *dominant* chord. The third phrase of *Drink to Me* ends with a half cadence. Most of the harmonic caesuras in the Prelude to *Tristan* are types of half cadence, in that they offer us a harmonic question to be answered.

Deceptive cadence. The expected answer to a harmonic question is not always desired by the composer. Sometimes he feels that he does not want to bring a period to an end even though the harmony may call for an authentic cadence. Then, in place of the tonic which the listener expects, he introduces a chord which is not anticipated. He deceives the listener; therefore, such a progression is called a *deceptive cadence*. Such a progression has two principal effects: (1) the surprise and freshness of an unexpected sound; (2) maintenance and increase of musical momentum by the avoidance of arrival. When a composer has used a deceptive cadence, it has often given greater point to an authentic cadence which will appear somewhat later. The composer has been using harmonic suspense. Listen for the cadences at the beginning of Mozart's *Prague* Symphony. Again and again Mozart seems to promise an authentic cadence, a fully satisfying point of harmonic arrival, only to thwart us at the last moment. Only when the slow introduction of this piece joins to the quick part of the movement do we hear what we have been waiting for during four minutes of music, the authentic cadence.

Plagal cadence. In literature, we shall sometimes find, after the main problem of a poem, essay, play, or novel has been settled, an epilogue that brings movement finally to a state of quiet. This is an afterthought which helps to provide a transition from our artistic experience to the realities of life itself. In music we also find such afterthoughts. The Amen at the end of a hymn is an example. Here we are likely to find the *plagal cadence,* a rather quiet progression. The settling, calming effect of the plagal cadence was used by Wagner to bring some of his great music dramas to a close. *Götterdämmerung,* the last of the four operas of the *Ring* cycle, ends with a plagal cadence, suggesting the end of the struggle for the gold, when the gold is returned to the Rhine maidens, the original and rightful owners. We sense, in this last cadence, a last resignation and reconciliation to destiny. At the end of *Tristan,* as the lovers find fulfillment in death, very much the same harmonic effect occurs.

Briefly, we shall list the progressions which make up these four main cadences:

1. Authentic cadence: V to I, with both chords in root (lower note of perfect in bass) position
2. Half cadence: a pause upon a dominant chord
3. Deceptive cadence: V to VI, or possibly some other chord
4. Plagal cadence: IV to I, the latter generally in root position

Ex. 2–39. Cadences within a phrase.

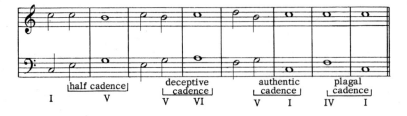

We can illustrate cadential action by showing its relationship to phrase structure. In Example 2–40, the first phrase ends with a half cadence; it leaves a question to be answered. The second phrase ends with an authentic cadence; it answers the question. The phrases and the cadences complement each other in a completely satisfying balance.

Ex. 2–40. Mozart: Sonata in A major, K. 331, first movement.

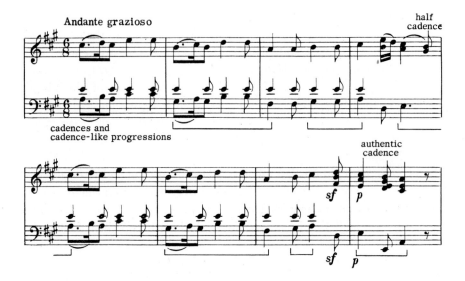

Many dance and song periods are built this way harmonically; *Old Folks at Home, Turkey in the Straw, Yankee Doodle* are examples.

Within phrases, we find progressions that are similar to these cadences. Such cadencelike progressions keep the sense of the tonal center well in mind, but, at the same time, keep the music moving. Music of the eighteenth century is saturated with such progressions; this is one of the main reasons that the music of Mozart is so easy to follow and to grasp. The brackets in Example 2–40 all mark off cadencelike progressions. You can find no cadencelike progressions, *cadential formulas,* in much modern music, as, for example, in Schönberg's *Pierrot lunaire.*

Distribution of Tonal Centers

A piece of music using familiar harmonic procedures will generally begin and end in the same tonal center or *key.* However, shifts of tonal center almost always take place during the piece. Such shifts of tonal center are called *modulations.* They are accomplished in various ways, sometimes by emphasizing a new tone until it takes on the aspect of a tonal center, sometimes by making cadences in the new key. When a piece begins in one key, shifts in turn to several other keys, and ends in the home key, it is like setting out from home, visiting various other places, and returning home again. Sit-at-home music can be very boring! A harmonic plan involving modulations gives some large-scale contour to the form of any piece of music. We could not bear to listen to the extremely long first movement of the Third Symphony of Beethoven unless it had the freshness and new interest that comes with well-planned shifts of tonal center.

Example 2–41, illustrating three shifts of tonal center, presents in miniature a plan that could occupy a composition several hundred measures in length.

Ex. 2–41. Shifts in tonal center.

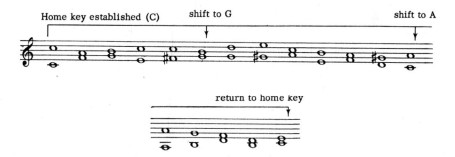

Sometimes the process of modulation is gradual; the listener may not even be aware that a change of tonal center is being made. Such modulations indicate a long-range plan; their purpose is to make and to secure an important change of tonal position within the piece. In other cases, modulation takes place abruptly, often with brilliant contrast of color. The purpose of such changes is to create a striking and bold effect, as in the first part of the second movement of Beethoven's Fifth Symphony. In this example, the contrast in key and color is associated with a contrast between a smooth, singing melody and a martial fanfare.

Ex. 2–42. Beethoven: Fifth Symphony, second movement.

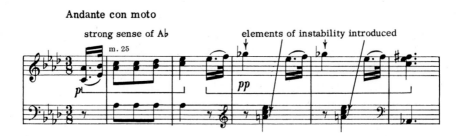

Scale and Mode

The harmonic effects we have been studying show harmony in action, harmony as a component of musical structure participating in effects of movement and arrival. These effects have been largely concerned with indicating, defining, or working around tonal centers. In order to accomplish this, it is necessary to select tones which will support a given note as a tonic; in order to assert itself the tonic needs the cooperation of other tones. These tones take positions with reference to the tonic, forming a system of tones. If we arrange these in stepwise order, beginning and ending on the tonic, we have constructed the scale for that particular tonal center. Example 2–43 illustrates the scale of C. On the diagram of Example 2–32, we should sound these tones if we play the white keys in order from left to right.

Ex. 2–43. Scale of C.

Scales differ in their characteristic qualities. The clue to these differences is the distribution of the intervals in the scale. Only two scales have equal intervals throughout, the *chromatic,* which has half steps, and the *whole-tone* scale, which has whole steps. (On our diagram, B to C is a half step; C to D is a whole step.) In these two scales the intervals give us no help whatsoever in determining a tonal center. Any impression of tonic will be arbitrary, and often uncertain and weak, as Example 2–44 shows.

Ex. 2–44.

a. Chromatic scale.

Passage using chromatic scale.

b. Whole-tone scale.

Passage using whole-tone scale.

The scales that represent traditional Western systems of harmony have intervals of two different sizes, half steps and whole steps. Within the range of an octave, there are two half steps; these are placed at the distance of a fourth or fifth from each other. The other intervals are whole steps. The effect, when we play such a scale, is one of coherence, evenness, and balance. The tones seem to belong together. Such a scale is called *diatonic,* in contradistinction to the chromatic scale. Example 2–43, above, illustrates a familiar diatonic scale; its half steps are found between the third and fourth, and the seventh and eighth tones. *Drink to Me* uses this particular scale or system, which is called the *major mode.*

Other Western scales show different positions of their half steps, although the distance between the two half steps does not change. A scale arrangement is called a *mode.* In Example 2–45, the modes that have been used in the last one thousand years are given.

Ex. 2–45. Modes.

a. Dorian.

b. Phrygian.

c. Lydian.

d. Mixolydian.

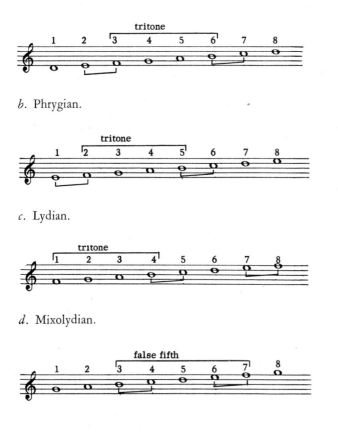

e. Aeolian.

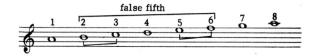

f. Ionian (major).

To realize the effects and the importance of different modes, play *Old Black Joe,* starting on each of the white keys. Of the seven versions, only the one beginning with C will result in the proper setting.

Thus, the half steps give character and distinction to each mode. Half steps are tight, binding intervals which give the effect of tying a knot, of turning a corner, of securing a position. Therefore, they are points of orientation in a scale. As we have heard, the position of the half steps in relation to the tonic note will have an important influence upon the character of the mode, and will give a special color to music written in a certain mode. Of all the modes, only the *Ionian,* which is our major scale, can use the tritone for reaching the tonic harmony. For this reason, the major mode gradually supplanted all the others as the most important scale used in musical composition. From about 1700 on, Western harmony centers upon relationships derived from the major scale. Even our *minor* mode, or scale corresponding to the *Aeolian* mode, has to borrow a tritone from the major scale. As you play this scale, you feel, reaching the seventh tone, that it should be raised, made a leading tone, in order to create a satisfactory binding effect. Toward the end of the nineteenth century, when composers began to look for fresh and exotic qualities of harmony, they turned to the older modes, and were careful to avoid leading effects. The beginning of Rimsky-Korsakov's *Russian Easter* Overture, is set in the *Dorian* mode, in order to suggest the solemn, archaic mood of an Orthodox Church service.

Summarizing, to orient ourselves harmonically, we proceed as follows:

1. We determine general effects of stability and instability.
2. We look for evidences of tonal center in the following manner:
a. Prominence of a given tone

b. Perfect fifth

c. Tritone and cadence effects

d. Combinations of processes *a, b,* and *c*.

3. We note special harmonic values, such as:

a. Mode

b. Types of chord used

c. Kinds of cadence and their relative strength

d. Distribution of tonal centers.

4. We try to fit our observations regarding harmony into the expressive picture of the piece.

Using these criteria, we shall summarize the harmonic values of the first movement of Beethoven's Third Symphony, which by now should be quite familiar to us:

1. There is sharp conflict between stability and instability. Unstable sections have a driving tension; stable sections have a grandiose sense of arrival.

2. Tonal centers are defined by strong cadential action, supported by prominence of the tonic as well as the presence of the perfect fifth in the tonic triad. The sense of a tonic is very strong at points of arrival.

3. While the principal mode of the piece is major, there are prominent sections in the minor mode. Traditional chord types are used, such as triads and seventh chords. The cadences are almost entirely authentic or half cadences. Strong cadences are widely spaced, acting as goals for long sections of directed instability. Arrival is generally accomplished by emphatic cadences. Dissonances are used specifically for their leading action, not as special effects of color. There are many shifts of tonal center, some following quickly upon each other, some resulting in long sections remaining in one key.

5. These harmonic values, combined with a richly varied motivic content, constant play between rhythmic balance and imbalance, and bold contrasts of texture, present the impression of a work in which giant forces are striving against each other.

PERCEIVING MUSICAL FORM

By now we have some idea of what takes place in a musical phrase with respect to melody, rhythm, texture, and harmony. As we listened for these elements and heard how they progressed within a phrase, we were making our first entry into the realm of musical form.

No one grasps the full meaning of the form of a piece upon first hearing. We all hear musical form on various levels. At first the attention may focus on interesting details and striking effects. As the piece moves on, a series of impressions will be stored up. Among these, some will strike the listener as being more salient or important than others. He will take these to be landmarks along the way. Listening again and more closely, he will recognize more and more of these impressions as being interrelated; and further, he will see that the composer has employed some plan, pattern, or formula in order to organize the effects of movement and arrival on a large scale. When these patterns become clear, much of the detail work will acquire a greater significance. It will no longer consist of one interesting effect following another; rather, the function of each gesture in the over-all scheme will make itself felt. Thus, by understanding the over-all plan of a piece and the working out of its larger sections, the listener can be more comfortable and sure in the evaluation and appreciation of specific effects and qualities.

Listening for musical form in this way is very much like watching a play. At first we are impressed by the setting, the appearance of the players, or striking moments and lines; these are immediate impacts upon our senses. Then we follow incident upon incident, watching the unfolding of the plot, in order to grasp the step-by-step continuity. In a well-constructed play we are led to important points of climax in an effective manner; perhaps these will balance or match each other. Finally, our experience is brought to some recognizable point of completion as the play ends. Later we reflect upon the various issues presented in the play, reliving certain moments; and we evaluate the author's, director's, and actors' skill or lack of skill in moving our emotions or delighting us with their offering.

Specifically, the listener should ask these questions as he gives his attention to the form of a piece:

1. What is taking place now?
2. What will happen next?
3. How does the present material relate to what has gone before?

The composer must also take these matters into account as he creates the successive phrases of his music; he must consider what has happened in one phrase in order to proceed effectively to the next phrase. He must assess one gesture or section in relation to what precedes and follows it. The flow of music is thus built up by such action, which can be expressed in the formula:

STATEMENT   answered by   COUNTERSTATEMENT

Statements and counterstatements overlap like links in a continuous chain. Each link is separate; yet the entire length and shape of the chain gives the observer a single impression of the outline or form of the whole. In order to find our way through the form of a piece we shall make use of the statement-counterstatement formula. It will enable us to relate motives, phrases, cadences, and other effects to each other.

Here are some ways in which statement and counterstatement relationships are manifested in musical structure:

STATEMENT	COUNTERSTATEMENT
Motive	1. Repetition
	2. Variation
	3. Contrast
Melody	1. Contrasting melody
	2. Repetition of melody
Half cadence	1. Authentic cadence
Tonal center or key	1. Contrasting key
	2. Return to home key as counterstatement to contrasting key
Phrase	1. Answering phrase of comparable length, giving rise to symmetrical construction
	2. Answering phrase or phrases of markedly different length, giving rise to nonsymmetrical construction.

By way of illustration, consider the relationship between (1) the two arresting chords that begin the first movement of Beethoven's Third Symphony and (2) the singing melody that follows. The two chords represent a bold statement; the melody comes then as a somewhat surprising but extremely effective counterstatement. This relationship exists on the *smallest possible structural scale*. On the *largest possible scale* within this movement, a final counterstatement to this first melody appears as it returns for the last time near the end of the movement, and is heard again and again, reiterating the principal melodic idea of the whole piece. As listeners, we make a connection, establish a link between the *first* statement and the *last* counterstatement. This *repetition* is one more item of rational organization that helps us acquire a perspective of the form of this movement.

Ex. 2–46. Sketch of first movement, Beethoven's Third Symphony. Statement and counterstatement.

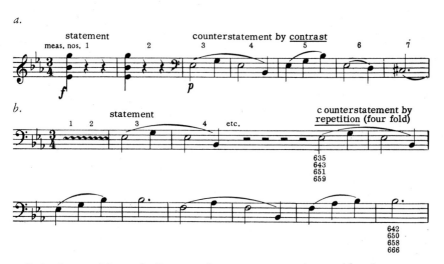

a.

b.

Indeed, repetition, of all types of counterstatement, provides the strongest and most convincing kind of binding action in musical form, as it does in other kinds of experience. Like its use in the process of learning, repetition in a musical form helps us to *learn* the music better. As a matter of fact, this applies not only to restatements of material within a given piece, but even more tellingly, to rehearings of the entire piece itself.

Like individuals, musical forms each have their own special characteristics. Each piece is a separate and unique organism, in some way different from all others. As with individuals, to know and appreciate a piece of music, we must go beyond passing acquaintance, we must test our reactions and impressions by renewed contacts. Then we can decide, if such a decision is indeed necessary, whether or not a given work belongs within the circle of our own taste.

Despite individual differences, musical forms run to type, just as human beings do. Recognizing a type of musical form will be of great assistance in developing better acquaintance with the piece itself. Basically, there are two ways in which a piece of music extends itself in time: (1) by adding well-defined phrases and periods to the original statement; (2) by spinning out movement continuously without clearly marked articulations.

In the first of these processes, phrases and periods have strong points of arrival; phases of movement tend to be comparable in length; a sense of balance and complementation controls the structure. In the second process, we sense few strong points of arrival; movement carries on continuously perhaps for a long time; continued momentum, rather than symmetry and balance, seems to be the controlling principle.

Within the first category, certain typical layouts occur. Of these the simplest is the *two-part* structure. This may operate on various scales of magnitude. Essentially, two-part structure rests on perfect symmetry and balance. It may consist of nothing more than a phrase answered by another phrase, a half cadence answered by an authentic cadence, as in Example 2–39. Going up the scale, we find two periods joined in such a form, as in *Drink to Me,* or in the first half of the march, *The Stars and Stripes Forever.* Later we shall see how the most monumental form in all music history, the sonata form, makes use of the statement and counterstatement plan of two-part structure.

Frequently, in somewhat larger two-part forms, the first part will be brought back at the end in order to round off the form more completely. This return is usually signaled by a restatement of the original melody. In such cases, a three-part structure has been created with the plan: A–B–A. Here the binding effect of melodic repetition is desired. Many dances and marches go through this cycle. The Menuetto of Mozart's *Eine Kleine Nachtmusik* has such a layout. Three-part form also can be realized on a broad scale, as in the Scherzo of Beethoven's Ninth Symphony.

As long as well-marked sections are involved, it is possible to extend the form simply by adding on sections or repeating sections previously heard. Johann Strauss, in his waltzes, exemplifies this procedure. In Chapter 6, we shall see how the eighteenth-century rondo grows in this manner.

It is quite easy to keep our bearings in musical forms that have clearly marked articulations and nicely balanced structural components. In a piece which spins out continuously, this becomes much more difficult. Such a piece may be organized according to the rise and fall of dynamic intensity or strength; it may involve a subtle and complex interweaving of motives in relationships of statement and counterstatement which change every few measures; it may be concerned simply with maintaining a steady and unbroken flow of sound for a given period of time. We will find such forms in the preludes and fantasias of seventeenth- and eighteenth-century music, also in music written contrapuntally, such as the fugues of baroque music and the motets of the Renaissance period. At first such forms may be puzzling to the listener, but the musical content which gives them their continuous flow is often more challenging.

These two types, the articulated and the continuous, represent ways of shaping musical materials. In most compositions they are both active in varying proportions. Each time a phrase begins, there is a forward push; each time a point of arrival breaks the flow, there is a check in momentum. Beethoven, in the first movement of his Third Symphony, played these two processes against each other with such powerful effect that the form of this movement became extended enormously. As you listen to any music, try to determine how the composer moves forward in the structure, and how he establishes points of articulation and reference.

In this chapter some tools have been provided with which the listener can work upon these problems. Each era in music and each musical style have found different solutions to the problem of form. They have arrived at these solutions because their materials and their expressive aims have called for certain forms. The survey of the eras of music history, which will be made in the following chapters of this book, will include some consideration of the important forms of those eras. The historical approach is adopted because it is in its own right a kind of form within which we can trace the building of style, the evolution of musical techniques, the change of expressive concepts, and the relation of music to culture and history. It is an orderly plan which has meaning to the layman himself, since it will enable him to project his imagination beyond the mere impact of pleasant or puzzling sounds, and give him an idea of what to listen for and in what manner.

As you study a musical composition or a distinctive musical passage, you might apply the criteria established in Chapters 1 and 2 as follows:

1. Qualities of sound
a. *Level of sound*: high, low, middle—wide or narrow range
b. *Color of sound*: rich, thin, _____ (indicate media)
c. *Amount of sound*: massive, light, medium
d. *Strength of sound*: great, moderate, light
2. Qualities of movement
a. *Pace*: quick, moderate, slow
b. *Regularity*: regular, irregular, (and to what degree)
c. *Flow*: vigorous, gentle, tense, relaxed (or perhaps some other designation)
3. Phases of movement and points of arrival
a. *Length*: short, long, relatively equal or unequal
b. *Arrival*: clear, unclear, strong, gentle, drive, lack of drive
4. Melody
a. *Intervals used*: principally conjunct, principally disjunct, combined
b. *Shapes*: _____ (use your own description)

   c. Motive relationships: repetition, variation, contrast

   d. Melodic treatment in piece: many melodies, few melodies, clear repetitions, development

5. Rhythm

   a. Meter: duple, triple, compound, regular, shifting

   b. Degree of accent: heavy, light, use of syncopation

6. Texture

   a. Single action

   b. Melody and accompaniment

   c. Polyphonic, imitation

   d. Give-and-take

7. Dynamics: degree of strength, increase, decrease, degree and manner of contrast

8. Harmony

   a. Tonal center defined by: prominent tone, perfect fifth, cadential relationships

   b. Harmonic quality: diatonic, chromatic, degree of stability and instability _____, modality

   c. Cadences: authentic, half, deceptive, plagal, strong, light, drive to cadence

9. Phrase relationships: degree of symmetry _____

Chapter 3. Medieval Music

UNTIL QUITE recently most of the music which has been available for listening, either in concert or on recordings, was written after the year 1700. Lately, thanks to musicologists, we have become acquainted with music composed during the Middle Ages and the Renaissance and have found much of it interesting and effective. Many excellent performances of this music are available today on recordings.

Unlike most of the concert music which is familiar to us, medieval and Renaissance music was not written expressly for a large audience of listeners who were expected to give all their attention to the music. Rather, music of these two eras made its appearance in connection with events of a religious or social nature. Many of the services and devotions of the church called for music; the entertainments of the court centered around singing and dancing, both of which made special demands upon music. Moreover, most of the music which has been discovered in musical manuscripts of the Middle Ages and Renaissance was intended for the highest social classes, the nobility and the clergy. We have few relics of popular or lower-class music, although it is quite clear that common folk and peasants had a vigorous musical culture. Thus, in any evaluation of music from these earlier times, we must recognize the limited size of the audience, the special background of the participants and observers, and the division of interest between music and some other form of activity. Try to imagine a scene at court or a service in a great cathedral as you hear this music.

PLAIN SONG

Listen to the first three numbers in the recorded collection, *Masterpieces of Music before 1750,* the antiphon *Laus Deo Patri,* the Alleluiah *Vidimus stellam* (We Have Seen the Star), and the sequence *Victimae Paschali* (The Paschal Victim).

These three pieces are taken from a tremendous body of music, called *plain song,* or *Gregorian chant.* From the sixth century until the end of the sixteenth plain song has been the most important kind of music in the Christian world.

Pay attention first to the quality of sound in this music. Voices are singing in unison, simply and in a straightforward manner; the music is deeply felt, intimate, and strongly evocative. Far back in human history the sound of the human voice has stirred the worshiper and prepared him to receive the word of God. Music set to a sacred text was intended to emphasize and intensify the emotional qualities and meanings of the sacred words. The steady, continuous intonation of the text on definite pitches certainly reaches the emotions of the hearer more surely and strongly than if the text were recited. The full effect of voices singing this music is felt only in a cathedral, where the echoes and reverberations intensify and amplify the sound, creating an all-pervasive effect.

In general these songs resemble each other. The quality of sound is the same. Movement is moderately slow, rather gentle, even, and flowing. Melodic shapes are rounded, using small, generally conjunct intervals. Points of arrival give the singers breathing spaces; they are not emphatic breaks in the flow of the music. Such qualities suggest calmness, security, and reflectiveness rather than extremes of emotion. Plain song is not geared to violent, nervous, and anxious states of mind, as is later music, especially in the contemporary age. Church song is music of the cloister, of retreat. Its features are not as bold and striking as those of latter-day music. Its distinctions are subtle, even elusive.

Yet plain song has a wide range of expressive values, and we can discover this in the songs we have heard. Listen for differences between *Vidimus* and *Victimae. Vidimus* moves much more smoothly, lightly, and freely than *Victimae. Vidimus* is a song of jubilation. The star of Bethlehem has been seen in the East; it is a time for joy. Alleluias are sung; the music breaks away from the text, giving many notes to a single syllable. The melodic flights in this song were called *melismas*; and the term *melismatic* has come to signify music which has elaborate melodic ornamentation beyond its text.

In *Victimae* we are told a story about the sacrifice of Christ, His death, and His resurrection. The words occupy the worshiper's attention. Since

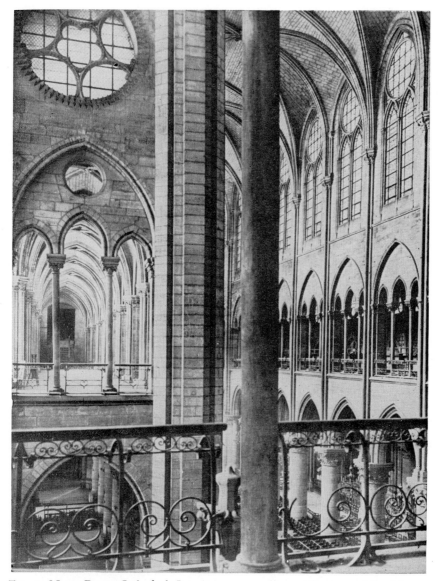

FIG. 1. Notre Dame Cathedral. Interior, upper gallery. (Courtesy of the Metropolitan Museum of Art.)

the words are declaimed, one tone to each syllable, in a *syllabic* style, the music has a much heavier quality of movement than the Alleluia. The narrative is told in poetry; the poetic meter thus brings about an even and regular pace in the music. In contrast, our Alleluia seems irregular and improvisatory in its quality of movement. *Victimae* gives a very comfortable feeling of balance in phrase structure, because its caesuras are regularly spaced and quite strong. Statement and counterstatement complement each other clearly and firmly. This strong impression of balance is missing in *Vidimus,* because we cannot detect the caesuras as clearly nor sense a balance of phrases.

Differences in style and structure in these two songs grew from their expressive values and aims; in one case, the emotion of joy gives impetus to a flight of melody; in the other case, the solemn tragic emotion calls for a deliberate manner and form.

Example 3–1 illustrates graphically the relationship between music and text in syllabic and melismatic styles.

Ex. 3–1. Syllabic and melismatic settings.

Syllabic

    music ⎯⎯ — ⎯⎯ — ⎯⎯⎯

    text ⎯⎯ — ⎯⎯ — ⎯⎯⎯

Melismatic

    music — — — — — — — — — — — ⎯

    text ⎯···⎯

In the plain song we shall now examine, neither the syllabic nor the melismatic style dominates. This combination of the two, where syllabic style is broken up by short melismas, is called the *neumatic style.* Now, in order to have a closer look at the structure of plain song, we shall use the *Laus Deo Patri.*

1. Melodic Aspects

a. Conjunct lines, with occasional thirds as the only larger intervals.

b. Range of less than an octave.

c. Gentle rise and fall, with melodic phrases tending to turn around one or two points.

d. Little or no differentiation between various motives; complete homogeneity of manner with the exception of the extended repetition on the recitation tone.

e. Some contrast on a broader scale due to the higher pitch of the phrase beginning *et tibi*.

2. Rhythmic Aspects

a. Gentle but steady pulse of moderate pace.

b. Size of pulse- or beat-groups varied, generally between two and three; articulation less clear in the recitation section.

c. Two kinds of note value: short equals one beat; long equals two beats.

d. Phrases comparable but not exactly equal in length.

e. As with melody, no salient rhythmic motives, but a homogeneity of rhythmic manner.

f. Legato performance.

g. At important caesuras, long notes used to give a sense of arrival; otherwise short notes used constantly; important caesuras clear as resting or breathing points.

3. Textural Aspects

Contrast between single voice and group.

4. Harmonic Aspects

a. Clear sense of arrival at the tonal center at each caesura.

b. Tonal center defined by prominence and by its presence at the caesura.

c. Shift of tonal center found only in recitation section, between caesuras of first and second lines.

d. Position of half steps between 1 and 2, 5 and 6 remains constant: Phrygian mode.

5. Form

a. Large three-part form, set up as *antiphon, psalm tone, antiphon,* or A B A.

b. Considerable extension due to the many repetitions of psalm tone.

c. Statements and counterstatements balanced in relative length; counterstatements tend to continue, vary, and spin out melodic material of previous statements.

d. Several gentle areas of contrast, i.e., *et tibi* phrase, and recitation tone, giving a large-scale contour to the song.

After you have noted the specific characteristics of the antiphon as indicated above, and perhaps added some observations of your own, listen to the piece once more as a complete, unified selection without making any particular effort to put every detail into place. You should find that you can follow the music much more easily, that you know where you are, and that many of the details *do* fit into place as the music flows onward. You have returned to the first general impression of the work, but this impression has become much firmer, broader, and richer for the better acquaintance which our study has developed. Not only will the idea of this song become more vivid, but its similarities to and differences from other kinds of plain song will loom larger and more important. It will not be difficult, then, to understand why musicians, musical theorists, priests, and worshipers in the Middle Ages were concerned with these distinctions, since plain song was the only organized body of music in Western civilization at that time.

Plain song was evolved from the cantillations, the chanting of verses, of Hebrew and Greek antiquity. In the early Christian era, a tremendous literature of church song developed. Each cathedral and religious center had its own repertoire. Differences and variants in music to the prescribed liturgy became so numerous that much confusion resulted. Led by Pope Gregory, a reform which aimed at codification took place. Various songs were grouped according to certain of their characteristics, such as range, style, typical melodic formulas, and final tone or tonal center. Thus the medieval *system of modes* was evolved. Each mode represented a final tone, a range, and also was associated with typical melodic formulas.

There were eight of these modes and to the trained listener and student, the distinctions between music in one mode and that in another were very important, although, to us, accustomed to much bolder contrast in music, the differences are at first very hard to detect. So strong was this feeling about different values and effects residing in the various modes that theorists assigned different emotional and moral qualities to the modes. They considered some proper for the expression of joy, others for sadness, solemnity, gaiety, etc. Whether or not these connotations seem valid to us, the important idea is the evidence they give of the power of music to stir men's feelings.

Plain-song texts are taken principally from the Psalms. The music was sung at two kinds of service, the *Mass,* the solemn commemoration service of the sacrifice of Christ, and during the daily rites of the *Office.* (See

Apel: *Harvard Dictionary of Music*, articles on Mass, p. 427, and Office Hours, p. 504, for a description of the details of these services.)

Although plain song was intended solely to support canonical, that is, Biblical texts, its melismatic sections, as in the Alleluia we have heard, represented a rather independent sort of procedure. Very soon, during the ninth century, new texts were set to the melismatic sections, making them syllabic. These texts were generally commentaries on the subject of the canonical text. Such additions were called *tropes*; they represent the first in a series of additions and elaborations of all sorts, textual and musical, that tell the story of musical evolution as far as the end of the Renaissance period. One especially important kind of trope was the *sequence,* such as *Victimae,* in which the melisma of the Alleluia was given a text. During medieval times many sequences were added to the literature of sacred music; independently composed pieces as well as new texts are found in this type of music.

During the fifteen hundred years and more of its existence, plain song has been the most significant musical factor in the life of the Roman church. Today it is the authorized musical language of that church. Throughout its history, plain song has been a rich source for musical materials, an inexhaustible fund from which composers have borrowed continuously. As an art form, it was highly polished, subtle, full of delicate shadings and nuances, and within its own realm, a complete and well-rounded mode of musical expression.

THE EVOLUTION OF POLYPHONY

Although life is short and art is long, the life of an art form undergoes growth, flower, and decay very much as living beings do. Some time before the year 1000 a drastic change in the history of plain song occurred. *Another voice or part was added,* at times, when plain song was being performed. Consider the implications of this practice, called *polyphony,* for the history of Western music. It caused changes in every aspect of musical art, and indeed, it is responsible for music as we know it today.

1. It created a *new sonority value,* giving a new dimension to musical sound and increasing thereby the range of its evocative power.

2. Potentially, although not at first, it carried the promise of *countermovement* between the various voices, both melodically and rhythmically; therefore, it led to the development of a greater intensity of movement.

3. It contributed to the evolution of *harmony*; some order in the distribution of intervals was necessary; conversely, preferences for certain types of intervals between the polyphonic voices were codified into systems which we call *harmony*.

4. It enforced *rhythmic order*. Thus, it required the development of a system of *notation* which would enable the performers and composers to communicate with each other and would give the performers some way of singing the right notes at the right time in order to stay together properly.

5. It set the text aside as the principal item of interest and the principal means for controlling the form. *Musical relationships* became more and more the central concern and interest.

6. It pointed the way continually to new and fresh ways of *extending* and *elaborating* music.

Polyphony began as an addition to an established melody. This should not be unfamiliar to us as a process nor hard to understand. When musicians perform, they have a natural, almost irrepressible tendency to add a few touches of their own to the established musical text. Only under the strictest conditions of propriety and coercion do they toe the line. Even today we hear conductors and performers taking liberties with the printed score. Thus addition and elaboration in music are part of the art itself.

From the tenth to the seventeenth century we shall follow the history of music largely through the additions which composers have made either to specific musical compositions or to established musical techniques. Music grew during this period through elaborations upon preexisting models.

Throughout the Middle Ages the Gregorian chant is the most important type of preexisting material. Much, if not most of the music written and performed during the Middle Ages and the Renaissance was used in connection with sacred ceremonies. The text and its proper music, the plain song, was of prime importance during the proceedings; therefore, whatever elaborations took place had to be built upon an appropriate plain song. Such a plain song was called a *cantus firmus*, meaning "a fixed melody." Thousands of complete, independent compositions used part or all of a plain song as the basic framework. During the Renaissance composers frequently turned to secular music, songs, and dances for their cantus firmi, even when music for the church was involved. Addition first grew as an extension of liturgical procedures; later, elaborations upon a cantus firmus broke away and became independent of liturgical associations. Eventually much music for social occasions was written upon a preexisting melody.

Once the trend of polyphony was set in motion, it developed and grew in many directions over a period of five hundred years and more. The main path from plain song to Renaissance music progresses in phases that are quite well defined, each of which is an elaboration or refinement upon a preceding phase. Like all growth, the development of Western music is an exciting thing to observe. Below are diagramed some of the important stages in this evolution, with particular reference to the qualities of movement created by each style.

Parallel Organum

This is the first stage of polyphony in Western music. *Organum* is the term applied to polyphony from the ninth to the thirteenth centuries. It probably refers to the fact that the voices were *organized* or fitted together. The plain-song voice was the *principal* voice; the added voices were *organal* voices. In this first phase of polyphony, the added voices were dependent both rhythmically and harmonically upon the principal voice. They moved along quite strictly with the principal voice, remaining at their allotted distance. The new feature in this music is its sound, the *richness of sonority* that comes about when the added voices move in the resonant intervals of the fourth, fifth, and octave. Due to this fuller sonority, parallel organum has a heavier quality of movement than plain song, which it otherwise resembles in its melodic shapes and patterns. There is also the impression of a rather rigid type of action, due to the parallelism, as if a squad of three or four men were marching perfectly in step. This type of music flourished during the ninth and tenth centuries. Listen to *Masterpieces,* no. 6, for a famous example of parallel organum, *Rex caeli domine* (King of Heaven).

Ex. 3–2. Diagram of parallel organum.

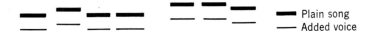

■ Plain song
— Added voice

Free Organum

We could hardly expect the added voices to submit for very long to the melodic and harmonic conditions established by a particular plain song. The first signs of growing independence appear when the added voice or voices create their own melodic patterns against the plain song. This is called *free organum.* We have the interest of two different melodic lines moving against each other. The effect of movement is somewhat smoother and lighter than in parallel organum. A play of different sonorities is created as the music progresses. The different melodic patterns create fourths, fifths, octaves, and unisons in a well-mixed variety. In addition, you will hear a few thirds, which provide a sweeter harmonic touch. Harmonically, points of arrival are indicated by the standard medieval intervals, fourths, fifths, unisons, or octaves.

Here and there you will notice that the added voice sings several notes to a single note of the plain song, suggesting the first move toward rhythmic independence. A feeling of melodic ornamentation is coming to life, something like the melismatic style we heard in the Alleluia. Still, free organum is *rhythmically* dependent upon the plain song, even though it has asserted its melodic autonomy. You may hear an example of free organum in *Masterpieces,* no. 7, the trope *Agnus Dei* (Lamb of God).

Ex. 3–3. Diagram of free organum.

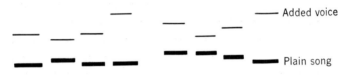

Melismatic Organum

We are still moving in the direction of freedom. In *melismatic organum,* the rhythmic and melodic independence of the organal voice comes into full flower. It sings many notes to each one of the cantus firmus. This has caused the cantus firmus to slow down its movement very much. It sings long notes, and, since it holds its notes for a considerable time, it came to be designated as the *tenor,* meaning "that which holds." The combined movement of the two voices suggests a flight which is not quite free, which is controlled by the deliberate changes of tone in the cantus firmus. When the cantus firmus changes, the impression of arrival becomes quite strong by contrast with the phase of movement in the melismatic sections. There is a great deal of florid ornamentation in the organal voice. Still, its shapes and patterns continue along the lines established in plain song; there is gentle rise and fall with smooth, even, and small intervals characterizing the movement of the melody.

Harmonically, the sound of open intervals, fourths, fifths, and octaves, dominates. Yet it was inevitable that the melodic voice would touch upon tones that were dissonant with the cantus firmus during phases of movement. Now and then you can hear some clashing dissonances quite clearly. Melismatic organum flourished in the twelfth century. *Masterpieces,* no. 8, provides an example. This is the *Benedicamus Domino.*

Ex. 3–4. Diagram of melismatic organum.

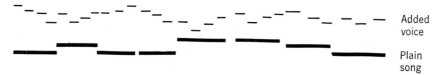

Added voice

Plain song

Measured Organum: Ars Antiqua

In measured organum we have turned a corner. The freedom of the added voice has been curtailed. This, too, was inevitable. Two voices singing together on completely different rhythmic planes need some method by which they can operate together with efficiency. At first the notes of the melisma were measured into short, self-contained rhythmic patterns; these patterns were based on the modes of poetry, which distribute syllables according to alternations of long and short in a triple meter. (See Chapter 2, Meter and Measure.) These rhythmic patterns in measured organum gave prominence to short, melodic figures which began to sound like motives. When there were two or more organal voices, these motives were interchanged in succeeding phrases, so that a simple kind of imitation resulted.

This all signifies a tighter internal organization of the music, a centripetal pull rather than a centrifugal flight. The continual statement and restatement of these short motives, piling up momentum, gives a vigorous, driving quality to this music. With reference to the quality of sound, it differs but slightly from that of previous polyphonic styles: open, sonorous, capable of much reverberation. One difference is very important: because of the regular, accented rhythm, dissonance and consonance are more strictly controlled. Accented points call for consonance, which in medieval music amounts to the usual open intervals. Unaccented points can accomodate dissonance. Still, here and there we hear the impact of a dissonance upon an accented tone; this but adds to the impression of strength which this style gives.

Measured organum appeared around the year 1200, and, as you can see, was the first important stage in the development of meter in music. No. 9 of *Masterpieces,* the *Alleluya* (*Nativitas*) illustrates two kinds of measured organum: (1) that in which the principal voice sustains one note of the plain song for a long time, while the upper voice moves actively in modal, that is poetic, rhythms:

Ex. 3–5. Diagram of measured organum (1).

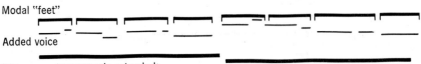

Modal "feet"

Added voice

Plain song (enormously extended)

and (2) in which the plain-song voice changes its tone with each *foot* of the upper voices. In other words, the cantus firmus becomes part of the entire pattern of movement, abandoning its role as a tenor. It has its own rhythmic patterns.

Ex. 3–6. Diagram of measured organum (2).

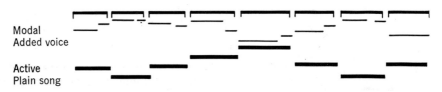

Modal
Added voice

Active
Plain song

Ars Nova

In the music of the fourteenth century in Italy and France one fundamental change developed in the quality of movement. Heretofore the rhythm had been measured by the rhythmic modes, which were basically triple in meter. The divisions allowed for two kinds of note value—longs and shorts. In the soloistic music of measured organum, however, many ornamental passages of very short notes were introduced. Again the impulse toward ornamentation asserts itself. In order to account for these when the music was written down, it was necessary to invent symbols and assign values to them. A system of *proportional* or *mensural notation* grew up as a result of this more florid and complex music. Composers began to use proportional values in many subtle ways; this undermined the regularity and driving momentum of the *Ars antiqua* style and substituted a highly refined rhythmic imbalance. It was music for experts in performance and listening.

Another result of this rhythmic revolution was the introduction of *duple* meter as an important rhythmic factor. Not all the music of the fourteenth century is complex and subtle in its rhythms. The *Agnus Dei* from Guillaume de Machaut's Mass, *Masterpieces,* no. 13, shows a vigorous, straightforward quality of movement, based principally on duple meter, particularly in the shorter note values. There are four different parts here, some sung, some played by instruments. Again, the sounds are those of the open intervals characteristic of medieval music. We can hear them reinforced by doublings and duplications, creating a larger amount of sound.

One special feature of Machaut's *Agnus Dei* is the well-delineated contrast between movement and arrival, harmonically speaking. Points of arrival are clear and emphatic. There is leading-tone action preceding the chords which act for arrival. We have no difficulty in hearing the difference between the clear resonance of the heavy caesuras, and the somewhat edgy, frequently dissonant sound within the phases of movement. The structural role of harmony in this music is well defined because of the distinctions between consonance and dissonance, assisted by the careful distribution of rhythmic motion and rest. The total effect of this composition by Machaut is very impressive; his Mass is one of the monuments of fourteenth-century music.

In the development described above, the plain-song melody, the central point of reference, is analogous to the liturgical text which would serve as the point around which a sermon would be expanded. You will notice, however, that the plain song is far from being the musical support to a text that speaks directly to the worshiper. The plain song is lost in the web of added voices; moreover, in many liturgical compositions, we hear but a fragment of the song. Plain song often alternated with the elaborate compositions we have been hearing; the entire music of a given song might be divided between original and elaborated presentations.

SECULAR MUSIC

Roman church music, represented by plain song and its progeny, ranked first in importance in the music of the medieval period. Still, not all medieval music was solemn, serious, or sacred. In the later Middle Ages an important secular art of music developed in connection with the rise of chivalry.

Poetry, music, and dancing were cultivated by the nobility, with the assistance of minstrels of low birth. This age is the source for many romantic stories about *troubadours* and *trouvères,* the poet-musicians of France and the *minnesingers,* their counterparts in Germany. Blondel, the faithful servant of Richard I, was said to have helped rescue his master from Leopold of Austria, discovering him by means of a minstrel song. Tannhäuser, the hero of Richard Wagner's opera, is a minstrel who vacillates between the unholy love of Venus and the pure holy love of Elizabeth. This is a curious combination of pagan and Christian ideas, a mixture quite frequently encountered in medieval culture.

The subject matter of medieval secular music had to do with stories of love, war, adventure, good living, fair weather, disappointment, jealousy, perhaps a bit of thinly disguised scandal—in short, the subjects that you might find in an opera or musical comedy today. Often the tone of these songs was moralizing or cynical. Naturally the principal interest would be in the text. Musically, the solo songs, the *monophonic* pieces, have much in common with plain song, as we can hear in nos. 4 and 5 of *Masterpieces,* the trouvère song, *Or la truix,* and the *minnelied, Willekommen mayenschein.* There is the same diatonic harmonic feeling, the smooth flow, the moderate pace, and the limited range.

Secular composers also adopted *polyphonic* techniques of composition. In fact, they invaded the realm of church music to put amorous texts to the upper parts of measured organum, a procedure which certainly does no credit to the piety of the author but at the same time betrays a certain venturesomeness. Many purely secular pieces in polyphonic style were composed during the fourteenth century. Of these, one of the most spectacular was the *caccia,* meaning "chase." In the caccia, one voice or part *chases* the other, singing exactly what the first voice has sung. In other words, the second voice is imitating the first exactly. This is called a *canonic* type of imitation. Caccias deal with stories of the hunt, or of fishing, and of market cries. Composers managed to include many descriptive and pictorial effects; they imitated the barking of dogs, the sound of hunting horns, the cries of hunters and street vendors.

Listen to the caccia of Ghirardellus, *Tosto che l'alba* (*L'Anthologie Sonore,* no. 59). Note its brilliant, sonorous, sparkling manner, its lively vigorous rhythm. Dogs bark, hunters sound their horns from the mountaintop, the excitement of the chase is caught and maintained by the clearly projected imitative figures. All this takes place within a transparent textural layout: two upper voices and a supporting lower voice, taken from the three-voice music of the thirteenth century. This layout represents a scheme which will become standard for musical composition in future centuries.

Dancing as well as singing was an important form of diversion in the court. The music produced for dancing not only has well-defined accents in modal rhythm, but, because of the patterns of the dance, musical phrases must balance each other in length. These phrases tend to have an even number of measures, often eight, bringing the impression of balance down to the very steps themselves. In the estampie, *Masterpieces,* no. 12, you can easily make out the eight-measure phrases from the beginning of the piece to the end. If you listen closely, you will hear that the lower voice repeats its melody, stating each phrase twice. The ending of each first phrase is *open,* corresponding to a half cadence in later music. The ending of each second phrase is *closed,* corresponding to an authentic cadence in later music. Each closed cadence, with the exception of one, ends upon the same tonal center. We have then the impression of a *harmonic digression* and a return with each pair of phrases. Such a pairing represents a very clear relationship of *statement and counterstatement.*

Ex. 3–7. Diagram of medieval dance form.

Part I   dance tune   . . . .) open cadence
Part II   counterstatement by repetition) closed cadence

Forms were built up by linking dances, such as the above, in a series of two, three, or more, retaining a general uniformity of style.

There is an enormous significance for later music in the clear formal layout of dances such as the estampie. This is an early appearance of the *two-part form,* a form which will grow in importance from this time until the middle of the nineteenth century. Symmetrical construction, which underlies many later forms, guides the shaping of these dances. Opposition of tonal centers, half and authentic cadences, and the control of *digression and return* in harmony by well-defined points of arrival in phrases and periods—all these are present on a small scale in medieval dances—and in certain types of sacred song, such as the sequence.

Other examples of simple two-part structure in medieval music can be heard in *L'Anthologie Sonore* recordings, no. 16. Especially well-known among these dances is *Il lamento di Tristan.*

Performance of medieval music involved voices, instruments, and combinations of voices and instruments. It was quite in order to substitute a voice for an instrument or vice versa in many kinds of music. Thus, in one ancient manuscript from the thirteenth century, the *Codex Bamberg,* there are motets, using a plain-song cantus firmus, expressly indicated for instrumental performance. We have no specific or accurate information covering the entire field of performance practice in medieval times, but we do know that it was considered adequate if each part had a representative performer of some kind. Therefore, contrasts and variations in tone quality, not only in different pieces, but in different performances of the same piece, could very well have occurred. Indeed, in view of the general transparency of the texture and the consistency of style, such variations in performance may have been quite welcome. Early instruments included plucked and bowed string instruments, wind instruments, keyboard instruments, and percussion. There was a tremendous variety within these groups; they were not at all standardized as at present. Recordings made recently of early instruments, including those in *Masterpieces,* show that the tone quality of these instruments was far less rich and full than that of present-day instruments. Still, there is a freshness and lightness of tone quality that well suits the performance of one-, two-, or three-voiced music.

SUMMARY

Sacred music in the medieval period was based on plain song, which in turn was developed from the cantillations of Hebrew and Greek music. Addition and elaboration were the processes by which the art of musical composition grew during this age. Briefly, the stages were as follows:

1. Addition of text to the melismatic sections of plain song; tropes and sequences
2. *Parallel organum*: Addition of voices moving in parallel fourths, fifths, or octaves
3. *Free organum*: Development of melodic independence in the added voices
4. *Melismatic organum*: Slowing down of the cantus firmus; extensive elaboration in the added voice
5. *Measured organum, known as the Ars antiqua*: Control of the melismatic voice by modal rhythms; rhythmic patterns in parts of the plain song
6. *Motet*: Texts set to the added voices
7. *Ars nova*: Rhythmic elaborations and complications leading to duple meter, proportional relationships, and mensural notation

Throughout medieval music, from the time that voices began to sing together, the general harmonic quality of sound remained constant. Points

FIG. 2. Notre Dame Cathedral. Exterior view from St. Julien-le-Pauvre. (Courtesy of the Metropolitan Museum of Art.)

of arrival, both for large and small phases of movement, were characterized by the sound of open intervals, principally the fifth and the octave. These gave a maximum impression of stability. Open intervals also fairly saturated the entire harmonic language. Between points of arrival, mixed in with the fourths, fifths, and octaves, there was a considerable amount of dissonance, brought about by the incidental clashes of melodic lines. Medieval harmony is thus characterized by rather sharp contrasts between the stable sounds of arrival and the active dissonances heard frequently between points of arrival.

Later medieval music, particularly that cultivated in France during the thirteenth and fourteenth centuries, has been called *Gothic* by analogy to other phases of culture operating at that time. Parallels between music and Gothic architecture have frequently been drawn. If we consider how each of these, Gothic music and the Gothic cathedral, took shape, that is, by the addition and juxtaposition of separate, distinct, and often clashing elements, growing out of the central idea of the worship of God, then the analogy seems quite valid. Indeed, throughout the entire history of Europe from A.D. 400–1400, the period we have been considering musically, the force of a central, all-powerful authority makes itself felt in every aspect of religion, politics, and art. Feudalism and the hierarchy of the Church dominated men's thoughts and, indeed, their very lives. As we have seen, music reflected this state of affairs; the only music of which we have record is that performed in church or court.

SUGGESTED LISTENING PROJECTS

1. **Easter Alleluia** *Pascha Nostrum, L'Anthologie Sonore,* Vol. 1, side 1, no. 2

Listen for: Melismatic melody; long phases of movement; repetition of phrases and melodic turns; manner in which melody winds around a given tone; narrow melodic range, sense of shifting points of arrival within a single mode; use of larger intervals, particularly the fifth, to create a dramatic contrast with usual melodic procedure; floating effect of entire piece suggesting the jubilation of the Alleluia.

2. **English Gymel,** *L'Anthologie Sonore,* Vol. 1, side 2, no. 8

Listen for: Short phrases; repetition of motives; prevalence of thirds in harmony; dancelike rhythms (trochaic rhythmic mode); cadential effect at end; the down-to-earth effect of the entire piece; compare with the estampie in *Masterpieces.*

3. **French secular song, fourteenth century,** *L'Anthologie Sonore,* Vol. 1, side 3, no. 3

Listen for: Intimate manner; graceful, supple melodic lines; fluid rhythm; short phrases; repetition of refrainlike phrases; open harmony (few thirds); transparency of the texture, especially the separation of solo and accompaniment; the syllabic setting.

Chapter *4.* Renaissance Music

IN THE history of man, the Renaissance is considered to be one of the great ages. From our present-day point of vantage, science, letters, art, discovery, all seem to have flowered with amazing richness during the fifteenth and sixteenth centuries. Moreover, we feel a strong sympathy with this age since many modern concepts were first evolved during it.

Similarly, music of the Renaissance is the first to deal with sound and movement in what has come to be known as *traditional procedure*. Renaissance music strikes a familiar and warm note for many listeners. Anyone who has sung in a choral group must have had experience with Roman motets, English madrigals, French chansons, or chorales dating from Reformation times. The pleasure and satisfaction which an ensemble singer derives from the play of voices and textures in Renaissance choral music is one of the great rewards of musical performance. The importance and vitality of this style is shown by the fact that for the past three centuries and more, composers, in many of their sacred compositions, have paid homage to the musical style of the Renaissance by emulating or paraphrasing it. Indeed, the Renaissance musical style is the first of the polyphonic styles to create a lasting tradition.

To illustrate the Renaissance way of musical composition, let us listen to Josquin Deprès' motet, *Ave Maria*. In this work we can note the following characteristics:

1. In contrast to medieval music, we hear a new quality of sound; a drastic reduction in the amount and impact of dissonance; thirds and sixths instead of fourths and fifths

2. Several very strong points of harmonic arrival

3. Very clear and distinct separation of voices; clear projection of gracefully turned melodic material; imitation

4. A sustained quality of movement; moderately slow beat; avoidance of extremes of brevity or length in note values; overlap of voice parts; telescoping of phases of movement

As an over-all impression, we can say that this music seems to have a balance, a control, an evenness, a sense of parts fitted together in a perfectly integrated and smooth manner.

These are general comments on this piece; yet they can well apply to much music written during Josquin's time. He was a great figure in the development of Renaissance music, representing the final crystallization of Renaissance techniques of musical composition. Before his time, Renaissance music was moving toward clarification; after Josquin, music, like art, began to develop special mannerisms.

Now, we shall look more closely at the various component qualities and procedures of Renaissance music.

QUALITIES OF SOUND

Triads

Around the year 1425, a new kind of sound began to filter into Western European music. The music has a fuller, richer, sweeter, and more thoroughly blended quality of sound. We hear many thirds and sixths in addition to the fifths and octaves which were the stand-bys of medieval music. Dissonances have receded to an unassuming position; instead of clashing head on at times, the melodic lines make way for each other. In Guillaume Dufay's *Kyrie* (1) from the Mass based on the secular song, *Se la face ay pâle* (*Masterpieces,* no. 15), an early manifestation of this new style is illustrated. This music has none of the strident, bold dissonances and little of the open sounds of Guillaume de Machaut's music.

The important fact about this new sound is that it is composed almost entirely of familiar major and minor triads. This is the moment in history when the traditional harmonic system of Western music began to take definite shape. The establishment of the triad as the basic harmonic unit was almost as important as the beginnings of polyphony itself. Each note in a chord had to be a member of a triad; if not, it had to be led gently to a tone which was a member. In this new style, the sense of harmonic movement from one triad to another, based on the play of different triad colors, was the principal harmonic interest. As an exceptional demonstration of the fondness of fifteenth-century composers for triad sounds, listen to

Dufay's *Gloria in excelsis,* ad modem tubae (in the manner of trumpets). Actually, the entire piece alternates between tonic and dominant harmony. The trumpets have a simple fanfare figure, while the voices decorate the harmonies with intertwining imitations. The incorporation of fanfares into highly elaborated musical compositions will become a favorite procedure of composers in later times. This is an early example and can be heard on the *2000 Years of Music* set, no. 7.

The impetus toward the new harmonic language probably came from England. During the Middle Ages the English seem to have had a preference for singing in thirds instead of fourths and fifths. As a result of the Hundred Years' War, which was fought in France, English ways became known to Continental musicians, and they began to use the sonorities they heard in English music. The sweetness of this new style was so captivating that frequently whole chains of such chords were sung, decorating the plain song in parallel movement.

You can discover for yourselves the effect of this technique, called *faux-bourdon* in the fifteenth century. At the piano select any white note. Play along with it the third above, and add to these the fourth above the upper note. You now have a chord of the sixth. Keeping strictly parallel, move slowly up and down the keyboard for a few degrees. The effect is pleasant on the piano, but in voices its sweetness is much greater. Indeed many popular singing teams today rely heavily upon this effect. In faux-bourdon, we receive the impression that a single melodic line has widened into a consonant, rich, and sonorous stream of sound. Thus, our first observation about Renaissance music is that it is primarily euphonious and consonant in its qualities of sound.

The Authentic Cadence

Throughout the Renaissance this feeling for harmonic euphony controlled the general quality of sound. Soon, however, distinctive harmonic procedures began to emerge from the play of triad sonorities. Among these, the most important is the Renaissance type of cadence, which we will recognize as our familiar authentic cadence.

We have heard harmonic points of arrival in medieval music. The leading-tone action in Machaut's Mass definitely points to a resolution. In most medieval cadences the action of the voices leading to the chord of arrival was stepwise:

Ex. 4–1. Stepwise cadence.

Thus, the idea of the cadence had already become important for indicating arrival. However, in music of the Renaissance, it was discovered that a much stronger, emphatic, and clearer sense of harmonic arrival could be projected if a leap in the bass voice from the *fifth* tone of the mode to the *tonic* were added to the stepwise movement from 7 to 8. Example 4–2 below illustrates the effect of adding the bass in such a manner.

Ex. 4–2. Bass cadence.

stepwise cadence

bass cadence

If you will refer to page 55 in Chapter 2, you will recall the strong effect of arrival that was created when the bass moved from 5 to 1, down a fifth (or upward a fourth). This is the *authentic cadence.*

It was only in music of the Renaissance that a genuine bass voice appeared in the harmony, acting as a support and harmonic guide. Previously all voices in a texture were almost equal in action, differing only in range. Now the bass behaved in its own fashion; it created a new kind of cadence. This distinctive action of the bass developed a new harmonic dimension, like the sense of visual perspective which was created in Renaissance painting in the fifteenth century.

Note, in the illustration, the feeling of distance; the eye is drawn by the vanishing point into the painting, so to speak, so that we have a greater sense of depth and position than in the somewhat flat representations of medieval painting. This was a new *horizontal* dimension. In music a new feeling of space distribution was developed in which voices were organized on a *vertical* dimension. Both the bass and the upper voices had their own areas of action, and they performed distinctly different roles within those areas. Throughout the Renaissance and during the seventeenth century, the feeling for organizing harmony around cadences guided by the bass grew continually stronger, until, in the eighteenth century, the cadential feeling saturated the entire harmonic language. Josquin's motet has several cadences of this kind. The strongest and most obvious cadence is the one we hear at the end; it creates a very convincing impression of finality. Such cadences thus serve important structural roles.

Dissonance Treatment

As we heard in Josquin's motet, Renaissance music deals mainly with consonances, triads, thirds, and sixths as the basic raw material of its sound; nevertheless, it does not disregard dissonance. The limitation of dissonance and its careful control opened new possibilities for musical expression. With fewer dissonances, each one became more important. The Renaissance approach to dissonance is a very special one. One of the principal procedures is as follows: if a dissonant tone is introduced, it is as a temporary *suspension,* i.e., *replacement* of a consonant tone and must move to, or resolve into, that consonant tone.

Ex. 4–3. Dissonance treatment (suspension).

The dissonance thus creates a special kind of tension calling for a specified resolution. This, in fact, is the basis of the consonance and dissonance relationship that will have a tremendous effect upon harmony for four centuries to come. Dissonance is not a special effect on its own; it has an obligation to its resolution.

In the final few chords of Josquin's motet we can hear such a suspension dissonance and the intensification of expressive quality which it creates. Listen to the topmost voice. Note that just before the end it holds back before moving to the leading tone, while the other voices go to their appointed positions in the chord. The suspension is the most thoroughly exploited technique of dissonance in all Renaissance music. It binds, and at

Fig. 3. Pieter Brueghel the Elder: *The Harvesters*, illustrating perspective in Renaissance painting. (Courtesy of the Metropolitan Museum of Art.)

the same time, by its contrast with the predominantly consonant sound, it creates a strongly expressive accent.

Later composers turned this quality of the suspension to use in expressing especially poignant or touching moments in their music. Dissonance was used for dramatic accent; it created a focus upon a critically important word or phrase. Sixteenth-century composers took delight in working out such relationships between music and poetry. An especially effective example of dissonance used pictorially can be heard in Luca Marenzio's madrigal, *S'io parto, i'moro,* in *Masterpieces,* no. 27, at the word *moro,* meaning "I die." Marenzio and some of his contemporaries represent a later and rather highly mannered aspect of Renaissance music, particularly in this respect. In Renaissance harmony, the dissonance became a special and valuable resource and remained such for five centuries.

Chromaticism

Another technique for creating special effects against the even flow of Renaissance harmony was chromaticism. In this technique chords belonging to very different tone systems were placed either next to each other or very close to each other. In chromaticism we have the impression of a colorful, somewhat unstable shift of harmonic position. In the Marenzio madrigal, at the words "and yet I must still leave thee," there is a chromatic relationship between the chords that begin and end the passage. This is a clever underscoring of the idea of departure by going from one tonal position to another. Such expressive and pictorial play upon music and words bespeaks the flexibility and richness of musical resources in the Renaissance. Chromaticism, as well as the use of dissonance, increases from rather restrained moderate use in Josquin's time to a high point of concentration in some very late sixteenth-century Italian composers, particularly Gesualdo. This is carried to the point where a sense of tonal center is almost entirely lost.

Range of Sound

The richer and more colorful harmonic language of Renaissance music is associated with a wider range of sound and a generally fuller quality than we have heard in medieval music. Medieval music was written principally in two or three parts, fairly close in range. Renaissance music was written typically in four or more parts, with a wider range than medieval music. Note in Josquin's motet the compactness and fullness when all four voices are singing. Observe also how Josquin took advantage of range differences to set pairs of voices against each other in textural contrasts. It is as if he were creating a third dimension, a sense of aural perspective in the contrasts of high and low. In later Renaissance music, the blend of five or more voices, full, rich, sonorous, and vibrant becomes a principal appeal, as we can hear in sections of the motet, *Tristis,* of Lassus.

The range of tone quality is quite broad in Renaissance music. Within Marenzio's madrigal, the first ten measures encompass ten changes in the amount of sound, from one to five voices being involved. The element of *contrast* in texture becomes very important. Toward the end of the sixteenth century, contrasts in quality of sound were exploited more and more; such contrasts represent one of the forces that eventually destroyed the consistencies of Renaissance music and ushered in the Baroque era. Indeed, contrast was the watchword in certain music of Venetian composers, who made a practice of alternating phrases in their compositions between choruses placed at different positions in the church. Instrumental groups, adding their sonorities to multiply the contrast, also participated in this type of performance, which depended largely upon the effects of reverberation possible in the great cathedral of St. Mark's in Venice. Giovanni Gabrieli's *Sacrae Symphoniae* are magnificent examples of this impressive style of composition.

Before we leave the matter of sonority values, a subject which is fascinating and absorbing in any age or style of music, we should refer to another aspect of the Renaissance musical practice, namely, the use of instruments. The sound of instruments pervades the musical life of the fifteenth and sixteenth centuries. During the Renaissance, performing on musical instruments appears to have expanded and flourished tremendously. Many compositions required a virtuoso command of the instrument to perform. Treatises on instrumental performance were written. Works that developed and exploited the special sonorities and agilities of different kinds of instruments, such as organ, harpsichord, strings, lute, and brass, were composed in increasing numbers. Instruments were used in entertainment, to provide dance music in the household, in the church where the organ was the chief instrument, and often to replace or augment vocal parts in choral or vocal ensemble music. These arrangements were generally quite optional; and many strikingly idiomatic works appear during the sixteenth century. With all of this interest, musical instruments of many kinds were developed or improved from early models. From this time on instrumental music established itself as an independent area of musical composition.

Summary

Establishment of triad sonorities, cadence effects, systematic and subtle use of dissonance, judiciously handled chromaticism, combined with a variety of instrumental effects—all these give evidence to the concern with sonority as a special value in Renaissance music. We cannot always reconstruct a Renaissance musical performance, nevertheless, it is apparent that in this age the sheer color and beauty of musical sound was a vital force in musical expression. Man discovered that voices or instruments, or both, chiming in upon the notes of the triad, formed a harmony that could be called *perfect*. From this time on, composers created countless effects that stemmed from these basic sonorities. Much later, Wagner went so far as to compose an entire prelude to a four-opera cycle, using but one single harmony, the E♭-major triad.

QUALITIES OF MOVEMENT

Renaissance music neither rushes along nor loses the steady momentum which seems to be so characteristic. We sense, in the works we have heard, a *moderate* pace that controls all movement. Josquin's motet provides an excellent example. As it proceeds forward, you can feel a gentle strength in the quality of movement, a deliberate pulse, even, regular, without the emphatic accent that invites foot-tapping in a dance or march. Yet the movement does not lag or lose vitality. The interplay of voices, each with its own action to contribute to the composite movement, creates the impression of a reserved but undeniably purposeful pace, a pace that establishes its own time scale. As a rule, we can say that Renaissance music moves deliberately.

Indeed, this moderate and regular pace was recognized at the time as a basic stylistic feature. Musical theorists of the Renaissance designated the unit of beat as the *tactus*. The tactus corresponds to the half note in a present-day andante tempo, approximately one second in length. The pulse we heard in Josquin's motet as a steady undercurrent represented the tactus.

Still, the manner of performance, the meter, and the style of the piece gave rise to differences of speed and accent. In Josquin's motet, the quality of movement changes when the meter changes from duple to triple and then back again.

Within this average pace, differences of speed and accent did occur. A choral piece using one or two notes for each tactus would give the impression of moving more slowly than an instrumental piece that might use four, six, or eight tones within the same interval of time. Let us take two highly distinctive examples. Contrast the lively effect of the lute dances, *Masterpieces,* no. 22, with the broad and deliberate quality of movement in the Lassus motet, no. 23; yet the basic tempos of the two are comparable. Moreover, the manner in which the lute performs must necessarily give a stronger impression of accent than would vocal music. The lute player strikes each tone with a plucked attack that creates accent, while voices set their tones in motion without noticeable impact.

Still another factor makes for contrast between the lute piece and the motet. Smoothness of movement comes very easily in vocal music; the voice can virtually glide from one tone to the next. On the other hand, the very manner in which the lute produces its tone by plucking tends to create an interrupted flow of sound. The accented, crisp style of the lute is ideally suited for dance music since every touching point can receive a stress. Perhaps you can realize more vividly just what effect a regular plucking has upon musical movement if you will think of the function that the string bass player serves in a dance orchestra. He helps to set the beat, the pace of the music, and at the same time provides a harmonic support as a bass instrument. The lute did this in many ensemble pieces of Renaissance music, and the jazz bass player is in this respect the counterpart, no matter how farfetched, of the lutenist of bygone days.

With respect to movement, we must remember that Renaissance music was still essentially polyphonic, although the combinations which the various voices made had to fit into the triad scheme of harmony. You will remember, as we studied polyphony, what its effect is upon the over-all sense of movement, how it creates overlaps, how it covers cadences and caesuras with fresh movement. This is all true of Renaissance music, particularly choral music. Many times you will hear the harmony focusing upon a cadence, yet the sense of arrival will be blurred by some melodic or rhythmic action in one or more voices. For this reason more than any other, Renaissance music has been described as a "long-drawn-out sweetness."

Melodic movement in Renaissance music contributes to the sense of moderate pace, balance, control, and subtle play. Renaissance melodic action seems to describe a rounded pattern, in which the melody dips and rises gradually with respect to a fulcrum that keeps it in comfortable balance. The Renaissance composer made his melody move so that it neither dis-

FIG. 4. Veronese: *The Marriage at Cana* (Louvre). Except for the figure of Christ in the center, this picture represents a sumptuous Renaissance feast, with entertainment by musicians depicted in the lower foreground. (Reproduced by permission of Caisse Nationale des Monuments Historiques.)

played too sharp a profile nor lost its momentum by insufficient action. In particular, you will hear very few large or striking leaps.

The opening of Josquin's motet serves us well as an example of this melodic style. The subject begins with a small downward leap; as a counter-statement, the melody rises gradually beyond the pitch of the beginning, turns around the high point several times, and makes its way downward gradually. You will notice also in this melody, that, as the music moves upward, rhythmic action becomes more lively with the appearance of shorter notes; and that with the descent action quiets and longer notes again predominate. Play this line, or sing it alone. One can hardly find anywhere a more exquisite example of a melodic period that creates, out of the gentle ebb and flow of movement, such a perfect inner balance.

The final flowering and the utmost concentration of the Renaissance melodic style is found in the music of Palestrina, which moves on with the greatest suavity and smoothness. If any of you have had occasion to study counterpoint based on sixteenth-century styles, you are well aware that one of the basic criteria is a melody that moves sweetly, gently, and yet with a clear sense of direction.

FORM-BUILDING FACTORS

After evaluating your initial impressions of a Renaissance composition, recognizing its characteristic sonorities, its triadic harmony, and its qualities of movement, your attention might well turn to the entire piece itself. How does it take shape? What can be grasped about its structure?

Certain general procedures typical of Renaissance composition can throw some light upon this problem. While no formula guarantees the structural strength of any one composition, it nevertheless provides a useful framework both for the composer and the listener. The typical form-building factors we shall examine here are:

1. Addition, elaboration, and improvisation
2. Imitation
3. Repetition and contrast
4. Text; familiar style
5. Dance music

Addition, Elaboration, Improvisation

As we studied medieval music, we saw it taking shape by addition and elaboration. One part was added to others; and the resulting patterns were expanded as elaborations were introduced between tones: rhythmic patterns were superimposed. Some of the most important types of music took shape by such accretions. In the Renaissance these procedures were still at work in many different ways. Josquin's motet illustrates one important method.

Its very title provides the clue: *Ave Maria, Gratia Plena* (Hail Mary, Full of Grace). This is the title of a plain song. Josquin has taken the plain song and elaborated it so that each phrase in turn becomes the melodic basis of a section or period of his motet. Josquin "borrowed" a plain song to create part of the framework of his composition. The length of the plain song then is a governing factor in the length of the motet. At other times Josquin, or others, might have borrowed a popular song such as Dufay did in his Mass *Se la face ay pâle*. Sometimes, as a play on words, the composer would invent his own "borrowed" material, by fashioning a motive from some phrase or name. Thus, Josquin Deprès wrote a Mass honoring the Duke of Ferrara and created a cantus firmus by tones that correspond to the vowels in the Duke's title. This is how it was worked out:

Ex. 4–4. Motto for the *Missa Hercules.*

re   ut   re   ut   re   fa   mi   re
HER - CU - LES   DUX   FER - RA - RI - E

In *Ave Maria* and in many other works, Josquin used a limited amount of precomposed material. But in the later sixteenth century, borrowing was carried so far that entire compositions were reworked into more extended or more highly decorated pieces. About three-quarters of the Masses of Lassus and Palestrina, the two most important composers of sacred music in the later Renaissance, are *parody masses*; they are elaborated from smaller sacred pieces or from secular polyphonic compositions. The parody mass represents the ultimate stage in the evolution that began during the early Middle Ages; that is, *the evolution of musical structure and texture by additions to preexisting material.*

Another striking example of borrowing is the *canzona francese,* in which Italian composers transcribed and reworked French secular songs, *chansons,* into instrumental compositions. We can hear what changes took place when this was done by contrasting nos. 20 and 21 in *Masterpieces.* These are two versions of the same song, *Pour ung plaisir.* The vocal piece is quite straightforward, brisk, and declamatory in manner. The keyboard piece derived from the chanson is florid, and its movement is less straightforward and vigorous. The florid effects in Andrea Gabrieli's piece arise from the process of *ornamentation*; in this process the composer or performer *breaks up a long tone into a number of shorter tones* which describe a pattern centering around the original tones.

Written and improvised ornamentation, both in instrumental and vocal music, was an important aspect of musical performance from the fifteenth to the middle of the eighteenth century. As we have heard, it made a profound difference in the musical effect, melodically, rhythmically, and harmonically. Ornamentation was extensively used in the numerous sets of *variations* written during the sixteenth century. In these, the basic melody or the harmonic plan of a preexisting model was given new treatment in the variations, of which there might be five, ten, twenty, or even more. Giles Farnaby's Variation for Virginals on the tune *Loth to Depart* (*Masterpieces,* no. 29) shows how ornamental figures were used in variations of the late sixteenth century. The appeal of such pieces, now as then, is the fresh quality of texture, movement, and expression given to a familiar musical idea.

No more striking example of elaboration in Renaissance music is found than in the *intonations, preludes, fantasias,* and *toccatas,* principally for organ, which preceded the singing of motets and other church music. These were originally intended to give the singers the *tone* on which they were to begin, or to make the tonic note of the mode clear to them. From a few simple chords and running passages that occupied a moment or two of time, these studies gradually became more and more elaborate until works of monumental scope were produced. As befits the situation wherein the performer is at liberty to improvise freely, these studies began to display brilliant virtuoso passages, making use of all the coloristic potentialities of the instrument. The great organ toccatas and preludes of Johann Sebastian Bach are direct descendants of these early organ intonations, themselves expanded from a single tone! Ponder this when next you hear the Toccata and Fugue in D minor of Bach.

Lute and string players also liked to exercise themselves upon their instruments, possibly before launching into the principal musical business, a dance, a song, or a set of variations. These exercises, called *ricercare,* from the verb meaning "to search," or possibly designated as *tastar de corde,* touching of the strings, exhibited the distinctive sonorities of the instruments and their special capacities for brilliant technical display. *Full chords,* to emphasize rich resonance, and *rapid passages,* to show off agility, alternated in such pieces. Thus, the form was built on bold contrasts. The term *ricercar* also applies to the sacred counterpart of the canzona francese, in which a motet was transcribed for instrumental performance.

Addition, elaboration, and improvisation represent typical attitudes toward the use of musical material, not only in Renaissance and medieval music, but also throughout the history of Western music to the present day. Here the emphasis is not so much upon originality or discovery as upon taste, distinction, and the resourcefulness of the composer to create an individual work. The amount of borrowing ranged from entire compositions, such as motets or chansons, down to small melodic fragments. In all cases the borrowed material helped to create a framework for the new piece, or at least to establish points of structural reference.

Imitation

Returning again to Josquin's motet, we can distinguish that the treatment of the plain song as a cantus firmus differs considerably from the medieval procedure. Here, the plain song is no longer an underpinning but becomes the melodic source for a series of *imitations* which carry throughout the entire piece. Imitation, then, is one of the principal structural features of this piece, as it is indeed in a great deal of Renaissance music.

Earlier we saw how melodic and rhythmic motives began to take shape in measured organum; frequently these motives were traded off between the upper voices. These voices were thus imitating each other from time to time; thereby, they created a clearly recognized kind of melodic statement and counterstatement. But the kind of imitation that began to permeate the music of the mid-fifteenth century was not the casual exchange of voices we heard in measured organum. Rather it was a systematic presentation of a distinctive subject in turn by a number of voices. Indeed, the form of a composition might be entirely built up by a series of such presentations. The effect of each set of presentations, called *exposition*, was cumulative in texture. As each new voice entered, those already singing would continue to spin out their own figures until all voices had entered; after a time, a cadence would be made, and a new exposition would take shape. Example 4–5 illustrates such an exposition, also called a *point of imitation*, and shows by diagram the imitated and the nonimitated material.

Ex. 4–5. Josquin Deprès: *Absalon fili mihi.*

Most of the imitation you will hear in Renaissance music is *free imitation,* in which the successive entries give the impression of dealing with the same basic motive yet are not required to copy exactly what the preceding voices have done. Actually much freedom could be attained without losing the sense of imitation which is all-important in this technique of composition. For example, in the Lassus motet, *Masterpieces,* no. 23, each voice enters with the characteristic three-note motive which is the subject of the first phase of imitation; yet some of the voices sing a different version of the motive and the first voice sings it upside down! Still we have no trouble in recognizing the basic motive in each entry. Working with such short flexible motives, the composer can handle his part-writing very freely, and will constantly discover opportunities for fresh movement. Not only was free imitation by far the most useful and prevalent type in the Renaissance, but it has dominated contrapuntal composition from that time to the present day. It is an ideal vehicle for retaining coherence in a composition and at the same time maintaining movement. Free imitation lends itself to the exposition type of structure whereby voices can merge at a cadence and then start anew.

Some imitative pieces were newly composed throughout, containing no borrowed or preexisting material. When borrowing did take place, the preexisting material was completely assimilated in so far as style is concerned. Compare the plain song *Ave Maria* with Josquin's motet: we no longer deal with the declamatory syllabic style of plain song but discover the cantus firmus altered rhythmically so that it assumes the typical quality of movement found in Renaissance music, a steady, continuous flow, governed by the beat or tactus, with a judicious, well-balanced distribution of tones of different lengths.

Repetition and Contrast

As a rule, Renaissance music tends to be *through-composed,* that is, each phrase, each section is freshly composed or worked over. Literal repetitions are relatively infrequent, yet the principle of repetition does operate to bind the music together thematically. Imitation itself is a kind of varied repetition. Moreover, in Josquin's motet, and in much Renaissance music, we hear responsory or echo effects in which one phrase is restated at a different pitch by different voices. This suggests a tiny, balanced, two-part structure embedded within the larger flow of the entire piece.

We do hear repetitions of phrases in the manner of refrains in many secular compositions of the Renaissance. Here an especially catchy turn or a particularly poignant phrase returns to emphasize the expressive quality and to bind the form together a bit more clearly. For example, in Luca Marenzio's madrigal *S'io parto,* the phrase *dolorosa partita* (this sad departure) is heard twice at different points in the piece with virtually the identical musical setting.

In a style as consistent and smoothly flowing as that of Renaissance music, contrast makes itself felt in a rather subdued and subtle manner. We have nothing of the bold contrasts we associate with symphonic music of a later age. Still, in Josquin's motet, the play of delicate contrasts throws light and shadow and gives distinct profile to the various phrases of the work. Consider the shift from one range to another, the change of motive from a relatively slow subject to one that is quicker, the concentration on major-triad sounds, as at the very beginning, as against the strong minor flavor elsewhere and at the end. We have already mentioned the shift in meter as a basic structural contrast. Later Renaissance music often veers toward bolder contrast effects, particularly those dealing with harmonic shifts, as in the example cited above from the Marenzio madrigal.

Starting with his subject or his model, the Renaissance composer worked out his composition by imitation or elaboration, or very possibly, both. He led the voices smoothly through the consonant harmonic combinations of thirds, fifths, sixths which made up typical Renaissance chord forms. The inner shape and the length of the form were controlled by the various cadences within the piece and by the length of the text or the cantus firmus. These were all quite flexible and were handled differently in each piece. Nevertheless, some well-defined plan is discernible in each piece, representing special applications of the general principles we have been discussing. For purposes of illustration, let us see how a contrapuntal work, the motet *Tristis est anima mea* (*Masterpieces,* no. 23), has been shaped.

1. Listening to the whole piece, we are aware of the continuing contrapuntal activity organized imitatively. Yet, by contrast, the two sections in chordal style, the *Nunc videbitis* and the *Ego vadam immolari* stand out as being particularly expressive accents.

2. Harmonically, most of the piece appears to remain in the tonal center first established. But we have a striking episode of harmonic contrast when the text gives the words *circumdabit me* (surround me). The motive used at this point is a pictorial representation of the act of surrounding, since it is circular in shape.

3. There are five points of imitation contrasted to the two sections in chordal style. These begin with the following texts:

a. *Tristis,* a slow and melodically quiet subject

    b. Sustine, a somewhat quicker subject with entries coming very quickly

    c. Et vigilate mecum, a quick, melodically active subject, treated more broadly and intensively than the first two subjects

Up to this point there is a steady increase in the pace and intensity of movement.

    d. Nunc videbitis, the first section in chordal style, representing a dramatically contrasted slowdown after the accumulated momentum of the previous music

    e. Quae circumdabit, an intensive treatment of the circular motive, representing the most striking harmonic digression within the piece

    f. Vos fugam, another tightly woven imitative section, again pictorial, in its representation of flight (the term *fugue* in music is derived from the Latin word for flight), the voices here continually chasing each other

    g. Ego vadam, in a slightly ornamented chordal style

4. In order to create a convincing sense of final arrival, the composer has established a strong harmonic drive. You can hear the bass sustaining the dominant tone of the mode, while the action intensifies by means of the running figures that imitate each other closely in the upper voices. The bass here is a center of gravitation that prevents the flight of the melodic voices from breaking away entirely. This drive to the cadence at the end of a piece is a characteristic feature of Roman and Flemish music of the Renaissance. In this piece, it establishes a large-scale contrast between the continuous and flowing movement within the structure and the sense of arrival at the end.

Ex. 4–6. Diagram of drive to cadence in Lassus: *Tristis.*

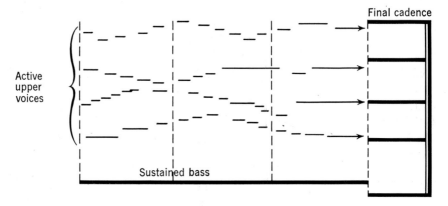

5. By close listening we have been able to appreciate the differences in the motives, to see how they grow from the sense of the text, and to recognize their function in providing contrast, albeit gentle, within the form.

6. Most of the inner cadences which ended points of imitation were covered by new movement, as in the following manner:

(new entry)
tristis est anima mea
tristis est anima mea
(arrival)

or:

(new entry)
vos fugam capietis
circumdabit me
(arrival)

From our discussion above, it should now be quite apparent that in listening to a polyphonic piece, it is well to become acquainted with the text beforehand. The composer frequently makes musical references to his poetic subject, either by creating a general expressive quality befitting the words, or by specific instances of pictorialism or expressive nuance. These can only be appreciated by a knowledge of the text as the piece is heard. Without knowing the text, the listener will become confused by the mixture of several voices singing different words at the same time.

Familiar Style

The polyphonic music we have been describing scans the text very freely, or not at all, in a poetic sense. One word, even a syllable, may occupy as much as an entire melodic phrase. With regard to the text this often becomes a melismatic style. At the other extreme is a style which we discover in many types of Renaissance music, a style in which the text is declaimed by a group of voices, all singing in a set rhythmic pattern according to the scansion of the text. This is a *chordal style,* which can be described texturally as *single action* (see Chapter 2, Texture). It has been given the name *familiar style*. Familiar style is similar to present-day church hymn music. Here the text occupies an important place in the attention of the listener from note to note. The length and structure of the text will then determine partly how the music will be put together. Familiar style appears throughout the sixteenth century in short sacred and secular works as well as in parts of more extended works. Its simplicity and directness commended it to Calvinists and it was the only kind of singing allowed in Calvinist churches. We heard several sections in familiar style in the motet *Tristis* of Lassus.

Dance Music

During the Renaissance there was an ever-growing interest in dancing and in dance music. Dancing was one of the essential items in the training of a gentleman or lady. The art and literature of the Renaissance provide ample testimony to the range and variety of dances during the sixteenth century. Thoinot Arbeau's *Orchesographie*, a work devoted entirely to a discussion of dances and dancing, lists many dances of various nations performed during the Renaissance. Most dances of the Renaissance were for polite society but some were popular tunes, such as the *Gassenhawer*, the street song of Germany, that curiously foreshadows the blues in its typical harmonic progressions. The prevalence of dance music, with its regularly balanced periods, its short phases of movement, its steady accents, and its penchant for what we would call *tunefulness* is evidence, in the sixteenth century, for the continually greater role that secular music was beginning to play.

Dance music ordinarily crystallizes into two-part structures, from measures through motives, phrases, and periods. The symmetry of physical motion is bilateral, step and counterstep, thrust and counterthrust. In Renaissance dance music, this two-part relationship of phrases and periods is carried out to the extent that separate dances would be paired. A fast dance would follow a slow dance; often in such pairs of dances, the second would be a variation upon the first, as in Lute Dances, no. 22 of *Masterpieces*.

There was a great variety of dances in the sixteenth century. Below are listed some of the more popular types and their special characteristics:

1. *Pavane*: a slow dance in duple time, performed with ceremonious solemnity after the manner of the peacock, *pavo,* from which it derived its name.

2. *Galliard*: a rather quick dance in triple time, the after-dance of the pavane.

3. *Allemande*: a dance of moderate pace in duple time, rather reserved in its motions; its name is the French word for "German."

4. *Courante*: a dance of moderately quick pace in triple time, deriving its name from the French *courant,* running; the after-dance of the allemande.

5. *Passamezzo*: a pavane of somewhat quicker pace.

6. *Saltarello*: the after-dance of the passamezzo, in triple time, quick pace.

7. *Branle*: a name given to a number of different dances in the sixteenth century, all characterized by being danced in groups, rather than by pairs of dancers.

8. *Morisca*: an exotic dance, danced in pantomime with grotesque Moorish make-up and costumes; the ancestor of the Morris dance.

Dance compositions were popular during this period; they circulated among musicians and frequently were used as subjects for sets of variations. From this time onward, the dance was an important medium of musical composition, and soon to become a formidable influence upon other kinds of music.

To summarize the form-building factors in Renaissance music described above:

1. Addition and elaboration
   a. Entire compositions, such as canzonas and parody masses
   b. Cantus firmus, taken from liturgical sources, secular sources, or created by the composer himself
   c. Sets of variations on dance or song tunes, or other familiar patterns
   d. Improvised elaboration, as in preludes and intonations
2. Imitation, strict and free
3. Control of the extent of a composition by the text
4. Distribution and strength of cadences and tonal centers
5. Balance of phrases and periods, in dance music
6. Repetition and contrast of sections

The techniques described above, and indeed, the typical Renaissance style which they define, were established by Josquin and his contemporaries. Consonance, even flow, and imitation in three, four, five, or more voices became the standard for musical composition until about 1600. This was especially the case in Catholic Church music, still the most important body of musical composition at this time.

NATIONAL STYLES IN RENAISSANCE MUSIC

During the first half of the Renaissance the countries in the northwestern part of Europe, the Low Countries, Burgundy, and France took the leadership in musical composition. Flemish composers were the acknowledged masters of their art in all Europe. After the defeat of Charles of Burgundy by the French in 1477 and the incorporation of Burgundy into the French kingdom, Flemish composers began to migrate to other centers of Europe, and particularly to Italy. Wherever they went, they introduced their own craft of composition, adapting it to the local conditions which they discovered. For example, in Venice they developed the polychoral style, taking advantage of the wonderful resonances in St. Mark's Cathedral, where the four arms of the (Greek) cross are equal. They set vocal and instrumental groups in the arms of the cross, answering back and forth.

In addition to the travels of Renaissance musicians, which carried musical information by word of mouth, the invention of a practical system of music printing about 1500 gave a tremendous assist to the dissemination of musical techniques. A give-and-take among composers was made possible; refinements and innovations were transmitted quickly. This is the musical counterpart to the invention of printing by Gutenberg.

From about 1500, throughout the century, Italy was the battlefield for the powerful rulers of Europe, those of France, Spain, and Germany, who took advantage of the internal struggles between the Italian states to form alliances and to claim sovereignty. Such struggles established lines of communication to various important points in Italy, Rome, Florence, Naples, etc., and musicians went along with the armies. It became the fashion to employ Flemish musicians in the chapels and courts of Italy, and so Italy, the theater of war, became also the center stage for the musical art of the sixteenth century, as it was for literature and painting. The first of the national styles to be described is the Italian madrigal.

Italian madrigal. In Italy, Flemish masters found a popular, attractive, yet undeveloped form in the *frottola*. The frottola was composed in familiar style to poetry that had popular appeal yet little elegance or distinction. By applying their learned techniques and their polished expressive manner to the clear, dancelike forms of Italian popular music, Flemish composers evolved the madrigal, which is perhaps the most representative and comprehensive embodiment of Renaissance music, both technically and aesthetically. The Italian madrigal is the secular counterpart of the motet, imitative in style, and rather similar in harmonic procedure. It became increasingly dedicated to the expression of intense and even violent personal feelings. Musically, this involved more pictorialism, a greater amount of dissonance, striking chromatic shifts, and bolder contrasts between sections and phrases. The Italian madrigal represents one of the forces that eventually destroyed the evenly flowing consistency of Renaissance music and ushered in the Baroque era.

Luca Marenzio's madrigal, *S'io parto,* represents the Italian secular choral style at its full flower. It has many special moments of striking emotional expressiveness, yet retains the sense of polyphonic movement that characterizes Renaissance music.

English madrigal. This was a secular form strongly influenced by the Italian madrigal. It was cultivated during the height of the Elizabethan period, from about 1590 on. Stylistically it is much like its Italian counterpart, but it shows distinctive qualities of its own, particularly in its touches of fanciful humor and its delightful play upon the rhythms of the English language, in which frequent shifts between various kinds of duple and triple meter create a buoyant yet subtle imbalance in the quality of movement.

Queen Elizabeth inspired the most important collection of English madrigals, *The Triumphs of Oriana,* Oriana being Elizabeth, of course. Many composers contributed to this collection. One of the most brilliant works of the entire set is Thomas Weelkes' *As Vesta Was from Latmos Hill Descending.* This piece has a most ingratiating manner; it is full of clever and subtle pictorialisms, some of which are noted below:

1. A declaratory opening, full ensemble: *As Vesta was from Latmos Hill*
2. *Running down amain*: descending figures succeeding each other in quick imitations
3. *Two by two*: two voices; *three by three*: three voices; *all alone*: solo
4. *Mingling with*: intertwining imitative figures
5. *Long live fair Oriana*: much-repeated fanfare figures using tonic and dominant harmonies; strong sense of cadential arrival

Chanson. The chanson was the principal French secular form of the Renaissance. It generally dealt with pastoral or amorous subjects, although some highly entertaining descriptive chansons were written in which vivid pictorialism abounded. The chanson was imitative in procedure, but the main interest lay in lively, dancelike rhythms, rather than in well-rounded melodic phrases. Indeed, this form and its instrumental paraphrase, the

canzona francese, can be identified by the rhythmic pattern ♩ ♩♩

(long and two shorts) which is found at the beginning of most chansons. In many chansons the harmony for long sections alternates between the familiar tonic, dominant, and subdominant chords, a procedure quite different from the subtle shifts of harmony found in the motet. This gives the chanson a modern sound at times.

Thomas Crequillon's chanson, *Pour une plaisir* (*Masterpieces,* no. 20), is typical of its genre. A very entertaining variety of chanson is the program chanson, which describes special scenes or actions with vivid pictorial effects. Clément Jannequin's *La Guerre,* which tells the story of the battle of Marignan with sounds that describe fanfares, drums, encounters, etc., is one of the most famous pieces of the entire chanson literature.

French vocal music has traditionally been concerned with a proper and clear declamation of the text, particularly in reference to the length of syllables. Hence, the chanson frequently employs familiar style. One group of poets and composers went so far as to set up strict conditions for measuring music according to the text. They created *vers mesuré,* in which the rhythmic independence of any voice, or of the entire ensemble, was subordinate to poetic scansion.

Chorale. One of the policies established by Martin Luther during the Protestant Reformation was the singing of sacred music in the native language, the vernacular, rather than in Latin. Although these songs were at first composed in the style of the imitative motet, using familiar melodies as cantus firmi, later, in line with the more direct, down-to-earth religious outlook of the Reformation, a simple type of chorale was evolved, employing familiar style. As a rule, then, the chorale tended to be shorter, simpler, and far less pictorial than the motet. The French counterpart of the chorale was the *psalm,* and in England the Anglican Church developed a form of sacred song called the *anthem.*

In no. 10 of *2000 Years of Music, Aus Tiefer Not,* we can hear an example of the early German chorale. Although it has some contrapuntal action, the interest centers on the chorale melody in the top voice. Note how rarely a major chord is heard. The dark, minor sounds of this piece suggest very strongly the sense of the text "Out of the deepest need, I call to Thee."

If we were to list the various media, forms, and styles of Renaissance music, sacred and secular, vocal and instrumental, Italian, French, Spanish, German, English, we would see that in spite of the general uniformity of style that governed music of this era, there was a rich variety of local color and expression. Indeed, sometimes the differences are much more easily seen than the underlying unity of style, as we can hear if we contrast a Lassus motet with a set of keyboard variations.

HISTORICAL SURVEY AND SUMMARY

Music historians have borrowed the term *Renaissance* from the history of art, literature, and ideas because music paralleled these other aspects of culture both in time and in certain characteristic features during that era. *Humanism* is the term which Renaissance historians have applied to the spirit of this age. Specifically it refers to a new interest in the ancient classic culture of Greece and Rome and the application of classic ideas in literature of the sixteenth century. In a broader sense, and this interests us much more, humanism refers to the new attitudes of the Renaissance, which, as Michelet, the French historian put it, led to the "discovery of the world, the discovery of man." Evidences of this spirit of inquiry are found in Da Vinci's scientific interest, particularly in his studies in anatomy, in Copernicus' new theories of astronomy, in the development of the science of perspective by Renaissance painters, and the penetrating and comprehensive search into human motivations and emotions which Shakespeare's plays embody. Musically, we find analogies to perspective in the creation of a true bass function in harmony. The awakening of the scientific spirit of inquiry might be compared to the development of a balanced, clear, and logical relationship between tones and voices which consonant, triadic harmony and imitation brought about. Strong personal feelings in drama and poetry are matched boldly by the emphasis on expressive devices and moods, both in the madrigal and the motet.

Historically, the Renaissance saw the first comprehensive effort to break away from the twin authorities of Church and Empire. Political and religious movements had repercussions in the field of fine arts. Much of the music we have examined in this chapter is secular in nature. Both the motivation and the means were present for the Renaissance man to express himself in a personal, warm, and often impassioned style. He no longer was concerned entirely with reframing and renewing hieratic, absolute values; rather his attention turned to his own feelings and the way in which he observed the real world around him, the world of senses and solidity.

In the area of religion, the great, conclusive event was the Reformation, the establishment of a new church, locally controlled, speaking the language of each country. Not long after, in the middle of the sixteenth century, the Roman Church took steps to counteract this centrifugal tendency that was manifested on all sides, and in the Counter Reformation, made efforts to reorganize itself and reestablish its supreme authority. The music of Lassus and Palestrina which we have heard was composed in the spirit of the Counter Reformation. Although in many respects it embodies the ideals of Renaissance art in its evenness, balance, smooth flow, and harmonious relationship between all parts, it avoids completely that sense of worldly delight and bold emotional projection which was the guiding spirit in the aesthetics of Renaissance art. In these respects, Roman polyphony is anti-Renaissance; it points to certain mystic qualities found in the art of the seventeenth century.

A great deal of Renaissance music was written to be performed on grand occasions, either solemn or festive. There was also music written for performance by musical amateurs, in the home, at court, or among friends.

Music was one of the graces that participated in the education of the ideal man of the Renaissance. Dancing, poetry, classics, art, and music were part of his accomplishments. The satisfactions he received from performing madrigals, dance pieces, or other compositions for ensemble can be re-created by the modern amateur if he has any training in vocal or instrumental performance. Indeed, he will receive a truer picture of Renaissance music and a deeper personal musical satisfaction if he can perform this music rather than listen to it in concert, a purpose for which it may never have been intended.

Briefly summarizing the points we have covered in dealing with Renaissance music:

1. *Qualities of sound*: consonant, triadic, careful use of dissonance; occasional striking chromaticism; development of a true bass; formulation of strong cadences; fuller sound due to greater number of voices; subtle effects of contrast

2. *Qualities of movement*: steady, evenly flowing, moderate pace; short, symmetrical phases of movement in dances; long, nonsymmetrical phases of movement with much overlap in polyphonic pieces; some variation within the basic pace due to note values and rhythmic patterns employed

3. *Form-building factors*: addition and elaboration upon cantus firmi; paraphrase of entire pieces; free ornamentation, imitation, dance forms, repetition, and contrast of material occasionally

4. *Style and expression*: growth of secular music and distinctions between national styles; development of an important instrumental music; concern with musical representation of personal feelings; faithful yet subtle delineation of the poetic text in music; control of expressive values by well-defined musical procedures, such as consonance-dissonance relationships; imitation; sense of steady rhythmic flow

SUGGESTED LISTENING PROJECTS

1. Canzona *Taat een meeskin,* in *L'Anthologie Sonore,* Vol. 1, side 8, no. 4

Listen for: Regular pulse; imitation; use of syncopation; systematic give-and-take among instruments; indications of sectional structure; contrast in change of meter; lack of harmonic contrast. Imagine the enjoyment of playing such a piece. With present-day instruments, this could be easily performed by guitar, flute, and two strings.

2. Frottola *Dal letto me levava* in *2000 Years of Music,* no. 7

Listen for: Emphasis on compact chordal texture; lively counter rhythms and give-and-take effects; strong cadences; short phrases; lack of melodic elegance; straightforward, gay manner of piece.

3. Motet *Miserere Mei* (Lassus) in *2000 Years of Music,* no. 12

Listen for: Emphasis on dark colors; fluctuation between imitative counterpoint and declamatory passages; low center of sound; suavity of movement; arching melodic lines; careful approach and departure from the melodic apices of the piece; strong sense of tonal center; powerful cadences; relate these to the tragic sense of the text.

Chapter 5. Baroque Music

THE Baroque era extends from 1600 to 1750 in music. As with Renaissance music, the term is borrowed from art history, this time from architecture. In architecture it refers to certain distortions and transformations of Renaissance architecture and was originally a term of opprobrium. Unlike the Renaissance, the Baroque period in music does not show a uniformity and refinement of practice throughout its one hundred and fifty years. Rather, the music falls into three fairly well-defined phases, designated simply as *early, middle,* and *late baroque.* We shall proceed in this order.

EARLY BAROQUE

Striking, unexpected changes in musical style took place around the year 1600. If you listen to such compositions as Giovanni Gabrieli's motet for two choirs with organ and instruments, *In ecclesiis,* or Giulio Caccini's madrigal for solo voice and lute, *Dovrò dunque morire,* or Claudio Monteverdi's madrigal for five voices, *Ohimè, se tanto amate,* you will find that they project an entirely different quality of sound and movement than do pieces which are typical of the late Renaissance. In Gabrieli's music we hear: (1) short phases of movement; (2) sudden changes in pace and quality of movement; (3) brilliant contrasts in qualities of sound; (4) striking dissonances and frequent cadences.

In the Caccini piece we hear: (1) a declamatory manner, intensely personal in feeling; (2) a solo voice separated from an instrumental accompaniment, instead of a number of equally important participants; (3) a stop-and-start quality of movement suggesting outbursts of feeling; (4) frequent cadences.

In the Monteverdi piece we hear: (1) contrasts in texture; (2) striking dissonances; (3) again a stop-and-start quality of movement; (4) abrupt changes of manner.

These pieces represent the drastic changes of style that seemed to overtake music about 1600, particularly in Italy. Striking, dramatic, intense, violent, and bizarre effects were sought, replacing the continuous flow and the carefully woven counterpoint of Roman sacred polyphony which, in each piece, embodied but a single, thoroughly controlled expressive idea. The conflict between the two styles was reflected in the writings of musicians at this time. Some, upholding the old style, or *prima prattica*, as it was called, spoke for the polish, skill, balance of the music itself. They believed music to be more important than the text. Others, championing the modern style, called the *seconda prattica*, felt that music should serve the words, that any device or effect that would intensify the dramatic value should be used, regardless of its consistency or lack of consistency with traditional usage. Music history shows no lack of such controversies between the old and the new. They have flared up as far back as the time of the Ars antiqua, and they rage today between the proponents of conservative and progressive music.

FIG. 5. *Music Party*. Seventeenth-century French engraving by Abraham Bosse. (Courtesy of the Metropolitan Museum of Art.)

In spite of the violent changes in musical style at the beginning of the Baroque period, signs of change were not lacking in later music of the Renaissance: (1) increasingly bold and sudden shifts of tonal center, particularly in the madrigal, coupled with poignant chromaticisms and dissonance that intensified special moments of feeling in the music and threatened the even, steady flow of vocal polyphony; (2) the growth of instrumental music led to the development of brilliant techniques of performance, as well as to the exploitation of the contrasting sonorities of instruments playing together in a group, particularly in the case of Venetian music, indeed, Venice being one of the centers of early baroque music; (3) when instruments were added to voices, the possibilities of contrast multiplied.

Indeed, the watchword of early baroque music is *contrast*. We have heard contrasts of sonority, contrasts of mood, contrasts of movement, frequently projected within very short phases of movement, as in the Gabrieli and Monteverdi pieces. The effect of such contrasts was, at first, to explode the musical structure, breaking the long line into many little pieces. We hear these following each other in short, distinctive episodes. This creates a sectionalized structure, but at the same time it enables the composer to highlight a single, striking musical idea. He can also work out repetitions throughout the piece, a process which acts to create unity. This is particularly apparent in the Gabrieli *In ecclesiis*. We hear many repetitions, some of which are immediate restatements of motives; others review entire sections heard previously.

Here is a diagram, sketching the plan of the work.

Ex. 5–1. Diagram of Gabrieli: *In ecclesiis.*

A. *In ecclesiis,* solo; declamatory style	10	measures
B. Alleluia, chorus; antiphonal (give-and-take)	9	measures
C. *In omni loci,* solo; declamatory	23	measures
B. Alleluia, chorus	8	measures
D. Sinfonia; instruments in canzona style	16	measures
E. *In Deo,* chorus; motet style (imitative)	45	measures
B. Alleluia, chorus	9	measures
F. *Deus meus,* chorus; motet style	43	measures
B. Alleluia, chorus	10	measures
G. *Deus adjuta,* chorus; chromatic, chordal	25	measures
B. Alleluia, chorus; broadened cadence	17	measures

Note the inner symmetry and the use of the Alleluia as a refrain which binds the structure tightly together.

One of the chief appeals of *In ecclesiis* is its range and variety of sonorities. Such contrasts of sonority, created by dividing the total ensemble into smaller groups or single parts and then setting them against each other boldly, represent the practice called *concertato*. This means "striving together." The concertato technique is the forerunner of the *concerto* procedure of later baroque music. From this time on, its influence pervades virtually all types of music even to the present day. When a modern symphony sets full orchestra against a few instruments in alternation or makes use of contrasts in color, it is employing a procedure descended from early seventeenth-century concertato style.

The play of sonorities in this piece is embodied in a texture which gives maximum brilliance and power to individual chord sounds. There is relatively little counterpoint, and imitation is reduced to a mere give-and-take. Solid, full *chords* are frequently used for the impact of their particular quality of sound. These chords are the familiar chord types of Renaissance music, but they do not take shape simply as the result of evenly flowing melodic lines accommodating to each other harmonically by combinations of consonant intervals. Rather Gabrieli seems to have used them for their special distinctive sounds; he has considered them as entities, important and valuable in their own right. Example 5–2 illustrates the difference between a chordal section from the Gabrieli piece and the typical Renaissance method of obtaining chords by contrapuntal action.

Ex. 5–2.

a. Gabrieli. Solid, separate chords; strong, immediate impact.

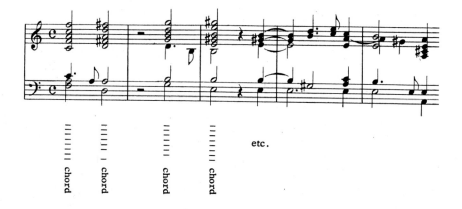

b. Renaissance. Combination of melodic lines to obtain chords.

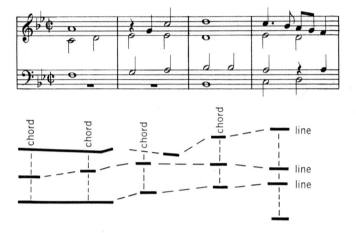

In this new style, then, each chord has considerable harmonic weight. Against such a center of harmonic gravity, it is possible to introduce melodic dissonances effectively for the sake of expressive accents and nuances. For example, at the very beginning of the recitative from Monteverdi's *Orfeo* (*Masterpieces,* no. 31) the voice sings *Tu se' morta, mia vita* (You Are Dead, My Life). The feeling of anguish is expressed by sharp dissonances in the voice against the sustained chord of the instruments.

Now you hear the solo voice separated from its harmonic support; it creates a contrast instead of a blend in the texture. In this opposition appears one of the principal harmonic aspects of baroque music, i.e., the *polarity* of the *chordal element,* represented principally by the bass voice, against the uppermost or melodic voice. In the music to Monteverdi's recitative, only the solo voice and the bass were actually composed. It was the responsibility of the keyboard performer to supply the inner notes, to fill out the chord; in this he was generally guided by numbers which indicated what intervals should be played above the bass tone as in Example 5–3.

This system of harmonizing was called *figured bass,* and, as we can easily hear, the principal musical interest lies in the outer parts. We have a reduction of essential parts from four or five to only two; whatever other tones appear do so in order to make the harmony clear and to give a fuller sound.

The result of pitting treble voices against the bass is a type of texture characteristic of a great deal of baroque music. It is generally designated as *trio-sonata texture,* since it is most clearly embodied in a form of composition

Ex. 5–3. Figured bass. Bach: *Sleepers, Awake,* cantata.

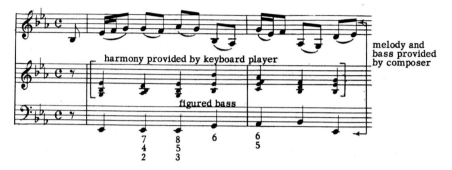

called the *trio sonata.* In this texture, two competing solo instruments are heard in the treble range; these are supported by a continuous bass part, played by the left hand of a keyboard instrument and a bass instrument. The right hand of the keyboard instrument fills in the harmonies. Occasionally we hear a lute assuming the role of the keyboard *continuo.*

In the trio-sonata layout, some of the most typical aspects of baroque texture appear in concentrated form. These are: (1) polarity between the treble and bass; (2) concertato action in the solo instruments; (3) chordal texture growing from the figured bass. Example 5–3A, taken from a late baroque piece, illustrates trio-sonata layout.

Ex. 5–3A. Handel: Trio sonata in G minor, first movement.

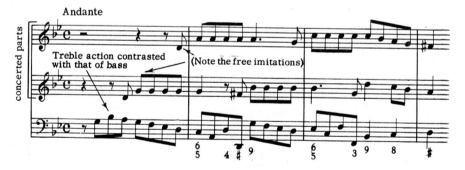

The separation of the melody from its harmonic web is most strikingly exemplified in the entirely new technique of composition which was described variously as *monody, recitative,* or *stile rappresentativo.* This manner, which we heard in the Caccini piece and the Monteverdi recitative, sets the voice free from the remainder of the texture, and assigns to it a declamatory melodic line which reflects faithfully the flow of the poetry and its expressive nuances. In the pure recitative, there is no steady, well-defined beat or pulse nor any organization of the melodic line by salient motives. The expressive aim of monody, when it was created by a group of Florentines at the very end of the sixteenth century, was, as Caccini himself put it, "to imitate the conceit of the words." Music was the servant and not the master of the poetry. These Florentine musicians and noblemen, designating themselves the *Camerata,* claimed to rescue music from the artifices of the contrapuntalists and turn it once again to the service of Platonic ideals, to revive the ancient Greek drama in which music was supposed to have played an important yet subsidiary role.

The poets of the Camerata took old Greek tales, such as that of Orpheus who lost his Eurydice, and gave them new dramatic form. These plays were then recited to music in the stile rappresentativo, the voice being accompanied by one or more instruments which furnished the harmony. This was the beginning of *opera.* Jacopo Peri's *Euridice,* composed in 1600, exemplifies this new idea of the relationship of music and language. It was composed almost entirely in recitative. Although certain moments in this work are projected with dramatic force and intensity, the unrelieved declamation does not create and hold interest throughout the entire composition. Opera, as a purely declaimed revival of Greek drama, lasted but a few years. Musical impulses began very soon to assert themselves. Older procedures from polyphonic music were taken up again and new techniques of composition were evolved, so that opera quickly acquired an independent inner strength based on the interplay of musical and dramatic values.

Claudio Monteverdi's *Orfeo,* composed in 1607, represents this new concept of operatic composition. It tells the same story as Peri's *Euridice,* but its internal structure is quite different. Instrumental sections, recitatives, and choruses, representing many different styles of composition, alternate in a lively and always interesting manner. The difference between Peri's and Monteverdi's works shows how opera grew quickly from a narrow, arbitrarily conceived process to one in which many different values and effects were gathered together into a unified yet diverse work. Peri's *Euridice* was conceived in the spirit of the Camerata; *Orfeo* already embodied those elements of dramatic contrast, of spectacle, of brilliant effect, that constitute, to this day, the principal appeal of opera.

Summarizing briefly the principal developments of the early seventeenth century in music, we have:

1. Sectionalism in structure, exemplified in the concertato style
2. Development of harmonic procedure, realized in the figured bass
3. The invention of recitative, with its most significant embodiment in opera
4. Expressively, a style based on bold contrasts, intense outbursts of feeling, striking impacts

The immediate appeal of this music must have been strong and compelling; much of it still is for today's listener. The first effects of these new processes were to destroy the continuity that characterized Renaissance music. But special qualities of sound, bold contrasts, and intense emotional outbursts were not enough to build musical movement and sustain it over any considerable period of time. Very soon after the turn of the century, as we have seen in *Orfeo,* composers began to strengthen the inner lines of their music. This period of strengthening and codification is the second stage in baroque music, the middle baroque.

MIDDLE BAROQUE

In order to see what direction the synthesis and codification of technique, form, and expression took during the middle Baroque period, we shall examine three works from the *Masterpieces* collection. These are:

No. 32 Giacomo Carissimi, Scene from *Judicium Salomonis*
No. 33 Heinrich Schütz, Sacred Cantata, *O Herr, hilf*
No. 36 Jean Baptiste Lully, Overture to *Armide*

Although the Carissimi piece is written entirely in the recitative style, it does not speak to us in the strongly felt, intensely affective accents of Caccini and Monteverdi. It is quite straightforward, indeed, matter of fact, with the exception of the music of the First Mother, whose poignant distress calls for dissonances, chromaticism, and a halting manner of movement. Generally, the accompaniment is extremely simple; many of the chords are sustained for a measure and one-half or two. The harmony is not venturesome; rather, it seems to be concerned with making cadences quite frequently. Structurally, we make out seven short but relatively self-contained sections; the last of these, being a resolution of the problem, and embodying Solomon's judgment in the case of the disputed infant, is somewhat longer than the preceding sections.

The principal distinctions between this music and its early baroque counterparts lie in (1) the simplification of the recitative technique, both in voice and accompaniment; (2) the clearer feeling for cadence; and (3) the reduction in the amount of striking dissonances previously used for affective purposes. The multisectional structure, on the other hand, suggests a retention of an early baroque formal layout.

The excerpt shows what happened to the recitative in the mid-seventeenth century. It no longer assumes the burden of intense musical expression; it moves on a level, at a rather even pace; it is proselike, declarative. As a type, this treatment of recitative turned out to be very useful for more than two centuries. In opera of the seventeenth, eighteenth, and nineteenth centuries, it served to compress a great deal of narrative or expository material into a relatively short period of time. In this kind of recitative, one does not linger; one hurries ahead. Only the few moments of the First Mother's music were more strongly evocative. In contrast to the prosy style, this kind of recitative represents a more songlike manner, also encountered in later dramatic music.

Like the recitative, the concertato style underwent changes during the middle of the seventeenth century. Schütz's Sacred Cantata illustrates what happened. This is a particularly apt example since Schütz was the pupil of Giovanni Gabrieli, the early Venetian master of the concertato technique of composition. First, we can see that striking contrasts of sonority no longer occupy the composer's attention. In line with this, each section carries out one idea for a considerable length of time. The quality of movement is purposeful and vigorous; momentum is maintained by the interplay of motives being worked over very thoroughly. The concertato procedure is embodied in this motivic interplay; actually, the give-and-take between voices and instruments is quite complex and close-grained. Gabrieli's stop-and-start effects are no longer present.

In this music long-range contrasts help to shape the form. There are three sections, varying in their qualities of movement. The first has a driving quality, in quick, energetic duple meter; the second section is smoother in movement, because of its triple meter; the third section picks up once more the driving quality of the first, but intensifies this vigorous manner by piling up closely spaced imitations and colliding dissonances within each phrase. In this third section, we feel a strong sense of cadential drive augmented by the accumulating dissonances. Thus the final part of this piece serves to round it off by aiming at emphatic points of arrival. Although the concertato procedure dominates this composition, the long-range harmonic drives, the steady vigorous pace, the systematic working over of motives, the elimination of striking contrast—all represent a drastic change from the early concertato manner of Gabrieli. With such compact and unified treatment, a strong sense of accumulation develops. Schütz's music foreshadows Bach's in this respect.

Lully's overture exploits the brilliance of instruments. The three sections of the piece carry out, at considerable length, (1) the movement of a stately ceremonial march, (2) a buoyant, swinging dance, and (3) return to the broad manner of the opening march. Within each section, movement continues, well-marked and vigorous. Again we feel that a drive toward a cadential point of arrival focuses the harmonic movement in each section or phrase. Within each section we hear little contrast; on the other hand, the contrast between sections is marked.

Although these three compositions differ from each other in manner and purpose, they do illustrate some of the underlying processes in the development of musical structure during the middle Baroque period.

1. In comparison to the very short phases of movement typical of the concertato manner in early baroque music, we have longer sections and a sense of unity within these sections, particularly in the Schütz and Lully pieces. Contrast takes place *between* sections.

2. In all three works a much stronger feeling for cadence seems to pervade the music. The harmony is directed to strong points of arrival. Naturally, this is associated with a well-defined sectional structure. The sections are fairly long. Strong caesuras and cadential points of arrival become necessary when phrases and sections become well defined. The cadential relationships in harmony begin to *saturate* the music.

3. Unity of manner within fairly long sections is associated with a consistent and skillful treatment of the melodic material, the figurations, the ornamentation, and the texture. In a given section the composer took one idea and worked it over systematically and intensively, imitating it, spinning it out, repeating it in many ways.

We might liken the structural tendencies of middle baroque music to a process of crystallization, in which small crystals are gathered slowly into larger and larger clusters. The diffusion, the centrifugal tendencies of the early seventeenth century are turned inward. Controls and codification occupy the composer's attention. This attitude is demonstrated by the fact that one idea, one quality of expression is carried out over a rather long phase of movement; the momentary nuances, the sudden contrasts of early baroque music have disappeared.

Before we proceed to the final stage of baroque music, one point must be made in order to set the record clear. Not all seventeenth-century music participated in this cycle of breakup and re-formation. You will recall that musical tastes at the beginning of the seventeenth century were divided between the new manner and the old, that is, the polyphonic style. Many pieces for sacred performance were written in the manner of Palestrina and the Roman school during the seventeenth century. Indeed, this style has survived, mostly in counterpoint classes, down to this very day. Therefore we cannot look for evidence in *all* baroque music of the developments we have described. Still, a close observer might discover that even the most conservative choral music of the seventeenth century had absorbed some of the modern ways, and that dance music began to employ the stronger harmonic language developed in early and middle baroque music.

LATE BAROQUE

If we listen to any music by one of the late baroque masters, a chorus by Johann Sebastian Bach, an aria by Georg Friedrich Handel, or a concerto movement by Antonio Vivaldi, we are struck by the greater sense of breadth and purpose which this music has over comparable works by earlier composers. This music seems to reach farther and to achieve its goals with more telling force than any music heretofore composed. We cannot help being impressed by the structural grandeur of late baroque music, fully realized in works of broad scope, but also reflected in the smaller compositions of this era.

It was no accident that musical forms developed coherence, breadth, and balance during the mid-seventeenth and early eighteenth centuries. The very techniques of musical composition changed so that inner strength and outer clarity were increasingly more apparent. Among these techniques, none was more important than the strengthening of the *key* sense in late seventeenth-century harmony.

We have already seen, in Chapter 2, how a cadence gives us a sense of key, or harmonic *position*. If we continue to use cadences systematically, we will have created a phrase or period which gives a clear and strong impression of a key. Moreover, by putting a heavier cadence at the end of such a phrase, the impression of the key is immeasurably strengthened. During the seventeenth century composers were developing ways in which such impressions of key could be projected in their music. At the same time they found that a *clear harmonic orientation* went hand in hand with *intensive motivic play and development.* Each cadential formula served to hold the music together, while at the same time the melodic and rhythmic energy of the motive propelled the music forward. It was a controlled and balanced flight, an interpenetration of harmonic, rhythmic, and melodic forces that enabled music to expand its phrases and periods to great lengths. In this plan, contrast was sacrificed, but later in the eighteenth century, as we shall see, contrast took its place in this structural scheme. An excellent example of a broadly scaled period which develops motives intensively and drives with tremendous force to its cadence is the very beginning of Bach's *Brandenburg* Concerto No. 3, in G major. The following example illustrates this kind of period, which is a basic structural plan for most baroque music:

Ex. 5–4. Bach: *Brandenburg* Concerto No. 3, first movement.

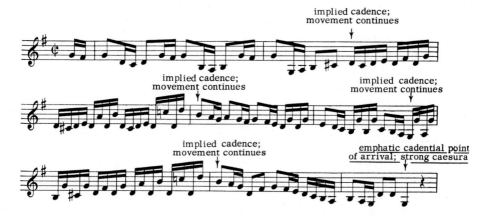

Such a period might be compared to the span of a bridge, anchored firmly by its cadential piers and possessed of great internal strength by virtue of its tightly knit construction and its solid materials. The clearness and the emphasis with which the impression of key is given in late baroque music enabled the baroque composer to build a movement in blocks of key *areas*. Each area represented a sharply defined harmonic *position*, established at a specific distance and direction away from the home key. In some cases the music would pause momentarily at a given position or area; at other times it would settle for a while in a new position. Here is the plan for the harmonic areas of the first movement of Handel's Concerto in C major, *Masterpieces,* no. 43.

Ex. 5–5. Handel: Concerto in C major.

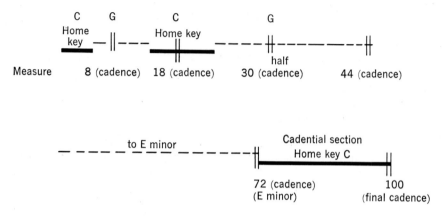

Briefly, then, the late baroque formula for structural units involves: (1) active, cadentially oriented harmony; (2) intensive play of motives, generally based upon one distinctive figure or style; (3) great rhythmic energy, manifested in a steady vigorous beat.

Proceeding from this technique of structure, late baroque music tends to carry out one basic idea or expressive value within a given composition or over an extended section within a composition. This reflects the general aesthetic attitude of composers and musical theorists during the Baroque era, an attitude which was codified in the theory called the *doctrine of the affections.* According to this theory of expression, certain types of musical figure were considered proper for the delineation of specific expressive values, especially when a text was involved. Rising figures suggested elation; falling figures suggested sorrow; chromaticism was proper for grief or other poignant, touching feelings. Both in vocal and instrumental music, the composer settled upon a suitable figure and then proceeded to write an entire piece based upon the rhythm, the style, and the *affective* quality of that figure. After he had established his initial expressive premises, after he had indicated the musical subject of his piece, the composer's main concern was to write as excellent a piece of music as he was able to do. The doctrine of the affections involved a formal symbolism; it belonged to an art in the grand manner, an art with more than a touch of absolutism about it.

In the foregoing pages we have sketched briefly some of the more important developments in music from 1600 to 1750. We have seen dis-

continuity give way to continuity, contrast yield to unity, experiment replaced by codification. Now for more intensive listening, we shall turn
our attention to some examples of late baroque music, works which represent the full fruition of more than a century of musical evolution.

The carrying power of late baroque music supported and intensified
expressive values, the affective qualities which were directed to the
listener's feelings and emotions, and which were so important in baroque
aesthetics. Nowhere is this relationship between technique, style, and
expression more vivid or dramatic than in the *Crucifixus* of Bach's B-minor
Mass and the *Et Resurrexit* which follows. The contrast between these two
numbers represents deepest sorrow followed by greatest joy. The sound of
the *Crucifixus* is dark; everything seems to gravitate downward to the
lowest notes of the bass. The bass line itself descends, as do the melodic
figures of the choral parts. Two aspects are especially to be noticed:

1. At no time does the pace lose its slow, triple beat, nor its grouping into
four-measure phrases. The descending bass figure is a *chaconne* pattern, taken
from a dance of slow and stately manner. Here the steadiness and clearness of a
dance rhythm supports, controls, and directs the tragic expressive flow of the
music. Fresh momentum develops each time the bass drops to its cadence note
and rises again to begin anew the downward path. Against the bass cadence, the
voices and the supporting harmonies create an overlap of harmonic and melodic
movement; thus the four-measure articulations are hidden though present, and
the renewal and intensification of the tragic affection by fresh entries takes place
in a free rhythmic scheme at variance with the basic chaconne pattern.

Ex. 5–6. Bach: B-minor Mass, *Crucifixus.*

2. The shifting, chromatic harmonies, saturated with many poignant dissonances, have set up a sense of harmonic instability throughout the piece. The general harmonic quality of the piece is *minor*; all the progressions work in the area of minor keys. At the very end of the *Crucifixus* the chromaticism reaches a point of greatest intensity; each chord brings a new harmonic inflection; the cup of sorrow is full to the brim. Then, the resolution of all of this is not to the minor, but to a sublime, transfigured *major* chord; the sorrow is completed by a touch of lyric softness. Surprising and unexpected as this ending may seem, it carries out the surprising and unexpected harmonic procedure of the entire piece. We cannot help being moved by the wonderfully affective contrast of minor and major at this point.

In utmost contrast to the darkness of the *Crucifixus* is the jubilation of the *Et Resurrexit*. The brilliant sound of trumpets, fanfare figures directed upward, long exultant melismas, a vigorous, quick, light quality of movement, the entirely fresh effect of a new and major key—all these combine to describe the most joyous moment in Christendom, the Resurrection of Jesus Christ. Just as the dissonances pushed downward, and the melodic lines sank in the *Crucifixus,* so does everything rise in the *Et Resurrexit.* The piece is treated in concertato style for chorus and orchestra; the exuberant give-and-take between elements of various types is proper to the feeling of renewed hope, energy, and joy that is given in the text. Only at the most important structural cadences does the steady driving movement come to a full point of arrival. Otherwise, throughout the *Et Resurrexit,* the driving pulse and the intensive development of two or three characteristic motives create an unbroken, continually growing sense of movement.

You may have noticed that Bach did not make any concession to the voices as far as brilliance or difficulty of material was concerned. The chorus is expected to handle the rapid virtuoso passages that interlace the entire fabric of the work. The broad and intensively searching techniques of composition are thus matched by the demands made upon the performers.

In the *Resurrexit* and *Crucifixus,* Bach used two very important procedures of composition, procedures that virtually dominate baroque music. These are: (1) *imitation,* as in the *Resurrexit,* and (2) *variation,* as in the *Crucifixus.* We have already discussed imitation and variation in Chapters 2 and 4. In baroque music, techniques of imitation were most intensively explored in the type of composition called *fugue.*

Fugue, strictly speaking, is a process in which a given theme or subject is presented and worked over in contrapuntal imitation by two or more voices or parts. In baroque music this process lent its name to compositions so worked out; therefore, we have a great number of pieces called *fugues*. Fugues in late baroque music shared in the general stylistic evolution we have described above; thus they are different in layout and procedure from imitative pieces of the Renaissance period. Briefly, the evolution took place as follows:

1. Points of imitation, of which there were many in chansons and motets, were reduced in number and their length increased.

2. Many canzonas and ricercare, after the beginning of the seventeenth century, dealt with one subject, instead of using a new subject for each point of imitation. The style of the subject was varied in each section, or a new contrapuntal setting was given to the subject in each section.

3. An increasingly stronger sense of harmonic drive within each section and the development of intensive techniques for working over short motives enabled composers further to increase the length of sections and at the same time to maintain and augment the sense of movement which gave unity and coherence to the structure.

4. Eventually, sectionalism virtually disappeared and the contour of the fugue structure was created largely by harmonic relationships and emphatic cadences.

Although their evolution was worked out along similar lines, the canzona and ricercar managed to retain their separate identities as far as style was concerned. The canzona became a quick fugue and very often used dance patterns in its subjects. The ricercar became a slow, serious fugue, retaining the even pace and something of the vocal style of the motet. The first two fugues in Johann Sebastian Bach's *Well-Tempered Clavier* illustrate the two different types. The first fugue is beholden to the ricercar, not only in style, but also in the very thorough way in which it searches through its subject, working it over in many ways, particularly in stretto, where new voices enter before preceding voices have completed the subject, as in Example 5–7.

Ex. 5–7. Stretto from Bach: *Well-Tempered Clavier, Book I,* Fugue in C major.

The effect of stretto is cumulative, intensifying. As a result of the stretto procedure, the subject is impressed much more upon our minds, and the whole piece seems very important. The second fugue, which gives us the subject nine times, as against more than twenty in the first fugue, uses the rhythmic style of the *bourrée,* an eighteenth-century dance. Its texture is thinner, its quality of movement lighter and more buoyant, its concern with the subject far less searching and serious than is the case with the first fugue. In spite of its skillfully worked-out counterpoint, this piece retains the spirit of the dance which was its source. We might reasonably expect, therefore, that it be performed in a rather dancelike manner.

Contrapuntal, imitative composition has always presented a challenge to the composer in so far as the treatment of subjects and themes is concerned. As far back as the fourteenth century, composers have displayed their ingenuity in setting a subject against itself in various ways. This procedure is called *canon,* meaning "law, rule." It signifies a relationship between two or more voices that remains constant throughout a piece or a section of considerable length. The simplest form of canon is to have the second voice follow the first exactly with respect to the intervals of the melody and the rhythmic values. Canon is opposed to *free* imitation. (See Chapter 4, p. 108.) The following diagram illustrates the pattern of canon.

Ex. 5–8. Pattern of canon.

As a rule, fugal composition has relatively little to do with canon. Bach has designated sections of larger works as being canonic in nature. Canons are found in his *Goldberg* Variations, *The Art of the Fugue,* and the *Musical Offering.*

A musical theme or subject can retain its identity for the hearer, even though it may be altered in some ways. This frequently happens in fugue composition. The theme may be turned upside down, *inverted*; it may be played backward, *retrograde*; it may be compressed in time value, *diminution*; and its time values may be stretched out, *augmentation.* These permutations often represent ingenuity. We are intrigued to hear the subject of the G-major Fugue in Bach's *Well-Tempered Clavier, Book I,* turned upside down. Bach achieves an effect of climax in the final section of the great organ fugue in E♭ major, the *St. Anne's* fugue, when he brings back the opening subject, the chorale melody, in long notes, in the bass. Example 5–9 illustrates graphically ways in which a subject can be altered.

Ex. 5–9. Alteration of a subject.

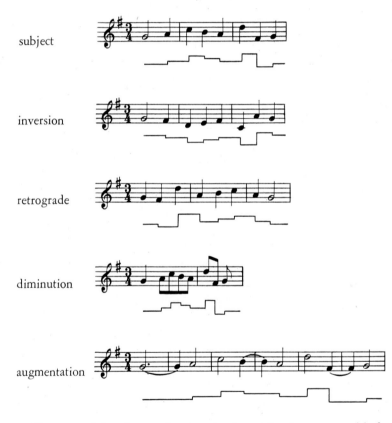

Elements of fugal procedure can be found in almost every kind of music during the Baroque era, although frequently an entire piece will not be handled fugally; rather, some sections may begin with fugal expositions. This you can hear in some sections of the *Et Resurrexit* from the B-minor Mass.

Ex. 5–10. Bach: *Et Resurrexit* from the B-minor Mass.

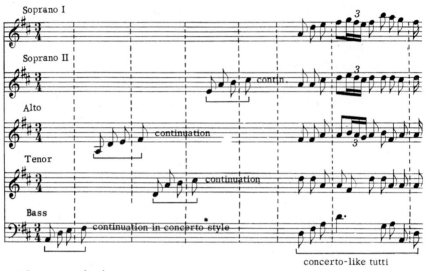

* See concerto in glossary

Another very important type of musical procedure in baroque music was the *variation*. This was an extension of the process of addition and elaboration which was so widespread in Renaissance music. Many variations were written for keyboard performers. This was to be expected, since only the keyboard performer had both the freedom of action and the command of the full range of sound which were desirable in the various settings of the model and its ornamentations. String instruments also partook in performances of variations because of their natural agility. Models for variations were taken from plain-chant melodies, chorale tunes, popular songs and dances, or from simple melodic patterns given to the bass voice.

Bach turned again and again to the variation procedure as a means of building a large-scale composition. His *Crucifixus* from the B-minor Mass, which we have already discussed, illustrates variation upon a bass theme. This composition, a continuously moving, searching, tightly woven work, exemplifies Bach's attitude toward variation procedure. He seeks out the possibilities of the subject and composes an entirely new work, using the theme as a scaffolding. We are not dealing here with decorative ornamentation. Several other examples will show further how Bach made use of the variation idea. In the Passacaglia and Fugue in C minor, the subject is a genuine tune:

Ex. 5–11. Bach: Passacaglia and Fugue in C minor.

The procedure in this piece consists of ornamentation surrounding the tune. The principal distinctions of the variation procedure in this piece are: (1) the striking rhythmic and melodic qualities of the added parts; (2) the sense of well-developed counterpoint in each variation as opposed to a rather decorative manner which was standard for pieces of this kind; (3) the bold and dramatic contrasts that are introduced strategically at certain connecting points between variations; and (4) the culmination of the variation concept in a broad fugue which employs a version of the tune as a subject.

In his Canonic Variations on *Vom Himmel hoch,* Bach used a familiar chorale tune, the first line of which is quoted below:

Ex. 5–12. Bach: Canonic Variations on *Vom Himmel hoch.*

The various phrases of this tune are treated as subjects for canonic imitation. Here the principal distinction is the superlative control of contrapuntal technique which gives evidence of Bach's unparalleled insight into the nature of musical relationships.

Another famous set of variations by Bach is the *Goldberg* Variations. Here the subject is the harmonic progression which supports a rather florid melodic voice. In the thirty variations which comprise this set, Bach has explored many types of musical composition and style characteristic of baroque music. We find dances such as gigues and courantes; we find one variation cast as a French overture (see p. 146); there are nine canons, each set according to its own plan. Each variation, moreover, has its own thematic material; only the rhythmic and harmonic skeleton provides the link between these pieces.

The ornamental type of variation which was a favorite vehicle for keyboard performance since the days of the Renaissance is represented by Handel's tuneful and sonorous piece, the so-called *The Harmonious Blacksmith.* In this piece it is not difficult to hear the tune, or, at least, to project it amid the figurations of each variation. The sonority effects created in this piece, ringing and vibrant as they emerge from the harpsichord, are perhaps the principal appeal of the work.

The Baroque period has been sometimes called the *age of variation,* since, in addition to the many compositions which systematically worked over a theme, numerous works used variation procedure in order to maintain interest and build up broader continuity. Variation as a means of composition has perhaps a longer history than any other. Indeed, there is one close resemblance between a Renaissance-baroque bass pattern that was very popular as a basis for variations, the *passamezzo moderno,* and the fast blues of today's jazz, the boogie-woogie. Both of these patterns move through the following degrees of the major key: I–IV–I–V–I. In all fairness, it must be said that the passamezzo does not dally with blue notes.

Both fugue and variation procedure represent a fundamental baroque attitude toward musical material, namely, the intensive treatment of one subject or theme. Countless compositions in baroque music involve some element of imitation, even though the imitation may not be as systematic nor as thoroughly developed as in works entitled Fugue. Variation, both the systematic sort, wherein a theme is taken through a series of permutations, and the ornamental treatment of a melody, were constantly in the forefront of baroque style. Indeed, ornamentation, representing one kind of variation, was part of the very lifeblood of baroque musical performance practice. It was not only permissible, it was virtually mandatory that performers be able to create ornamental elaborations upon the written melodic line.

PERFORMANCE OF BAROQUE MUSIC

One of the most important tasks of musical historians recently has been to ascertain how early music was actually performed. This has been most illuminating. In establishing valid methods of re-creating this older music in sound, these scholars have shown us the beauties and the charm, the freshness of sound, the buoyancy of movement, the piquancy of arabesque that emerges from Renaissance and baroque music. One result has been the recorded *Masterpieces* set which has been used as a reference here. The delight which this music can give would be lost to us if it were performed with the heavier, broader tones of today's instruments or in a manner of playing based on Tchaikovsky and Wagner.

The sound of baroque music, particularly music for groups of instruments, therefore, is quite different from the sound of chamber or orchestral music of the late eighteenth and nineteenth centuries. This is partly due to the different qualities of instrumental tone, and partly due to a different disposition of the instruments themselves. As far as the constitution of an instrumental ensemble was concerned, there was no strict standardization. An orchestra might consist of ten, or it might consist of thirty, forty, or even more performers. Whatever instrumentation was used in any particular piece, however, the instrumental layout exemplified the three character- istics described above on page 125. When a number of concertato instru- ments were employed, they would share the responsibilities of the upper parts. Without exception, a keyboard instrument would be on hand to fill in the harmonies from the written-out bass part. We thus have a kind of layered texture, which preserved its essential uniformity of manner, regard- less of how many or how few instruments were playing at any time.

With respect to the amount and strength of sound, the dynamic levels, increase and decrease, we have not, as a rule, heard either very loud or very soft passages. Still, in the concerto, for example, the contrast between solo and tutti inevitably creates a contrast in dynamics, a sharp rise or fall between relatively loud and relatively soft. This sudden change is typical of much baroque music, particularly that laid out along the lines of the concerto. This type of dynamic style is called *terrace dynamics*. As far as crescendo and decrescendo are concerned, while they probably occurred in performance, they were not a primary resource of expression, as, for example, in Wagner's or Tchaikovsky's music.

Historians are still seeking answers to the question, "How was baroque music performed?" We may never reach a complete solution to this problem because we cannot turn time back and duplicate the conditions of per- formance. Yet even the approximate solutions have opened a new world of sound and expression to the listener of today.

We have a good deal of information as to *where* and *when* music of the seventeenth and early eighteenth centuries was used. Generally speaking, there were three kinds of occasions that called for music. Representing the oldest tradition, was *worship music* and its concomitant, solemn public ceremony. *Domestic music* was performed for the entertainment of a court or household. It also included pieces used for teaching purposes. *Theater music* was embodied, of course, in opera and ballet. These were classified by baroque theorists as *church, chamber,* and *theater styles.* Ordinarily, the church style leaned toward a contrapuntal exposition of musical materials; the chamber style employed dance idioms or dealt with brilliant studies for solo performers; the purest embodiment of theater style was recitative. Church, chamber, and theater music intermingled, however, as far as style was concerned; they traded and borrowed from each other to such an extent that by the beginning of the eighteenth century, these classifications referred to occasions, but not necessarily to techniques or styles of composition.

Church, chamber, and theater music were performed all over Europe during the seventeenth and eighteenth centuries. Still, due to political and economic conditions, the leading musical countries of Europe, Italy, France, Germany, and England, took different directions in the cultivation of various media and idioms of performance. The particular forms in which late baroque music was written developed and flourished according to the environments and to performance conditions. We shall look at these forms now, taking into account the type of occasion and where pertinent, the type of environment.

Theater Music

Italian opera. The intense activity in all the arts that characterized Italy during Renaissance times continued with the fullest vigor into the seventeenth century. Italy remained a wellspring of culture, musical and otherwise, during the Baroque period. The magnificent establishments of court and church in Rome, Florence, Venice, and elsewhere were maintained by aesthetic-minded princes and popes, who stopped at no point in their support of the arts. Italy was still a battlefield in the seventeenth century, contested for by the great Continental powers, and divided internally; nevertheless, the protection given artists and thinkers enabled Italy to maintain a level of high achievement, culturally speaking. This was particularly true of music.

The most important single development in Italian music was, of course, opera. Both church and court gave encouragement to this new and exciting vehicle of expression. For the court it was the summit of lavish, grandiose entertainment, because, in addition to the dramatic representation, it gave full scope to ballet, massed ensembles, scenery, and novel stage effects. The Roman opera of the early seventeenth century was among the most lavish that has ever been staged. The Church, striking back during the Counter Reformation, used every means at its disposal to bring the people once more into its orbit. Thus it used the techniques of opera in the oratorio, and staged operas on sacred subjects as well. This double blessing, from temporal and spiritual authorities, gave tremendous momentum to opera composition so that, quite early in the century, thousands of operas had already been written and many opera houses sprang up in Italy. Indeed, the first *public* opera house opened in Venice in 1637, although the patrons and subscribers were still members of the aristocracy.

Venice, a republic, was certainly the most appropriate locale for the initiation of public musical performances. At first public opera imitated court opera, staging elaborate spectacles, but soon it was found that costs were outrunning income. The result, a profoundly significant one for the history of music, was the establishment of operas that featured brilliant soloists, spectacular virtuosi who became the idols of the Italian public. Thus, Italian opera was standardized for a century to come. One might expect the rather colorless recitative to recede in favor of an acrobatic, coruscating style formed into arias that would give the singer frequent and extended opportunities to display his power and agility. Italian musicians, performers, and composers traveled all over Europe in the seventeenth and eighteenth centuries, and wherever they went, they conquered. Italian opera, with one exception, became European opera. The one exception was French opera, and even so, in its early stages French opera was stimulated by Italian importations.

When musical values began to reassert themselves in the early opera, one of the most important forms of vocal music started to take shape. This was the *aria*. In contrast to the amorphous, wandering recitative, the aria had some consistent, regular, and fairly extended plan. It leaned toward song or dance rhythms; its melodic material was more continuous and rounded in quality; it made use of repetitions and neatly balanced contrasts. Its quality of movement was more flowing than that of the recitative, and its points of arrival clearly indicated the ends of long phrases or periods. It worked over one idea at considerable length, thus paralleling the structural evolution we have described in instrumental music.

The specific forms in which arias were cast were quite varied, but toward the middle of the seventeenth century one type began to dominate. This was the *da capo aria. Da capo* means "return to the head, or beginning." It comprised (1) a first section, in rather brilliant style, followed by (2) a contrasting middle section, perhaps slower (the reverse order of manner was also possible), and (3) a return to the first section. The da capo form was especially suited to the musical styles of the later seventeenth and the eighteenth centuries in which consistent and thorough exploration of a single musical value or effect had become the principal procedure, and contrast occurred between movements or extended sections.

The excerpt from Handel's *Rinaldo* (*Masterpieces,* no. 44) shows a number of different musical procedures associated with opera. We first have a recitative similar to that which we heard in the Carissimi piece; next a canzonalike instrumental interlude, indicating furious action on the stage. The da capo aria which follows is a slow, tragic piece; it takes advantage of the halting, somewhat imbalanced rhythm of the sarabande; and a hint of fugal exposition is heard at the beginning to suggest a serious, even grave expressive quality. The middle section, changing to a mood of defiance, takes up again the brisk canzona style. The entire scene is rounded off by a return to the principal expressive value, the sense of tragic loss, as projected in the first section of the aria. This aria is based on a dance style.

In Italian opera of the late seventeenth and eighteenth centuries, some arias assumed the proportions and manner of a vocal concerto, with brilliant ornamental passages, difficult figures, and a generally flamboyant style. Indeed, dramatic values in Italian opera receded in favor of the brilliant, highly polished, and stereotyped music. Operas featured virtuosi; the elaborate arias were frequently extended by interposed passage-work of enormous difficulty, negotiable only by a very few singers. The composer had to write this music to order; he was not free to experiment with new musicodramatic ideas. In reaction to this rigid, highly popular commodity, some composers in the middle of the century, notably Christoph Willibald von Gluck, proposed and composed operas that achieved a fairer balance between musical and dramatic values. This was the famous opera reform of the eighteenth century, which reduced vocal display, strove for simplicity and truth of dramatic expression, and aimed for a more continuous flow of action than was possible with the vocal concertos of the Italian opera. Gluck's *Orfeo* and *Alceste* are the most noted representatives of this more direct kind of opera.

In early Italian operas, it was the custom to perform a canzona before the main presentation began. This canzona, called *sinfonia,* on such occasions was likely to show the sectional structure of most seventeenth-century instrumental music. The sections became standardized into a three-movement form. The first was a brilliant, quick piece, sometimes imitative, at other times a rousing fanfare; the second borrowed the style of the aria, in a rather slow tempo; the third, again quick, was dancelike, most often using gigue style. The Italian opera sinfonia is the ancestor of the great symphonies of the later eighteenth and the nineteenth centuries. The sinfonia was intended to collect the attention of the audience for the performance to follow. Thus it began in a rather noisy, brisk manner with fanfares, running figures, unisons for full orchestra designed for emphasis, and bold strokes that punctuated the movement frequently. It rarely lingered over any idea for long, nor did it develop a thread of meaning that carried out a single phase of movement broadly. It simply made more brilliant use of the sectional contrast effects of the early canzona. Indeed, many critics of the eighteenth century considered this genre to be a most superficial kind of piece. The sinfonia preceded an opera given as a public commercial venture for a rather mixed audience of nobility and wealthy middle-class merchants. The commercial aspect grew in importance when, in the middle of the eighteenth century, sinfonias were programmed independently on the first public orchestra concerts in the history of music. This was the decisive step that led eventually to the imposing symphonic masterpieces of a later age.

Unlike other kinds of baroque music, the Italian opera sinfonia did not survive to be performed by musicians of the twentieth century. Very few recordings are available and the operas themselves are not performed. A very good idea of the style of the sinfonia, however, can be obtained by listening to the earliest symphonies of Mozart.

French opera. In France political conditions led to a very different kind of musical situation from that found in Italy. Politically the Italian peninsula was broken up into many kingdoms, principalities, and minor states, most of which were under the control of some foreign power. There was great dispersal, no strong center. France, under Richelieu and later Louis XIV, became a highly centralized state, independent of the Papacy, the embodiment of monarchical absolutism, and the strongest kingdom of Europe. Controls were set upon many aspects of French life; order was established by court edict, and style was dictated. Supporting and glorifying this centralized absolutism, magnificent displays in all the arts were offered during court entertainments.

Mirroring the absolutism of the king, French music had its own dictator, its own absolute monarch during the late seventeenth century. This was Jean Baptiste Lully, who was granted supreme powers over French music by express order of the king. With power, funds, and resources at his command, Lully created the finest orchestra in Europe, the "twenty-four violins." Indeed, the formation of the modern orchestra is largely traceable to the great interest and activity in orchestral music, stimulated and directed at first by the example of Lully, and expanded during the first half of the eighteenth century.

French opera developed distinctive characteristics in response to the grandeur of Louis XIV's court. Instead of a series of brilliant solo numbers which gave musical heroes opportunities to show off, French opera was a spectacle affair. Ballet was of primary importance in the scheme; there was more instrumental music than in Italian opera, due to the superlative orchestral establishment; arias were shorter, often dancelike in style; the

Fig. 6. Patel: *View of the Chateau of Versailles taken from the avenue de Paris.* Note the spaciousness and the absolute classical symmetry of the entire plan. (Reproduced by permission of Caisse Nationale des Monuments Historiques.)

dramatic situation was given a greater place in the total scheme, and a special kind of recitative, declaimed in fluctuating time values and fitted to the peculiarities of the French language, was developed instead of the matter-of-fact recitative of Italian opera. One further distinction: Italian opera was performed all over Europe, and often had to pay its own way; French opera centered at the court of Louis XIV and was heavily subsidized.

Lully displayed his superlative orchestra at its greatest brilliance in the overtures which opened the festivities of a grand entertainment, accompanying the king as he was making his way into the theater. These pieces acquired the name *French overture.* They begin characteristically with a stately marchlike pace, and are distinguished by the snappy dotted rhythms which enabled the orchestra of Lully, with its matchless precision, to display its famed virtuosity. The slow ceremonial pace of the opening section of the French overture also gave the orchestra a chance to show off its richness and fullness of tone. Example 36, from *Masterpieces,* the Overture to Lully's opera *Armide et Renaud,* illustrates these qualities of the genre. Following the slow opening section, a quick canzonalike piece provides a contrast, with lively rhythms and imitative layout.

Throughout the eighteenth and nineteenth centuries, the pattern of a slow, solemn introduction followed by a quick, brilliant movement represents, in sonatas and symphonies, the heritage of the French overture. Mozart's *Prague* Symphony, Beethoven's Second Symphony, and Haydn's *London* Symphony, all begin with stately, serious introductions that recall the manner of the French overture.

English theater music. England's musical position during the Baroque period suffered through the years of the Commonwealth. A ban was placed on the English court entertainments, the masques which were produced on a remarkably lavish scale during Tudor and Stuart times. There was a considerable amount of domestic music performed throughout the century, but the luxuriance and vigor of musical activity needed to define a distinctive style were lacking in England. Upon the Restoration, French and Italian music were imported, intermingling with English dances and songs in the revived masques and in opera. English music of the late seventeenth century is party to a strange and curious paradox in the history of opera.

Despite the lack of a concentrated home-fed musical style, the one opera, Italian, French, or English, that appears in today's repertory, dating from the late 1600's, is an English work, Purcell's *Dido and Aeneas.* We rarely hear any French or Italian dramatic music from the middle or late Baroque period, although we would certainly be impressed by this music if it were available. But *Dido and Aeneas* has such a poignant and moving dramatic appeal, its music is so wonderfully fresh and colorful, it offers no sticky problems of staging, and it has such a wealth and variety of styles and attitudes that it has commended itself to modern concert or dramatic performance with equal ease. It has been staged effectively by both amateur and professional groups. Since it represents, structurally, the middle baroque style, its individual numbers are relatively short, make their dramatic point, and move on to the next without the intrusion of the personality or prowess of the singer. (The work was composed for a girls' school.) *Dido's Lament*, at the end of the opera, is one of the most touchingly sorrowful expressions in the entire history of opera. Like the *Crucifixus* of Bach's B-minor Mass, it discovers its basic affective quality in the descending chromatic line of an ostinato bass, above which the perishing Dido sings a melodic line burdened by dissonances and particularly expressive intervals. Example 5–13 shows both the bass line and Dido's song. Compare this with the example from the *Crucifixus*.

Ex. 5–13. Purcell: *Dido and Aeneas*: Dido's Lament.

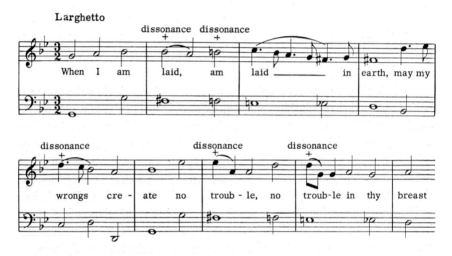

Within the short space of little over an hour, Purcell takes us through a grand sweep of events, from Dido's awakening love, through the plotting of the sorceress to force Aeneas's departure, to the final tragic death of Dido. Note the brilliance of the triumph music, the imaginative tone painting of the sorceress's music, the infectious buoyancy of the sailor's dance.

Aside from this more or less isolated English masterpiece, the British developed no momentum in the composition of opera. But a foreign product, Italian opera, was being imported in vast quantities; by the beginning of the eighteenth century and until the very end, Italian opera was à la mode in London.

Most of the music we have been describing was composed and performed for the benefit of the aristocracy, for kings, princes, nobles, and for the great personages of the church. This was upper-class music, and, just as the upper classes took themselves seriously, so was their music serious. The opera which was performed at court or in opera houses dealt with serious subjects. Indeed, such opera was called *opera seria*. Gods, antique heroes, mythological personages—these were the characters in opera seria. The plots dealt with serious and noble events and emotions, qualities which were supposed to reflect the nature of the patrons of opera. Generally, the conflict between love and duty was the central dramatic theme.

Popular music, music intended for the middle and lower classes, had existed for centuries before the Baroque era. We have few documents relating to this music before the seventeenth century, but we know that much of it was performed in connection with improvised stage presentations, the most celebrated of which was the *commedia dell'arte*. In this form the traditional characters of broad farce, Harlequin, Punchinello, Columbine, Pantalon, etc., were first encountered. The nobility liked to have episodes of

FIG. 7. Nicolas Tournier: *The Concert* (Louvre). About 1600. (Reproduced by permission of Caisse Nationale des Monuments Historiques.)

FIG. 8. Pannini: *Concert given at Rome by Cardinal de Polignac in the court of the Embassy, November 26, 1729, on the occasion of the birth of the Dauphin, son of Louis XV* (Louvre). This picture is particularly interesting for the documentary evidence it provides about a grand baroque concert in a large, heavily ornate theater with numerous singers and musicians. (Reproduced by permission of Caisse Nationale des Monuments Historiques.)

comedy as relief between the acts of their serious operas. As this custom grew, a new form of opera took shape, the comic opera or *opera buffa*.

Aristocratic opera tells us something about the façade of seventeenth- and eighteenth-century history, the magnificent courts, the absolute monarchs, the ideas of grandeur and power. Comic opera hints at the forces gathering strength from below, the growing middle class which was beginning to gain control of finance and commerce, and which was eventually to become the patron of music in the late eighteenth century. Naturally, the subject matter of opera buffa would show the middle class or the servant class as heroes, and the nobility would be cast as villans, appearing in the

most ridiculous light. Comedy thrives on punctured pomposity and out-
raged dignity. The classic theme of opera buffa shows the servant winning
over the master. Pergolesi's *La Serva padrona* (The Maid as Mistress) is
the most famous early eighteenth-century opera buffa. It created a sensation
when it was performed in Paris in 1752, and, as its title clearly indicates,
represents a triumph for the servant. Indeed, as far back as we can pene-
trate into the history of folklore, the king for a day theme echoes and
reechoes. In Mozart's great comic operas, Figaro masters Almaviva, the
count; the buffa characters of *Don Giovanni,* Leporello, Zerlina, and
Masetto, come out best in the end. In a more serious vein, the middle-class
philosophy of Sarastro, whereby a man can succeed on his merits alone,
overcomes the absolutism of the Queen of the Night in the opera, *The
Magic Flute.* Note here that Zerlina, Figaro, Leporello, and others in these
works are transformations of the old *commedia dell'arte* types.

Musically, opera buffa also represents a contrast to opera seria. Instead
of grandiose arias which developed one affective quality at great length
and displayed the arts of the virtuoso singer, we find short, tuneful songs,
with emphasis upon a sparkling, witty text. One of the most amusing techniques was *parlando,* a quick patter in an even, steady tempo. Parlando
became virtually a trade-mark of comic opera, surviving many changes of
style. (A Gilbert and Sullivan piece would certainly lose much of its appeal
without its patter songs.) Comic opera did not have the stars of the opera
seria; rather it relied upon quick-witted acting and singing, and particularly,
upon the ability of the performer to etch sharply parodied characterizations
or to splash about with broad farce. Needless to say, it focused attention
upon incident and plot much more than did opera seria. As a result of the
interplay of incidents and characters, opera buffa developed the ensemble
number, in which a number of characters sing together in a lively give-and-
take, often using figures and motives that are sharply contrasted to each
other. We might take this to be a lighthearted concertato procedure. Later
Mozart was to transplant the ensemble technique to serious moments in his
operas. In Chapter 6, we shall see how this was done during the first scene
of *Don Giovanni.*

All in all, this middle-class entertainment, the opera buffa, probably did
more to undermine the grand, somewhat severe musical art of the Baroque
period than did any other single factor. Comic opera won the heart of
Europe in the eighteenth century. Its tunefulness, its easy, regular rhythms,
its simple harmonies, and its transparent textures asked little from the

listener in the way of concentrated attention. It was a predigested form of musical nourishment. It is one, although not the only, symptom of the decay of musical absolutism.

Church Music

Church music in Baroque times reflected social and political conditions in the various countries of Europe. Nowhere was this more clearly demonstrated than in Germany. Germany's musical history during the seventeenth century reads quite differently from those of Italy or France. Germany was the battlefield for the last and most bitter phase of the conflict between Catholicism and Protestantism, the Thirty Years' War, 1618–1648. The country was devastated and its resources were exhausted. Grand entertainments at the courts of the warring princes were out of the question, regardless of the attractiveness of French and Italian ways. Opera, therefore, did not find the conditions which caused it to flourish in Italy and France.

On the other hand, the ideological strength which Protestantism was able to gather in this religious struggle gave great encouragement and impetus to church music. Germany, of all the countries in Europe, was the only one in which a fresh, vigorous, and extensive art of sacred music was cultivated.

Of all German church music, probably the most important was the *cantata*. The cantata, meaning a "sung piece," had several different forms in the Baroque era. As far as we are concerned, however, the most important type is the church cantata, which evolved in North Germany as Lutheranism became more and more firmly established. Each Sunday and feast day of the year called for a cantata, based on a liturgical text, to be sung in German and performed by the musical establishment of the church for which it was composed. Hence, the cantata is a type, rather than a specific form of composition.

Cantatas consisted of a number of movements embodying various styles and forms. Some movements might be grand concertato pieces, using orchestra and chorus; others might be solo songs, preceded perhaps by recitatives; in the event that the cantata used a chorale melody as a cantus firmus, one or more movements might be settings of the chorale melody. Numbers 46 and 48 from the cantata of Bach which uses the chorale melody, *Christ Lay in the Bonds of Death,* illustrate the chorale and the concertato methods of composing cantata movements.

During the seventeenth century, the melodies which were used as cantus firmi in the chorales and cantatas of Lutheran worship became subjects for many kinds of elaboration, generally by organists. The congregation sang the chorale proper; and this was preceded by an organ *chorale prelude* by way of introduction. The forms of the chorale prelude are those of other types of baroque music. The melody might be broken up into its phrases, and each subject treated as a point of imitation, as in a ricercar; it might be given in long notes, while a considerable amount of contrapuntal activity takes place in the other parts. (The first number in the cantata *Sleepers, Awake* represents this kind of chorale prelude.)

The chorale might be treated as a set of variations, a fugue, or an ornamented aria. The original melody was felt to be the musical counterpart of the sacred text upon which a sermon would be based; the elaboration, the exegesis, corresponded to the preacher's development of the subject of the sermon. Unlike the motet, which used the plain chant as an invisible skeleton within the contrapuntal web, the chorale and the chorale prelude give bold prominence to the chorale tune. This reflects the Lutheran attitude of worship; the message must be direct, simple, clear, and understood by all.

Many of you have heard the organist in a church perform a chorale prelude on such traditional tunes as *A Mighty Fortress Is Our God, From Heaven on High,* and *Christ Lay in the Bonds of Death.* As the theme proceeds forward, supported and strengthened by its elaborations and imitations, the sense of overpowering conviction, an idea of faith, is conveyed to the worshiper.

Church music in North Germany developed, through its intensive and widespread activity, an important school of organists. Bach was the culmination, and indeed, the end of an era in Germany dominated by organ playing and by composition for the organ. In the early Baroque era, German organists studied in Italy and elsewhere, borrowing techniques of composition from the Italian canzoni and ricercare. Through Froberger, Pachelbel, Reinken, and Buxtehude, noted predecessors of Bach, North German polyphony matured, and techniques of fugue composition were evolved that found their ultimate realization in the great preludes, toccatas, fantasias, and fugues of Bach. The growth of the fugue can be traced in very much the same manner as we followed other types of baroque music, embodied in a steady expansion, strengthening of harmonic lines, and intensive exploration of the possibilities of a given subject.

In Italy a distinctive form of church music arose through the transplantation of opera techniques into chapel music. This was the *oratorio.* Since medieval times, religious stories were often presented in dramatic fashion, with characters and scenery. The medieval church dramas are the ancestors of modern drama, and, in so far as they employed music, might be considered to be indirect forerunners of the oratorio, a dramatic presentation of a religious or throughtful subject or story. The oratorio, as a form, became established in the seventeenth century, and resembled opera in its component parts, using recitatives and arias; it relied however, more than opera upon the chorus. Sometimes a narrator, who helped guide the story, was used as a framing element. In its musical aspects, the oratorio might be considered a large-scale cantata, but both oratorio and cantata, as we have observed, borrowed much from opera.

Handel's *Messiah,* familiar to all, and one of the most celebrated works ever composed, not only exemplifies the oratorio but is a treasure house of musical riches and a compendium of baroque techniques of composition. As a rule, we find Handel's music less dense than that of Bach; Handel's counterpoint is more likely to give way to massive effects of sonority and brilliant passage-work; the intertwining of contrapuntal lines is more loosely carried out. Handel more than makes up for this by a wonderful sense for the dramatic nuance, by the elegance of his melodic lines, and by the brilliance and power of his sonorities. All these are illustrated in the *Messiah,* and, lest we overlook his contrapuntal skill, one of the most impressive movements of all is the fugue *And With His Stripes.*

Chamber Music

In the seventeenth and eighteenth centuries, the borderlines that separated theater, church, and chamber music were constantly being crossed. Nowhere was this intermingling more pronounced than in the type of composition called *sonata.* Originally the title was *canzona da sonar,* a canzona to be sounded instead of sung. This was shortened to the more terse name, *sonata.* Early sonatas, calling for various types of instrumental performance, either in chamber or church, followed the pattern of other music of the early Baroque period. They were composed principally in short, contrasted sections involving a number of different styles or manners. These sections became longer in line with the general trend of middle baroque music and were more or less standardized into an alternation of slow and fast movements. In many sonatas dance movements were included. About 1650, the typical layout of the sonata for the next century was defined. It consisted of a pair of quick movements using free imitation, separated by a middle movement in a somewhat slower, dancelike style. Later, a slow introduction was added, making a four-movement form.

Sonatas were used in two different connections: (1) in the church, where they were called *sonate da chiesa*; (2) for domestic use, where they were called *sonate da camera*. Sonate da chiesa were supposed to use a more serious style than the sonate da camera; nevertheless, dancelike movements are found in both types. Corelli's Sonata da Chiesa in E minor, *Masterpieces*, no. 39, illustrates the ecclesiastical type. You will observe the severe style of the slow movements, the purposeful polyphony of the first quick movement, and the dancelike manner of the final quick movement. Notice, particularly in the slow movements, how skillfully Corelli used tightly bound dissonance-resolution patterns to create a strong harmonic forward drive, aimed at broadly gauged cadences.

A companion form to the sonata was the *suite,* essentially a group of four or more dances. In the late Baroque period, especially, sonatas and suites might trade movements. That is, a suite might begin with a serious slow movement and then proceed to its dances; we have already mentioned the reverse procedure, the borrowing of dances by the sonata.

The suite evolved from the pairing of dances in Renaissance music. Eventually, about 1650, the sequence of dances was standardized according to the following order:

Allemande. A dance of moderate pace, duple meter, and rather heavy quality of movement.

Courante. A moderately quick dance in triple time, frequently employing momentary shifts of accent, creating a rather blurred and imbalanced rhythmic feeling.

Sarabande. A rather slow dance in triple meter, generally with an accent of length upon the second beat of the measure, as in the following pattern:

Ex. 5–14. Sarabande rhythms.

Gigue. A quick dance, often handled imitatively, in triple meter.

The four movements of the suite show its international flavor, since the allemande is German, the courante is French, the sarabande Spanish, and the gigue English. After the standardization of the suite, the practice of adding optional dances to the basic four grew up. For example, in Bach's French Suite, No. 6 in E major, the movements are: Allemande, Sarabande, Gavotte, Polonaise, Bourrée, Menuet, and Gigue.

Number 35, Suite in E minor by Froberger from *Masterpieces* illustrates the mid-seventeenth-century suite at about the time of standardization. From this time on, dance music invades virtually all kinds and media of music, either obviously carrying its titles, or, in disguise, through its characteristic patterns and qualities of movement. This will be explored more thoroughly in Chapter 6. Like the sonata, suites were written for solo instruments, small ensembles, and large groups approximating an orchestra in size.

Suites were a favorite genre of composition in France. The French cultivated dance music passionately, but the kind of music we find in French seventeenth- and eighteenth-century dance suites is quite different from that composed in England, Germany, or Italy. Indeed, a very distinctive kind of chamber-music style evolved in France. French musicians preferred the lute particularly as a domestic instrument.

The lute, a plucked string instrument, could neither play in a genuine polyphonic manner nor sustain a tone, once it had been plucked. In this respect it is similar to the present-day guitar, of which it is a direct ancestor. The role of the guitar, when we hear it now, is to provide a rhythmic-harmonic support to a singer or some instrument that can take a melody conveniently. Likewise, in the seventeenth century, the lute was used as an accompaniment instrument, very often as the continuo-bass element. However, by ingenious modifications, French lute composers managed to bring that instrument up to the level of solo performance. They interspersed runs of rapid notes and arpeggios between the principal tones of the melody to create a more continuous effect of movement; they alternated melodic motives between several strings, giving the impression of polyphony; and they created ornamental clusters of rapid tones around the principal tones to give the illusion of a sustained sound. All in all, French lute music had an airy, insubstantial, highly ornate, delicate, and quite precious manner, entirely in contrast to the monumental style of the French orchestra. This suggests the picture of French court society as it was at that time. The court individual was frivolous and of little weight and the music he might play likewise. The King was all: *l'état, c'est moi,* "I am the state," and the music associated with royal functions reflected this state of things. In the latter part of the seventeenth century, French musicians turned to the harpsichord as the principal solo instrument, but they transferred the style of the lute to the keyboard.

This gave rise to a typical French manner of performance, well-known in the eighteenth century, and called the *stile brisé,* the broken style. François Couperin's piece for clavecin, *La Galante,* illustrates the ornamental French style. (See *Masterpieces,* no. 40.) Bach turned to the French

Fig. 9. François Boucher: *Dispatch of the Messenger*. French rococo painting illustrating a great deal of ornamental detail. (Courtesy of the Metropolitan Museum of Art.)

manner again and again, providing many of his slow movements with a rich embroidery of ornaments.

Increased activity and expanded techniques in instrumental performance not only gave impetus to sonatas and suites in the chamber-music field, but toward the end of the seventeenth century the *concerto* was evolved, and it became the most important type of baroque orchestral music. Like the fugue, the concerto is as much a procedure as it is a prescribed form. Two things are important about its procedures: (1) the give-and-take between various combinations of instruments; (2) a characteristic type of brilliant figuration. These are both very clearly represented in the first movement of Bach's *Brandenburg* Concerto, No. 2 in F major.

As you listen to this piece, you will have no difficulty hearing the contrasts of the full orchestra, called the *tutti,* with the brilliant solo instruments, the violin, the bell-like high trumpet of Bach's time, the oboe, and the flute. The opening theme of this piece, announced boldly by the tutti, is a typical concerto theme, somewhat square, vigorous in effect, angular in shape, anchored upon the principal tones of the major or minor triad. Here is this theme and some other examples:

Ex. 5–15. Bach: *Brandenburg* Concerto, No. 2 in F major, first movement.

Ex. 5–16. Handel: Concerto Grosso in D major.

Ex. 5–17. Handel: Concerto Grosso in F major.

Ex. 5–18. Bach: Concerto for Violin in E major.

Themes such as these have a great deal of propulsive power. As you can hear in the first movement of the *Brandenburg, No. 2,* they break out easily into florid passages, generally taken by the solo instruments. These florid passages consist of chains of rapid, mechanically regular notes put together in stereotyped patterns. They are supported by a vigorous, regular motoric beat in the bass instruments and the supporting parts.

The concerto absorbed its characteristic manner of figuration from English keyboard music of the seventeenth century. English musicians and actors traveled throughout Europe, often by necessity to escape from the authority of the Commonwealth. Wherever they went, their keyboard style was taken up by local composers and also transferred to other instruments. These figures, originally employed as a means of variation, became the staple ingredient in the late baroque instrumental concerto. Example 5–19, from the *Brandenburg, No. 2,* shows the solo performers working through a set of such figurations. Notice here the sense of progression created by the systematic rise and fall of the various parts.

Ex. 5–19. Bach: *Brandenburg* Concerto, No. 2, first movement.

Over the entire movement which we have taken as an example, the form builds as an alternation of tutti and solo. Typically, in the concerto, the tutti opens and closes the movement with its bold thematic statement in the home key. Within the movement, the treatment of tutti and solo will vary according to the style and the type of instruments used. Our present example, with its brilliant solo participants, emphasizes the contrast between these and the tutti. The solo episodes stand out. In the *Brandenburg* Concerto, No. 6, Bach has a thoroughly homogeneous group of instruments, *viola da braccio, viola da gamba,* cello, and bass. He therefore concentrates upon an intense and compact interweaving of melodic material and does not attempt to project a brilliant soloistic quality, although we can detect the tutti-solo alternation if we listen closely. Harmonically, the concerto follows the plan of other late baroque music. A key is set at the beginning. The music moves out from this key in one direction and another, sometimes returning. The harmony circles around the home key, but is never far away, as we can see in the diagram of the example we are using.

Ex. 5–20. Diagram of key scheme. Bach: *Brandenburg* Concerto, No. 2, first movement.

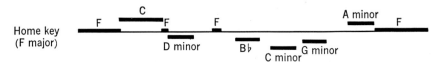

In Example 5–20 the heavy black lines represent areas of harmonic stability; the thin black line represents the home key as a level of reference throughout the movement; areas where no heavy black line shows represent shifting, relatively unstable harmonic action.

Like the fugue, French overture, sinfonia, and sonata, the concerto is a descendant of the canzona. Actually, we might say that it is a canzonalike piece, treated in concertato style. It developed from the canzona into a three-movement piece. The first movement displays most typically the concertato and virtuoso aspects; the second movement is frequently patterned after the slow arias of opera; the last movement may take up again the manner of the first movement, or it may assume the style of a dance, such as a gigue or minuet. Its most important function in baroque music was to provide baroque musicians the opportunity to exercise themselves boldly and exuberantly, to work together for no other purpose than the sheer pleasure of fitting the music into place.

We can get some idea of the importance of the concerto in eighteenth-century music when we realize that not only did its style pervade much other music of its time, but that it is the *one* form that provides a link for the important music of Baroque times with that of the later eighteenth century. When you hear the first movement of Mozart's *Prague* Symphony, many brilliant effects based on concerto style will come to your attention.

Finally, in our list of baroque instrumental types, is a kind of piece which is restricted to no specific procedure whatever, except those imposed by the limitations of performance and the conventions of harmony. This type, called *prelude, toccata, introduction, fantasia,* might consist of flourishes, runs, and arpeggios in an improvisatory style; sometimes such pieces, or sections within them, might assume the manner of a dance, an overture, a fugue, or a systematic development of a given figure, in the manner of an exercise. The toccata of the Toccata and Fugue in D minor, is a thoroughly improvisatory piece. It gives the impression of probing, searching, exploring, almost at random. On the other hand, most of the Preludes from Bach's famous work, the *Well-Tempered Clavier,* are cast in one established form or another, although the most familiar of these, the First Prelude, is an improvisation.

Not only were the types we have described above well-defined in late baroque music, they were sufficiently flexible to be combined or set against each other in juxtaposition. Thus, a fugue might borrow dance rhythms, or a dance might be handled imitatively, as though it were going to become a fugal piece. The instrumental concerto style was borrowed both in choral and solo vocal music. The *Et Resurrexit* of the B-minor Mass is a choral concerto, carried out even to the point of using the structural plan as well as the style of the concerto. On the other hand, the concerto appropriated the slow aria style of the opera for its slow movement, and the last movement was frequently a dance. This transference, this intermingling of style and procedure is a symptom of a highly developed, thoroughly codified art, an art which can enrich its individual products by stylistic and idiomatic cross-fertilization. The late Baroque era was unusually wealthy in idioms, techniques, and styles; all of these were, nevertheless, controlled and rigidly supervised by a logical and vigorous harmonic discipline.

The four principal areas of musical activity in the seventeenth and early eighteenth centuries, Germany, Italy, France, and England, each contributed something distinctive to the synthesis of style in late baroque music. Of these, Italy's activity, while not productive of such great monuments as those of Germany, was more pervasive and persuasive than any. The Italians worked out brilliant styles of instrumental performance just as they had done for solo vocal music in opera. They were also responsible for the final evolution of the modern violin. Such names as Stradivari, Amati, and Guarneri are legendary in the history of violin making, and the Italian violins have not been equaled to this day in beauty of tone. As with opera, wherever Italian musicians traveled they carried their style of playing and the musical forms which they had evolved. The very language of opera and chamber music was Italian, as the titles and terms bear witness.

Such widespread popularity grew from the pleasing nature of Italian music itself. Ingratiating melody, sensuous appeal of sound, brilliant and facile passage-work, regular rhythms, a feeling for easily perceived order, a sweetness and logic of harmony: all these were qualities which combined to gain for Italian music a popular success all over Europe and to establish the Italian style as a kind of norm, even into the nineteenth century, as witness Rossini's *Barber of Seville*.

While these qualities appeared in various guises and in different degrees of saturation, there were few forms or styles, or for that matter, individual compositions, which did not bear some Italian stamp. In its grand tradition Baroque inherited the contrapuntal technique of the Renaissance and applied it consistently, reaching a level of ultimate grandeur in the fugues of Johann Sebastian Bach. Nevertheless, contrapuntal composition in the motet-fugue sense also reached a final point of historical arrival in Bach's music. The Italian influence, leavening and lightening musical texture, represents another stream of musical evolution in the seventeenth and eighteenth centuries. Frequently, in Italian music, fugues and extended imitations give way to spectacular sonorities, to exciting alternations in the concertato manner, to electrifying runs of rapid notes. The importance of the Italian music becomes perfectly clear when we realize that the next era in the history of music, the Viennese classic, drew most of its procedures from Italy.

SUMMARY

Baroque music began as a violent explosion that utterly destroyed the steady continuous flow of Renaissance music. Violent feelings were expressed; striking gestures and colorful sonorities were projected. Interest in harmonic effects and relationships developed as a result of the play of sound masses. Harmonic techniques gradually combined with certain procedures carried over from the Renaissance, such as imitation, variation, cantus-firmus treatment, and dance forms to crystallize in forms and procedures of the late Baroque period, such as the concerto, the cantata, the sonata, the suite, the fugue, the overture, etc.

The principal structural aspects of late baroque music were: (1) systematic long-range focus upon key definition; (2) consistent and unified treatment of a single basic idea or affection throughout a single movement, the idea being represented by a distinctive motive or group of motives.

Whatever title or purpose might be assigned to a piece, whatever its medium of performance, whatever its special style, this harmonic logic and internal unity are found. Baroque music dealt with a continuous yet forceful flow of sound. Points of arrival were rarely points of rest; rather, they were concentrations of cadential action. Aside from dance music, long-range symmetry and balance did not much enter the structural picture.

When the continuous flow and expansion began to break up, when the long line became a series of short fragments, when cadences and caesuras occurred frequently and regularly, showing shortening of breath, then the baroque itself no longer lived. There was a foreshadowing of this in the Italian opera sinfonia. In opera buffa, in salon pieces for keyboard written in the middle of the eighteenth century, and in short and simple songs and dances that appealed to middle-class listeners, the process of breakup spread. Eventually, this disintegration opened the way to a new re-formation of musical structure which took place during the Viennese classic era of the late eighteenth century.

SUGGESTED LISTENING PROJECTS

1. Monteverdi, Claudio: *Lamento d'Arianna, 2000 Years,* no. 18

Listen for: Stilo rappresentativo; poignant, often chromatic supporting harmonies; strong cadential effects; particularly expressive intervals in solo voice line; varied settings of the refrain *Lasciatemi morire* (Let Me Die).

2. Vivaldi, Antonio: Concerto in G minor, Op. 3, no. 2, Vox PL 7423

Listen for: Very clear distinctions between tutti and solo; mechanical stereotyped figures, especially in solo passages; continuous motoric drive; cadential drive, particularly toward end of a section. Compare the transparent part-writing of this piece with the densely woven counterpoint of the first movements of Bach's *Brandenburg* Concertos, Nos. 3 and 6.

3. Handel: *The Messiah,* For unto us a Child is born, Victor LCT 6401

Listen for: Concertolike style and layout; contrast between the three principal motives: *For unto us, And the government, Wonderful!*; incidental imitations not thoroughly carried out; virtuoso demands upon chorus; transparent textures; four important points of arrival; stretto and broadening effects at end.

Chapter *6.* *Classic Music*

Today's listener needs no introduction to classic music. Haydn, Mozart, and Beethoven are familiar concert names. Mozart is a best-seller in recordings of serious music. For almost two centuries classic music has offered a tremendous appeal to listeners, performers, composers, and scholars.

Let us begin by listening to a work that is familiar to most concert-goers: the first movement of Mozart's Symphony No. 41 in C major, the *Jupiter*. In many respects this music is different from any that we have thus far heard in our survey of music's growth. There is a greater brilliance and fullness of sound; there is a tremendous variety of texture and color; we hear many sharp contrasts of style and dynamics. The marchlike pace builds up into long phases of movement projected on a grand scale; the points of arrival are emphatic and act as long-range goals, indeed, as areas of arrival following intense action. The shift from one expressive value to another is striking, often surprising. Marches and flourishes, a song, a dance, vigorous contrapuntal wrestlings, and grand climaxes—all find their place within the framework of this piece, a piece that impresses also by its imposing length. Throughout we sense undercurrents of dramatic force, ready to explode at any time. With all this variety and richness of content, we are constantly aware that the form, long as it is, remains entirely under control, that it seems to pursue its ends with clarity, breadth, and force.

From our listening, we know that classic music contains many works that are comparable to the *Jupiter* Symphony in scope and in richness of content. How did this come about? What are the conditions and procedures that underlie the classic style and its forms? To answer these questions, we must first set the stage.

STYLISTIC SOURCES OF CLASSIC MUSIC

In the first movement of the *Jupiter* Symphony, we heard a considerable number of musical styles. Some of these had a popular flavor. There were march patterns, a number of charming songlike moments, and a captivating little dance that Mozart let us hear a number of times. These are all symptoms of what was taking place culturally and socially during that era.

During the eighteenth century a new audience began to exert a strong influence upon musical style and taste. The middle class, growing in prosperity and strength, became an important patron and consumer of music. The preferences of the middle class ran to simple dances and songs, to short and easy pieces of obvious and strong popular appeal. This represented a drastic shift in musical taste from that of the aristocratic connoisseurs of the Baroque period. Dances themselves reflected the change in style. For example, earlier in the eighteenth century, at the court of Louis XV, dances were intended for a small group of experts. There were many subtle variations of movement in the dances themselves and a corresponding free ornamentation of the music with which they were accompanied. This was an art meant for the delight of sophisticated noblemen. On the other hand, the popular dances of the later eighteenth century were mass dances, characterized by a vigorous, simple, and down-to-earth quality; and the music for these dances corresponded in style.

The history of the minuet, the most popular dance of both eras, illustrates the change strikingly. In the earlier period, the minuet was an elegant and elaborate dance of rather moderate and restrained quality of movement. By the time of Haydn and Mozart it became a sturdy and forthright dance with a briskly swinging quality of movement. Contrast J. K. F. Fischer's Menuet with the Menuetto from Haydn's *London* Symphony. In the former the very pace seems uncertain, because of the elaborate ornamentations; we hear no strong sense of accent. The Haydn Menuetto, on the other hand, has a direct, earthy manner, arising from its vigorously accented beat and its unadorned melody.

Ex. 6–1. Change in style of minuet.

a. J. K. F. Fischer: Menuet.

b. Haydn: Menuetto from *London* Symphony.

The ever-growing influence of popular idioms, which we have been tracing during our survey of the medieval, Renaissance, and Baroque periods, reaches its point of saturation in Viennese classic music. In the later eighteenth century, dances, songs, and marches were so strong in their appeal and influence that they became common denominators for musical style. The principal materials for many sonatas, symphonies, and concertos were drawn directly from these idioms.

Listen to the opening of Haydn's Sonata in C major. It is in the manner of a march.

Ex. 6–2. Haydn: Sonata in C major.

The Allegro of the first movement of Mozart's Symphony No. 39 in E♭ major, K. 549, begins as a *ländler,* a German dance resembling the waltz.

Ex. 6–3. Mozart: Symphony No. 39 in E♭ major, K. 549.

The final movement of Beethoven's Concerto in G major for Piano and Orchestra, Op. 58 is in the style of a contredanse.

Ex. 6–4. Beethoven: Concerto in G major for Piano and Orchestra, Op. 58.

Another strong popularizing influence in music was comic opera. In its various forms, as *opera buffa, opéra comique, Singspiel,* and *ballad opera,* this type of stage entertainment was enthusiastically patronized everywhere in Europe during the eighteenth century. As in other times, comic opera of this era made use of popular song and dance idioms. In fact, it often acted as a kind of central clearinghouse. Well-known tunes might be inserted into the music of a comic opera; and, on the other hand, a fetching new song from a comic opera often became a current favorite. In those times it was perfectly in order to "adapt" great music to popular usage. In a letter to Baron Gottfried von Jacquin in 1787, Mozart said, "all these people (in Prague) flew about in sheer delight to the music of my 'Figaro' arranged for quadrilles and waltzes." To be sure, the line between popular and serious music was a bit more difficult to draw in the eighteenth century than it is at present.

Mingled with popular idioms we find, in classic music, many serious styles and idioms drawn from the reservoir of eighteenth-century musical practice. A bird's-eye view of these will help us to appreciate the stylistic content of classic music. In doing so, we can better understand one of the basic principles of classic musical aesthetics, namely, *the contrast and the reconciliation of divergent and often opposing musical qualities.*

The division below has been made according to: (1) *types,* which represent fully-formed pieces or sections thereof, and (2) *styles,* which represent a manner of composition. In practice, the two categories often overlap; for example, a march is a style as well as a type.

Types

Dance music. There were many distinctive kinds of dance music in the eighteenth century: minuets, gavottes, polonaises, gigues, écossaises, contredanses, etc. Each type of dance had a characteristic rhythm, tempo, and manner. The *Little Music Book* that Leopold Mozart gave to his son Wolfgang on his seventh birthday contains many examples of dances current at that time. It provides evidence of the importance that dance music had as an ingredient in the musical nourishment of Wolfgang. Examples 6–1, 6–3, and 6–4 illustrate some eighteenth-century dance types.

Marches and fanfares. Marching music and fanfare signals were heard everywhere in eighteenth-century Europe. Every court, large or small, had its military music. Entertainments opened with festive little marches. In opera and concert the march style was also a great favorite, so much so that the first movements of many symphonies and concertos are saturated with it. Fanfare signals, often used as the basis for march tunes, ring the changes on the tones of the major triad, exactly as we hear in military bugle calls. Examples 6–2 and 6–5 illustrate march rhythms.

Ex. 6–5. Mozart: *Little Music Book.*

Songs. These were lyric pieces of flowing melodic quality, often intended for amateur performance. Many songs were dances to which words had been added. Example 6–6 is a passepied, a dance in moderately quick triple time. It also is from Mozart's *Little Music Book.*

Ex. 6–6. Mozart: *Little Music Book.*

The French overture. See Chapter 5, p. 146. The opening of Mozart's Symphony in E♭ major, K. 543, illustrates the French overture manner in classic music.

Ex. 6–7. Mozart: Symphony in E♭ major, K. 543.

Recitative. Two kinds of recitative were standard in the eighteenth century. (1) *Secco,* meaning "dry." This was a close approximation to ordinary speech. It was accompanied and punctuated with occasional chords played by a keyboard instrument. Secco recitative told a great deal about the plot or the situation in a very short space of time. Frequently it lent itself to the sharp thrusts of comedy. The example below, from the first scene of Mozart's *Don Giovanni,* comes immediately after Don Giovanni has killed Anna's father. The matter-of-fact, flippant manner is a shocking contrast to the tragic death scene which has just run its course. Nowhere in his music has Mozart projected the contrast of serious and comic elements so boldly as at this point.

Ex. 6–8. Mozart: *Don Giovanni.*

(2) The other type of recitative is called *accompagnato,* meaning "accompanied." In its strongly emotional quality, accompanied recitative recalls the

stile rappresentativo of the early opera. Here we have fragments of expressive melody, pathetic touches, outbursts of strong feeling. Anna's recitative, after she has discovered the body of her father, is set in this manner. Here is an excerpt from this passage:

Ex. 6–9. Mozart: *Don Giovanni.*

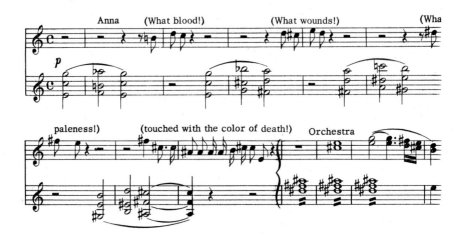

Styles

Hunt style. In the courtly world that existed before the French Revolution, the hunt had for centuries been one of the supreme sports and diversions. An entire literature of hunting calls had been developed, based on the fanfare figures of hunting horns. Classic composers made much of these figures. Again and again the hunt echoes in the great masterpieces of the Viennese classic era. Mozart's *Hunt* Quartet, his Quintet in E♭ major (see Example 6–10), the finale of Haydn's *Drumroll* Symphony, the finale of Beethoven's Violin Concerto—all combine the characteristic figures and flavor of hunt music with typical dance manners.

Ex. 6–10. Mozart: Quintet in E♭ major, K. 614, opening of first movement.

Oriental effects. Eighteenth-century interest in the Orient, stimulated by travels to the East and by the presence of envoys from Eastern potentates at the courts of Europe, led, in music, to occasional use of Orientalisms. Mozart's *Alla Turca,* his Overture to *Seraglio,* and the Turkish march from Beethoven's *Ruins of Athens* illustrate this curious exotic aspect of eighteenth-century musical style.

Bagpipe and musette effects. In imitating country-dances, one of the most popular devices was the bagpipe effect. One tone is held as a drone, while the melody travels its way in a rather simple manner. The trio in Mozart's Quintet in E♭ major is a lovely little drone-bass piece. Haydn, in the finale of the *London* Symphony, also made use of a bagpipe effect. *Musette* is the name sometimes given to such pieces, the musette being the French bagpipe.

The singing-allegro style. The lyricism which eighteenth-century music had acquired from Italian opera was incorporated into instrumental music in a characteristic manner called the *singing-allegro.* In this manner, a songlike melody with rather long notes and a rounded contour was accompanied in quick, even notes; a rapid, dancelike pace was typical of this style. The singing-allegro was particularly favored in piano music; and many of Mozart's piano sonatas begin in this fashion.

The learned style. Classic composers not only absorbed the popular idioms of their time. They were thoroughly trained in counterpoint, fugue, figured bass: the heritage of an earlier musical era. This was designated as the *learned* or *strict style.* The learned style stands in opposition to those we have been considering up to this point, the so-called *galant music.* Indeed, in the eighteenth century many theorists and critics discussed the pros and cons of the learned and galant styles. Rousseau, in line with his return-to-nature ideas, preferred the galant; and Quantz, a highly trained German musician, had much admiration for the subtleties of the learned style. This controversy among advocates of one style versus another reflects the sociologic changes that took place in the eighteenth century. The galant or free style superseded the learned or strict style as the principal mode of musical composition. This parallels the decline of absolutism and the rise of democracy. Classic composers seldom wrote entire pieces in the learned style, with the exception of sacred music, which traditionally required contrapuntal treatment. Generally, in later classic music, learned procedures were applied in works that were essentially galant in manner, as in Example 6–11.

Ex. 6–11. Mozart: Quartet in C major, K. 465, finale.

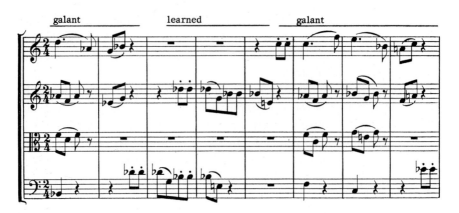

The soloistic style. This was a style in which the soloistic capacities of the performer were displayed. It consisted of brilliant passages in bold style, in both instrumental and vocal music. Soloistic music was generally laid out according to the concerto-grosso plan, that is, alternation of passages for full ensemble with passages for solo. Example 6–21 shows an unusually brilliant use of soloistic style, beginning at the ninth measure.

The Storm and Stress style. Both the Storm and Stress style and the Sensibility style—which will be described next—represented later eighteenth-century metamorphoses of aesthetic values cultivated in the Baroque period. They were concerned with the delineation of certain well-defined, expressive, and emotional qualities. Both involved relationships between music and literature. In the case of the Storm and Stress, it was drama and opera; in the case of the Sensibility, it was poetry and song.

Although the doctrine of the affections still influenced the Storm and Stress and the Sensibility, emotional values in these styles were much less stereotyped and well defined. The composer and performer were supposed to show that they were moved intensely at every moment in the composition. Instead of working out a piece consistently with one figure, the composer introduced many striking changes and contrasts. General feelings and kaleidoscopic shifts of mood were portrayed instead of a single, specific emotional value. Baroque music had the aspect of an objective, universal, aesthetic system. The Storm and Stress and Sensibility had the aspect of subjective and personal aesthetic systems. These latter, in fact, are early manifestations of romanticism in music and literature. There is actually a closer connection between them and the romantic age to follow than there is with any other aspect of classic style.

The Storm and Stress style had a stronger impact on classic composers than had the Sensibility. Storm and Stress qualities were more challenging, and, when merged with the sustained structural strength of classic music, could create a tremendously dramatic impact. The specific features of this style, illustrated in Example 6–12, are rhythmic agitation, chromaticism, dissonance, minor mode, compact texture, and the expressive qualities which the name itself so well describes.

Ex. 6–12. Mozart: Fantasia in C minor, K. 475.

Most of the first movement of Beethoven's Fifth Symphony is in the Storm and Stress style.

The Sensibility style. The Sensibility style and its German equivalent, the *Empfindsamkeit,* were intimate and capricious in manner. There were rapid changes in mood and feeling. Phrases were irregular; there were many stops and starts without strong rhythmic propulsion. Example 6–13 is typical of this style.

Ex. 6–13. Mozart: Fantasia in D minor, K. 397.

Example 6–13 begins with a plaintive little melody. Suddenly at the fifth measure a strong, impulsive exclamation is interjected. There is a suspenseful pause and the music continues with an uncertain, broken, chromatic descending figure, suggesting perhaps sighs or the spasmodic breathing that attends weeping. Again a pause of suspense, then an emphatic figure hammers away at one tone while the accompaniment descends, the dissonances accumulate, and the music finally reaches a highly ornamented cadence. Such sudden changes of mood and expression called for an intimate type of performance. Sensibility and *Empfindsamkeit* were typically keyboard and song styles, by which the performer could make as direct a contact with the listener as possible.

All these idioms were familiar to the eighteenth-century listener. He took delight in observing how a composer managed them during a composition; he, as well as the composer, appreciated the richness of content which the interplay of these various styles provided. And the better he knew the musical language of the time, the keener would be his judgment with respect to the skill and imagination of the composer. He could recognize the winning, the elegant melodic phrase, the moving harmonic gesture, the well-placed effective contrast, and he could distinguish these from music that was commonplace, dilute, and awkward. To us today, these values also can come alive if we develop some acquaintance with classic ideas and means.

If you listen once again to the first movement of the *Jupiter* Symphony, checking carefully as to how and when Mozart uses material in various styles, you will notice that he is not content to use this material in a matter-of-fact way. Rather, he makes something of each gesture, repeating it, developing it, returning to it at strategic moments. There is balance, control, and drive, a grand scheme in which each measure and motive has its place. Here is a monumentally conceived form, giving evidence, like so many other works written at this time, that classic composers were vitally concerned with building form on a big scale. They had the raw materials, the techniques, the impulse of expression, and the imagination to accomplish this. Our next step is to get some idea of the ways in which classic forms are built.

FORM IN CLASSIC MUSIC

We would probably all agree that the principal impression we receive from classic form, large or small, is the idea of balance. By the time a classic piece has run its course all problems have been solved and a satisfying sense of equilibrium has been established. This, of course, is more readily felt in short pieces, in which our aural perspective, our overview of the entire work becomes clear upon the first hearing and in which the symmetry and balance between the various sections can be immediately and directly felt.

For this reason, then, we turn once more to classic dance forms, where symmetry governs musical events in a most apparent fashion. We shall find, later, that there is a strong family resemblance between dance forms and the larger structures of classic music.

Symmetry in music grows by statement paired with counterstatement. Motive answers motive; phrase answers phrase; cadence answers cadence.

Nowhere is this more obvious than in dance music, where movements of the dance itself prescribe symmetry in the music. When one phrase ends with a half cadence and is answered by another phrase ending with a full cadence, we have a symmetrical period. When such a period is answered by another of comparable length, we have a symmetrical two-part form. With few exceptions the popular music of the eighteenth century is made up of periods and phrases arranged symmetrically.

To build small pieces, eighteenth-century composers connected two or more periods, arranging matters so that a final sense of arrival came only at the end of the piece. Let us have a look at some of these.

Small Forms

The most prevalent structural plan for small pieces in eighteenth-century music embodies *two* relatively equal periods, or two groups of periods; this is called *two-part form*. We became familiar with the genealogy of two-part form, in the dances of medieval, Renaissance, and baroque music, the estampies, the pavanes, the allemandes, etc. Classic composers found the small two-part form quite sufficient to contain some of their most delightful and winning music, as the examples below bear witness.

As you listen to the following pieces in two-part form, try to determine how completely balance is maintained, or where it has been disturbed. Also, listen for the strong cadence points within the piece, and at the end.

Ex. 6–14. Mozart: Menuetto from *Eine Kleine Nachtmusik*.

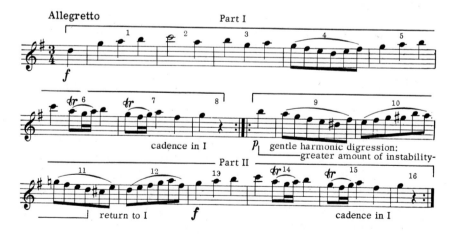

We sense perfect balance in this piece. The two parts are exactly equal in length. The cadences are equal in strength. The cadence at the end of

Part I is, to a certain extent, final-sounding because it ends solidly in the home key. Yet we do not accept it as the end of the form because the music has not been in progress sufficiently long to call for a full stop. However, when the very same cadence appears at the end of Part II, we can accept its finality because it completes a symmetrical pattern involving two periods. Here is an example of the simplest kind of counterstatement, an answer by literal repetition. To be sure, the slight harmonic digression at the beginning of the second period makes a great difference, enough to give the cadence of Part II a greater feeling of weight and arrival. As you listen for the harmonic flow of classic music, you will become aware that the broader and bolder a harmonic digression is, the stronger will be the cadence which subsequently will bring matters back into balance.

Ex. 6–15. Haydn: Rondo from Sonata for Clavier in D major.

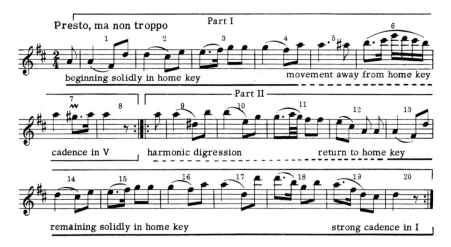

Certainly this is different from the Mozart example. First, we cannot make out perfect balance between Parts I and II, because Part II is longer again by one-half. How did this come about? Part I provides a clue. If you listen carefully, you will hear that the cadence in Part I goes afield; it does not end in the home key. This is a modulation that is secured by a strong cadence in the new key, the dominant. (See Chapter 2, Cadences, Distribution of Tonal Centers.) Since the harmony has digressed, has gone off base, it must make its way back home. Having set up such a problem, Haydn felt an obligation to explore before he turned back to his home key. In making such explorations, the mathematically perfect balance of two equal parts was destroyed. No matter; he finished the period solidly in the home key and we have a satisfying sense of completion. The cadential question of Part I is balanced by the cadential answer of Part II. Here is a diagram of this two-part form:

Ex. 6–16.

	PART I			PART II	
If the piece is in the major key	I	V I		"X"	I
If the piece is in the minor key	I	III		"X"	I
	Presentation of tonic key	Contrast key: strong cadence		Harmonic digressions	Return to tonic: final cadence

You may have noticed that the melody presented at the beginning returned again toward the end. To be exact, it returned when the music came back to the home key. Indeed, the reappearance of the theme acted as a kind of signal for the reestablishment of the tonic key. Thus, *the melodic layout* might be taken as *three-part*: (1) the theme, in the home key; (2) other melodic material; (3) return of the theme, as music returns to the home key; thus giving us an A B A form. These forms then, and many others like them, are hybrids; *their cadences and their periods crystallize into two-part structures; their melodies shape into three-part forms,* as the following diagram shows:

Ex. 6–17.

Thematic plan:

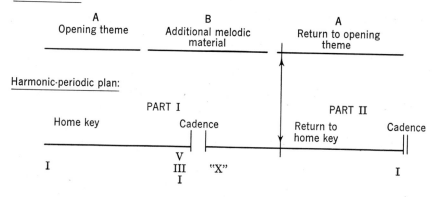

Harmonic-periodic plan:

To illustrate the widespread and virtually unlimited possibilities offered by the two-part form, let us look at still another example, the duet *La Ci Darem La Mano* from Mozart's opera, *Don Giovanni*. Mozart, with his superb insight into the relation of music and dramatic action, has ingeniously used a formal dance as the musical setting for Don Giovanni's attempt to lure Zerlina away to his castle. A symmetrical period form is apt here, since there is a regular give-and-take between the two singers in alternate phrases. Don Giovanni has a rather forceful melodic line; Zerlina sings the same material, but with graceful ornamentation suggests a yielding quality. This ornamentation provides the springboard for a somewhat extended form with broader and more elaborate cadential effects, especially in Part II. In its elegance and grace this melody is one of the choicest examples of Viennese classic music.

Small two-part forms are rarely offered as complete compositions. They were combined with each other to make up larger pieces. This procedure stems from earlier music, in which dances were often played in pairs or groups. For example, in minuets there was a first dance, rather vigorous in style, followed by another minuet, possibly more lyric in style. This second minuet was played by a smaller group of instruments, often a trio; thus the second minuet acquired the name *trio*. After the trio, the first minuet was repeated. This plan was taken over in classic music with or without modifications. Listen to the trio of the Menuetto from Mozart's *Eine Kleine Nachtmusik*. In this middle piece, we hear a more flowing manner, a lighter texture, and a change of position since we visit another key. Mozart here has contrasted a sturdy minuet that seems to *walk* along with an elegant trio that floats and touches ground but occasionally and lightly.

As you may surmise, it was not difficult to turn out a routine piece in two-part form. Literally, hundreds of thousands of such pieces appeared during the later eighteenth century. This was the bread-and-butter music upon which Haydn and Mozart and all the other composers of the time were nourished and raised. Dilettantes and amateurs also tried their hands at writing little dances and minuets. They were taught to compose these pieces along with their lessons at the keyboard. Among the teaching manuals we find such titles as *The Ever-Ready Minuet and Polonaise Composer* by Johann Philipp Kirnberger and the *Philharmonic Game* attributed to Haydn. These books provided simple melodic fragments; by throwing dice, the rankest amateur could put together a minuet from certain of these fragments.

Broader Phases of Movement

Popular idioms and their neatly balanced little forms were common property in eighteenth-century music. The Viennese masters' distinction in small genres lay in the elegance of their melody, the fine detail work of their texture, and the subtlety of their harmony. But they truly showed their genius in going beyond this small scope to marshal many forces and to build on a grand scale. This was done in many ways, a few of which will be described below. These deal principally with techniques for breaking the symmetry of a period. It is not often that the lay listener has the opportunity to follow closely and clearly the constructive processes of a great style. In much music the materials themselves are difficult to shape or even to understand. But in the case of classic music, the sense for balance in period structure and the disruption of that balance are so well projected and address themselves with such telling force to the listener, that we can proceed quite far toward an understanding of the ways in which classic structure takes shape.

Listen to the following example from the Violin Concerto of Beethoven:

Ex. 6–18. Beethoven: Violin Concerto in D major, first movement.

Just when you expect the cadence, the music suddenly crashes forward with a completely unanticipated surge. A new motive, a deceptive cadence, a change of rhythmic intensity: all these give a new momentum to the music, causing the period to become enormously extended. The cadence we wanted, and which we still hope for, arrives—but twenty-eight measures later.

Meanwhile, what a wealth of musical interest has been added to the original material of the period! The critical moment for this period was the *deceptive cadence* at measure 28.

Ex. 6–19. Beethoven: Quartet in C minor, Op. 18, no. 4, opening of first movement.

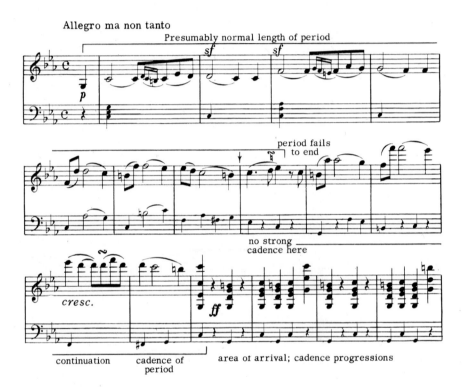

The driving quality of this period sets up a momentum which overrides the normal cadential point at measure 8. At this point a light cadence articulates but does not halt movement. The music reaches forward, rising dramatically to a climax just before the broad cadence which resolves the tension. At the cadence, the idea of arrival is pounded home by violent strokes of tonic and dominant. The extension of this period is certainly its most engrossing moment. The structural plan of this extended period, and, indeed, of many such periods in classic music might be drawn as follows:

Ex. 6–20.

Despite the absence of perfect symmetry, a psychological sense of balance is very effectively projected by this kind of structure. It both challenges and satisfies our feeling for movement and arrival.

Ex. 6–21. Mozart: Quintet in E♭ major, K. 614, first movement.

At measure 66, the harmony moves afield: this not only initiates an extension, but actually prepares for a greatly extended cadence. At first we hear a comfortable give-and-take (measures 62–65), but when the digression interferes there is a tightening of movement which explodes into a soaring, brilliant, climactic flight that settles to a point of arrival only at the cadence. The extension has exactly doubled the length of the period.

Here is still another example of a broadening of the phase of movement.

Ex. 6–22. Mozart: Quartet in C major, K. 465, first movement.

more elaborate part-
writing begins here

part-writing continues the movement

At measure 31 in Example 6–22, the instruments become very active in working against each other; this is in contrast to the simpler and lighter texture of the first phrase. The singing, lyric melody of the first phrase descends to a lower register and becomes more impassioned and eloquent; tension is increased by the tug and pull of the voices accompanying the melody. So strong is the momentum developed that the melodic action does not quiet at the cadence but carries on directly into the beginning of the next period. Here we have heard an active interplay among the component parts. This interplay had an intensifying effect and caused momentum to carry beyond the point of arrival for the period. Classic composers were always alert to give accompanying or subsidiary parts some rhythmic and melodic life of their own.

Still another way of generating more intense and sustained movement is *contrast*. The classic style makes bold contrast a basic principle of structure. Much of the dramatic quality we hear in Haydn, Mozart, and Beethoven arises from skillfully placed, often sudden, contrast. We might compare the expansive effect of such contrast to the energy that is released when two forces collide or two substances work against each other in friction. The opening of Mozart's *Jupiter* Symphony is an excellent example. The alternation of two highly contrasted, juxtaposed motives sets off a momentum that eventually runs down only some thirty measures later.

The expansion of the period provided the classic composer with a structural resource that lent itself to broad-scale forms. Not every period in Haydn's, Mozart's, and Beethoven's music is of this type, yet it is principally this structural procedure which distinguishes their forms from the ordinary layouts of eighteenth-century popular music. These techniques for expansion are some of the principal resources classic composers had for conveying the sense of exhilarating excitement, dramatic climax, and logical resolution that characterizes all classic music.

Treatment of Motives

Listen once again to the extended periods discussed above. Note what happens to the melodic material while the extensions grow. The melodic phrases are broken up into their constituent motives and the motives are worked against each other in a tightened interplay. They contribute their own push to the increasing momentum of the period.

Such play with motives represents one of the greatest skills of classic composers. As you listen to the first movement of the *Jupiter* Symphony, you find that much of the interest it carries is created by the resourceful methods Mozart employed to work over the dozen or so salient motives in the work. One great tour de force of classic composition is the finale of Haydn's *Drumroll* Symphony. The melodic material of this entire movement consists of but *two* motives. Observe the amazing variety of treatment which Haydn has given to one of these motives.

Ex. 6–23. Haydn: Symphony No. 103 in E major, finale.

a. Motive, answered by a variant, four measures later.

b. Four and one-half statements of motive, two measures apart, answered by a swiftly descending contrasting figure; tighter construction than in *a.*

c. Motive answered by totally contrasting figure.

d. Shortened statements of motive piled on quickly; very tight construction.

e. Motive used against itself in learned manner.

Now listen to the entire movement and notice how Haydn uses this motive again and again to propel the music forward. He rarely lingers; the motive constantly gives the music fresh momentum.

Classic Harmony

All that we have described so far in classic music, its styles, its phrase structure and periods, its melodic and motivic material—all the salient and rather easily noticed aspects—would not add up to the classic style itself were it not for the highly characteristic classic treatment of harmony. The classic sense of harmony, particularly the classic sense for key, is a framework that encompasses all classic procedures of composition. Observe, in the simplest period, the neat opposition of half and authentic cadences that projects the key so clearly and sweetly. Observe, in the grand extended periods of large works, how their cadences drive toward the goal which is the confirmation of key.

No other style in the history of music makes as clear and emphatic a point of setting forth the key as does classic music. The entire cycle of a classic form, large or small, involves presenting a key, departing from it, and returning to end the piece with conviction in the home key, as in the plan, I–V; X–I. Thus a sense of key in classic music is very much like the sense of spatial or geographic orientation in the physical world. Home, the tonic key, is the point of departure and arrival. Regardless of the excursions one takes, far or near, long or short, the return to home is made, and there, in the home key, one remains. The difference between classic music and its predecessors in this respect is the dramatic emphasis and the extensive preparations which classic music gives to the various points and areas in this cycle of departure, exploration, and return.

Nothing can demonstrate the importance of a triumphant affirmation of key better than the very end of Beethoven's Fifth Symphony. For many measures we hear nothing but fanfares and flourishes on the tonic chord, C major. Again and again Beethoven drives the impression home, so that, by sheer weight and mass, he will create the harmonic area of arrival he feels is necessary to anchor the entire symphony in the home key. Such gestures you will hear at the ending of almost any movement in the classic repertoire. It is not enough simply to reach the tonic chord; the impression must be deep, lasting, and final.

Intimately associated with this key sense is the periodization we have observed. Periodization provides the light and strong cadences, those points of arrival which are necessary to give clarity and dramatic emphasis to the projection of a key.

With this basic idea of classic structure in mind—the interaction of a

key sense with period structure, framing a rich and varied melodic content
—we can now proceed to describe the larger forms in which classic music
is most fully realized.

Large Forms

Classic symphonies, concertos, quartets, sonatas, and other comparable
works are large-scale, ambitious compositions that require perhaps as much
as twenty-five to thirty minutes or more to perform. They are made up
of three or four movements, each of which stems from a slow or fast type
of movement found in a baroque concerto, sinfonia, sonata, or suite. The
extensiveness of classic form is a reflection, in part, of the circumstances
in which the music was performed. For example, the symphony and concerto were presented to a large public audience, sitting in a large public
concert hall, listening to an orchestra that was larger than those customary
in the private courts of the earlier eighteenth century. Moreover, the
audience was listening to the music itself, not associating it directly with
dance, dramatic action, ceremony, or worship. Nor was the music taken
as casual entertainment; it was intended to absorb the listener entirely.

The individual pieces in the three- or four-movement cycle drew upon
the standard idioms of the time. Following is a brief description of the
typical styles of the movements:

1. The opening movement was serious, broad, brilliant and searching; it
brought all the skills and imagination of the composer into play. Often its basic
pace was that of a march; sometimes it assumed the manner of the eighteenth-
century concerto grosso, or a dance, or the singing-allegro. The first movement
of the *Jupiter* represents the first movement of the eighteenth-century symphony
in the grandest manner.

2. The slow movement appealed to lyric sentiments. Here composers sought
for broadly singing, well-rounded, winning melodies. The style was generally
that of a song or aria, but occasionally it was a slow dance or march, as in the
slow movement of Haydn's *Drumroll* Symphony. These movements gained
breadth by their slow pace rather than by extensive and searching development.

3. In four-movement cycles, one of the middle movements was generally a
dance, a minuet or scherzo. Mozart and Haydn preferred the minuet, but
Beethoven quickened the pace to establish the scherzo as the dance movement.
We observe, in spite of the dance style and form, much play with motives and
part-writing, many surprises, contrasts, and unexpected turns of phrase in most
of the minuets and scherzos of classic music.

4. The last movement often matched the first in brilliance and treatment.
This is particularly true of the *Jupiter* Symphony. Many times the last movement

achieved a pitch of excitement toward the very end unequaled by anything previously heard in the entire work. This, of course, was intended as a fitting climax and wind-up to the whole composition, as at the end of Beethoven's Fifth Symphony. Frequently, the last movement was a quick dance, often in hunt style.

In compositions intended for entertainment purposes primarily, such as serenades, divertimenti, and cassations, there was likely to be a greater number of movements. These would be additional minuets, dances, or slow movements. The order of movements given above represents the usual plan; nevertheless, the arrangement is by no means fixed and many pieces show a different order. In all cases, slow movements were placed so as to provide a strategic contrast in style and pace with neighboring quick movements. Moreover, a work might begin with a slow movement, but it would rarely end in such a manner.

Sonata Form

A movement from such works as Beethoven's Third, Fifth, or Seventh Symphonies or Mozart's *Jupiter* Symphony is a complex structure; its musical path traverses many kinds of terrain and the distance covered is great. There is a tremendous difference between the simple, small, and crystal-clear structure of the two-part dance forms of the eighteenth century and the imposing masterpieces which represent the culmination of classic musical art. Yet despite the vast gulf which separates the dance from the symphony, structurally there is a family resemblance between the two. We can use this resemblance to help us get a clear picture of large-scale classic form. To use an analogy: in architecture the motive of the rectangle may be taken as a basic principle of structure. We recognize the function and position of the rectangle when we see it, whether it be realized in a skyscraper or a small house. Similarly, there are certain points of reference which classic structure uses very consistently, both in large- and small-scale forms. No matter what the scope of the form may be, these points of structural reference react upon each other in much the same way.

By reason of usage developed in the nineteenth century, the large-scale classic form we are going to describe has acquired the name, *sonata form*. We shall use this term, since it is a very convenient designation. Still, we must remember that eighteenth-century musicians no more conceived of this term than did Schütz and Lully think of themselves as baroque composers.

Returning to our two-part form, especially that represented by the Haydn, Example 6–15, we can picture it as a bridge, in a harmonic sense.

Terra firma is represented on both sides, or at the beginning and end, by the solid sense of the home key. There are two spans to this bridge, anchored in the middle by a strong cadence in the dominant key. The illustration below gives this scheme graphically:

Ex. 6–24.

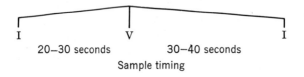

I   V   I

20–30 seconds   30–40 seconds

Sample timing

In point of time, this is a small structure, taking less than a minute to traverse its harmonic ground. Now, imagine this same structural plan to be extended, to cover an enormous area. The pillars would have to be anchored much more strongly; the spans would have to be strengthened and perhaps supported by subsidiary pillars. Perhaps also the bridge itself would have to be reached and left by approaches. Yet the basic plan can very well be unchanged, regardless of size, as illustrated in Example 6–25.

Ex. 6–25.

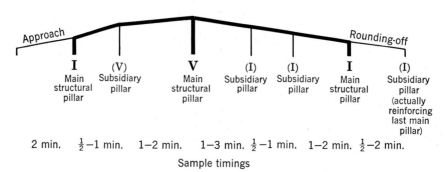

Approach   Rounding-off

I   (V)   V   (I)   (I)   I   (I)
Main   Subsidiary Main   Subsidiary Subsidiary Main   Subsidiary
structural pillar   structural pillar   pillar   structural pillar
pillar   pillar   pillar   (actually
                                                            reinforcing
                                                            last main
                                                            pillar)

2 min. $\frac{1}{2}$–1 min.   1–2 min.   1–3 min. $\frac{1}{2}$–1 min.   1–2 min. $\frac{1}{2}$–2 min.

Sample timings

On the large scale that the sonata form represents, it is not easy for the listener to hear the harmonic progress of the form, particularly during the first time or two that he gives attention to it. He is attracted principally by the more apparent qualities, the themes, the contrasts, the textures, the dramatic gestures. Still, underneath these surface manifestations, he may sense, without realizing it, the broad and purposeful onward flow of the music toward its grand points of harmonic arrival. At critical moments these harmonic objectives assert themselves in unmistakable terms; these correspond to the pillars of our bridge. Such points can be recognized by the emphatic cadential gestures which anchor the form at spaced intervals.

Listen to the final movement of Mozart's *Prague* Symphony. You should have little trouble in locating two extremely important points of arrival, one shortly before the movement has run half its length, and the other at the very end of the movement. Try this also: compare the two cadences by putting the phonograph needle down on the record just before each passage. The two cadences use the same melodic material, yet you should hear easily that the first is in the dominant key and the second in the tonic. This corresponds perfectly to the I–V; V–I plan described in Chapter 2, section on harmony.

It should also be apparent that strong cadences and the harmonic stability they embody can be anticipated for a long time; during the course of this expectation the composer can introduce many striking, interesting, ingratiating, or impressive musical details. Relying on the *unity* and strength which his harmonic objectives provide, he can achieve an amazingly rich local *variety* of expressive content. The two processes work hand in hand. *Broad scope invites richness of content; richness of content gives fresh momentum and energy toward the mounting of a broad-scale phase of movement.*

As you listen to a sonata form, you will notice one or more salient themes. For both the listener and the composer themes are landmarks; they help us to get our bearings within the form; they act as areas of arrival and departure. As we studied the small two-part form earlier in this chapter, we noticed how the theme, stated at the beginning of the piece and in the home key, returned later to signal the reestablishment of the tonic, or home key. It is the same with the sonata form.

At the beginning of the form, when the home key is presented, we hear what is generally the most important theme of the entire movement. This is the theme which the composer associates with the tonic key. Therefore, at the moment of recapitulation, when the home key returns, it is almost invariably signaled by the opening theme. When the music moves to the contrasting key of the exposition, it, too, will be announced in many cases by a distinctive thematic statement. We shall also hear this in the recapitulation, *but in the tonic key.* A very clear example of the association of themes with keys is the first movement of Mozart's Quintet in E♭ major. There are two salient themes, one in hunt style, and the other in a singing-allegro manner. The first announces the tonic key, the second introduces the dominant.

Composers differ in the treatment of thematic material in their music. Haydn is well known for using a variant of the opening theme to begin the second key area. Mozart and Beethoven have tended to use several distinctive themes in each key area. Mozart's use of many themes came from the Italian influence in his music, characterized by the appeal of ingratiating melodic materials. Mozart was also fond of striking contrasts in texture; there was no better way to highlight such contrasts than to introduce them with new themes. Often when Beethoven introduced new themes other than at the beginning of key areas, it was to establish additional areas of departure and arrival for his more extended forms. A thematic statement is like a station that acts as a point of rest in a long journey. We shall see how this comes about when we discuss the first movement of his *Eroica* Symphony.

It is possible that you may have heard somewhere about the *first* and *second themes* of sonata form. Most descriptions of this form proceed, from the very first, to characterize a bold or *masculine* first theme and a lyric or *feminine* second theme. This thematic contrast is supposed to establish the fundamental structure of sonata form. However, in classic music this is not always clear to the listener. We can see sharp local contrasts; we can hear many more than two salient themes in some forms; and we also note that Haydn will frequently use the same theme for both key areas. All this would make it difficult, indeed impossible, to apply the thematic contrast idea generally to classic sonata form. The principal themes become sharply differentiated in style as a basic rule only in sonata forms of the romantic period.

In order to come to terms with the conventional idea of sonata form proposed in most textbooks, the following plan is given:

HARMONIC PLAN		CONVENTIONAL DESIGNATION OF SECTIONS		
Part	*Home key area*	A.	*Exposition*	Main theme
I	Contrasting key area			Subsidiary theme
Part	Harmonic explorations	B.	*Development*	Themes worked over
II	*Home key area*	A.	*Recapitulation*	Themes restated

You will notice that the same discrepancy between harmonic plan and thematic order that we discovered in the small two-part form is present in the sonata form. If we turn our attention to the themes, we make out a three-part form. If we recognize the organizing power of the harmony, the two-part form appears to be basic. The two-part versus three-part controversy concerning sonata form is still alive today. Here we shall recognize its two-part origin and harmonic layout, and at the same time acknowledge that it was becoming a hybrid form as its thematic relationships became stereotyped.

When we listen to a sonata form movement, our concern with themes should be to appreciate the skill and imagination with which the composer has introduced and used them. Are there many or few? How are they introduced, restated, worked over, and in what manner? Frequently the number of themes has much to do with the character of a piece. One salient theme developed extensively gives the impression of compact structure and driving momentum; many themes in a movement convey a broad and luxuriant quality to the listener. The presentation of an appealing theme is essential to the balance of the form and a grateful contrast to the tensions of development and cadential drive. We rest awhile and enjoy the melody before resuming the business of moving ahead. In the themes of sonata form we have the manifestation of the popular eighteenth-century manner which established so strong a contact with the listener.

With the foregoing in mind, let us have a look at some movements in sonata form. Take, for instance, the Mozart *Jupiter* Symphony, first movement.

Exposition. Contrast of two large key areas. We have already described the extended period which comprises the *first key area* of this piece. (See Example 2–6.) This key area is marked off by a grand pause in the full orchestra. When the opening theme starts again, gently, and with a delicate contrapuntal texture, Mozart has begun his journey to the second key. He takes his time about arriving, making a few excursions along the way. Another full stop after a great deal of flourish prepares for the *second key area,* introduced by a graceful theme in singing-allegro style.

Ex. 6–26.

Mozart does not linger long; suddenly the Storm and Stress breaks in, driving the music forward. This excitement builds, maintains a high level for a while, then rather quickly trails off. After another complete stop, a sprightly little dance tune, a grateful contrast to the foregoing struggle, settles the quality of movement and the harmony into an area of arrival. A few measures of flourish, recalling motives heard earlier, drive home the impression of arrival. We have made our way as far as we shall go into the dominant key. Here we pause before turning back.

Development. Movement away from second key, harmonic exploration, and return to home key. When the sonata form reaches the final cadence in the second key, it has come to a critical point. From this moment on the ultimate harmonic objective will be to make a way back to the home key and to complete the form by means of an extended section in the home key. This will prove that, after all, the tonic key is the most important element in the harmonic scheme. The first stage in this return is to undermine the feeling of assertion which the second key gave at the end of the exposition. There are countless ways of doing this; each sonata form seems to take another road. This is one of the points where the resourcefulness and imagination of the composer is tested. As a rule, the section called the *development* goes far afield harmonically, creating a great deal of instability; toward the end the harmony settles so that a cadence to the home key is first promised, then accomplished.

In the later classic era, composers found the development to be a great challenge. They worked their thematic materials over intensively, guided the harmony at bold tangents, introduced sharp contrasts, often in a most unexpected way. The development was becoming the most exciting part of the form.

Mozart, in our example, throws the listener off balance immediately. Starting on the tone which ended the exposition, he engages in a bit of harmonic prestidigitation, which lands us, in four tones, in a faraway key. Blithely, then, the little dance tune takes up again as if all were calm and placid. This cheerful latecomer is destined for great things, however. Hardly has it come to a cadence when it breaks apart and begins to struggle with itself in a tight contrapuntal duel that goes on for many measures. When matters are finally settled, we find ourselves arriving at the opening theme. But still we are not home. *It is not the right key!* After a momentary rest, we resume our harmonic wanderings, while the opening motive is being whipped around mercilessly. Finally, there comes a sense of leveling off. We are being made ready to hear the advent of the home key, and with a grand gesture, it arrives.

Recapitulation. Reestablishment of home key. Officially, the recapitulation stays firmly in the home key and reviews the thematic material given in the exposition, and in the original order. The thematic material first heard in the second key area now appears in the home key. The hegemony of the tonic key is acknowledged by this harmonic adjustment. We might think of the sonata form in this connection as being one immense musical rhyme, in which a specific sound at the end of a line is given a different meaning at the end of a subsequent line, as follows:

MEANING		SOUND		
tonic	A	thematic material		
dominant	B	"	"	⎫
X				⎬ rhyme
tonic	A	"	"	⎪
tonic	B	"	"	⎭

As a matter of fact, such musical rhymes frequently occur in small two-part forms, where the cadence to Part I is repeated at the end of Part II.

As you come to know a particular movement in sonata form, look for local changes in the way the material of the recapitulation is handled as compared to the exposition. To the alert eighteenth-century listener, such changes represented freshness, cleverness, and imagination. One such change is the shift into minor after the first period of the recapitulation in the first movement of the *Jupiter*.

Coda. Cadential area for entire movement. In many sonata form movements, the composer has felt that the cadences which end the exposition are not broad and emphatic enough to bring the entire movement to a proper conclusion. He then joins on a section which is primarily devoted to this purpose, but which may concern itself with other matters before it discharges its cadential commission. In the first movement of the *Jupiter* Symphony, Mozart added just four measures of fanfare. In the finale he engaged the music in a tremendous contrapuntal development before winding up with brilliant cadential formulas. Sections which are so added to the end of a form are called *codas,* meaning "tailpieces."

The thematic content in a coda is taken from material previously heard in the movement. In some codas, before the composer settles down to make his cadences, he will engage in some harmonic exploration and development.

Each movement in sonata form represents a distinctly individual way of working within the general harmonic and stylistic framework. For example, the exposition in the first movement of Haydn's *Drumroll* Symphony is quite short and deals mostly with the motives from the opening theme. There is no break in movement until the very end of the exposition, when, in refreshing contrast, we hear a bouncing waltz tune. The development, on the other hand, is extensive and searching, working over all the material heard in the exposition. There is also a coda in this movement, prepared for by a sudden harmonic digression, an interruption in pace, and a reference to the motive heard in the slow introduction.

In the first movement of Mozart's Quintet in E♭ major, there is constant alternation between two contrasting elements, the hunt music and a brilliant soloistic style. With dramatic surprise the development introduces a completely new theme, in a new mood, the Storm and Stress. Listening carefully, you will hear that neither the exposition nor the recapitulation end with a full sense of arrival. At the very last moment, in each section, an element of harmonic instability is introduced. In the case of the exposition, this leads directly into the development. In the case of the recapitulation, it makes way for a brilliant, expansive coda full of excitement, with the instruments moving at striking tangents to each other.

As sonata form evolved in the classic era, it was adapted to many types of expression. Quick movements, slow movements, brilliant, gay, reflective, lyric qualities: all found the sonata form a proper vehicle of structure. One element of the form became increasingly important during the late eighteenth century. This was the dramatic contrast inherent in the opposition of two key areas, and to a great extent, of two groups of themes. Such contrasts and their reconciliation when the tonic key returns to establish its harmonic rulership for the remainder of the movement lend themselves to operatic exploitation. Mozart has given us some felicitous examples of sonata form in certain arias and ensemble numbers; and of these, none is more apt than the duet which concludes the opening scene of *Don Giovanni*. The lovers, Don Ottavio and Donna Anna are singing; Anna's father has just been killed in a duel with Don Giovanni. The harmonic and dramatic form parallel each other as follows:

HARMONIC FORM	DRAMATIC FORM
Part I First key area, minor key.	Anna sings; rejects Ottavio in her despair.
Second key area, related major key.	Ottavio offers consolation; contrast to opening mood.
Part II Shifting harmonies.	Both swear revenge; emphasis and accent of accompanied recitative.
Return to home key.	Firm resolution for revenge; Anna's key and the mood of her opening music overcome the contrast of Ottavio's mood and key of consolation.

Special gestures within this form highlight the dramatic situation and help to clarify the underlying structure. The exposition has ended with a somewhat more relaxed quality of movement than we heard at the beginning. Suddenly the music stops short, underlining the change of mood and dramatic meaning. The incisive strokes of the recitative section tell us that a grim purpose has been formed. The restatement of the recitative drives the sense of purpose further home and the duet moves steadily to its end from that point on with an accumulation of momentum, shaping a broad area of arrival for the entire form. The regular, unbroken movement of the final section is proper to the sense of high resolve that finally unites the lovers after their despair. There is hardly a more perfect example of the dramatic possibilities of sonata form than this duet, yet, strangely enough, in spite of its melodic elegance and richness, there is not one theme by which the listener can find his way through the form. Mozart does not develop or recapitulate the thematic material of the exposition!

During the later eighteenth century, the harmonic plan I–V, X–I, which is embodied in both the small two-part form and the sonata form, controlled a great deal of classic music. We have already seen how broadly it can be projected in sonata form. But much as they had done, eighteenth-century composers had not explored the full possibilities of sonata form. It remained for Ludwig van Beethoven, representing the second generation of classic composers, to achieve what is to this day the ultimate stage in grandeur and monumental scope as far as the sonata form is concerned. In certain movements in his music, the expansion of the form and its concomitant inner strengthening seem to have reached the maximum degree possible. It is his power to scale his forms so broadly that has ranked Beethoven along with those other titans of the creative arts, Shakespeare and Michelangelo.

Of all the single movements in Beethoven's music, perhaps the most impressive from a structural point of view, and certainly one of the most significant in its impact on the future history of music, is the movement we have already come to know quite well, the first movement of the Third Symphony. In sheer length it is virtually double any sonata form heretofore composed. (This fact impressed later composers.) But this, of course, means very little unless we understand some of the circumstances surrounding this great length.

How is this gigantic form justified? The answer to such a question remains essentially a mystery, nevertheless we may point out some clues. In Chapter 2 we have looked at some of the special qualities of this piece.

Principal among these was the immensely vital and vigorous quality of movement, especially intense when syncopations pile up at strategic moments. (See p. 36.) As compensation to this purposeful, broad-scaled quality of movement, important points and areas of arrival are reached with great dramatic emphasis. In every measure of this work there is furious activity, an electric quality of action. We might draw an analogy with physics; the microscopic collision of musical particles sets free a tremendous outburst of energy which must necessarily give rise to an extended form. Moreover, in this movement, much of the expansion takes place at points that the eighteenth-century sonata form was content to pass over rather quickly—in the development section, and at the cadential area of the entire movement that completes the recapitulation. Both the development and the coda of this movement are extremely long. In order to support and give point to this length, Beethoven established new piers to his structural bridge, new areas of arrival within the form. The diagram below illustrates what happens:

Ex. 6–27. Diagram of Beethoven: Symphony No. 3, first movement.

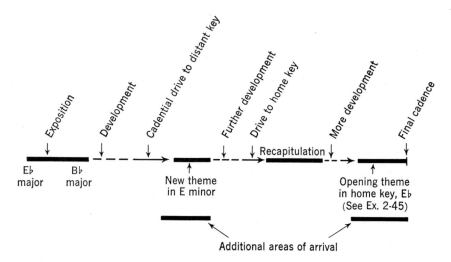

In the development section, a new theme is presented in E minor, a key far removed from the home key, E♭ major. This section represents a kind of apex, the point of farthest exploration, or of greatest distance from home. From here onward, the harmonic objective is the return to the home key, a return which takes considerable time to accomplish. It is this development section, of such length and dramatic power, that has been responsible for the concept that the development is the crucial area of sonata form, that it is a psychological climax.

A counterweight to the section just described, and an additional strong point of arrival in the form, appears at the final return to the home key in the coda of this movement. At this point the opening theme, for the *first* time in the movement, appears in a normal balanced arrangement, its phrases alternating in simple fashion between tonic and dominant harmonies. Here the theme is allowed to project its original quality, that of a straightforward melody. This is the area of arrival for the entire movement. Here we find the classic viewpoint made clear. The form must be rounded off; it must finish properly; all instability must be set to rights; full compensation must be made. It is remarkable that in a movement of such grandiose conception and realization, the music returns to its origins, to the straightforward, sturdy values of a popular art.

Historically Ludwig van Beethoven stood with Haydn and Mozart as one of the three great masters of the classic style. His sense of form shows him to be a classicist. In most of his works we find the basic premises of balance-imbalance adjustment worked out in proportions that conform to classic use. Yet the expressive content of his music represents such an intensification over that of Haydn and Mozart that a greater momentum was developed, a more violent surge forward created. Since classic premises governed his forms, this more intense content naturally caused an expansion in dimensions. This was one of the most significant aspects of Beethoven's classicism: his forms became very broad.

Yet Beethoven had a strong kinship with the age that followed, the romantic period of the nineteenth century. Romantic composers were strongly influenced by Beethoven in many respects. For example, the thematic concept of romantic sonata form is already realized in the first movement of Beethoven's Sonata for Piano in F minor, Op. 57, the *Appassionata*. There are three distinctly different episodes that constitute the exposition, each with its salient theme and each in a different key. This is quite different from the integrated exposition of the typical classic sonata with its drive from the tonic to the structural cadence in the contrasting key. In addition to its form, the first movement of the *Appassionata* Sonata contains a number of striking effects, each of which shows a romantic flavor:

1. Extreme contrasts in range
2. Extreme contrasts in dynamics
3. Constant use of Storm and Stress values

4. Brilliant virtuoso passages

5. Sudden, unexpected changes in pace

Other qualities that attracted and influenced romantic composers were:

1. Striking orchestral effects, as in the *Pastoral* Symphony, and in the *Leonore* Overtures, Nos. 2 and 3

2. Recitative passages for instruments, as in the first movement of the Sonata in D minor for Piano, Op. 31, no. 2, and in the last string quartets

3. Passages of great harmonic instability, as at the beginning of the String Quartet in C, Op. 59, no. 3

4. The idea of the hero, so dramatically presented in the *Eroica* Symphony.

Beethoven inherited Mozart's sense for the dramatic and contrasting relationship; he also learned a tightness of development and motivic interplay from Haydn. He lacked Mozart's spontaneous lyricism; therefore, he did little in the field of opera. He lacked Haydn's spontaneous sense for the play of phrase and effect; therefore, he had to wrestle mightily with stubborn materials. Rarely does a Beethoven phrase or period wind its way comfortably to its end. His imbalances were the grim crises of the romantic age to come, not the inflections and nuances of the eighteenth century. Still, the explosion had not yet come; the centrifugal forces contained in Beethoven's music are controlled by a sense of musical balance, of *gravitation to a long-range point of arrival.*

The sonata form was a kind of synthesis, a summing up of all the different techniques, idioms, and styles of the eighteenth century. It used harmonic logic, period structure, and thematic clarity from the song and dance styles; it took richness and variety of manner from the Storm and Stress, the soloistic, and the Sensibility styles. It developed its exciting and lively handling of voices from the learned style; it acquired both a singing manner and the idea of dramatic contrast from the Italian opera. Most important, music written in the sonata form was intended primarily to be listened to, not to accompany singing or dancing. It was concert music, and therefore, could make a strong challenge to the listener, to say nothing of the composer himself. Its principal distinction was its breadth of dimension, which came about from the interplay of strong propulsive forces and compensating emphatic points of arrival. The most imposing sonata forms were those found in music intended for literate and appreciative audiences, audiences which learned to enjoy the combination of galant and learned styles. Such listeners frequented the concert halls of Paris, London, Vienna, and Prague in the late eighteenth and early nineteenth centuries. Mozart's piano concertos, Haydn's *London* Symphonies, and Beethoven's orchestral and chamber music represent the zenith in the evolution of sonata form.

Rondo Forms

From the grandeur of the sonata form, we shall return for a while to entertainment music of the eighteenth century as we become acquainted with rondo forms. Listen to the entire finale of Haydn's D-major Sonata, of which we have already heard the opening two-part section. Try to determine its layout. Certainly its most prominent structural feature is the main section, the tune which returns a number of times. This periodic return identifies the piece as a *rondo*.

Rondo forms rank second in importance in classic music, the sonata form, of course, ranking first. The principal idea of the rondo was to entertain, to please the listener without particularly exciting him or taxing his intellectual powers. Therefore the rondo presented a group of attractive song or dance tunes. One of these tunes, generally the first, was the most important, and was heard interspersed between the others. The rondo comes *around* to its *refrain,* or main tune, again and again; thus it acquired its name. The intervening tunes are called *episodes.* Rondos differ in form according to the distribution of refrains and episodes. Here are some examples:

A B A C A	Haydn: D-major Sonata, finale
	Mozart: C-major Sonata, K. 545, finale
	Mozart: C-minor Piano Concerto, K. 491, slow movement
A B A C A B A	Mozart: D-major Sonata, K. 311, finale
	Haydn: D-major Quartet, Op. 64, no. 5, finale
A B A C B A	Mozart: C-major Sonata, K. 309, finale
	Haydn: B♭-major Symphony, No. 102, finale
A B A C A D A B A	Mozart: B♭-major Sonata, K. 281, finale
A B C A D C A B	Mozart: G-minor Quintet, K. 516, finale

In earlier eighteenth-century music, rondo forms were used to frame dances and songs. They had, therefore, the following characteristics: (1) normal period structure; (2) strong melodic appeal throughout; (3) steady, even movement; (4) a minimum of harmonic instability and exploration within a given section. The finale of Haydn's D-major Sonata exemplifies this type of rondo.

In the simple rondo forms, where each section is a complete little two-part form, we do not receive the impression that a long-range problem is working its way to an important solution. We are concerned here with local excursions, each of which starts out from home. The form can grow simply by adding on excursions, as the diagram shows:

Ex. 6–28. Diagram of rondo forms.

A	B	A	C	A	(B or D)	A	
Refrain	Episode	Refrain	Episode	Refrain	Episode	Refrain	etc.

Conceivably the piece could end after any refrain except the first; on the other hand, new episodes and additional refrains could be added very easily.

As an example of how the rondo fared at the hands of the Viennese masters, let us have a look at the second movement of Mozart's E♭ Quintet.

We hear first a graceful, beautifully poised theme, set out in normal periods as a small two-part form. Mozart does not let us forget this tune. As a matter of fact, it is the only melody in the entire movement; but changes in key, structure, and mood provide the contrast necessary for the episodes of a rondo.

The most remarkable feature of the movement is the way in which Mozart handled the texture. By this time in his life (1791), he was the transcendental master of part-writing, of elaboration, of the precious detail. In every moment of this piece some new delight of ornamentation, give-and-take, filigree work, or texture appears. It is like a closely woven tapestry, a masterpiece of decorative art.

Later eighteenth-century rondos, those that served as final movements of sonatas, symphonies, or concertos, show the same kind of internal expansion that we have seen in the sonata form. Moreover, they approach the style and manner of the sonata, exhibiting the following characteristics:

1. Extended periods, except when themes are being presented
2. Much development of motivic material
3. Broad-scale phases of movement, frequently with contrasts of strong dramatic impact
4. Extended harmonic digressions and broad cadential drives

Probably the most remarkable example of the later rondo is the finale of Haydn's Symphony No. 103 in E♭ major. The entire motivic material of this movement is presented in the first eight measures. Two motives, a hunting fanfare and a lilting dance tune are set against each other contrapuntally. How typically classic this is: to set galant themes against each other in the learned manner!

Ex. 6–29. Haydn: Symphony No. 103 in E♭ major, finale.

Hardly a note in the entire movement is not related to these two figures. (See Example 6–23.)

The form of this movement is delineated by key relationships in the following manner:

Section	A	B	A	C	A	B	Coda
Key	I	V	I	'X'	I	I	I
Measure	1	91	158	182	264	300	351

It is apparent that this movement approaches the sonata form very closely. Movement and interest are maintained by an incredibly imaginative treatment of harmonies, part-writing, contrast, and motive relationships. Not only in the opening subject but throughout the entire form, this piece represents a complete interpenetration of the dance style with the learned and serious techniques of later classic music. Visualize the situation when this rondo was first performed. The listener was familiar with rondo forms and with the usual procedures of late eighteenth-century music. From the very beginning, every figure, every turn involved a surprise. Yet not one bit of logic was sacrificed; the thread of the musical discourse remained clear. The effect must have been electrifying. No wonder Haydn was cheered when his music was performed in London, for all of it had the same lively, attractive, fanciful, and at the same time, profoundly logical quality.

Variation Form

The variation form, another legacy from an earlier age, consists of a two-period dance or song-type subject which forms the basis for a number of small pieces or variations. Each variation retains the general rhythmic and harmonic layout, particularly with reference to phases of movement and points of arrival. Style, texture, melodic configuration, incidental harmonic effects are changed but often retain some similarity to the original pattern. Often a variation in the middle part of the piece changes the mode from major to minor or vice versa. This contrast gives the piece a broader outline. The subject of the variation may be original with the composer, or he may have taken it from some other source. The appeal of the variation form is the resourcefulness with which the composer elaborates and alters the details of his model without changing the essential structure. Each variation presents a new light upon an old subject.

Variation form has been used for opening movements, as in Beethoven's Sonata in A♭ major, Op. 26, and Mozart's A-major Sonata, K. 331. Haydn's Symphony No. 103 in E♭ major has a slow movement in variation form, as has Beethoven's Quartet in A major, Op. 18, no. 5. The finale of Mozart's D-major Sonata, K. 284, is also in variation form.

Beethoven employed the technique of variation extensively, developing ever more searching and imaginative ways of treating his original theme. One of his greatest works, and a monument in the history of the variation is his *33 Variations on a Waltz of Diabelli,* a work of the last years of his life. Diabelli's tune has all the common features of a popular two-part dance form: symmetrical construction, a simple tune built on the notes of tonic and dominant chords, a stock harmonic digression to the dominant and then back. There is also a sequence in the tune itself. Beethoven enriches each of these formulas in incredibly imaginative and subtle ways, intensifying every gesture, creating in each variation a new composition, and yet retaining the skeletal structure of the model.

Another remarkable work of Beethoven that uses variation procedures is the finale of his *Eroica* Symphony. Here he has taken a tune and its bass:

Ex. 6–30. Beethoven: *Eroica* Symphony, finale.

This happens to be a contredanse which Beethoven had used before as melodic material in several compositions. In this movement we can see that it was a favorite of his. He treats each of these, tune and bass, in many different ways. We hear after the opening rush of the orchestra:

Home key
{
1. Decorative variations on the bass
2. The melody with ornamental garlands
}

Other keys
{
3. A fugal passage on the bass subject
4. A dance, using the melody
5. A march, using the bass
6. A songlike variation, using the melody
}

Home key
{
7. A fugal passage, on the bass, with the melody chiming in
8. A slow aria, using the melody
9. A grand chorale, using the melody
}

At this point Beethoven abandons the variation procedure. He is making a coda; thus, we hear some free harmonic exploration preparing the final exultant cadential section. The movement winds up with fanfares and rushing passages, picking up the exciting figure that began the movement with a challenge.

As you can see, Beethoven was not content merely to put together a set of interesting elaborations upon his subject. Instead, he gave the form a broad over-all structure by: (1) large key areas: tonic—shifting keys— tonic; (2) an integrated phrase structure, in which cadences were often not clear-cut. Thus two neighboring variations would be linked without a break. As with so much of Beethoven's music, the impression is one of broad gestures, violent drives, and grand ideas; the whole piece is "written large."

Variation procedure is often applied to pieces in other forms so that when a distinctive theme returns, it is altered in its texture or melodic details. The diverting effect of a new dress adds interest at such points. Variation then becomes a resource for heightening the interest of a counter-statement, which would ordinarily be a simple repetition. Example 6–31 from the slow movement of Mozart's Quartet in C major, K. 465, illustrates such elaboration. The first excerpt is from the exposition; the second from the recapitulation.

Ex. 6–31. Mozart: Quartet in C major, K. 465

a. Exposition.

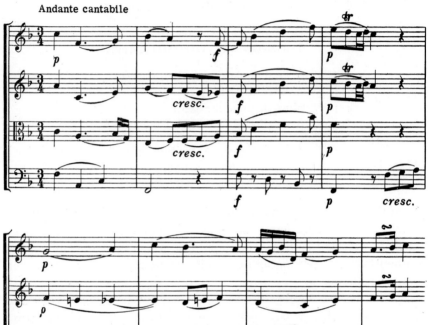

This is a simple theme, in relatively long-note values.

b. Recapitulation.

original theme

The long notes of the theme are divided into shorter ornamental notes, giving a rather decorative quality to the restatement.

Three-part Forms

Since the melodic material of slow movement is lyric rather than energetic, the forms of such movements sometimes involve no more than several
broadly singing, well-rounded melodies. In the simplest versions there is a
principal melody, a contrasting melody in a different key, and a return to
the first melody. A three-part form is created, as in the slow movement of
Haydn's Trio in G major. The outline of the movement is given below:

A (E major)	B (A major)	transition	A (E major)
1–16	17–36	37–44	45–69

In more highly organized three-part forms, some of the harmonic and
periodic techniques of sonata form are used. In the slow movement of
Beethoven's Piano Sonata in Eb major, Op. 7, extensions, harmonic explorations, and broad cadences give the movement a very impressive air.

The designation, *three-part form,* is also applied to dance-type movements in which two dances are performed in succession, and then the first
is repeated. The most familiar example of this form is the minuet-and-trio.

The Introduction

The first movement of a symphony, sonata, or quartet sometimes has an
introduction in slow tempo. This is derived from the opening section of
the French overture, which was described above, p. 146. In the introduction
of Mozart's Symphony in Eb major, K. 543, the typical dotted rhythm of
the French overture is used. In other introductions, the slow tempo was
retained, but a more singing style, as in Italian opera, was substituted, as
in the introduction of Haydn's Symphony in Bb major, No. 102. In either
case, French or Italian style, much of the introduction was dedicated to a
cadential preparation for the beginning of the main part of the movement.
The introduction of Mozart's *Prague* Symphony, K. 504, is by far the most
impressive section of its kind in all eighteenth-century music. Here is a brief
description:

The piece opens with the three *coups d'archet* so frequently found in eighteenth-
century music. The quality of movement is broad, impressive. Striking contrasts
pile up in a very short time; *texturally* by tutti-solo contrasts; *rhythmically,* by
changing patterns; *stylistically,* by fragments of *Empfindsamkeit* and the singing
style; *harmonically,* by exploration. Three times we move toward a cadence;
three times the resolution is held off by deceptive cadences. The third time there
is a cadence to the minor (not the major, as expected). Such a change is a far-

reaching shift of tonal center; key regions remote from the home key are now being explored. The exploration becomes systematic, the phrase structure balanced. The whims, the surprises of the first part are answered here by a purposeful drive which gradually focuses on the dominant of the home key. The resolution to the tonic major, the home key, comes only when the quick part begins. This introduction takes thirty-six measures of very slow four-four time and lasts about four minutes. The quick part of the first movement is a worthy counterstatement to the introduction which it matches with its brilliance, verve, and its great skill in handling a rich variety of materials.

The Concerto

The classic concerto, along with the symphony, represented the most impressive type of instrumental music in the late eighteenth century. Carrying on the tradition of baroque music, the solo or concertino element might be drawn from the orchestra itself. Concertos were written for clarinet, flute, horn, bassoon, cello, and harp. But as classic music expanded its techniques and intensified its expressive qualities, the more brilliant, the more impressive instruments, the violin, and particularly, the piano, became the leading solo instruments in the classic concerto.

The late piano concertos of Mozart, those he wrote for performance by himself in Vienna, give a panorama of concerto composition that has had implications for concerto procedure over a period of almost two hundred years. In these works, we have (1) the lively give-and-take that characterizes the baroque concerto grosso; we also have (2) the dramatic opposition of forces that distinguishes classic musical expression; further, in Mozart's piano concertos, we meet (3) the brilliant virtuoso soloist, the immediate ancestor of the romantic hero-musician of the nineteenth century.

Structurally the concerto is laid out like other works of big scope. Generally there are three movements. The first is a quick piece in sonata form, modified to include an orchestral tutti in the tonic key at the opening before the actual sonata form begins to unfold. The orchestral tutti replaces the repeat of the exposition in other sonata form movements, although the tutti and the repeated exposition do *not* come from the same source. Classic music, in the first movement of the concerto, combined the baroque concerto-grosso layout with the sonata form key scheme: it thereby created a synthesis, much as it did in other areas of style and structure. The middle movement is a slow piece. The finale is again quick, and usually has a frankly dancelike quality.

Of all Mozart's piano concertos, perhaps the most unique of all is the

C-minor Concerto, K. 491. From the very first tones, we can perceive immediately that this work will not move in any standard eighteenth-century groove. Instead of a flourish, a fanfare, *coup d'archet,* or even perhaps a singing melody—gestures which might be expected to begin a concerto—we hear a disembodied, winding, chromatic, and harmonically ambiguous line, a motive that suggests doubt and emotional unrest.

Ex. 6–32. Mozart: Piano Concerto in C minor, K. 491, first movement.

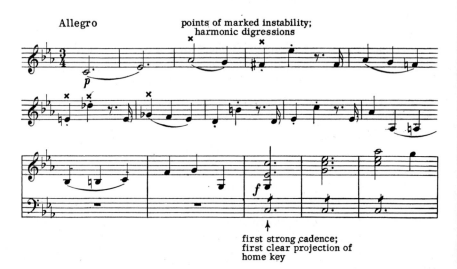

Such imbalance at the very beginning certainly betokens a series of crises that will force the movement to be worked out on a broad scale, structurally, expressively, and texturally. We are not disappointed in this expectation. Throughout the first movement we find a tremendous wealth of melodic material, a breadth of periodic structure, and a fantastic variety of textures. Here is no solo display discreetly supported by accompaniment figures in the orchestra. Listen to the bold manner in which Mozart uses the wood winds, setting their airy, fluid tones against the percussive, crisp quality of the solo piano. Listen for the various roles the piano plays in this piece, solo, ornamental, contrapuntal, and even accompaniment. Only the piano, among all solo instruments, can match the orchestra in range, fullness of sound, power, and complexity of action. Like Beethoven in his *Eroica* Symphony, Mozart has searched deeply and ranged widely in this concerto, which is, in a sense, his own *Eroica.*

The Fantasia

Classic forms are based upon clear-cut period structure. The fantasia is a different kind of piece. It appeals to the sense of the improvisatory; the element of surprise is cultivated; the music seems to wander freely without balance of phrase or well-defined cadences. The figures in a fantasia are brilliant; the harmony is boldly exploratory. Now and then, a period or two of more balanced quality appears by way of contrast. The Sensibility, the Storm and Stress, and the soloistic styles are favored in this kind of piece. Since it changes pace and manner quickly, the fantasia is best suited to keyboard performance. The impulsive moods of the fantasia foreshadow similar pieces for the keyboard written by Schubert, Chopin, and Schumann in the romantic era. Mozart's Fantasia in C minor, K. 475, is probably the most celebrated example of this kind of piece. It is organized as follows:

1. Exploratory section, many deceptive cadences—1–25
2. Stable section, singing theme—26–41
3. Exploratory section, brilliant virtuoso style—42–90
4. Stable section, new singing theme—91–129
5. Exploratory section, brilliant virtuoso style—130–155
6. *Stable section,* area of arrival using material of Part 1, and in C minor—156–172

Each section, except Part 6, uses new material. Harmonically and thematically Mozart rounded the form of this piece by Part 6.

Summary of Classic Forms

In the preceding survey of classic forms, we have seen that they represented ways of using harmony and the period forms of late eighteenth-century music. There were two general methods of building forms: (1) in *sectional arrangement,* as in dances, small two- and three-part forms, and simpler rondos; (2) in *integrated arrangement,* as in the sonata form and the concerto.

In the *sectional arrangement,* we had normal period structure; the forms grew by addition and repetition of sections. There was a straightforward rhythmic and melodic appeal in such movements. *Integrated arrangement* involved internal expansion and a more closely knit connection between succeeding periods. The forms grew from within. The principal appeal of such movements was the challenging excitement that broad-scale concepts could stimulate. As the classic style evolved, integrated forms grew more and more impressive while sectional forms acquired some of the continuity and expansion of integrated arrangement.

Analysis of a movement according to the methods worked out here would proceed along the following lines:

1. Establishment of a large-scale perspective by determining the harmonic plan and the nature of the period structure
2. Noting the highlights, the important landmarks by examination of thematic distribution
3. Observation of significant detail work, such as specific harmonic progressions, interplay of parts and motives, handling of texture
4. Consideration of the general expressive qualities of the piece, especially in relation to the style or styles used

Particularly interesting will be the relationship of statement and counterstatement. When a progression, a theme, or a texture is repeated later on in a movement, it very often is changed in some way. Fresh interest is thus given to the counterstatement; and to the perceptive listener, this new light thrown on a familiar musical quality is one of the great pleasures of the classic style.

MEDIA OF PERFORMANCE IN CLASSIC MUSIC

The styles, forms, and techniques we have described were all used in the principal media of performance in classic music. Although one style may have been evolved in a particular medium, it would be borrowed for use in a different setting. Transferring styles and idioms from one type of medium to another was characteristic of late baroque music, and this trend was maintained in classic music. Thus, a section in an orchestral piece might be in the aria manner of Italian opera, or a piece for keyboard alone might emulate the tutti-solo arrangement of the concerto. Nevertheless the medium of performance did have some effect upon the music that was written. The amount of sonority available, the types and varieties of color values, the size of the place in which the music was to be performed, the kind of audience and the sort of attention it would give: all these influenced the composer's decisions with regard to form and style.

The principal media of classic music are as follows:

1. The orchestra (including concerto)
2. Chamber music for various combinations

3. Solo keyboard music
4. Opera
5. Choral music

The Orchestra

Orchestras differed in size and personnel in the eighteenth century. Small opera houses and court orchestras generally had few string instruments, a pair or two of wind instruments, such as oboes and flutes, two horns, perhaps timpani, and a keyboard player who directed the orchestra while filling in the harmony at his instrument. Mozart's early symphonies use this orchestration. The large orchestras, which furnished the instrumentation for music of the late eighteenth century and became models for nineteenth- and twentieth-century orchestras, functioned in large cosmopolitan centers and in celebrated courts, such as Mannheim and Berlin. They had many strings, pairs of flutes, oboes, bassoons, horns, trumpets, timpani, and often clarinets. Although the keyboard leader was still present, he was no longer needed to complete the harmony and keep the music going. This was because of the much fuller sound of these larger orchestras, their greater competence, and the ability of the brass and lower strings to provide a strong support to the harmony.

The principal advantages of the orchestral style were brilliance and full mass of sound as well as variety of color. There was a tremendous range of dynamics; striking contrasts between loud and soft effects were exploited; crescendo and decrescendo passages added to the excitement of an orchestral performance. The classic orchestral style, evolved principally in Mannheim and Paris, made use of these "new" orchestral values, and yet retained the tutti-solo procedure of the baroque concerto grosso.

Early in the eighteenth century, a major field for orchestral performance was opera; from about 1730, orchestral concerts became important areas of activity. Many of the items in the programs of these early orchestral concerts were sinfonias borrowed from Italian opera. Opera sinfonias are the ancestors of the classic symphony. Indeed, many of Mozart's early symphonies are typical examples of this kind of composition.

It was in the late eighteenth century that the modern procedures of orchestration were developed. In order to see how a typical orchestral composition might be worked out, let us return once more to the first movement of Beethoven's Third Symphony. It is scored for the following instruments:

2 flutes	2 timpani
2 oboes	1st violin (14 to 16)
2 clarinets	2nd violin (12 to 14)
2 bassoons	viola (10 to 12)
3 horns	cello (8 to 10)
2 trumpets	string bass (8)

Playing all together, as they frequently do, these instruments can create a very large amount of sound. Most of the time, however, they are set against each other both with respect to tone color and action. Generally, there is one principal melody; the majority of the time this is carried by the first violins, although flute, clarinets, or oboes often partake in the melodic leadership, particularly in lyric moments. Now and then, a horn or trumpet is given a solo passage appropriate to its style of performance. Against the principal melodic line, much subordinate action takes place. We hear typical accompaniment figures; these are generally taken by the middle string instruments, second violin and viola, and sometimes the cello.

In Beethoven's orchestra, the underlying support is assigned principally to the lowermost strings, the cello and the bass. If we listen closely to what these low strings do, we can see that Beethoven has managed to give them an amazing variety of figures and functions. They support the harmony; they provide rhythmic spark to a passage; they punctuate; and now and then they take on the principal melodic role. Aside from their occasional fanfare themes, the brass give body to orchestral sound; also, because of their bold attack, they can accent a chord or a point of arrival. The timpani also serve a purpose of accent; their other role is to reinforce the bass.

As with form, Beethoven took orchestral procedures from late eighteenth-century music and expanded them notably. His orchestration set the pattern for nineteenth-century scoring. Berlioz, Wagner, Brahms, Liszt, and many other romantic composers stem directly from Beethoven, taking the cue from his boldness of effect, his fullness of sound, his variety of texture, and his brilliance of manner.

Chamber Music

In the middle of the eighteenth century and before, instrumental ensemble music could often be played with one or more performers to a part. Trios or quartets, for example, might be presented by single players for each part, or by a small string orchestra with a leader at the keyboard, as in the first quartets of Haydn and the orchestra trios of the Mannheim

School, about 1750–1760. As the new orchestral style evolved, a split took place between orchestral and chamber music. Composers wrote either with orchestral sonorities in mind, or they wrote with the knowledge that a few expert players would perform the piece. Often these experts were the principal instrumentalists in the large orchestras.

In chamber music there is a great flexibility of part-writing. The relationships of texture and sonority are more intimate, less dramatic than those of the orchestra. Contrasts are not as sharp as in other media of performance. Hence, in chamber music, we are likely to find more extended lines, a considerable amount of fine-drawn ornamentation, and a great deal of interweaving among the parts. Since the performers were skillful, there was a great deal of soloistic writing, often to compensate for the inability to create a massive sound, as in the symphony.

Many varieties of chamber music were written, according to the number of performers and the purpose of the performance. There were two general types of chamber music:

1. Serious, thoughtful works intended for small-scale concert performance. The broad forms and all the stylistic resources of classic music were used. Mozart's, Haydn's, and Beethoven's string quartets represent this type.

2. Pleasantly entertaining pieces intended for amusement at a party or festive occasion. Dance-, song-, or march-style movements comprised these works; each contained four, five, six, or more of these popular pieces. Very little serious material was introduced. Wind instruments were often used, particularly when the performance was to take place out of doors; the sound of wind instruments carries better in the open air than does the sound of strings. *Serenade, divertimento,* and *cassation* were names given to such pieces.

Beethoven's Quartet in F major, Op. 59, no. 1, and Mozart's Quartet in C major, K. 465, represent the serious style; Mozart's *Eine Kleine Nachtmusik* is a very famous serenade, whereas Mozart's Quintet in E♭ major, K. 614, has elements of both styles.

Solo Keyboard Music

Keyboard music has the advantage of the flexibility that comes when one performer has control of the musical performance. The principal keyboard media in the later eighteenth century were the harpsichord and the early piano, neither of which had the massive quality of sound that the modern piano can command. Classic keyboard music is transparent. It was often composed in two actual lines, one for the right hand and one for the left;

that is, frequently no more than two notes were sounding at a given instant. Contrasts could be made very easily, but the range of contrast was not great, due to the homogeneity in the tone quality of the instruments. There was much figuration in rapid notes. Sometimes this was brilliant, in order to try the prowess of a virtuoso performer; sometimes the figuration was restricted and modest, in order to accommodate the modest abilities of the student or amateur for whom a piece may have been written.

A characteristic type of figuration, called the *Alberti bass,* was taken over by classic composers from the earlier school of Italian keyboard composers. This figuration consisted of a regular alternation, in a narrow range, between tones of a chord in the left hand. The right hand played a singing melody. In addition to the Italian style which reached the classic composers via Johann Christian Bach, the music for solo keyboard received much from the German *Empfindsamkeit* through the influence of Karl Philipp Emanuel Bach. Anyone who has had some training in piano has probably become acquainted with samplings of classic solo keyboard music. The sonatas of Mozart are standard items in the teaching repertory, as are those of Beethoven, and to a lesser extent, the piano sonatas of Haydn.

Opera

Opera offered the classic composer the ultimate in dramatic contrast of sonority values. The human voice, with the strong and immediate emotional quality of its impact, was contrasted with the variety of sonority in the orchestra. Because of the plot and the text, gesture and emotion have a much more specific meaning than they have in instrumental music. Musical figures can underscore and highlight these dramatic values. The Baroque doctrine of the affections was concerned principally with the use of appropriate musical figures when a text was being set. Classic opera continued this tradition, but, thanks to the flexibility of classic techniques of composition, was able to add sharp contrast to strong affective quality. In Mozart's last operas, each character is portrayed in a musical style fitting to his nature and his dramatic function. Furthermore, within the general style for each character, subtle musical nuances reflect shades and variations of meaning.

We have already mentioned the rise of opera buffa in relation to the change in social structure during the eighteenth century. Opera, like instrumental music, achieved a synthesis in the works of Mozart. Comic opera, that is, buffa, and opera seria were merged. For example, consider the order of events in the first part of his *Don Giovanni*:

1. The overture begins with a slow introduction, after the manner of the French overture. We have here the Storm and Stress style, forecasting the tragic doom of Don Giovanni. The principal part of the overture is a total contrast to the introduction. It is a brilliant example of the galant style, in which fanfare, singing-allegro, concerto, and even the learned styles intermingle.

2. The overture makes a surprising shift of key at the very end, pausing upon the dominant chord of the key in which Leporello, a comic character, will make his entrance. This sudden harmonic nuance is a typical buffa gesture.

3. Leporello's song is typical buffa music. It is perky, simple, tuneful, and set in a light texture. It, too, does not come to a full close but moves into a transition that picks up the pace and leads into the scene of the struggle, the duel, and the death.

4. This scene of conflict is an ensemble piece, an example of vocal chamber music in which the music for each character reflects faithfully the role being played. Anna and Giovanni are struggling; their music is tense; it tends to rise in pitch; Leporello retains his buffa manner. Suddenly, the action focuses more sharply; the key changes abruptly, and the pace slows to a more deliberate and ominous tempo. The Commandant enters. The quality of his voice, a basso, and the slow, dignified nature of his music give a more weighty and tragic aspect to the action. As the duel between Giovanni and the Commandant begins, the music is quite literally pictorial; the parries and thrusts are portrayed by rapid scale passages and at the death blow all movement stops, while the orchestra sustains a sharply dissonant chord. As the Commandant dies the harmonies are minor and chromatic and the melodic lines all descend. Yet, at this point, when Leporello sings, he retains his buffa manner!

The forms of opera are even more diverse than those of instrumental music. The action of the opera, or the text of an aria or recitative will often determine the form of a number. Yet, in all cases, musical relationships provide the inner coherence as well as the over-all plan. Operatic music depends upon key contrast, period structure, and development of motivic material just as does instrumental music. Sonata forms, dance forms, and rondos have been used frequently.

A special type of form is the composite number, of which the section analyzed above is an example. This provides a more fluid type of movement, more continuous action, and yet allows for a number of varied or contrasted dramatic values. The stereotyped forms of earlier opera seria appear occasionally, but these are shortened. The more dynamic quality of movement, sharper dramatic contrasts, and the exquisite sense of timing derived from opera buffa—these did not permit the composer to dwell too long upon any one value or affective manner.

Choral Music

Choral music in the late eighteenth century was practically all intended for church performance or for other purposes of devotion. There was a strong influence of conservative traditional practice in choral music, most of which consisted of Masses or individual numbers from the liturgy. Traditionally certain portions were handled in a fugal style; other sections, not bound by tradition, showed operatic and galant qualities. In the sections not dedicated to the learned style, the forms were those of other music: sonata, three-part, rondo, etc. Like orchestral music, the texture of choral music (almost always accompanied by instruments) varied from transparent and thin to the mighty effect of massed voices and instruments. These contrasts were often juxtaposed.

All serious composers in the eighteenth century had a thorough training in church music. Much of the early output of Mozart and Haydn was in the form of music for sacred services. It was principally from this source that they acquired the discipline and strength of part-writing and harmony that enabled them to transform the somewhat frivolous popular music of the time into important and enduring masterpieces.

SUMMARY

Regular dance and song patterns and a well-defined sense of key provided classic composers with a sturdy framework upon which to build extended phases of movement and large-scale forms. Richness and variety of expression were drawn from idioms that were available in eighteenth-century musical life. Change in the type of audience and less restrictions upon the kind of musical idiom provided a powerful stimulus in the late eighteenth century for more imposing compositions. At this time the sonata form became the most important structural plan. Its importance lay in its long-range harmonic scheme which could organize and focus the activity and momentum of a large number of periods. As the inner content of a movement grew more intensely expressive, the form broadened.

There is a strong temptation to draw a parallel between rationalistic thought in the eighteenth century and classicism in music. Actually this is only partly valid as a comparison. Rationalism might be compared to mid-eighteenth-century music in which a balanced, clear, uncomplicated, and down-to-earth quality was predominant.

Toward the end of the eighteenth century, unsettling forces were at work. The middle-class revolutions in America and France had taken place.

Early romanticism had made its first appearance in the *Sturm und Drang* period of German literature and in the writings of Rousseau. German idealism, with affinities to the romantic movement, was being developed by Fichte, Kant, and Hegel. We have seen the analogy to this unsettling influence at work within the harmonic and rhythmic structure of the classic period form. Yet, in no way did this unseat the fundamental premise of classic music, which was the final and complete victory of stability after an engrossing musical experience that involved strong elements of instability. Classic music, through its synthesizing power, was able to assimilate the incipient romanticism of the Sensibility and the Storm and Stress qualities, and to assign these qualities their proper function in the stream of musical movement. Thus, it turned what might have been a hostile force into an ally.

The musical objective of the classic composer was to entertain, stimulate, and challenge the listener, and at times to touch his emotions more profoundly. Neither he nor the listener were supposed to lose themselves in the tide of the music, as was the case in a later era. Classic music was neither a purely rationalistic art in which all terms save those that were easily reconciled failed to qualify; nor was it a mystic art reaching for goals that were unattainable. Somehow, it managed to stand poised between two opposing forces and receive maximum benefit from both.

Thus, classic music faces both ways. This ambivalence is also seen in many details of classic composition. Very often a chord or melodic figure was approached in one meaning, as an item in one pattern, but was given a different meaning as the point of departure in another pattern. The very fact that any musical idea can be both statement and counterstatement gave rise to this equivocality. Classic composers delighted in making a play with ambiguous relationships; like Shakespeare with his puns, they liked to assign more than one value to a musical term. Nevertheless, this uncertainty was only an internal detail of action; it was a contribution to the sense of movement within a form. Never did it become so powerful as to weaken the strength of the form itself. The last phase of the classic relationship between form and content was reached in Beethoven. Afterward, the individual moments of intensity or color in the music began to assume more importance for the composer and the listener than did the balanced perfection of the form. This was the way to romanticism.

SUGGESTED LISTENING PROJECTS

1. **Haydn, Joseph, Quartet in D major, Op. 76, no. 5, finale. Col. 4 ML–4924**

Listen for: Intensive working over of two contrasting motives stated in the first twelve measures; shaping of form entirely by key areas; interweaving of parts; striking harmonic surprises; absence of many strong cadential points of arrival; imbalance of phrase relationships; two strategically placed pauses, one in the middle, one near the end, just before the cadences in the dominant and tonic, respectively; the new melodic material used to make these cadences; the general country-dance quality of the entire piece.

2. **Bach, K. P. E., Sonata in B minor, last movement.** *Columbia History of Music* **DB 831**

Listen for: The general sentimental quality, *Empfindsamkeit*; the elegant ornamentation; expressive intervals; the exactly regular phrases and periods, four and eight measures in length; a complete sense of balance in phrase structure; chromaticism; thin texture; rondo form; small-scale concept; gentle quality of movement.

3. **Mozart, *Magic Flute,* Aria of the Queen of the Night, *Die Holle Rache* (Mortal Vengeance). Col. SL–115**

Listen for: Storm and Stress character of entire aria; contrast of key areas; emphasis on pointed figures and motives rather than upon fully formed themes; active give-and-take between voice and orchestra in concerto manner; the breaking into coloratura at the moments of greatest passion; dramatic effect of recitativelike passage at the cadential section of the entire aria, as if the Queen's rage had crystallized into a decisive plan; compare with the revenge duet at the end of Scene I of *Don Giovanni* (same key, similar idea, same harmonic plan, similar use of recitative).

4. **Beethoven, Symphony No. 7, Scherzo. Col. 4ML–4507**

Listen for: General headlong pace of Scherzo; setting of short opening motive as statement, long-spun-out melody as counterstatement; striking, unexpected shifts of tonal center; use of orchestration to contribute to off-balance effects of movement; striking contrast of Trio to Scherzo in every respect: sonority, movement, melodic style, texture, phrase structure.

Chapter 7. Romantic Music

CLASSICISM and romanticism are so closely linked in so many respects that it would be difficult to draw a line that would separate the two styles. Romantic expression first stirs in music sometime in the middle of the eighteenth century, while classic ideas of structure still exert much influence beyond the end of the nineteenth century. Nevertheless, in its most typical manifestations, romantic music is very different from classic music. In order to get the clearest idea of romanticism's distinctive expressive qualities we shall go to the music that represents marked departures from classic ideas of composition.

Romanticism appears in its fullest flower in such works as the Prelude to Wagner's opera, *Tristan und Isolde,* Chopin's Preludes for piano, Schumann's *Carnaval,* Berlioz's *Symphonie fantastique,* Schubert's song cycle, *Die Schöne Müllerin,* and Liszt's Sonata for Piano in B minor. Each of these works has some qualities which mark it especially as being romantic; they will comprise the principal material for study in this chapter. And of all these compositions, probably the most typical of romanticism, and at the same time, a unique work in many respects, is the Prelude to Wagner's *Tristan.* For us, it can be a central area of reference from which we can start down the devious paths of musical romanticism.

QUALITIES OF SOUND

Harmonic Tension

Wagner, the wonder-worker of harmony, draws us into the mood of the entire opera with the very first chord. What a world of intense feeling, of longing, of frustration, and unhappiness it seems to suggest! Restless, unstable, dissonant, and tense, it has a rich, almost luxuriant quality of sound, produced both by the intervals and by the manner in which the chord has been set for instruments.

223

Ex. 7–1. Wagner: Prelude to *Tristan und Isolde.*

This chord has become famous in music; it has been labeled the *Tristan chord* and is felt to symbolize the world of romantic harmony. Indeed, an entire book has been written upon it and its implications for the history of harmonic expression.*

As the music moves forward, the first impression is maintained and augmented. Every chord, every sound has a richness of color as well as some element of dissonance or instability. At no time do we reach a point of final arrival, an authentic cadence, or for that matter, an entirely stable chord. We listen for a clear definition of tonal center; yet the music only hints at keys, and refuses to establish or confirm them. *Harmonically,* everything seems to be in a state of flux. This constant movement is the harmonic basis of what Wagner himself called *endless melody.*

Melody, rhythm, and texture add their share to this general impression. At first the flow of sound proceeds without a defined beat or pulse; only later, when activity becomes more animated, does the underlying *meter* of the piece make itself felt. *Texturally,* the music is dense; the component voices all move slowly, shifting constantly and subtly. Above and through this dense mass of sound, the *melodic line* floats and spins out. *Expressively,* the music seems to be reaching, groping, striving; yet it never reaches a final goal. We are not certain where we are going, nor exactly why, but the striving itself is portentous, and each moment in the music stirs us deeply.

Most of the chords in the Prelude to *Tristan* have one feature in common: they are chords which have been traditionally used to *create the tension* which is necessary to make a cadence. They have a strong leading-tone action. Play almost any chord from this piece separately, and your ear will wait for a resolution. Such unstable harmonies convey a sense of movement in addition to projecting an effect of richness in color. The example below illustrates some of these wonderfully evocative combinations:

* Ernst Kurth, *Die Romantische Harmonik und ihre Krise in Wagner's Tristan,* Berlin, 1920.

Ex. 7–2. Typical chords in the Wagner vocabulary.

unstable intervals marked

How did Wagner arrive at such a harmonic vocabulary? We must retro-spect a bit in order to see Wagnerian harmony in its true historical per-spective. As we watched the evolution of music from the early Middle Ages on, we noticed that there was a gradual increase in the strength and the frequency of leading-tone action in harmony. In plain chant, Ars antiqua, and Ars nova, cadential action took place only at the ends of phrases, simply to round off a phase of movement conveniently. In Renaissance music, we began to see more concentration on arriving at the cadence; the action of leading tones became more prominent. Also chord progressions began to group themselves around tonal centers. In baroque and classic music, this process became increasingly more important. Dominant har-monies and leading tones occupied a more and more prominent place within the phases of harmonic movement, creating more and more fre-quent cadences.

At times in eighteenth-century music, and much more in nineteenth-century music, the leading-tone factors became so densely concentrated that they pushed the tonic harmonies, the chords of resolution, entirely out of a passage. Leading-tone harmonies were beginning to saturate the music. In *Tristan*, the leading-tone factor reaches its point of greatest concentra-tion. Tonic harmony is more conspicuous by its absence than by its presence. Afterward, as we shall see, the process will continue; those elements which create tension will be isolated and used independently. The other tones, those which create a body and a rich sonority for the chord, will be elimi-nated. This will take place in the music of Mahler and Schönberg, as well as in the music of many other twentieth-century composers. So, Wagner represents a critical stage in the history of harmony. In his music the acme of cadential tension is reached by the avoidance of chords of resolution. After Wagner, the tension elements in harmony lose their contact with any specifically indicated resolution and they are used as independent free agents.

Harmonic Color

Listen again to the beginning of *Tristan*. This time, pay particular attention to the characteristic qualities of the individual chords. They can attract us simply as a play of kaleidoscopic, shifting effects. In so listening, you will be less aware than before of the urgency in the harmony; each combination of sounds will have its own appeal within a generally consistent mood. Again and again in romantic music we encounter moments and perhaps even extended passages in which the composer seems to be drinking deeply of the effect that a special chord or sound creates. Here are the first few measures of Schubert's song *The Phantom Double*. Note the weird, ghostly effect created by the low-placed, slowly moving chords.

Ex. 7–3. Schubert: *The Phantom Double*.

In such music, the principal appeal—and it is generally a very strong appeal—centers upon tone color and its ability to establish and maintain a consistent and evocative mood. In contrast to the growing and collapsing tension of the music we have been discussing, which relied on *instability,* this other kind of romantic music assigns a relatively *stable* quality to its harmonies, even though there may be dissonance contained in the sounds. The harmonies are not used primarily for their tensions nor their driving quality of movement; rather, they are precious for their intrinsic qualities of sound. Perhaps this explains partly why the music of Wagner exerts such a strong appeal. The sense of urgent emotional necessity created by his unbroken chains of tension chords is clothed with a rich luxuriance of immensely attractive sound.

As a virtually pure example of a mood created by a steady flow of one kind of sound, listen to the song *Wohin* from Schubert's song cycle, *Die Schöne Müllerin.* The song describes the flow of a brook and the wistful speculation which this flow suggests to a wanderer in the country. The murmur of the water is depicted by a rapid little figure in the piano, repeated over and over again within very simple and sweet harmonies. The steady flow is embodied in a gentle pulse which gives life to the sound. Over this current the melody floats, giving point to the glow of the harmony and texture. The entire song envelops us in one sustained mood, which, although it fluctuates somewhat, is faithful to its first impression.

Now, in order to obtain a clear view of romantic music, we must look beyond its harmonic surface to discover some of the attitudes and ideas that impelled musical composition. More than at any other time in history, the relationship between music and various literary ideas becomes explicit.

EXPRESSIVE VALUES

Emotional Intensity

Tristan's harmony symbolizes a new world of expression in nineteenth-century music. We meet violent emotional outbursts, restlessness of the spirit, ideas of foreboding, tragedy, and doom, intense desires and yearnings.

If we recall the duel and death in the first scene of *Don Giovanni,* we see a foreshadowing of this type of expression in the strikingly dissonant chord that accompanies the death stroke. Also, the overture of *Don Giovanni* creates an impression of doom by the dark and unstable harmonies at the beginning. In these respects Mozart points to musical romanticism. The impression of terror and doom, of damnation, is projected in the Wolf-Glen scene from the opera *Der Freischütz* by Weber through a similar concentration of unstable, shifting harmonic effects. Violent, impetuous feeling is frequently suggested by the music of Schumann; this quality is supported by restless shifting harmonies, as at the beginning of his Overture to *Manfred,* after the poem by Lord Byron.

All these qualities of expression seem to involve personal feelings, personal destinies. Art, music, literature, and philosophy during the nineteenth century are passionately concerned with the individual and his fate. They deal with personal reactions, experiences, and emotions. Man quests and probes, seeking the solution of the problem of good and evil. Nineteenth-century music draws heavily upon such literary and philosophic concepts. The power of music to convey strong emotional effects was geared to such grand and profound ideas. Let us have a look at some of these concepts.

Good versus Evil

In nineteenth-century thought, the conflict between good and evil took many forms. Certainly the most celebrated version of this theme was the Faust story, which tells of a compact made with the Devil for the sake of worldly power and personal advantage. Faust's redemption comes about through the intercession of Marguerite, a heroine whose pure and holy love for Faust overcomes the power of the Devil. To be sure, Faust is not saved in every version of the story, but in each case, the struggle between the diabolic and the angelic forms the body of the story. Berlioz, Wagner, Liszt, Gounod, and Boito all took the Faust theme as a subject upon which they based musical compositions. Moreover, we do not have to look very hard to find the Faust story in disguise in Weber's opera *Der Freischütz.* Max, the hunter hero, represents Faust; Zamiel is the counterpart of Mephistopheles, the Devil; the magic bullets represent the temptation of power and worldly success; and Agatha is Weber's Marguerite.

Wagner, himself, was deeply concerned with such problems. In each of his music dramas the central issue seems to be a metaphysical conflict. In *Tristan,* it is love against death, in *Tannhäuser,* sacred love against profane love, in *Parsifal,* the holy against the pagan, in the *Ring* cycle, the godlike race against the giants and dwarfs, honor versus power.

We can find some of these ideas prefigured long before the romantic era. For example, Don Giovanni pays his price in Hell for his thoroughly evil and selfish life on earth. In Mozart's *Magic Flute,* the line between good and evil is drawn again, this time with a sociologic and political intent. Good is represented by Sarastro; only those who are proved worthy may enter into his temple; evil is personified by the Queen of the Night, whose power lies in spells and incantations. Sarastro thus stands for the newly rising *individual,* who was coming into his own during the latter part of the eighteenth century; the Queen is the symbol of centuries-long entrenched hereditary *autocracy.* In this bold, searching, imaginative kind of dramatic material, Mozart anticipates romanticism.

Closely linked to the idea of good is the search for the ideal in romanticism. This might have religious connotations, as in Parsifal's search for the Holy Grail. In the case of Tristan and Isolde, it involves the longing for the bliss that only a perfect realization of love can embody. Siegfried is the ideal of a hero; Wotan seeks the absolute power that only the Ring can confer. At the end of Liszt's *Faust* Symphony, we hear the words, "The eternal woman draws us onward." Strauss's Don Juan seeks but never finds the perfect woman. As we might expect, the ideal is rarely attained. Frustration and death are the answers to all the seeking and yearning.

Evil, especially the diabolic, seemed to fascinate many romantic composers. Moussorgsky's *St. John's Night on the Bare Mountain,* Liszt's *Mephisto* waltz and his *Totentanz,* the Witches' Sabbath from Berlioz's *Symphonie fantastique,* the Wolf-Glen scene from Weber's *Der Freischütz,* all depict the Devil and his cohorts afoot in the dead of night.

In suggesting these concepts and themes, the music explores and develops those qualities of harmony which are unstable, agitated, restless, and dissonant. All these qualities are highly concentrated in the harmonic materials of *Tristan und Isolde.* This kind of harmony seems to be the principal ingredient in the emotional compound of musical romanticism. In addition to restless harmony, you will hear many strange effects in these works. These we shall have occasion to discuss later.

Nature: Descriptive Music

The coloristic aspects of romantic harmony and sonority were employed for specific purposes of description. These were frequently associated with images of natural phenomena. Nature, in many forms, attracted composers of the nineteenth century.

The play of water, the rhythm of sea-waves, the murmur of the countryside, the rush of wind and rain, the shepherd's and the hunter's horn echoing over the hills—all these and many other fancies provided frameworks for the play of colors, figures, and textures in music. Let us mention a few examples:

1. Beethoven's Sixth Symphony, called the *Pastoral,* projects a distinctive quality of sound in each movement. The first movement, with pleasantly monotonous dronelike sounds, sustained or endlessly repeated, describes pleasant feelings upon arrival in the country. The slow ambling of a brook is suggested in the gently swinging motion of the second movement. The fourth movement creates the impression of a sudden storm with sound effects borrowed from eighteenth-century Storm and Stress music.

2. Wagner, himself, set the stage for his gigantic work, *The Ring of the Nibelung,* by describing the flow of the river Rhine in the Prelude to *Das Rheingold.* This is a most remarkable piece of music, since it contains but one harmony, the chord of E-flat major, upon which all the flowing, rolling figures are based.

3. Mendelssohn's *Hebrides* Overture, descriptive of a sea voyage to Scotland, is a landmark in the history of descriptive music. Listen to the strange harmonies

Ex. 7–4. Mendelssohn: *Hebrides* Overture.

within the first few measures. How striking is their suggestion of bareness and desolation on a tossing open sea! The whole piece explores such harmonies, balancing them, to be sure, with the traditional cadential progressions of classic harmony. Worked into the harmonic fabric, we hear a short motive, repeated again and again. These are like little points of color worked into a painting. The scene, the harmony, the melodic arabesques: these point the way to *musical impressionism,* a style of the late 1800s and early 1900s that devoted itself almost entirely to the description of strange and exotic scenes. Figure 11 depicts a seascape such as Mendelssohn might have observed.

4. Carl Maria von Weber begins the overture to his opera *Oberon* with a slow sustained call on the muted horn that seems to come from deep in the midst of the elfin woods of Oberon's realm. Fairy flutes and trumpets add their bit to the atmosphere of magic which Weber so effectively creates in the introduction to this piece. Strikingly enough, the body of the overture, the Allegro, is worked out very much as a classic type of piece, in which Weber shows his great debt to Beethoven in matters of orchestration, part-writing, and development.

The descriptive aspect of romantic music has been designated as *program music.* Much has been written for and against the propriety of composing music with a story or scene in mind. While pictorialism and affective values had for centuries been part of the aesthetics of music, it was in the nineteenth century that the tendency to link music with extramusical ideas became so strong and all-pervading that it was a basic issue among musicians and critics.

Such interest in a program for musical composition was inevitable in the intellectual and artistic climate of the nineteenth century with its grandiose, picturesque, sentimental, and nostalgic feelings and concepts. Moreover, the increased resources of harmonic color and texture lent themselves to special effects of pictorialism and mood. Program music, as a genre, is neither good nor bad. Each composition has to be taken separately and judged according to general standards of effectiveness, imagination, and taste.

Richard Strauss, in his tone poem, *Till Eulenspiegel,* managed to link an amusing yet pathetic story to a composition that is a masterpiece. The mischievous humor of Till is delightfully suggested by capricious turns in the music, by an effervescent manner, and by a highly imaginative set of musical materials. Although each can stand alone, the story and the music complement each other beautifully. The very same composer, Strauss, fails to convince us of the validity of his intention in another work, the *Sinfonia Domestica,* although this piece has many realistic touches of description.

FIG. 10. Pierre Rousseau: *Edge of the Woods.* (Courtesy of the Metropolitan Museum of Art.)

Nationalism

The romantic artist's interest in nature represents an escape from the dull or oppressive realities of everyday existence. Such flights are typical of romanticism. The artist wants to explore different, faraway, and strange worlds; he wants to free himself from the center of gravity which is his own mundane life; he strives to expand the world of his imagination in every direction. All the favorite subjects of romanticism typify this expansion, this centrifugal motion. The nineteenth century, itself an era of expansion on a broad scale, finds a true reflection of its trends in its music. Nowhere is this better demonstrated than in the nationalisms which developed in music. Folk music, the legends of the national past, the funda-

Fig. 11. Gustave Courbet: *The Sea.* (Courtesy of the Metropolitan Museum of Art.)

mental truth of the national spirit were all expressed with great vehemence, particularly by composers in those countries which had been on the periphery of European music during the preceding centuries. These were especially the Slavic and the Scandinavian countries.

Russia, with Moussorgsky, Borodin, Rimsky-Korsakov, and others, developed a new and highly significant musical language, based upon folk rhythms and Oriental qualities of color. These characteristics give a special distinction to such works as Moussorgsky's opera, *Boris Godunov,* Borodin's opera, *Prince Igor,* and Rimsky-Korsakov's *Russian Easter* Overture. In all of these you will hear brilliant flashes of color, odd-sounding melodies based on exotic scales, and a violence of rhythm not encountered in Western music. These represent a deliberate effort to break away from Western European style; they assert the distinction and separateness of a national culture.

Music and Language

The titles and subjects that we have discussed above show that romantic music has close ties with literature and with ideas borrowed from the world of language. But these connections extended beyond the use of literary associations in musical compositions. Many composers were both writers and critics. Weber, Berlioz, Schumann, Liszt, and Wagner produced interesting and often excellent prose in their writings that dealt with musical criticism and aesthetics. Conversely, E. T. A. Hoffmann, one of the strongest spokesmen for romanticism in his writings, and the source of the story of the fantastic opera, *The Tales of Hoffmann,* was a composer of some prominence in his time.

The connection between music and literature went even farther. Composers and poets tried to borrow and implant the expressive values of the opposite art into their own. Music became poetic, and poetry strove to become ever more musical. Thus music tried to approximate the declamatory accents of poetry and dramatic speech in its effort to become more eloquent and persuasive. Liszt, at the beginning of his B-minor Sonata, suggests a profound and impassioned soliloquy; within this piece we hear passages in recitative style, as if a text were being declaimed. Indeed, in Wagner's later music dramas, the entire vocal content is cast in the manner called *Sprechgesang,* "speech-song," in which the inflections and rhythms of the German language are delineated in the music.

Ex. 7–5. *Sprechgesang.*

The entire song literature of the nineteenth century, one of the most distinctive contributions of romantic music, depends upon the close union of words and music. The eloquence, charm, and pathos of poetry is closely matched by the music which romantic composers set to lyric poetry.

While music was striving to become ever more poetic and speechlike in its expression, poets, on the other hand, made efforts to create a musical quality in the sounds of their words. The dark mood of the following excerpt from Edgar Allan Poe's *Ulalume* is measurably enhanced by the vowel sounds he has chosen, framed by a singsong alliteration among the consonants:

> It was night in the lonesome October
> Of my most immemorial year.
> It was hard by the dim lake of Auber
> In the misty mid-region of Weir.
> It was down by the dank tarn of Auber
> In the ghoul-haunted woodland of Weir.

In an entirely different mood, John Keats enhances the richness of the scene he is depicting in *The Eve of St. Agnes* by choosing words which have a strongly resonant quality:

> While he from forth the closet brought a heap
> Of candied apple, quince, and plum, and gourd;
> With jellies soother than the creamy curd,
> And lucent syrops, tinct with cinnamon;
> Manna and dates, in argosy transferr'd
> From Fez; and spiced dainties, every one
> From silken Samarcand to cedar'd Lebanon.

One of the finest songs of the nineteenth century is that which Schubert set to Goethe's poem, *The Erlking*. Goethe tells the story of a father riding home through the storm with his child in his arms. The Erlking, the embodiment of Death (again the supernatural element) first tries to coax the child to come with him, then threatens, and finally takes the child by force. By subtle changes in the music Schubert manages to give the solo voice the appearance of singing four different parts: the narrator, the father, the child, and the Erlking. He mirrors the emotional values of the poetry in subtle, yet telling fashion. Here are samples of each part:

Ex. 7–6. Narrator.

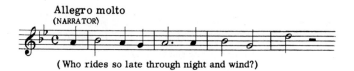

(Who rides so late through night and wind?)

First, the narrator tells of the father hurrying home through the storm and wind. The music begins in a somewhat level, matter-of-fact manner, although the agitation which the storm music in the piano creates tells us that this quiet manner is but a foreboding. As the narrator continues to sing, his melodic line grows active, to signify greater tension.

Ex. 7–7. Father.

(My son, why do you hide your face in fear?)

The father's music, Example 7–7 above, begins on a low pitch, and throughout the piece, is generally placed low, with the exception of his last phrase, when the terror of the situation seems to communicate itself to him. The sturdy interval of the perfect fourth, rising from dominant to tonic, characterizes the father's music.

Ex. 7–8. Child.

(My father, my father, do you not hear?)

The child, in contrast, is given a high-pitched melodic part, of which the example above is the most characteristic excerpt. Three times we hear this outcry, each time a major second higher, and each time it is a refrain that answers the Erlking's persuasions. Schubert has assigned to the child's music the most unstable harmony in the piece; the pleas of the child are sung over dissonant, unstable harmonies.

Ex. 7–9. Erlking.

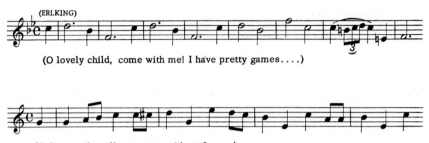

(O lovely child, come with me! I have pretty games....)

(O fine youth, will you come with me?.....)

The two melodies above represent the Erlking's music. Notice how sweet and ingratiating they are, like candy offered to a child. This is a master touch in composition, to coat the deadly intent of the Erlking with cloying sweetness. Listen also to the manner in which Schubert lightens the driving accompaniment figure whenever the Erlking sings.

Ex. 7–10. Narrator; recitative.

(In his arms the child was dead!)

At the very end comes the finest touch of all, as the momentum which carried throughout the piece is broken, and the narrator announces in halting recitative, that the child is dead. Nothing could portray so well the absolute horror of the tragedy as this bare final statement.

The affinities which music, poetry, drama, and pictorial art have had for each other during the many centuries of Western civilization concerned Wagner deeply. The idea of merging arts reached its climax in his book, *The Art Work of the Future*. In his plan Wagner not only brought music and poetry together, but included the graphic arts and pantomime to create his idea of a timeless, universal composition whose subject matter was neither current nor historic, but rather drew upon the legends of German antiquity in order to develop the simple and monumental values associated with man's origins. In Wagner's scheme, music was to play a secondary role, supporting and assisting the dramatic idea. Wagner himself described the relative importance of various arts in this scheme. He said:

True drama can be thought of only as arising from the drive of all arts to communicate in the most immediate way to a general audience. . . . All of the richly developed possibilities of individual arts will be used in the comprehensive art work; in this form, these possibilities will reach full stature.

Paradoxically, the artistic residue of Wagner's work is almost entirely musical. We are no longer stirred by his grandiose scheme or his racial pageants, but we find that his music is a living experience for us today.

The two harmonic tendencies we have observed in romantic music, harmonic tension and harmonic color, each proceeded farther in its own course; each gave rise to a distinct style of composition in the late nineteenth and early twentieth centuries. The emotional conflicts, the introspection, and unrest suggested by harmonic tension led to the style called *expressionism*. The shadings, nuances, and textures suggested by color in harmony led to the school called *impressionism*. In Chapter 8 we shall again pick up the threads of these particular lines of musical evolution.

INSTRUMENTS AND PERFORMANCE

Returning once again to the beginning of *Tristan,* we can very easily see that much of the color effect comes from the way in which the instruments themselves are used. The rich chords would lose much were they to be played by light or thin-bodied instruments. The scoring is for low-pitched wind instruments, massed together; they merge and blend to produce a full, throaty, and vibrant sound. Indeed, throughout the piece, our attention is drawn to wind and brass instruments used with great prominence. We hear the orchestral effect at the beginning expanded, varied, and developed as the Prelude unfolds.

Such concentration on the special effects that instrumental sounds can produce is to be found in much nineteenth-century music. Romantic composers give special attention to instruments in two general ways:

1. They are concerned wth instrumental color and sonority.
2. They are concerned with virtuoso, soloistic treatment of instruments, both singly and in groups.

As we shall see, these two areas often overlap.

The Orchestra

The development of the art of orchestration involved the efforts of many composers; writing for the concert or symphony orchestra had already grown into an important branch of musical composition in the eighteenth century. Instruments had assumed the state and function which they occupy at the present time, except for some refinements and improvements that developed more fullness of tone, greater accuracy of intonation, and greater ease of handling. By the beginning of the nineteenth century, the orchestra and its instruments were ready to participate in the flights of exploration that romantic composers were about to take. No one exemplifies the imaginative treatment of the orchestra better than Hector Berlioz. His *Symphonie fantastique* represents him best in this vein.

As we listen to his *Symphonie fantastique,* we are struck immediately by the entirely different qualities of sound which distinguish this piece from the Prelude to *Tristan.* In the music of Berlioz there seems to be a brilliance, a sharpness, and a transparency of tone which borders upon thinness. In *Tristan,* the composer seeks a richness and a fullness that borders upon heaviness and opacity. Wagner's tone color suggests a massive emotional upheaval; Berlioz's tone color connotes an intense nervous excitement. Wagner broadens and weights the line of melody by assigning it to a number of instruments which may duplicate each other in several octaves. Berlioz prefers to emphasize the play of melodic fragments against each other, projecting brilliant flashes of color in mid-air. The center of Wagner's tone mass is rather low; he fills in the spaces, from top to bottom, with tones that add body and richness to the sound. In contrast, Berlioz's center of tonal gravity is high, and open spaces may be sensed between the various levels of pitch. Thus, the texture of Berlioz seems well layered; Wagner's is thoroughly mixed.

Continuing with our comparison, we find that Wagner creates, varies, and develops one general quality of sound throughout an extended passage. His orchestration is dedicated to the same expressive purpose as his harmony: to carry out a special mood to its peak of intensity. On the other hand, Berlioz appears to seek out change and contrast, often in the boldest and most unexpected manner. We have unusual juxtapositions of high and low sounds, sometimes together, sometimes in alternation. The tone colors themselves often represent explorations of regions previously untrod.

As we might expect, the expressive purpose of Berlioz is far removed from Wagner's. Berlioz has a darting, lightninglike imagination; like the

Viennese classic composers, he projects and reconciles contrasts, although in his case, the boldness of the contrast frequently overrides the resolution. With respect to melodic material, Wagner uses motives that resemble each other in general style; these he works over intensively, and he returns to them constantly for the very fabric of his musical discourse. The component voices in Wagner's music wind in and out in a semi-independent manner, suggesting a constant undercurrent of movement. Berlioz's material shows great variety and sudden contrast. When two or more voices are set against each other, they frequently project a bold conflict in the respective qualities of movement; they proceed at striking tangents to each other. This effect comes about through sharply contrasted rhythmic patterns and the deliberate avoidance of blend between the instruments involved.

Berlioz and Wagner each represent a characteristic attitude of romanticism, and the above comparison only underscores the rich variety to be discovered in the music of this time. Moreover, we shall find much in both composers that is similar. Each was well grounded in the standard orchestral techniques of nineteenth-century music. Each learned much from Beethoven in the way of orchestration. But, in his characteristic vein, each struck out in a different direction. Wagner sought greater fullness and richness of sound to support his grandiose conceptions; Berlioz sought to evoke new impressions by exploring new techniques of scoring, and he highlighted them with a transparent quality of sound.

By way of illustration, listen to these passages from the *Symphonie fantastique*:

1. Distant thunder is suggested by the roll of four timpani at the end of the third movement, *In the Country*. This is certainly one of the most striking passages in all orchestral literature. Tuned to four different tones, these instruments project a strange, muffled, and veiled quality, in which the listener may detect, but cannot fix a pure pitch. Beethoven had already, in his *Leonore* No. 3 Overture, and in his Symphonies Nos. 8 and 9, used the timpani as a solo instrument, but only in its normal function, projecting a bass line. Berlioz goes far beyond this usage, and his low, murmuring chords for timpani, associated with a description of a scene in the country, constitute a bit of pure musical impressionism.

2. In the country one hears the shepherd's horn echoing in the distance. Berlioz evokes this picture by using the English horn, an oboe of rather low pitch and full sound. Its rather dark tone quality suits it admirably for playing the *ranz des vaches*, the herder's theme in the third movement. Ordinarily, the English horn did not figure prominently in early nineteenth-century music.

3. The last movement describes a diabolic orgy. At one point, the doom of

Fl.
Ob.
Cl.
Fg.
Cor. { (B) (Eᵉ)
C.à p. (B)
Tr. (B)
Tbni.
Tb.
Timp.
Ptti.
G.C.
Vl.
Vla.
Vc.
Cb.

muta B in H.

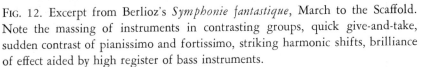

Fig. 12. Excerpt from Berlioz's *Symphonie fantastique*, March to the Scaffold. Note the massing of instruments in contrasting groups, quick give-and-take, sudden contrast of pianissimo and fortissimo, striking harmonic shifts, brilliance of effect aided by high register of bass instruments.

The key to the abbreviations of the names of the instruments which appear on this score is given on the facing page.

Fl.	— Flute(s)	C. ap.	— Cornet(s)	G. C.	— Bass Drum
Ob.	— Oboe(s)	Tr.	— Trumpet(s)	Vl.	— Violin(s)
Cl.	— Clarinet(s)	Tbni.	— Trombone(s)	Vla.	— Viola(s)
Fg.	— Bassoon(s)	Tb.	— Tuba(s)	Vc.	— Violoncello(s)
Cor.	— Horn(s)	Timp.	— Kettledrum(s)	Cb.	— Double-Bass(es)
		Ptti.	— Cymbal(s)		

sinners is foretold by a quotation from plain chant, the *Dies Irae* (Day of Wrath). We hear this solemn tune first intoned by tubas and large bells, as it might resound in a cathedral, but immediately each phrase is taken in turn by different groups of instruments, higher, more quickly, and with increasingly grotesque effect, as the devils take over.

4. In the second movement, the hero's dream of a grand ball is told. At the beginning, the misty atmosphere of the dream is depicted by murmuring strings and an ensemble of harps playing brilliant, skyrocketing arpeggios.

Throughout this entire piece, Berlioz tends to bring instruments that would ordinarily take subordinate or accessory roles to a more prominent position than usual by highlighting them and by giving some special value to their figures. More than any other composer of the nineteenth century, he seems to create his ideas for the orchestra directly, to conceive a figure or effect as it would be performed by instruments. His electric, kaleidoscopic boldness and verve of effect grew out of his keen feeling for the evocative power of the grand romantic orchestra. One interesting concomitant of this superb orchestral mastery was a sense for contrapuntal action whenever a figure made its appearance in the texture. Berlioz's instruments, as they work against each other, project that sense of counterthrust which is the essence of counterpoint.

By and large, during the nineteenth century, orchestral music leans toward the Wagnerian idea of orchestration, with its fullness and power, its richness of color. Brahms, Tchaikovsky, Dvorak, Franck, Liszt, Bruckner, and the earlier Mahler, all seem to be concerned with the massive, the grand, the heroic sound of the orchestra. As a reaction, toward the end of the nineteenth century, the orchestral qualities we have observed in Berlioz's music began to exert more influence. Transparency, strikingly unusual effects, economy, and lightness appear in the music of Debussy and Ravel, in some of Strauss and Mahler, and in much contemporary music.

As evidence of the tremendous appeal of nineteenth-century orchestral music, one has but to tabulate the orchestral repertoire of present-day symphony orchestras. They lean heavily to the large-scale works composed during the romantic era. Indeed, to many listeners, the entire world of music consists of compositions which embody the romantic orchestral idea of sound. Nowadays, the voicings of many jazz orchestras represent a modified version of Wagner's or Brahms' scoring, rich, compact, and full. Motion-picture music, not only in its scoring, but in its way of appealing to the feelings and sentiments of the movie-goer, echoes the sound of romantic orchestral music.

Virtuosity

The search for new, more impressive, richer, and more striking effects in orchestral music is all part of romanticism's urge toward expansion. Scoring was not the only aspect of performance that was affected. New effects made new, and often greater, demands upon the performers. Greater virtuosity was required in all fields of performance. This applied particularly to solo performance. The nineteenth century begins the era of the musical hero, the Paganini, the Liszt, the Rubinstein, the von Bülow, the Wagner. Both the difficulties of performance and the strangeness of the music itself acted to create a tremendous chasm between the artist and the listener. It was as if the artist were endowed with mysterious magic powers that set him apart from ordinary human beings. It was said of Paganini, the great violin virtuoso, that he was in league with the Devil. Not only the performer, but the composer himself was being separated and estranged from his audience, largely because of the elusive or difficult music he wrote in his search for individuality. It was said of Brahms that his violin concerto was not *for,* but *against* the violin. Here is a sample of the sort of figuration the violinist was expected to negotiate:

Ex. 7–11. Brahms: Violin Concerto, first movement.

The Piano

Aside from the orchestra, the principal medium in which this tendency of virtuosity developed was the piano, which, like the orchestra, received its definitive form in the nineteenth century.

Refinements and improvements in the structure and action of the piano were developed that gave it a much wider range of tonal effects and a more brilliant sound than its predecessor of the eighteenth century. The limits of pitch were pushed both higher and lower and the new registers were effectively employed.

Ex. 7–12. Piano ranges.

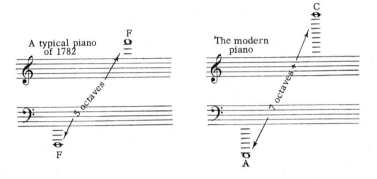

Romantic piano music shows an amazing variety and range of effects. We find the sharpest contrasts between loud and soft, high and low, full and thin, and these seem to have been negotiated by the performer with perfect ease. Of all the refinements, possibly the most important was the perfection of the sustaining pedal, which allowed a tone to reverberate for a time after it had been struck. This one resource opened an entire new world of tone color. (You can easily test this effect for yourself. At the piano, hold down the sustaining pedal, that is, the pedal at the right, and play the chord C–E–G. Release the keys and keep your foot on the pedal. Not only will you hear the reverberations of the tones that were struck, but you will hear, accompanying these tones, *all* the Cs, Es, and Gs above chiming in by *sympathetic resonance*.) Such atmospheric, delicate effects were exploited to the utmost in romantic piano music. Moreover, the sustaining pedal augments the mass of tone, so that grandiose effects are easier to achieve. Finally, much of the singing quality and warm tone which one hears from a fine piano performance comes from wise use of the sustaining pedal.

With its increased resources, the piano stimulated the development of distinctive personal styles. In each of the three works for piano mentioned at the beginning of this chapter, Chopin's Preludes, Schumann's *Carnaval,* and Liszt's Sonata in B minor, we discover a highly characteristic treatment of the keyboard.

Of all nineteenth-century composers, Chopin probably explored the capacities of the piano most thoroughly with regard to texture and coloristic effects. The first Prelude gives us a typically Chopinesque miniature. We hear a singing melody floating above a fine network of sound. Although the melody itself is straightforward and symmetrical, the coloration of the tune by use of inflections seems to create a kind of urgency. A complex figuration supports this melody, but the pattern is repeated under each motive, and is carried out during the entire piece. Chopin was a master at devising such figurations, such sonorous and airy laceworks of sound.

Ex. 7–13.

a. Chopin: Prelude in C major.

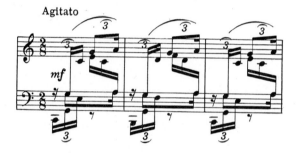

b. Chopin: Prelude in F♯ minor.

Naturally, these arabesques would require the use of a sustaining pedal, to create the desired atmospheric mood, and to maintain an adequate body of sound throughout the duration of the chord. Actually you are hearing just a few notes struck at any instant, perhaps no more than one or two. Thus, in Chopin's music, we receive the impression of easy but swift and soaring movement, sometimes gentle, sometimes stormy, but rarely heavy

or strained. Chopin's keyboard effects lend themselves best to compositions
in which a single mood prevails, or in which episodes of different moods
alternate. The first Prelude sings, but has an undercurrent of agitation. The
second, an unusual work of Chopin's, moves lugubriously, with a dark and
tortured effect; it exploits the heavy, obscure lower sounds of the piano.
The third is completely light and effervescent, the sixth is elegiac, the
eighth, stormy, the ninth, broadly singing, and the eighteenth is an explosion of violent melodramatic fury. Each of the pieces in this work is a
short, highly characteristic piece, in which strongly provocative expressive
qualities address themselves to the listener. At the same time, they are not
so specific in their emotional connotations that the listener is prevented
from finding his own particular or general reactions.

Robert Schumann, contemporary of Chopin, and very close to him in
stylistic and aesthetic respects, nevertheless developed quite a different
manner of composing for the piano. As we listen to Schumann's *Carnaval,*
we hear much that is similar to Chopin in general mood. But the quality of
sound in Schumann's music for piano is heavier, more massive than
Chopin's. The center of sound seems lower. Therefore, the quality of movement appears to be less light, and to involve something of a strain. Typically, Schumann uses more notes at a given time than does Chopin. Often
the performer has to negotiate massive chords which move rather quickly.
While Chopin's harmony seems to change at an even, rather slow rate,
whether the piece be slow or fast, Schumann's chords change quickly; the
harmony boils up, exploring and restless. We hear greater rhythmic imbalance in Schumann than in Chopin. This, together with the restless harmony,
gives an impression of instability and constant massive motion.

Ex. 7–14. Schumann: Chiarina from *Carnaval.*

Passionato

Briefly, Chopin gives the impression of an elegant ease of movement and
a transparent quality of sound, while Schumann gives the impression of a
rather heavy movement with a denser quality of sound. For that reason

Schumann frequently has a more forceful emotional impact upon the listener than does Chopin. There is a personal quality, often impulsive and fantastic, to his music. Chopin's texture and manner point the way to musical impressionism. Liszt, Ravel, and Debussy are his stylistic descendants. Schumann's texture, both in piano and in orchestral music, was adopted by his protégé, Johannes Brahms, and his harmony is a direct forerunner of the harmonic style of *Tristan und Isolde.* Franz Liszt also learned much from Schumann, as, indeed, he did from many of his nineteenth-century forerunners and contemporaries.

The demands made upon the pianist by nineteenth-century composers exceed anything which had been required previously for piano performance. At the summit of virtuosity stands the Sonata in B minor of Franz Liszt. This work embodies all the varied styles and techniques of piano performance that had been evolved up to this time; it also represents the trend of the later nineteenth century to encompass an entire world of expression and feeling in a monumental composition. Everything in this piece seems to have the air of bigness. Most of the music is phenomenally difficult to play. The range of sound covered is tremendous. The volume of sound moves from the loudest possible sonorities to the merest whispers. Most important of all, the range of expression in this piece covers a huge gamut. The low-pitched hollow passages at the beginning, with their uncertain harmony, suggest a kind of thoughtful foreboding. Suddenly this mood is broken by an explosive outburst, a wild crash of dissonant harmonies, spearheaded by a boldly arresting theme. Later, a grandiose and sweeping melody enters, to provide a contrast to what has preceded it. Lyricism, impassioned declamation, delicate fantasy, grim purpose set up in fugal manner, and finally, beatific resignation at the very end are some of the moods that succeed each other in this piece, much as scenes in a tableau.

In its effort to encompass a gigantic range of expression, this sonata seems to go far beyond the idiomatic style of the piano at many points. Most of the music is what we would call *pianistic,* yet many passages appear to imitate orchestral sounds. We can imagine bassoons and horns sustaining the first low tones while the string basses and celli take the slowly descending figure. Certain lyric passages call for flute or oboe; other massed effects suggest a compact sound of brasses. On the other hand, Liszt is apparently seeking the eloquence which is the special property of vocal music when he composes recitative and declamatory passages in this piece. Everywhere, in almost every respect, there seems to be some kind of push outward, an effort to exceed the limits of usual or ordinary sound, technique, and expression. Thus, like *Tristan,* the Sonata in B minor is truly a representative work of musical romanticism. Further evidence along these lines will turn up when we turn to form in romantic music.

Considering the dominating position of the virtuoso in the musical scene of the nineteenth century, it is not surprising that many important concertos were written during this period. Indeed, most of the solo concertos you will hear at symphony programs were written after the year 1800. Beethoven, Mendelssohn, Schumann, Chopin, Liszt, Brahms, Tchaikovsky, and Rachmaninoff wrote concertos for solo violin or piano and orchestra, all of which are in the vein of the grand virtuoso style. Today we are still under the spell of the musical wonder-workers; it is the soloist who captures the imagination of the audience and draws the full houses.

Throughout this chapter we have been concerned with the basic techniques and the expressive content of romantic music. From its harmonic tension and its harmonic color, we were able to proceed toward general aesthetic implications. We dealt with intense emotional expression, ideas of good and evil, of the ideal, of the supernatural, of the heroic, the faraway, the long-ago, of simplicity and the charm of nature, and generally, we considered that this all represented a flight from reality, from the everyday world. Associated with this trend, lending it material assistance, was the expanded world of performance, involving new sounds, greater brilliance, range, and virtuosity.

The rich content of romantic music is somewhat difficult to manage, particularly on a broad scale. We ask, "How can such materials shape themselves into musical forms?" Having learned much about the expressive values of romanticism, we can turn our attention to form in romantic music. As always, the proper way to understand musical form is to see how it grows out of the nature of the thing to be expressed.

FORM IN ROMANTIC MUSIC

First, we must say that there is no consistent principle of structure that governs romantic music. A prelude of Chopin and Liszt's sonata are not manifestations of the same guiding plan, as was the case with the classic minuet and sonata form. The harmonic and rhythmic forces in classic music set up lines of attraction which held both large- and small-scale forms in tight control. The *antigravitational* impulse of romantic music destroyed these lines, or at least made them much less powerful. The tremendous variety of expression and style in the nineteenth century created new problems of coherence and contour with virtually every composition. So, we have to look at special and particular structural phenomena, and we must restrict our generalizations somewhat.

The Dynamic Curve

Again we return to our source piece, the Prelude to *Tristan und Isolde.* We recall its dissolving harmony, its fluid rhythms, and its dense interweaving of melodic lines. The hearer has difficulty to orient himself, to grasp the structure of the piece. If we listen for landmarks, for clear points of structural arrival, we shall remain confused. But if we enter into the romantic world of expression, to sense the rise and fall of emotional intensity, we can get a fairly good idea of the structure of the Prelude. Each phase of movement begins on a relatively low level of pitch and intensity and builds up to a climax; after each climax, the music drops, and new tension begins to develop. Moreover, each successive phase of movement seems to reach a slightly higher point of climax. The entire piece builds up to the final climax, which is the most violent, impassioned, and sustained of all. Correspondingly, the collapse afterward is the most complete; exhausted, the music sinks back to its first gropings. Structurally, we sense a contour, rather than well-defined positions. The form takes shape in successively larger waves of sound, upon a curve of rising dynamic intensity. Its outline might be illustrated graphically as follows:

Ex. 7–15. Pattern of dynamic curve.

This rise and fall in strength of sound, this *dynamic curve,* is an important resource for building structure in nineteenth-century and early twentieth-century music. (You will recall in *The Erlking* how the emotional value of terror is steadily intensified by the higher pitches of the successive outcries of the child. Schubert has here used a dynamic curve as a form-building factor.)

In the dynamic curve of the Prelude to *Tristan,* Wagner has epitomized the entire dramatic idea of the opera. Such a plan corresponds very much to the way in which our own emotions grow and ebb. In this music, the composer seeks an empathy with the listener; he wants to bring his hearer entirely into the state of feeling set up by the music, so that the listener will lose himself in the music. Such an attitude is quite different from the seventeenth- and eighteenth-century idea of projecting affective qualities, wherein the sympathetic response of the listener was evoked without any intention of overwhelming him.

In its plan of mood value, the Prelude assumes rounded form; the piece ends very much in the mood of its beginning, although a literal repetition does not take place. We receive the impression of an A–B–A form, without the usual balance of sections and the clear definition of the boundaries of each part. Again, the emotional conditions indicated by the music help to define the form. The uncertainty at the beginning is matched by the collapse at the end. The final section, as in all A–B–A forms, acts as a counterstatement to the first section; therefore, it serves as an area of arrival. But the return does not sound like the triumphant and glorious achievement of a goal, as it would in sonata form; it is rather a sinking back, an exhaustion, a surrender, and a defeat.

Weakening of Cadences

In its lack of authentic cadence, in the absence of a sense of unequivocal completion, the Prelude to *Tristan* represents another important aspect of romantic form. By now we have some idea of the role that the cadential feeling plays in musical form. Not only does a cadence round off a section, but it acts as a goal, as a point of arrival toward which the music pushes. While much romantic music does arrive with a flourish at the end of a section or movement, a great many compositions of this era fail to arrive emphatically; they trail off, leaving a question unanswered. Liszt's sonata, for all its heroic wrestling and searching, evaporates into thin air at the end. Schubert's song *The City* ends with the sound of a dissonant chord; his song *Teardrops* clouds the major mode of the song with an ending in the minor mode. Chopin's first Prelude trails off; so does his A-major Prelude, that brief, delicate, and wistful fragment of a waltz. The lack of cadence seems to leave something unsaid, so that the mood will continue and the listener will furnish, in his imagination, the resolution of the story. Romantic poetry frequently employs this device. In the two short poems given below, much more is hinted at than is actually said. In Shelley's poem, we are awakened to the lingering fragrance of flowers, the reverberation of tones, the recollection of love, all of which echo far beyond the actual time of experience. In Wordsworth's poem, the simple lines hint at a deep and lasting sentiment.

To—

Music, when soft voices die,
Vibrates in the memory—
Odours, when sweet violets sicken,
Live within the sense they quicken.

Rose leaves, when the rose is dead,
Are heaped for the beloved's bed;
And so thy thoughts, when thou art gone,
Love itself shall slumber on.

Shelley

SHE DWELT AMONG THE UNTRODDEN WAYS

She dwelt among the untrodden ways
Beside the springs of Dove,
A Maid whom there were none to praise
And very few to love:

A violet by a mossy stone
Half hidden from the eye!
—Fair as a star, when only one
Is shining in the sky.

She lived unknown, and few could know
When Lucy ceased to be;
But she is in her grave and, oh,
The difference to me!

Wordsworth

In both the musical and poetic examples described above, we might very well consider that the form does not end when the music or words do. An essential part of the experience, and thus, of the form, is the echo, the reverberation which continues after the actual sound has ceased. Thus, the indeterminate limits of such musical forms associate themselves with the intimate, personal quality of expression in the pieces themselves; one's feelings linger afterward.

The two poles of romantic expression, the intimate and the grandiose, are embodied in two different kinds of structure, in so far as size itself is concerned. One is a short composition which explores one type of effect; the other is an extended form, frequently in one unbroken movement, which may include many different episodes.

The Short Piece

The short composition which deals with one expressive value, be it a song or piano piece, is most typical of nineteenth-century music. These pieces take their momentum from the impulse of the original idea; the brevity of the form needs no contrast or additional force in the way of development or extension. The inner structure of these short compositions tends to accommodate the expression of a single mood or feeling. In other words, their lyric value is best projected in a song or dance form. Thus, in Schubert's *Moments Musicales,* Chopin's Preludes and Etudes, Mazurkas, Waltzes, and Nocturnes, Schumann's many piano works, and Mendelssohn's *Songs Without Words* (note the title!), the form comes out typically as a series of well-defined, balanced periods and phrases, recalling the small two- and three-part forms of the eighteenth century. Here we find relatively little extension, although frequently, as we have mentioned above, the final cadences of these pieces are not calculated to bring matters sharply to an end. Indeed, the composers we have mentioned tend to be even more rigid in their phrase structure than were Haydn, Mozart, and Beethoven. The classic composers had a flexibility within the period which was balanced by a strong sense of cadence at the end. The romantic composers had an automatic, almost singsonglike evenness in the phrases of their short pieces, but they often surprise us by their indeterminate endings.

These short compositions have a wonderfully spontaneous charm. Composed in series of six, twelve, or more to a set, they can touch upon many different moods in succession. Chopin and Schubert preferred to give them general, nondescriptive titles, such as Impromptu, Nocturne, Ballade, etc. Mendelssohn and Schumann made a point of assigning characteristic titles to such pieces, as, for example, *Spring Song, Venetian Boat-Song, Papillons* (Butterflies), etc. In one set, his *Kreisleriana,* Schumann went so far as to identify each piece with an imaginary character, either *Florestan,* the impulsive spirit, or *Eusebius,* the introspective spirit.

To study the forms in which songs were written in romantic music, we can best refer to Schubert. We have already discussed one song of Schubert, *The Erlking,* in some detail. In form this was not scaled as a miniature but rather as a fairly extended dramatic scene. It was *through-composed,* meaning that to each line of text new melodic material was provided. This is opposed to *strophic* form, wherein the same music serves for all stanzas. Through-composed music tends to develop the ideas being expressed, the music sharing significantly in the unfolding of the idea. In strophic settings, the music, charming as it may be, eventually becomes a suitable framework for the stanzas and nothing more.

The song, *Thränenregen* (Teardrops) from *Die Schöne Müllerin,* just misses being a fully strophic song, and by just that much becomes an exquisitely touching work of art. The poem speaks of the reflection of the stars and the moon in the brook for the first three stanzas. Schubert has set this as a sentimental melody, with a few melting chromatic nuances; but the mode is *major.* The fourth stanza breaks the spell. Schubert suddenly places his music in *minor,* makes a turn back to major, but no! at the very end, the minor, the question, the doubt returns and leaves the final impression. Nothing could better suggest this melancholy, this clouding of intimate romantic mood than the sudden darkening of the harmony.

Another song, a familiar one, *Ungeduld* (Impatience), is entirely strophic. The basic form is short; each stanza is but eighteen measures long. But notice how convincingly Schubert suggests impatience by a quick pace and restless piano music. Each phrase of the voice is short; there are no real points of arrival, only momentary rest before picking up the pace. Each phrase reaches higher than the previous, until finally the dynamic curve achieves its peak with its refrain, "You are my heart!" Only at this end do we reach our cadence! This is truly a miniature, yet the fervor and the expanse of feeling it suggests carry far beyond its actual extent in time.

Large-scale Form

In building larger forms, nineteenth-century composers followed the general schemes which they inherited from the classic era. They used the sonata, the rondo, the two-part dance forms; to a large extent, their symphonies, concertos, sonatas, and overtures are modeled after those of Beethoven. Yet the changes in style and expression that took place in the nineteenth century affected the manner in which extended forms were built. This applies particularly to the ways in which romantic composers modified sonata form.

You will recall that classic sonata form, as it appeared in the symphonies, sonatas, etc., was a big structure. Much of the expressive content of a classic sonata form was buoyant, tuneful, even popular in vein. Nevertheless, much was serious, important, and challenging; and this aspect of expression was responsible for the expansion of the form.

Romantic composers, who were concerned greatly with mood, manner, and gesture, addressed themselves directly to the characteristic grand and serious style of the sonata, the symphony, and the concerto. Relatively few nineteenth-century pieces in sonata form are light or cheerful in mood. It was Beethoven, principally, whose music had the greatest effect in this direction.

Many romantic symphonies, in developing the grandiose manner, became extremely long. Some of Mahler's and Bruckner's works exceed an hour in length. Beethoven's *Eroica* Symphony and his Ninth Symphony stood as models for later compositions on an extremely broad scale.

Together with the increase in size, we often find an increase in the performing personnel. Beethoven's use of the chorus in the final movement of his Ninth Symphony was taken by romantic critics as a sign that the power of Beethoven's expression had exceeded the ability of instruments alone to realize. Henceforth, the chorus was used in a number of symphonies, particularly those that Mahler wrote. The sound of massed human voices was intended to provide the transcendental, the apocalyptic touch, especially toward the end of the symphony; it was necessary to make a fitting climax. Unlike Beethoven, however, romantic symphonists seem to lack that active inner logic and strength which, in his works, gave rise to broadened forms. Indeed, of the two tendencies in romantic structure, the minute and the monumental, the former often seems much more attractive. Now let us have a closer look at the way in which romantic composers used the sonata form.

The differences between classic and romantic sonata form stand out very clearly in the ways in which the expositions of the two forms are built. Classic sonata form was set up in two large key areas, with a considerable variety of material, much local contrast in style, and a broad drive to the cadence which ended the exposition. The composer was free to introduce a new theme as he saw fit, at any place; or, he might be perfectly happy working over one theme. Nevertheless, we observed a tendency to introduce an important new theme at the beginning of the second key area, a theme which might represent a contrast to the opening subject of the movement.

The vividness of expression, the search for distinctive, impressive moods in romantic music led its composers to underscore the characteristic thematic content of sonata form. To them it was important to find an arresting, serious subject, to work this theme over for a time, and then to introduce, as a large-scale contrast, a songlike theme which would be the counterstatement to the opening theme. The *personalities of the themes* and their dramatic opposition became the basic structural idea, not, as in the eighteenth century, the *opposition of two keys* and the harmonic-rhythmic pull of grand cadences.

Here are some examples of thematic contrast in nineteenth-century symphonies:

Ex. 7–16. Schumann: Symphony No. 1 in B♭ major.

a. First or masculine theme.

b. Second or feminine theme.

Mahler: Symphony No. 2 in C minor.

a. First theme.

b. Second theme.

Such a sharply marked thematic contrast between a bold, masculine, aggressive theme and a lyric, gentle, feminine theme can also be heard in the first movements of Brahms' Third Symphony and in César Franck's Symphony in D minor. Each theme, in these examples, has something of the character of an independent piece or episode; thus, there is a kinship with the small-scale lyric pieces we described earlier.

Because of the episodic structure in the romantic symphony, momentum over an entire movement has been sacrificed for the sake of highlighting individual moments of striking intensity or appeal. The price paid for this was a looser, less compact form with many stop-and-start effects. Such a structural plan is in line with the basic aesthetics of romanticism. The individual moment, the individual idea, the individual person himself, demands and receives room for expression, even at the expense of the structure of the entire organism. We are handsomely compensated, of course, by the special charm or the bold impact of the individual gesture.

Even in the symphonies of Johannes Brahms, who, of all nineteenth-century composers, represents the spirit of classicism most vigorously, we find points where the romantic loosening of structure is apparent. One of his finest movements, and one which represents the grand manner of the romantic symphony, is the first movement of his First Symphony. The description of this movement, given below, touches upon certain characteristic features of his style and summarizes the over-all structure of the movement.

We know immediately, in the first few measures that we are going to hear a big piece. Not only the fullness of sound, but the breadth and sustained manner of the melodic line and the quality of movement indicate spaciousness to the listener. Curiously enough, the first few notes in the upper line are very similar to one of the motives at the beginning of *Tristan*. Also Brahms' harmony has strong chromatic flavor. Yet the contrast is even more striking than the similarity. Listen to the inexorable beat, hammered out by the timpani. There is no question about the rhythmic meaning here. Also, despite the chromaticism in the upper voices, the sense of key is set and maintained through the pedal-points (the repeated and sustained tones in the bass) which hold firmly to the tonic note of the key. This introduction builds to a series of strong cadences, and thus prepares very effectively for the main part of the movement. It is an introduction conceived in a classic vein.

The chromatic motive of the introduction is built into the opening theme of the Allegro. In the first key area, note how Brahms has taken the syncopation of the opening motive and used it again and again to lead to a strong cadence. In this respect he follows his master, Beethoven. Here is the motive, and the maner in which it is used later:

Ex. 7–17. Brahms: Symphony No. 1 in C minor, first movement.

a. Introduction

b. Allegro of first movement.

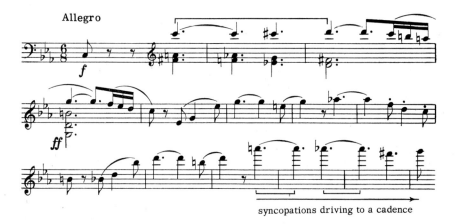

syncopations driving to a cadence

For the second key area, Brahms has actually composed two different pieces. The first is the usual lyric section with a theme that is the antithesis of the opening theme in most respects:

Ex. 7–18. Brahms: Symphony No. 1 in C minor; principal theme, lyric section.

The second section, used as a closing theme, picks up again the manner of the opening Allegro:

Ex. 7–19. Brahms: Symphony No. 1 in C minor, closing section.

Note, in the second phrase of this period, how Brahms creates a striking counterstatement by reversing the positions of the upper and lower themes: a technique of *invertible* counterpoint which adds stress to the stormy manner of the theme. Most of the first movement embodies the stormy, vigorous style. The second theme appears only as an episode.

Brahms' development section, spacious, yet closely knit, has the driving quality which brings him so close in spirit to Beethoven. This is most dramatically evident in the manner in which he planned the development. Less than half of the one hundred and seventy-four measures is devoted to harmonic explorations which move outward and away from any fixed tonal center. The remainder centers upon the dominant harmony of the main key. Like Beethoven, in the first movement of the *Eroica* Symphony, Brahms creates a tremendous drive toward the tonic key at the beginning of the recapitulation. The binding, the integrating effect of this gigantic cadential drive is entirely classic in its intention, although many incidental nuances betray the richness of harmonic detail we find in romantic harmony.

Brahms' recapitulation carries out the usual restatement of material heard in the exposition, but his coda is another matter. Instead of building up another and still more emphatic closing section in the manner of Beethoven, Brahms shows how strongly romantic procedures affected his thinking. Listen to the ending of the movement. After all the Storm and Stress, the coda relaxes into a calm, reflective sort of afterthought. The slowing down and the final cadence with its poignant plagal quality (see Chapter 2, page 61) create the kind of ending which we find in so many romantic works, and which we described above as being inconclusive and suspended.

Thematic Role in Romantic Form

The growing importance of thematic contrast in romantic sonata form is a symptom of a general tendency in nineteenth-century music, namely, to assign greater importance to themes in the structural and expressive aspects of composition. Individualism, as a creed, becomes very significant in romantic philosophy and aesthetics. Musically, the epitome of individualism, its very signal, is the *theme*. A striking, distinctive, and imaginatively conceived theme is a very precious thing in music. The theme becomes a landmark in nineteenth-century musical form, much more so than before. Themes, instead of cadences and key areas, are points of arrival and reference. This is particularly true of music that has a great deal of harmonic tension and instability, as in the Prelude to *Tristan* where, for all its spinning out, its endless flow, the melodic material consists of a few well-defined and salient motives which are worked over in many ways. This is an important means Wagner has chosen to bind the music together. His harmony wanders, his rhythm is imbalanced, but his melodic material is striking in its ability to hold the music in place.

Ex. 7–20. Beginning of Prelude to *Tristan und Isolde*.

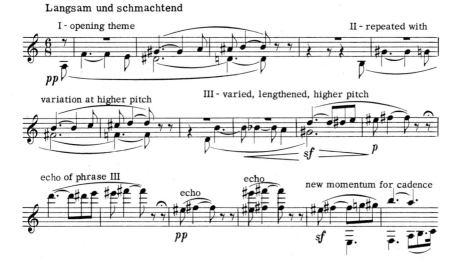

Listen to the first phrase; note its motive. The second phrase takes up the same motive at a higher pitch, the third phrase still higher and noticeably altered. Most of Wagner's melodic structure takes the form of statements and varied counterstatements of a salient motive, announced two, three, four, five, or even more times. Moreover, you will hear motives recurring frequently. Such recurrences help us get our bearings within this vast sea of movement that seems to have no shore. Thus, at the climax of the entire Prelude, we hear the opening motive thrust forward by the horns, expanding the emotional implications of this motive.

Thematic Transformation

Perhaps the most important contribution that romantic music made to large-scale form grows from its preoccupation with important thematic material. Liszt's sonata exemplifies this approach. Before, we have listed its styles and manners, its many different moods which succeed each other in such bewildering variety that the thread of continuity seems to disappear at times. Liszt endeavors to compensate for this seeming confusion by drawing most of his melodic material from four salient themes, which he transforms in many ways throughout the piece. These themes are changed drastically to conform to the various manners we have described above, yet at no time is it difficult to recognize them. The process of *thematic transformation* at the same time heightens interest and creates points of structural reference that help to hold the piece together for the listener. Here are some examples of Liszt's procedures:

Ex. 7–21. Liszt: Sonata in B minor. Thematic transformations.

a. Theme I—brooding, introspective.

Transformation—brilliant passage work.

b. Theme II—bold, impassioned, electrifying.

Transformation—lyric, fanciful.

c. Theme III—active, percussive.

Transformation—songlike.

To give the entire work some definite contour, Liszt has taken elements from the sonata form. He sets the bold theme against the lyric theme, with the usual contrast of key areas. In the center of the work, he builds a tremendous area of development, and the sonata winds up with a recapitulation of the two principal themes. This we can recognize as the outline of a sonata form, but, from phrase to phrase and section to section, we frequently lose that sense of purposeful arrival and clearly directed movement which gave rise to the classic sonata form. As we said before, the episodes are so different from each other, and, frequently, so loosely connected, that they would need little to make them independent pieces.

Liszt turns this particular fact to advantage; the contrast in style between the first and second sections is so great that they take on the roles of an opening and a slow movement respectively. The development is still another movement, a grand fantasy, while the recapitulation acts as a broadly scaled epilogue. Liszt took the cue from Beethoven in this respect; a number of the later works of Beethoven display this multisectional form. A very familiar orchestral version of this multisectional form, with serious, lyric, stormy, grandiose episodes, based on the transformation of two important themes, is the *symphonic poem, Les Préludes,* also by Liszt. The introspective, metaphysical idea of the title, that life is but a series of preludes, again demonstrates romanticism's preoccupation with destiny and the meaning of life. Liszt wrote the following about the piece, drawing his ideas from Lamartine's *Méditations poétiques:*

What is our life but a series of Preludes to that unknown song, the first solemn note of which is sounded by Death? The enchanted dawn of every existence is heralded by Love, yet in whose Destiny are not the first throbs of happiness interrupted by storms whose violent blasts dissipate his fond illusions, consuming his altar with fatal fire? And where is to be found the cruelly bruised soul, that having become the sport of one of these tempests does not seek oblivion in the sweet quiet of rural life? Nevertheless, man seldom resigns himself to the beneficent calm which at first chained him to Nature's bosom. No sooner does the trumpet sound the alarm, than he runs to the post of danger, be the war what it may that summons him to its ranks. For there he will find again in the struggle complete self-realization and the full possession of his forces.

Leitmotif

The multisectional form, held together by thematic relationships, is probably the most characteristic of large-scale romantic formal types. It certainly accommodates to romantic modes of expression; indeed, it came into being through the necessities of structure created by these modes of expression. The binding action of important themes, which can establish a long-range statement and counterstatement relationship within a musical form, has been used by many composers since the end of the eighteenth century. For example, Berlioz, in his *Symphonie fantastique,* refers again and again to the theme which represents the hero's beloved. It follows the hero everywhere, in his dreams, in his retreat to the country, up the steps of the scaffold, and in the nightmare of the Witches' Sabbath. Thus, it was called the *idée fixe.*

Ex. 7–22. Berlioz: *Symphonie fantastique, idée fixe.*

In order to achieve a measure of unity and, at the same time, shape the contours of his tremendous music dramas, Wagner assigned significant motives to persons, ideas, or situations. These have been given the name *leitmotif,* or, as Wagner himself designated them, *basic themes.* Here are some:

Ex. 7–23. Leitmotives.

Love-slumber motive from *Tristan* (Wagner)

very quiet

Sword motive from *Ring* Cycle (Wagner)

bold, angular
fanfare

Valhalla motive from *Ring* Cycle (Wagner)

chorale-like

River Rhine motive from *Ring* Cycle (Wagner)

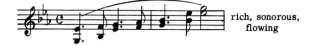

rich, sonorous,
flowing

They are used constantly as the source material for most of the content in a given opera. Important themes were treated differently by different composers. Berlioz, Weber, and Verdi generally quoted themes or motives verbatim, as they appeared earlier. These were *remembrance motives*. Wagner developed a motive intensively, as a rule, whenever he introduced it or reintroduced it. He might vary it somewhat in harmony or rhythm, but he rarely changed its basic character or mood. Liszt and Strauss often made drastic changes in the style of a given theme or motive, so that the theme was truly transformed.

Greater concern with thematic values as the central point in musical composition went along with the subordination of harmony as a form-building factor. Finally, in some styles this led to the complete elimination of harmonic elements as means of organization. The final step, when all musical material is drawn from a basic and generating melodic pattern, comes with *tone-row* music and will be a subject for our next chapter.

As a final word on the subject of form in romantic music, one particularly brilliant and distinctive solution to the problem of structure should be mentioned. We have heard Berlioz's *Symphonie fantastique* in connection with a number of topics discussed in this chapter. The first four movements each conform to a standard structural type. The first is in *sonata* form; the second is a *waltz with trio*; the third is again in *sonata* form; and the fourth movement is a *march*, also *with trio*. But the last movement is quite unique, structurally speaking. For a clue to its structure, let us glance at

Berlioz's scenario appended to the score: ". . . a Witches' Sabbath . . . a fearful crowd of spectres, sorcerers, monsters . . . strange noises, groans, shouts of laughter, distant cries . . . the melody of the beloved . . . trivial, grotesque . . . the *Dies Irae* . . . the *Rounds of the Sabbath.* . . ."

Berlioz has framed this picture of ancient and timeless evil exulting in its night of revelry as a *fantasia* and a *fugue*! Consider the fantasialike procedure of the first half of the movement, the short, weird episodes, often interrupted by violent contrasts. The effect is one of a monstrous improvisation. The devilish company is gathering. When all have arrived, the dancing begins; the dance is a fugue. Here Berlioz regards the fugal procedure, the imitations, as a means of building an excitement he might not otherwise have created with homophonic means. In this movement, an archaic form, the fantasia and fugue, turns out to be the ideal vehicle for the scenario of the piece and the type of expression contained therein. Berlioz's forms generally are worked out with keen insight and a sense for the justness of the relation of structure and expressive content.

Summary

By way of summary, we shall review the tendencies by which romantic music has developed its forms:

1. Developing emotional intensity, the surge of increasing excitement created the *dynamic curve,* as in *Tristan.*

2. Desire to avoid breaking off a mood sharply often led to the weakening of cadences.

3. Intense, characteristic moods, often intimate and deeply felt, took shape in short pieces whose regular and unbroken movement accommodated a single expressive value.

4. The grandiose manner expanded the scope of sonata form; mood qualities shifted emphasis in sonata form from harmonic-rhythmic structures to thematic contrasts and relationships.

5. Thematic relationships played an increasingly greater part in holding romantic forms together.

OPERA

Opera deserves separate consideration in this chapter because, of all musical forms, it lends itself best to the expression of the emotional and pictorial values especially cherished by romantic composers. These values—terror, tragedy, triumph, transfiguration, ecstasy, magnificent scenes of pageant, the mysterious solemnity of the cloister, the weirdness of the supernatural, and many others—hinted at or suggested in instrumental music, could be projected with tremendous impact by the combination of plot, scene, and music.

Opera, like instrumental music, was not one, but many things in the nineteenth century. As romantic opera has come down to us, we know it best in two different types: the opera of Wagner and the opera of Verdi. In order to point up the special expressive qualities of each composer, we shall consider them in comparison and contrast, using excerpts from Wagner's *Tristan* and Verdi's *Aida* as models.

Listening to an excerpt or section from either work, it would not be difficult to recognize which we were hearing. In general, the qualities of sound which each composer preferred are sharply different. Verdi's sound, as a rule, is thinner, more transparent, less richly mixed, higher in its center, and lighter than Wagner's. We hear the voice as the principal carrier of musical interest in Verdi, no matter what is going on. In Wagner, the voice is often but a single part in a complex web of intertwining lines; often the greater musical responsibility seems to be carried by the orchestra. Verdi's voices sing lyric songlike material that is idiomatically suited for them. Wagner's melodic lines contain difficult intervals and imbalanced rhythmic patterns. Verdi's harmony is less unstable and searching than Wagner's; he stays in one key longer, makes cadences frequently, and is a master at creating striking contrasts of harmonic color.

Movement in each work tells us much about the expressive values. Verdi almost always manages to create a strong sense of pulse or beat. His movement has a physical energy and strength. Each impulse creates fresh momentum. Together with his lightness of texture, Verdi's active beat creates a buoyant sense of movement. Notice that the bass instruments often punctuate the flow, establishing points of rhythmic arrival. They do not fill in the lower ranges of the harmony to create the typical thickness of Wagner's sound and the heaviness of his movement.

Verdi's emphatic quality of movement, linked to a feeling for action, tends to coalesce into well-marked phrases and periods. Thus movement reaches arrival points with strong cadential effect. Wagner's phases of movement, characterized by a much less accented pulse, lack the clean-cut points of arrival we hear in Verdi. The phrases often trail off; elsewhere, the expectation for arrival is thwarted by deceptive cadences. Due to his well-defined phrase structure, Verdi can project contrast with maximum effectiveness and thus give fresh momentum to his music at critical points. Wagner does not deal with the element of contrast in so sharp or clear a manner. His music tends to accumulate intensity and strength by the expansion of one particular idea over a long period of time.

These qualities of sound, movement, and arrival have arisen from essentially different expressive aims in Verdi and Wagner. Verdi was concerned with the bold projection and the sharp contrast of specific emotions and the striking impact of dramatic incident. Wagner constantly tried to overwhelm the listener with the power, extent, and mass of a general emotional drive. Verdi's dramatic values are electric; Wagner's are hypnotic. The sense of time becomes more urgent in Verdi; in Wagner, we lose the sense of ordinary time passing.

The emotional content of *Aida* deals with love, patriotism, jealousy, power, and revenge—emotions that strike us with a strong sense of reality. We have felt them ourselves. The emotional content of *Tristan* deals with an obscure hate that is magically turned into love by a mysterious potion. This love reaches a state of blind ecstasy and comes to fulfillment in death. These are emotional experiences far beyond the realm of ordinary human joy and suffering. Verdi's plot is a complex set of interwoven motives and events, all pointing to the final tragedy. Wagner's plot is relatively much more simple with fewer events. Therefore, Verdi's music is dedicated much of the time to developing *action*; Wagner's music, on the other hand, is devoted principally to developing emotional *moods*.

By way of illustration, we shall look at an excerpt from each opera. From *Aida,* we take Aida's soliloquy and prayer from Act I, beginning with the words, *Ritorna vincitor* (Return Victorious). From *Tristan,* we shall examine Isolde's recital of the curing of Tristan's wound. This is also from Act I, and begins with the words, *Wie lenkt er sicher den Kiel* (How Surely He Guides the Boat); it extends to the outcry, *Tod uns Beiden* (Death for Us Both).

The two scenes have a certain parallelism. Each comes early in the opera. Each sets up an intense conflict of emotion that bears upon the plot of its respective opera. Each scene is projected on a large scale, and at the end both Aida and Isolde invoke a power that is beyond human understanding as the only answer to their inner conflicts. These similarities, however, serve only to make the essential contrasts more vivid.

First, there is a fundamental emotional difference between the two scenes. Aida's motives are clear; her feeling for Rhadames and her love for her father and her country, although they conflict, are both strong and genuine. Isolde's motives are shadowy and mixed; she, like Aida, is a captive; she hates her captor, not for his triumph, but for his unworthy role in acting for another in the question of love. Somehow, we sense that

Isolde is already in love with Tristan. Her scene is charged with subtle psychological complexities and symbolisms. For Isolde the only answer is death; for Aida the answer must come from the gods, from whom she asks pity.

Each scene embodies its particular expressive qualities in form and movement. Wagner builds increasingly, with ebbing and flowing, expanding the range of movement and intensifying the emotional effect until the tremendous outburst is reached at the very end and Isolde collapses. Regardless of the quickening or slowing of pace, there is a constant flow of movement, maintained by the typical unstable harmony of Wagner, his shifting, imbalanced rhythms, the active development of motives and the constant crescendos and decrescendos. The dynamic curve, which dominated the form of the Prelude, is here used to carry Isolde's emotional outburst to the point of frenzy. Whatever gestures or motives may be used are swept up by the current. Example 7–24 gives an approximate outline of this scene:

Ex. 7–24. Diagram of Isolde's scene.

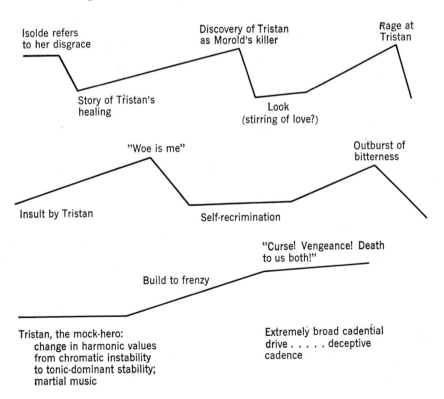

In contrast to the continuous flow of Isolde's scene, Aida's music shows distinct changes in pace and in intensity of movement. Moods change kaleidoscopically as Aida considers first one, then another of her conflicting desires and emotions. At the very beginning of the scene, the music underscores the emotional pull from two sides. Aida repeats the phrase she has just been singing with the chorus, *Ritorna vincitor*. Listen to the orchestra's chord on her last syllable: the upper instruments play a brilliant major chord, suggesting victory, while the bass adds an unstable tone which undermines the position of the harmony and suggests Aida's misgivings. The following example illustrates this penetrating bit of musicodramatic insight:

Ex. 7–25.

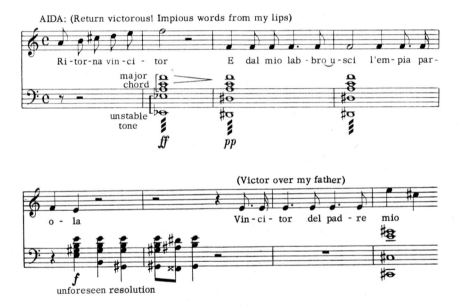

In the first recitative, the harmonic shifts are addressed to Aida's grave problem. Her feeling of loyalty rises to supplant, for the moment, her love for Rhadames. Following this recitative, Aida decides, momentarily, to remain with her father. This decision is set in a short, but perfectly balanced two-part form, that moves in a swift and agitated manner. Here the regular form and the crystallization of feeling complement each other. At the end of this song indecision returns and the moment of uncertainty is emphasized by a deceptive cadence. Again a recitative, rather songlike, in which Aida reflects on her love for Rhadames, follows; this is succeeded by a second aria, in which the decision is to place love above duty.

This second aria is set in a remote minor key, to suggest the impending tragedy which this decision will call forth. Finally, Aida, despairing to find answer within herself, turns to the gods in prayer. Verdi has set this final section again as a song, with rounded and balanced phrases. The texture in this section, high, remote, shimmering, transparent, and vibrant, captures the spirit of mysterious invocation and stands in contrast to all of the four preceding sections, each of which had its own characteristic texture. The last section, in its gentleness of movement and steady continuity of sound, acts musically as an area of arrival for the entire scene; thus, it corresponds with the sense of dramatic resolution in the prayer. Verdi, as in his other music, plays contrasts effectively and theatrically against each other with an eye to the final reconciliation.

Ex. 7–26. Diagram of Aida's scene.

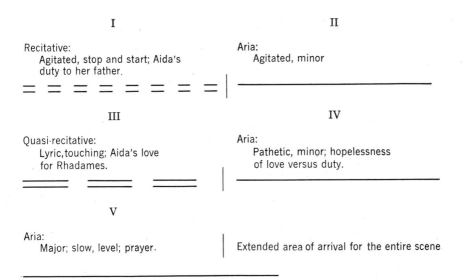

These two scenes show Verdi and Wagner in their typical mature style. Of the two, Wagner represents romanticism much more intensely than does Verdi. The continuously expanding flow of Wagner's music is much more in the spirit of the romantic age than are Verdi's well-defined articulations of movement. Verdi becomes romantic in his use of lyricism, in certain uses of chromaticism and harmonic instability, and in his exploration of color values, as in Aida's final song. Wagner shows a debt to classicism in his development of motives, harking back to Beethoven. Wagner's music drama, however, is entirely a creation of the nineteenth century. Verdi's opera is the nineteenth-century version of Italian opera, a genre with a long history and established traditions.

After Wagner and Verdi, the styles they represent continue to live in somewhat altered guise. Richard Strauss used many of the techniques of Wagner, his orchestration, his rich harmony, and the leitmotif, but departed from the grand metaphysical area of expression. Rather, Strauss's operas tend to deal with personal issues, often with morbid psychological connotations, as *Salome* and *Elektra.*

Giacomo Puccini is the chief heir of the Verdi tradition; also, he is the principal representative of the manner called *verismo,* which sought its subject matter in the realism of nineteenth-century city life. In this respect, Puccini is the counterpart of Zola, De Maupassant, and Flaubert in literature, and of Daumier in art. *La Bohème* of Puccini is one of the best-known operas in the entire repertory. It must be said, however, that Puccini does not use a *realistic* musical technique; rather, his music offers a very sweet, colorful, and ingratiating manner, sentimental instead of brutal.

Opera, in the nineteenth century, was written in other styles than those of Verdi and Wagner. In the 1820s and 1830s the most spectacular form was French grand opera; this was an elaborate type of production involving vast resources of chorus, ballet, and scenery, as well as the usual apparatus of orchestra and soloists. Grand opera centered upon subjects of historical interest and was directed principally toward the politically élite society of Paris under the rule of Louis Philippe, the "citizen king." Grand opera, whose chief exponent was Giacomo Meyerbeer, adopted the Italian musical style of composition, the ingratiating, nicely shaped style of Rossini. But the appeal of such works as *The Prophet, The Huguenots,* and Halévy's *The Jewess* was in their extremely effective combination of spectacle, popular plot, and assimilable music. Verdi, much later in the century, was to employ grand opera's spectacle in his *Aida.*

Comic opera also had a vigorous life in the nineteenth century. Many of the tunes from this genre are familiar to us today, such as the Barcarolle from Offenbach's *Tales of Hoffmann,* Figaro's Largo al Factotum and Rosina's Una voce poco fa from Rossini's *Barber of Seville,* the waltzes from Johann Strauss's *Gypsy Baron* and *Die Fledermaus,* as well as a whole bouquet of tunes from Gilbert and Sullivan's *The Mikado, The Pirates of Penzance,* and other amusing and familiar favorites.

One important opera of the nineteenth century, Moussorgsky's *Boris Godunov,* was written in a manner entirely different from those of Italian, French, or German opera. Moussorgsky's work epitomizes the new Eastern European nationalism that developed in the later nineteenth century. In line with this tendency, Moussorgsky has given a central dramatic position to the chorus, which represents the Russian people. He has turned his back on the sophisticated musical language of Western Europe, the language of Wagner or Verdi; instead he has used idioms, sounds, rhythms, expressive qualities suggestive of the native culture of Russia. Here are two examples which illustrate two important aspects of Moussorgsky's style: (1) his sense for color and immediate impression, as represented in the bell sounds of the Coronation Scene; (2) his preference for simple, straightforward, down-to-earth music, as represented in an excerpt from Varlaam's song from Act I.

Ex. 7–27. Moussorgsky: *Boris Godunov.*

a. Coronation scene.

b. Varlaam's song, Act I.

Moussorgsky disliked the academic development procedures of Western symphonic and operatic composition. Instead he preferred to create fresh effects, to spin out his material in a somewhat improvisatory manner, ringing the changes upon a few very simple motives. Tone color and rhythmic drive are central points in his style. Thus, Moussorgsky has influenced both the impressionists and the folkloric composers of the early twentieth century.

SUMMARY

We have presented the romantic era in music as being motivated toward expansion; it reaches outward in many directions, propelled, it would seem, by a centrifugal impulse. Considering the enormous variety of styles, forms, and procedures wherein each composer seems to strike out for himself in an unexplored direction, it follows that romanticism is a time of individualism, not a time of common practice. Growing in different directions, two composers, each truly romantic in spirit, can be utterly opposed to each other in specific features of style and aesthetics, as for example, Mendelssohn and Wagner. In our summary, therefore, we shall not attempt to establish a general set of criteria applicable to romantic music generally. Rather we shall list the important points covered in the chapter and indicate some of the important composers associated with these points.

I. Qualities of Sound
  1. New and striking instrumental textures (Berlioz)
  2. Exploitation of piano sonorities (Chopin, Schumann, Liszt)
  3. Continuous play upon a special sonority (Schubert, Mendelssohn, Chopin)
  4. Harmonic instability (Liszt, Wagner, Schumann)
II. Qualities of Movement
  1. Gentle, steady movement (Schubert, Mendelssohn)
  2. Impulsive, explosive movement (Schumann, Liszt, Berlioz)
  3. Continuously intensifying movement (Wagner)
III. Forms
  1. Short characteristic pieces (Schumann, Schubert, Chopin, Mendelssohn)
  2. Standard classic forms (Weber, Schumann, Schubert, Mendelssohn, Brahms, Tchaikovsky, Verdi)
  3. Forms based on leading motives
    a. Liszt—symphonic poem in a single movement
    b. Wagner—leading-motive technique
IV. Expressive Aims and Subjects
  1. Intense, immediate emotional impact (many composers)
  2. Interest in the faraway, the long-ago, nature, the homeland (Moussorgsky), Weber)
  3. Pictorialism (Mendelssohn)

4. The grandiose, the ideal, the superlative (Wagner, Liszt, Mahler)

5. The supernatural (Berlioz, Liszt)

6. Eloquent musical declamation; musical speech and poetry (Wagner, Schubert)

7. Conflict between good and evil (Wagner, Liszt, Mahler)

V. Technical Devices

1. Greatly expanded use of leading-tone harmony

2. Deceptive cadences

3. Increasing rhythmic imbalance

4. Leading motive as a binding factor

5. Greatly extended range and variety of sound

6. Increased brilliance and difficulty in performance

All the special characteristics of romantic music, those which set it apart from its predecessors, are gradually exploited more and more as the nineteenth century moves to its close. The process of separation, by which elements found in classic music were taken out of context and highlighted, continues, so that by the beginning of the twentieth century a number of special techniques and styles were developed. There are refinements of certain qualities of romanticism, appearing under such names as *expressionism, impressionism, folkloric music,* and *neoromanticism.* These we shall examine in our next chapter.

As a final word on romanticism, we might speculate that it represents a phase of development in the growth of musical self-consciousness. Rationalism and authority might embody a sort of *supra*-consciousness, reflected by the concern with large-scale problems that found their solution in a classic balance. Romanticism represents nineteenth-century *self*-consciousness, the individual regarding himself as the principal focus of interest and importance. We might carry the analogy further and point to the concern with the *sub*-conscious which marks so much of twentieth-century art, philosophy, and psychology. Here, indeed, is the process of separation at work on a grand scale over centuries of thought and expression. Rejecting the answers of the eighteenth century, self-contained but incomplete, the romantic artist sought solutions in his own imagination, feeling, and mystic ethic. His inability, or his unwillingness to reach a convincing resolution eventually engendered a disillusionment and a strong counterwave to the expressive ideas so cherished in the nineteenth century. We are still living in an age in which romanticism is somewhat suspect; but we have been learning to accept romantic expression, not for what it claims to do, but for what it *is*, a fascinating, distinctive, colorful tour of the human spirit.

SUGGESTED LISTENING PROJECTS

1. **Schubert, *Der Lindenbaum* (The Linden-tree)**

Listen for: Folk-song quality; exquisite but simple shaping of the melody; basically strophic structure of song; changes which Schubert made to integrate the structure, such as fluctuation between major and minor mode, variation in piano accompaniment for successive stanzas, changes in pace (hurrying forward and holding back) in piano accompaniment; picturesque touches such as chromatic figures at "wind;" use of horn figures to suggest rural setting.

2. **Chopin, Scherzo in B♭ minor, Victor LM–1132**

Listen for: Intensely dramatic contrasts; wide range; fluctuation between broadly singing melodic lines and extremely brilliant virtuoso figuration; check beginning and ending of piece to see how Chopin began in one key and ended in another; variations in quality of movement although the pace remains relatively constant.

3. **Mendelssohn, Symphony No. 3 in A minor, first movement. Vox 7080**

Listen for: Elegance of melodic material; songlike nature of themes; chorale style of introduction; emphasis on minor harmonies, suggesting a melancholy, nostalgic quality; neat balance of phrases; luminous orchestration; easy, swinging pace of Allegro.

4. **Wagner, *Die Walküre,* introduction and opening scene**

Listen for: Contrast between introduction and opening scene, storm mood versus the suggestion of awakening love; single tone held throughout the introduction (the tonic) while the harmony shifts above and below it; change in quality of movement from steadily driving pace to uncertain fluid manner; consistent development of motives in both sections; use of the dynamic curve.

5. **Moussorgsky, *St. John's Night on the Bare Mountain.* Victor LM–1816**

Listen for: Short, colorful, pointillistic effects; modal harmony; tunes suggesting folk dances; tendency to repeat most phrases at least once; sectional structure.

Chapter 8. Modern Music

MUSIC IN the twentieth century continues to exhibit those trends which were so characteristic of romantic music, the search for new and striking techniques of composition, the development of personal styles. To the person who is trying to obtain a perspective, a bird's-eye-view of modern music, the heterogeneity of styles is far more evident than any underlying unity which may exist. To point up this individuality of styles, few contrasts would be more striking than those offered by the Second Symphonies of Roger Sessions and Walter Piston, respectively. These works, recently made available to the listener through recordings, show completely different ideas of musical expression. In each work, the style is epitomized by the first few moments of the opening movement.

Piston's work begins with a broad, sweeping melody which has a distinctly romantic flavor and contour in its rather somber and reflective manner and its undulating rise and fall. Rhythmically, the Piston work has a regular, deliberate quality of movement, and at the beginning the phases of movement are projected on a broad scale. Texturally, the sound seems to have a solid *core,* to be anchored to a strong base, giving a sense of fullness and richness. Harmonically, we have no difficulty sensing a tonal center. The tone on which the opening melody begins, the lowermost note of a minor triad, announces itself as the tonic; the harmony itself has a modal flavor, due to the use of a raised sixth degree. You can hear this tone very prominently, since it stands just below the climax, the uppermost tone of the melody. Generally, this particular place in Piston's music suggests the serious, thoughtful manner of late nineteenth-century symphonists; the music of Brahms and Franck comes to mind.

We are not able to orient ourselves so successfully at first in Roger Sessions' Symphony. There, instead of a broadly scaled melody, motives and fragments are hurled at us with explosive force. Immediately there is a sense of development, of working-over; we are plunged directly into the

Fig. 13. The New York Philharmonic-Symphony Orchestra Dmitri Mitropoulos, Musical Director.

middle of a profound struggle. Although we may feel subconsciously that a pulse is present underneath the furious give-and-take, it certainly is entirely different from the stable and steady meter of Piston's music. The texture contributes its share to the feeling of tension and instability. There is less of a core of sound; contrapuntal activity, a layering of component parts seems to be Sessions' idea of texture. On the other hand, the energetic propulsion of the motivic fragments requires less contact with the "earth" of a solid foundation of sound. Harmonically, Sessions has taken his cue from the post-Wagner trend; his music employs, to a high degree of saturation, the elements of instability and tension we have already described, *minus* the chordal matrix from which these elements originally had sprung. In this work Sessions' genealogy appears to stem from various sources, from Beethoven in his serious manner, from Berlioz, possibly, in the technique of orchestration, from Wagner, in the harmonic procedures. Nevertheless, once we adjust ourselves to the somewhat forbidding façade of this music, we can feel the impact of a strong, and in its way, eloquent style; moreover, as we listen, it becomes evident that Sessions has a convincingly dramatic way of carrying his music forward.

The contrast between Piston and Sessions is even more striking when we realize that these two composers have had very similar backgrounds, are of an age, and that these two works were written within a few years of each other. We could multiply the contrasts of style by many times by introducing other examples of American and European music. But the point of this demonstration, *the extreme diversity of modern music,* should be quite clear by now.

In addition to the aesthetic and philosophical motivations which led composers in the nineteenth century to strike out for themselves, stylistically speaking, several additional stimuli arose in the twentieth century that gave added impetus to the search for different modes of musical expression:

1. Circulation of modern music through performance, radio, recording, and publication has made it possible for a composer to acquaint himself with virtually any current mode of musical expression.

2. Research in music history by modern musicologists has made musical values of past eras available to the composer of today.

3. Modern technology, particularly that concerned with electronics, has opened new areas of exploration in the field of creating sound itself.

In today's musical Tower of Babel, the composer, critic, and listener are faced with a sticky problem at the very outset. They must define, in the case of each musical composition, the very premises upon which its values and meanings are based. Today's music has no basic grammar upon which all agree, as in the eighteenth century with its sense of key and period structure. As a result we must first concern ourselves with the anatomy and physiognomy of modern music. This is as it should be. In music, as in any other mode of communication, we must have a pretty good idea of what is being said before we make up our minds whether or not we agree with the content of the expression or accept the manner in which it is being uttered.

Stylistically, today's music is not entirely helter-skelter. Since the end of the nineteenth century, certain lines of development have had significant strength, direction, and continuity. We shall describe these principal trends, considering them along the following lines:

1. Their expressive values and feeling for movement
2. Their techniques
3. Their solution of the problem of form
4. Their historical antecedents
5. Where pertinent, their association with other aspects of culture

It was in the period directly following Richard Wagner that modern trends of musical composition began to crystallize. From this era, the saturation point of musical romanticism, two very different musical styles evolved. These were *impressionism,* developed principally by the French composers, Claude Debussy and Maurice Ravel, and *expressionism,* cultivated by Austrian and German composers, such as Arnold Schönberg, Anton von Webern, and Alban Berg.

IMPRESSIONISM

Expressive Values

Impressionism represented a reaction against the philosophic and aesthetic ideas of Richard Wagner. It rejected his grandiose idealism, overdrawn heroic manner, and his mysticism. Impressionist composers wished to project vague and evanescent moods; they avoided strong or violent emotional values. They created instead a feeling of subtle, subdued restlessness that did not seek resolution or arrival but gave the impression of movement being poised in mid-air.

Fig. 14. Claude Monet: *Bridge over Pool of Pond Lilies.* (Courtesy of the Metropolitan Museum of Art.)

Subject matter in impressionism centered around fantastic, faraway, nostalgic, and pastoral ideas. The music depicted the play of water, wind, and the sea, the drifting of clouds, or the moods of colorful and exotic scenes. The titles of compositions are strongly evocative, such as *Delphic Dancers, Ondine* (The Water-Nymph), *What the West Wind Saw, The Engulfed Cathedral, Footsteps in the Snow,* etc. At all times, the object was to give a personal impression of some aspect of the external world in a form whose outlines were blurred and whose colors tended toward the pastel.

Techniques

Impressionism used any musical device that had the power to evoke such moods and values. Particularly in the field of harmony new, strange, and colorful effects were developed. Impressionist composers were unsympathetic to the Wagnerian conception of artistic expression, nevertheless, they found much in Wagner's harmonic language that could be used for their own purposes. As we know, Wagner used tone combinations that gave an effect of instability, of need for fulfillment and resolution. The opening of Wagner's *Tristan und Isolde* symbolizes romanticism's hopeless yearning, its sense of deep tragic emotion. This mood is established by the harmonic tension of the richly dissonant chords. (See Examples 8–1 and 8–2.)

Impressionism seized upon this quality of harmonic color and instability, but used it in an entirely different musical situation. Ravel's *Ondine* begins with a combination of tones quite similar to that which begins *Tristan*. But, as we can see, both the texture and the quality of movement are quite different.

Ex. 8–1. (Note the tones marked by squares.)

a. Wagner: *Tristan und Isolde,* opening.

Langsam und schmachtend

b. Ravel: Ondine from *Gaspard de la nuit,** opening.

Ravel, in contrast to Wagner's profound metaphysical introspection, created a vague, fairylike atmosphere. There were many chords of this type used by Wagner and borrowed by the impressionists solely for the sake of color. Example 8–2 shows a series of these.

Ex. 8–2. Debussy: Prelude, *Footsteps in the Snow.**

It is remarkable that Debussy was able to use such rich harmonic effects in a short piece meant to portray the plaintive and melancholy mood of winter. The harmony actually contributes to the mood; each harmonic effect becomes a separate phase of movement; there is no building up of tension by piling on momentum.

The impressionists not only picked and chose from late nineteenth-century harmony. They were alert to utilize any harmonic resource that was available. Frequently they turned to the musical systems of the Middle Ages, of folk music, or of exotic countries.

Each of these had possibilities for color that were entirely absent from the traditional harmonic system of Western music. In fact, the cadential formula of eighteenth- and nineteenth-century music was the one type of

* Permission for reprint granted by Durand et Cie, Paris, France, copyright owners. Elkan-Vogel Co., Inc., Philadelphia, Pa., agents.

harmonic effect that impressionist composers generally avoided. They tried also to circumvent the major scale, the best representative of a key sense. As we have seen, the major scale represents the last word in clear harmonic definition. This potential for clear harmonic definition is closely associated with well-defined points of arrival in the structure of a piece. But such clear articulation was not sympathetic to the expressive ideals of impressionism. Moreover, scales other than the major had a strangeness, an intriguing quality that attracted the impressionists. Their color effects were suitable for the palette of musical impressionism. Here are some examples. The excerpt is given and below it, in each case, the scale upon which the excerpt is based.

Ex. 8–3. Ravel: Quartet in F, first movement.*

Example 8–3 is a graceful, floating melody that takes advantage of the plaintive quality of the Phrygian scale upon which it is based. The Phrygian scale has a half step between the first and second degrees as well as between the fifth and sixth degrees. These half steps, being low in the scale, tend to suggest a resigned, rather than an energetic effect.

Ex. 8–4. Debussy: Prelude, *Footsteps.**

* Permission for reprint granted by Durand et Cie, Paris, France, copyright owners. Elkan-Vogel Co., Inc., Philadelphia, Pa., agents.

This halting, forlorn, broken melody also uses a scale which has the half steps placed low. This is the Aeolian scale, with half steps between 2 and 3, 5 and 6. Again the color of the scale sets up the mood.

Ex. 8–5. Debussy: Prelude, *The Hills of Anacapri.**

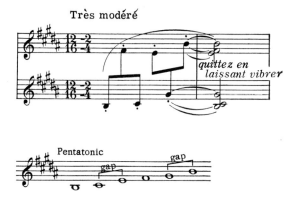

The pentatonic scale, a gamut of five tones, is used in Example 8–5. Notice that it skips two notes on its way upward. It is a primitive kind of scale and has been used in folk music in many parts of the world. Debussy employs it here possibly to suggest the echoing reverberation of bells or shepherd's horn through the hills.

When a scale has intervals of different size, as those we have examined, it retains some power to establish points of reference. The special intervals are melodic landmarks. In the whole-tone scale, on the other hand, all the intervals are equal to each other, being whole steps. Therefore, this scale cannot establish a point of melodic reference. This vagueness is admirably suited to the aims of musical impressionism; hence, it has been intimately linked with this style, but its actual use has been somewhat less than its reputation would lead us to believe. Sometimes, as in Debussy's Prelude, *Sails,* it forms the basis for a large section of a piece; at other times it

* Permission for reprint granted by Durand et Cie, Paris, France, copyright owners. Elkan-Vogel Co., Inc., Philadelphia, Pa., agents.

appears fragmentarily. In *Sails* the whole-tone effect helps create the impression of a slowly swaying passive motion, the easy, indolent mood of a sailboat upon the sea.

Ex. 8–6. Debussy: Prelude, *Sails*.*

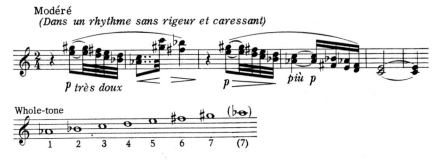

It is interesting to note that Debussy introduced a striking effect of contrast in the middle section of this piece by using the pentatonic scale.

Impressionist composers worked out many special effects of harmony that were new to music at that time. We have looked at a few of these, enough to realize that harmony in this style cannot be separated from texture and color. In impressionism, the chord is a resource for sonority effect, not a carrier of a dynamic quality of movement.

Indeed, texture was one of the principal concerns of the impressionist composer. Whatever he used in the way of instrumentation, wherever he placed his sounds, he was careful to create a transparent, luminous, self-sufficient quality of tone with a distinctive color value. Ravel and Debussy were especially fond of exploiting the pedal resources of the piano, which allow tones to reverberate long after the tone has been struck and give the effect of music floating in the air. The excerpt from the *Hills of Anacapri*, Example 8–5, shows how Debussy used this device.

Form in Musical Impressionism

It is rather apparent that such techniques of harmony and sonority would not be dedicated to building up extended or highly organized forms. On the contrary, the forms tend to be rather simple. The principal technique of structure was to string out a series of minute and relatively separate effects; at the same time, a consistency of texture was maintained as well as smooth

* Permission for reprint granted by Durand et Cie, Paris, France, copyright owners. Elkan-Vogel Co., Inc., Philadelphia, Pa., agents.

connection between chords. Small and gentle phases of movement were repeated and varied but they did not develop any emotional intensity.

Many pieces in this style consisted of a series of episodes, sometimes in A–B–A form, sometimes in rondo form. Sonata form was rarely used. Impressionism found no use for the harmonic, rhythmic, and motivic contrasts and development which gave rise to sonata form. The effect of contrast between episodes was created by changes in texture, pace, or harmonic quality. Thus, in *Sails,* Debussy managed to project a striking contrast by using the pentatonic scale for the middle part and the whole-tone scale for the first and last parts.

One form-defining procedure was taken over from the romantic technique of building up to tremendous climaxes. This was the *dynamic curve,* in which a steady increase or decrease in the volume or intensity of sound provided a method for organizing small musical fragments into a larger line; the dynamic curve thus gave some over-all shape to a section of considerable extent. The dynamic curve, however, *did not serve an emotional purpose in impressionism,* as it did in romantic music. Rather, it controlled the rise or fall in the intensity of an impression. Its function was pictorial, descriptive. As such, it made an effective framework for *Lever du jour* (Daybreak), the first number in Ravel's *Daphnis et Chloé* Suite No. 2. Daybreak, the rising of the sun, and increasing action of the shepherds and shepherdesses—all describe a rising dynamic curve. Ravel begins the piece with the slightest murmur of sound, created by gliding harps and winds and muted, sustained strings, a perfect example of impressionism's pastel tone painting.

After some measures which expand this quality somewhat, a melody takes shape in the lower strings, crystallizing, as it were, out of the amorphous fragments heard at the very beginning. This melody, built principally from one-measure figures, grows by linking its motives together in a general upward direction. The broad dynamic curve of the entire piece is given point and focus by the wide sweep of this melody, which always begins low and rises gradually. Several climaxes are reached, attaining successively higher peaks, and the last, of course, is the highest. In its general contour, this piece resembles the Prelude to *Tristan,* but the details and nuances of style bring about a totally different result. Note in this piece how steady and even the rhythm seems, how stable and placid the general harmonic effect is, and how calmly the bass instruments support the texture. In these respects, Ravel's piece is diametrically opposed to *Tristan.*

Other examples of use of the dynamic curve may be heard in Debussy's *Fêtes* from his Nocturnes for Orchestra, which pictures an approaching and departing group of dancers and merrymakers, and in Ravel's *Bolero* and *La Valse,* which build up an impression of increasing physical excitement.

Historical Antecedents

Impressionism was only in part a reaction against Richard Wagner. Throughout the nineteenth century many pieces written in a pictorial vein to evoke certain moods forecast the impressionism to come. For example Beethoven's Sixth Symphony, the *Pastoral,* is a series of five impressions of various aspects of rural life.

In Mendelssohn's *Hebrides* Overture, constant repetition of a short but graceful motive suggests the play of water, a typical impressionistic subject. Chopin was a valuable source book for the impressionists with his treatment of the piano pedal for sonority and his incredibly imaginative and delicate keyboard figuration. Wagner himself created the impression of water flowing when he spun out rolling motives at the beginning of *Das Rheingold.* These examples are but a few of the pictorial pieces that abound in nineteenth-century music. They serve to show how impressionism grew out of one aspect of romanticism.

Impressionist Painting and Symbolist Poetry

Impressionism in music was closely allied with other activities in the creative arts that were taking place in Paris just before the turn of the century. Actually, musical impressionism acquired its name from painting, from the school of Monet, Pissarro, Sisley, and Renoir. These painters achieved the same blurred outlines, the same misty luminous effects that the composers worked out in their music. *Pointillism* was the painter's technique, a method of combining separate tiny bits of color suggesting the prismatic effects of light broken up into its constituent colors. Pointillism created much the same effect in painting that specific small moments of texture and sonority did in music. Both in painting and in music the quality of movement was floating, gentle, disembodied. Monet's *Bridge over Pool of Pond Lilies* represents impressionist painting in its earlier, somewhat romantic phase. (See Fig. 14.)

Symbolist poets and writers furnished much material for impressionist vocal music. Verlaine, Mallarmé, Maeterlinck, and others cultivated a style characterized by nuance, ideas half-formed, suggestion, exotic and fantastic atmosphere. This manner of the symbolist writers found a strong response among impressionist composers. The trailing word image could be enhanced by the trailing musical phrase. Frequently symbolist poets tried to develop a purely decorative or musical quality in their texts, a play on sonorities without special reference to meaning. Consider the colorful, mellifluous quality of the following excerpt from *Apparition* by Stephen Mallarmé:

> La lune s'attristait. Des séraphins en pleurs
> Rêvant, l'archet aux doigts, dans le calme des fleurs
> Vaporeuses, tiraient de mourantes violes
> De blancs sanglots glissant sur l'azur des corolles.

Debussy's *Prelude to the Afternoon of a Faun* was inspired by Mallarmé's poem of the same name; his opera *Pelléas et Mélisande* is based upon Maeterlinck's drama; and he wrote songs to poems of Paul Verlaine.

Ravel wrote much that was impressionist in flavor, such as *Gaspard de la nuit, Daphnis et Chloé,* and *Rapsodie espagnole,* yet in all his works there was a sense for the long line not entirely compatible with the pointillistic techniques of impressionism. This linear aspect of Ravel's music led him to write works in traditional forms, particularly the sonata form, and to write much music that had no pictorial or special mood values. Frederick Delius in England, Alexander Scriabin in Russia, Charles Loeffler in America, Manuel de Falla in Spain, all wrote music in the impressionist style. Today impressionism has long died out as an active school. Indeed, toward the end of his life Debussy himself veered away from the pure impressionist style. Yet much of the harmonic vocabulary of today's music was first defined by the impressionists, and here and there, in music written much later, atmospheric touches recall this style.

EXPRESSIONISM AND TONE-ROW MUSIC

Expressive Values

Musical expressionism represented the most complete contrast possible to impressionism. Its object was to suggest the innermost world of feeling, not the external world of picture and mood. Expressionism tried to give an idea of the struggles, tensions, and contradictions working within the subconscious. This inner world has strange qualities of meaning; its drives are often perverse and destructive; disparate concepts are linked in an obscure manner. Expressionism deals with strange shapes, odd juxtapositions, disembodied fragments; there is no central core of substance, little contact with familiar realities. There is a striking parallel between the emergence of expressionism and the development of psychological techniques to explore the subconscious. Freud and expressionism are both aspects of man's concern with his inner psychic states. Naturally, the qualities of movement in expressionism would not be clear, direct, and smooth; rather, they are capricious, unpredictable, shifting, angular, irregular, brief, and incomplete.

Although Richard Strauss and Gustav Mahler did not go as far in this direction as did later composers, they dealt with subject matter that showed a strong tendency to portray distorted states of mind and escape from reality. Strauss's *Elektra* deals with matricide and insanity; *Salomé* centers on sadistic lust; *Till Eulenspiegel* upsets the whole world; *Don Juan* allows himself to be killed out of disappointment after surfeit; *Don Quixote* yearns for a lost world and tilts at windmills. Mahler's *Song of the Earth* combines late Viennese romanticism with some artificial *chinoiserie* in a work whose mood shifts from deep despair at the futility of life to momentary solace in toy scenes. In all of this music there is little to suggest regeneration, of good struggling with evil and winning out, perhaps in a better world. The object is to report as strikingly and effectively as possible the nature of the problem, the state of mind; the resolution is not given.

Techniques

Expressionism was drawn to Wagner's dissonances, to his melodies that gave an effect of distortion through wide jumps and jagged outlines, and to his rhythmic patterns that conveyed a sense of conflict and restlessness. These all were techniques that created a feeling of instability. Expressionism wished to avoid well-defined points of arrival. Through constant use of arbitrary dissonant combinations it avoided giving any sense of tonal center. This was called *atonality*. Melodies that flowed evenly and rhythms that were regular also came under the ban since they can easily create a sense of stability. Yet the most important factor of all in creating expressionism's spidery, grotesque effects was its texture. We no longer have a substantial central core of sound, a merging of voices that gave body to the texture in music of earlier periods. Rather, there was a use of ornamental melodic voices generally placed at great distances in range from each other. Contrapuntal activity of great intensity was supposed to create musical interest and to compensate for the removal of the musical *terra firma*. One might draw a parallel with aviation.

If impressionism borrowed a specific idea of tone quality from Wagner, expressionism developed his melodic, rhythmic, and harmonic techniques. The richness of sound that appealed to impressionism was exactly the value that expressionism eliminated. The diagram below shows the relative historical positions of impressionism and expressionism, with reference to Wagner.

Ex. 8–7. Historical positions of impressionism and expressionism.

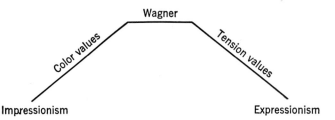

Arnold Schönberg was the leader in the school of musical expressionism. Probably the most celebrated work of this school is his *Pierrot lunaire,* a set of twenty-one melodramas set for voice and five instruments. The subject matter of the poems deals with the nocturnal adventures of Pierrot of the Moon, a fantastic spirit. The imagery is vivid, but the meanings are elusive and dreamlike. Many of the poems have grotesque ideas, but at the same time they invoke an almost painfully nostalgic mood. The voice half-sings and half-speaks; this technique, developed from Wagner's declamatory recitative style, is called *Sprechstimme.*

Number 5 from *Pierrot lunaire,* Valse de Chopin, illustrates the compositional techniques of expressionism.

Ex. 8–8. Schönberg: Valse de Chopin from *Pierrot lunaire,* No. 5.*

* Copyright 1914 by Universal Edition, Vienna; used by permission of Associated Music Publishers, Inc., New York.

Notice in this example the disembodied texture, the fragmentary bits of melody, the lack of a strong point of reference, and the constant tension. Schönberg here composed a nightmare parody of a waltz. The tiny melodic and rhythmic fragments of this piece could well fit into a romantic waltz if they were set together in a clear statement and counterstatement relationship, and if they were supported by a vigorous rhythmic and harmonic accompaniment. The nostalgia of this work and its debt to romanticism emerge most clearly in the final piece, No. 21, *O Alter Duft.*

Ex. 8–9. Schönberg: O Alter Duft from *Pierrot lunaire,* No. 21.*

The harmonic progression in this excerpt is a cadence (!) but the distortion of the lines disguises the sense of arrival and retains for the piece something of characteristic expressionist tension.

The values established by expressionism strongly pervade the styles of the present era. More than any other single factor, expressionism is responsible for the complexity of idiom that characterizes much modern music, as we heard in Roger Sessions' Second Symphony.

Form in Musical Expressionism

With regard to form expressionist composers faced a difficult problem. They eliminated all the factors that made for clearly perceived stability and for creating a well-defined structural contour. Unpredictable, often contradictory qualities of movement prevented the music from reaching strong points of arrival. Relationships between statement and counterstatement were not easily projected. Large-scale form was not the answer to the problem of structure in expressionism. On the contrary, expressionist music suggested that much was happening in a very short time. Every note and figure seemed an outward symbol of profound inner states of mind and experiences. Hence, a significant musical message could be hinted at in a very short piece. All twenty-one numbers of *Pierrot lunaire* are short; so

---

* Copyright 1914 by Universal Edition, Vienna; used by permission of Associated Music Publishers, Inc., New York.

are the Six Little Piano Pieces of Schönberg, dating from this period. The laconic manner and the compressed form were the most characteristic aspects of expressionist structure. Some works with expressionist qualities, however, retained an expansive late romantic manner and were cast in broad forms, such as Gustav Mahler's *Das Lied von der Erde* and Richard Strauss's opera, *Elektra*.

Within a given movement we find that the form takes shape by repetition and variation of distinctive melodic figures or by contrasts in texture or manner. The form is no longer outlined by harmonic or rhythmic strong points. For example, consider how Schönberg organized the first nine measures of No. 1 of *Pierrot*.

A	Measure 1	Statement of motive
A′	Measure 2 to Measure 6	Counterstatements of first motive
B	Measure 7	New motive, textural contrast
A″	Measure 8	Repetition and variation of first motive
C	Measure 9	New motive, textural contrast

Motive A, a tinkling little arabesque figure that suggests the liquid quality of moonlight, returns throughout the piece as a refrain. We could say then that No. 1 of *Pierrot lunaire* is a rondo.

Expressionist music frequently relied upon a text to give some over-all contour to its forms. More than half the works of Schönberg's early period involve a text. The highly charged emotional quality of this style was certainly effective as a setting for words with remote and elusive connotations.

As expressionism developed, certain tendencies became more and more manifest. Habitually a literal repetition of any kind was avoided, since it would create a static effect and break the tension. At the same time, a distinctive melodic figure was used in many varied ways throughout a piece as a means of obtaining some underlying unity. Eventually this led to a systematization known as the *tone-row technique* or the *method of composing with twelve mutually interrelated tones*.

The tone row represents an application of the principle of nonrepetition, of continual progress to the chromatic scale itself. A characteristic melodic pattern, using all twelve of the chromatic tones, provides the bulk of the material for a piece of music. This pattern could be handled in many different ways: it could be played backwards or upside down; it could take on any rhythmic pattern; it would be compressed into chords, or distributed in different textures. This technique was codified by Arnold Schönberg in 1924 after many years of observing his own procedures of composition. It was first applied consistently in his Serenade, Op. 24.

The tone-row technique provided a point of reference for the composer; he could range freely among traditional forms and manners, adapting them to the basic twelve-tone procedure. This system did help the composer to write more quickly and fluently.

Each of the three composers who formed the early tone-row school, Arnold Schönberg, Alban Berg, and Anton von Webern, were able to project their own personal styles into their music without any loss of individuality. Schönberg retained his romantic connections; works like his Fourth String Quartet and his Piano Concerto show a strong flavor of Brahms. Berg affected a more spectacular, and often more immediately assimilable style. His opera, *Wozzeck,* which uses tone-row procedures at various points, suggests the expressionism of Richard Strauss. This work, one of the great musicodramatic achievements of the twentieth century, is quite comprehensive in its range of style and expression. For example, Berg occasionally uses a simple, affecting melodic style, as in Marie's lullaby *Ei-o-po-peia.* Here and there, one hears the sound of a major or minor triad, strategically placed for expressive nuance; also, fragments of march-like rhythms (Wozzeck is a soldier) crop up now and then. Moreover, Berg's idea of sound leans rather to the rich side than to the spare, open manner of other composers in the expressionistic school. In his Lyric Suite for String Quartet, Berg has created atmospheric effects not unlike musical impressionism.

Anton von Webern continued in the terse manner of expressionism, along the lines of the procedure exemplified in *Pierrot lunaire.* He represents the antiromantic wing of the tone-row school, and his influence is perhaps the strongest among younger tone-row composers. Webern's technique of writing very short pieces with very few notes has been particularly attractive to younger French tone-row composers; they have progressively rarified the musical atmosphere of their compositions until the individual tones have become virtually disengaged from each other in pitch and texture.

For illustration of tone-row techniques of composition, we shall examine some excerpts from Schönberg's Fourth Quartet.

Ex. 8–10. Schönberg: Fourth Quartet.*

a. The basic row.

b. This is the opening theme of the first movement, in a vigorous, square-cut style.

Allegro molto, energico

c. A transitional passage in the first movement, in a capricious, arabesquelike improvisation.

d. A waltz, from the second movement.

Comodo

Tone-row composers have used traditional forms of eighteenth-century music, such as sonata form, rondo, fugue, and variation, in an effort to reconcile themselves with music of the past. These traditional forms were originally based upon clear harmonic orientation and sharply demarcated rhythmic groupings; yet, these were the very values the tone-row composers rejected. Whether or not a successful merger of traditional forms and the perpetual variation procedure of tone-row music has been effected is a matter to be decided in each individual case. There exists no area of common structural practice in the tone-row technique, as yet.

The number of composers using the tone row at present is considerable, both in the older and younger generations of modern music. Ernst Křenek, Luigi Dallapiccola, Wallingford Riegger, and many others have devoted themselves to composition based on the premises of the tone row. We can discover an even more interesting phenomenon in the partial use of tone-row techniques by composers such as Bartók, Samuel Barber, and Stravinsky. This indicates a recognition of the organizational and expressive potentialities of the tone-row procedures, an acknowledgment that the tone row is a genuine and idiomatic product of twentieth-century musical culture.

Historical Antecedents

Expressionism and the tone-row school are the direct descendants of the metaphysical tendencies of the nineteenth century and their attendant chromaticism and dissonance. From the Sensibility and the Storm and Stress down through Beethoven, Liszt, Wagner, and Mahler, runs a current of supercharged emotional values. Romantic preoccupation with the dark and sinister aspects of human imagination—witches, unholy talismans, the Devil himself—leads directly to the fantastic world of expressionism.

In retrospect we can see that certain musical techniques point the way from romanticism to expressionism. Prominent among these was an increasing reliance upon thematic values to organize the form of a composition. (See Chapter 7, Examples 7–21 to 7–23.) Harmony became involved and complex; it could not give as clear an outline of the form as it did in classic music. Themes became more distinctive and important; they were made points of reference, *leading motives.* In some works, such as Liszt's B-minor Sonata and Strauss's *Till Eulenspiegel,* themes were constantly being varied or transformed. Thus the opening theme of Liszt's Sonata has at different times a brooding, a demonic, a plaintive, a masterful, and an apocalyptic quality. This is not far from the perpetual variation of tone-row music.

Beethoven's last string quartets influenced the expressionist composers profoundly. They were impressed by the deeply introspective quality, the tightness of structure, and the rich elaboration of motives that these works exhibited. For example, Beethoven's Grosse Fuge, Op. 133, which takes about fifteen or sixteen minutes to play, is built up entirely of two subjects which are developed and varied in an incredibly imaginative way. One of these subjects shows incipient tone-row features.

Ex. 8–11. Beethoven: Grosse Fuge, Op. 133.

Compare the first four notes of this subject with the beginning of Schön-berg's row for his Fourth Quartet, Example 8–10. Note that they are varied inversions of each other.

We sometimes receive the impression from tone-row composers and their spokesmen that theirs is the most significant school of musical com-position operating today. The basis for this assumption is the genealogy we have just described. They feel that the logical continuity of musical evolu-tion passes to them from Bach through the classics and Wagner. No doubt this is true, but we know enough of history to recognize that the last stage in an evolution is not necessarily the greatest. Moreover, the history of musical taste is not strictly evolutionary but shows a swinging back and forth between the galant and the learned manners.

Relationships with Art and Literature

Musical expressionism was part of a general reaction against late roman-ticism and impressionism, a reaction that took place as well in literature and art. The term *expressionism* was taken from the German school of painting led by Paul Klee and Vassily Kandinsky. As in music, expression-ist painters sought to convey intense and subjective qualities, characterized by strange shapes, odd relationships, and elusive meanings. An analogy between surrealist painting and expressionist music might be drawn con-sidering the ways in which each mode of expression places familiar items into bizarre and unfamiliar contexts, removing them from their ordinary frames of reference.

In literature the dreamlike quality and the hidden meanings of symbolist poetry attracted expressionist composers. Stefan George provided the texts for a number of compositions by Schönberg and his colleagues. We can also see a parallel between expressionism's flow of compact, yet obscure asso-ciations and the *stream-of-consciousness* technique being developed by James Joyce at that time in his *Ulysses* and other works.

FOLKLORIC MUSIC

Expressive Values

At the time that expressionism was coming into full stature, another significant trend was making itself felt strongly in European music. This was the folkloric style. You have heard music from the expressionist school; now listen to the Dance of the Adolescents from Stravinsky's *Le Sacre du printemps*. There could scarcely be two kinds of music farther apart than expressionism and the folkloric style, as represented by the excerpt from *Le Sacre*. Here is a dance; but it is no dance such as we have encountered before in our study. This is no graceful court dance, nor even a jolly village whirl. It is primitive, tribal, pagan; it suggests a purpose far more serious than the dances which have traditionally provided entertainment in Western culture. The purpose is religious. We are told, in the scenario of the ballet for which *Le Sacre* was composed, that this is a dance of spring. Homage is paid to the earth in the hope of reaping good crops.

Certainly the most salient feature is the emphatic, percussive beat that carries the sound along. All the profound reflections and personal manner of romanticism are cast aside, and the aboriginal values of music, the play of quantities and durations of sound are substituted in the evocation of a raw sense of activity. The beat is in charge!

As a contrast to this expressive quality, we hear, from time to time in *Le Sacre,* a simple folk-song manner, often improvisatory in style. Thus, the two aspects of a folk music, the dance and the song, provide the raw material for a work that is highly stylized, strikingly imaginative, a work that created one of the most celebrated "scandals" in the history of music, when it was first presented in Paris in 1913.

Techniques

Principal among all the technical features of this style is the beat and its treatment. We can hear quite easily that the distinctive rhythmic manner arises from two factors: (1) the ways in which beats are organized, and (2) the ways in which beats are performed.

In earlier styles we heard characteristic ways of treating the beat. Medieval and Renaissance music tended to generate an easy, steady flow of gentle beats. Baroque music also set up such a flow, but with considerably more emphasis. Dance music and music of the classic style organized beats in groups of two, three, four, or six, with regularly spaced

FIG. 15. Vassily Kandinsky: *Composition III*. 1914. (From the Collection of the Museum of Modern Art, Mrs. Simon Guggenheim Fund.)

periodic accents. Romantic music often displayed irregularities and uncertainties in the flow of beats. But folkloric music, as represented in our excerpt, developed its own distinctive way of organizing rhythmic groups.

In order to demonstrate to yourself the effect of handling rhythmic groups in the distinctive folkloric manner, try the following experiment:

1. First, count out a series of four-beat measures, making a stroke at each strong beat, as in Example 8–12.

Ex. 8–12.

stroke

beat

1 2 3 4 1 2 3 4 1 2 3 4 1 2 3 4 1 2 3 4 1 2 3 4 1 2 3 4 1 2 3 4

As you continue, notice that the beats, the accented strong beats, and the general quality of movement remain regular, smooth, and virtually automatic. You lose awareness of the rhythm as an immediate or challenging element.

2. Now try the same flow of beats, but after the first two groups of four, introduce a strongly accented beat after three, two, five, three, and four beats, as in Example 8–13.

Ex. 8–13.

stroke

beat

1 2 3 4 1 2 3 4 1 2 3 1 2 1 2 1 2 3 4 5 1 2 3 1 2 3 4

What a world of difference there is in the whole rhythmic concept! Instead of becoming dormant, the accent develops a life of its own, asserts itself in an electrifying way. The periodicity is broken and the impact of an unanticipated accent gives new energy and momentum to the musical flow.

Example 8–14 from the Dance of the Adolescents of *Le Sacre* illustrates this kind of rhythmic organization. Try tapping it!

Ex. 8–14. Stravinsky: *Le Sacre du printemps,* Dance of the Adolescents.*

Tempo giusto

In order to secure and emphasize this rhythmic quality, the entire orchestra must participate. The usual custodians of the underlying beat, the percussion, are not sufficient to give the kind of weight, body, and color to the rhythmic strokes of this music. Thus, in Example 8–14 the burden is carried by the strings; they become quasipercussion instruments, and in the mass that they constitute in the grand symphony orchestra, they carry off the effect brilliantly.

Colorful scoring is closely associated with this rhythmic style. A rhythmic gesture not only involves a stroke; it has arresting, often unique qualities of sonority. As you listen to *Le Sacre,* you hear at every moment strikingly evocative sounds, tone colors splashed on brilliantly and barbarically, yet with a subtle insight for the justness of the effect.

In contrast to the rhythmic violence and the flashing colors, the melodic material often has a simple folk-song flavor. Melodies tend to be short in phrase; their range is small. They gain length by spinning out; fragments are often repeated with small melodic or rhythmic variations. These melodies tend to center around a single tone or to move back and forth between a few tones. The melodies frequently use the modal scales described in the section on impressionism. The total effect is rather singsong, as in Example 8–15.

Ex. 8–15. Stravinsky: *Le Sacre du printemps,* The Games of the Rival Cities.*

Molto allegro

f ritenuto pesante a tempo

The harmonic language of this style frequently sounds opaque and crashingly dissonant. Yet if we pull all the pieces apart we find that the harmony is made up of simple, familiar, diatonic units, such as triads, open fifths and fourths, and scales which are put together in layers on top of each other or succeed each other in odd ways to create a dissonant effect. In other words, the harmonic values of folk song represent the starting point for the complex chord structures of the folkloric style. Example 8–14 illustrates the use of two chords from different keys sounded together but kept distinct by well-defined layering. This device is known as *polytonality.* Example 8–16 is an illustration of *pandiatonism,* a harmonic device in which notes from a diatonic scale are combined in nontraditional

* Copyright 1921 by Edition Russe de Musique. Copyright assigned to Boosey & Hawkes, Inc. Used by permission.

ways. Both polytonality and pandiatonism represent efforts to retain some of the stability and orientation value of triads and homogeneous scales while introducing special and piquant harmonic effects.

Ex. 8–16. Stravinsky: *Le Sacre du printemps,* Rounds of Spring.*

Form in Folkloric Music

Listening for the definition of form in folkloric music, we discover, as probably the most apparent feature, *contrasts* in texture and mood. The form takes shape in well-demarcated episodes. Within an episode the principal structural unit is a phrase or period whose length is determined by the composer's feeling that a certain effect has been sufficiently exploited. The phrases themselves take shape by varied repetition of figures and harmonies. A sense of movement within the phrase is projected by the permutations of rhythm, melody, and texture which we have described above. A natural concomitant of such structure is the dynamic curve, built by the accumulation of intensity, volume of sound, and increase of pace, at times. Points of arrival in phrases and in episodes are rarely familiar cadences; rather, arrival is signaled by some sort of climax in the dynamic curve, or by the beginning of a new effect, texture, or harmonic procedure. In this music, statement and counterstatement show a simple, down-to-earth relationship.

It was no accident that this style, with its colorful associations of primitive culture, its dominating dance rhythms, and its episodic forms based on sharp contrasts, should have been developed in connection with modern ballet and stage arts. Most of Stravinsky's early music was stage music; his connection with the great choreographer, Diaghilev, is one of the celebrated associations in the history of music and dance.

By way of illustration, let us have a look at the way the first few episodes of *Le Sacre* are fitted together.

* Copyright 1921 by Edition Russe de Musique. Copyright assigned to Boosey & Hawkes, Inc. Used by permission.

The very opening sounds presage the strange and exotic music to come. The improvisation of the bassoon in its highest, most tortured register, the interjected fragments by the clarinets in their lowest, most somber register, the curious pointillism of structure: all these create a world of musical imagery far removed from Western experience. Bit by bit the fragments coalesce, new motives dart in and out; an excitement is growing. The texture, transparent at first, becomes increasingly clouded and heavy. Suddenly the rising dynamic curve breaks off, and the bassoon, alone again, recalls for a moment its speculative thought of the beginning. In schematic terms, the form thus displays an A–B–A plan. The final A, while it may act for arrival, still has a tentative quality that enables it to serve as a transition to the next large episode, the Dance of the Adolescents. This dance is dominated by the rhythmic figure we first hear plucked by the strings. Around this rhythmic motive, above and below, melodic fragments are superimposed; these figures possess a tremendous rhythmic vitality. When they are combined with the driving rhythmic ostinato, the impact is explosive. As we might expect, the over-all form of this episode turns out to be a dynamic curve; the dance works itself up to the point of frenzy and rushes directly into the next episode, The Play of Abduction, at which point the tempo becomes headlong. Indeed, this quickening of pace was perhaps the only effective way the music could move ahead from the climax of the previous dance. The remainder of this work should also be evaluated structurally by its gestures, textures, and rhythmic effects, rather than by harmonic or melodic analysis, at least, if it is the layman making the analysis.

Historical Position of Folkloric Music

As we mentioned above, the first impetus toward the use of folk idioms came from composers in the nineteenth century. The composer who made the sharpest break with Western music was Moussorgsky. His phrase structure, percussive rhythms, folklike melodic style had much influence on Stravinsky. Another representative of Russian nationalism, Rimsky-Korsakov, taught Stravinsky much in the way of orchestration. It was only when Stravinsky abandoned the folkloric manner for neoclassicism that he turned aside from Rimsky-Korsakov's conception of scoring.

The heyday of the folkloric style was during the second decade of the twentieth century. In addition to Stravinsky, Béla Bartók, who did a monumental study of Eastern European folk music, was the other principal figure in the folkloric trend. Both in its techniques and its attitudes, this style has been tremendously influential upon later music. The free play of small, well-defined rhythmic groups is a strikingly characteristic manner among contemporary American composers. Nowhere do we find this better illustrated than in Aaron Copland's *El Salón Mexico,* in which an exuberant offbeat rhythmic manner is combined with brilliant orchestration and a winning melodic content. Walter Piston frequently uses this calculated rhythmic imbalance, as we can hear in the last movement of his Second Symphony.

FIG. 16. Thomas Hart Benton: *Homestead.* 1934. (From the Collection of the Museum of Modern Art, Gift of Marshall Field.)

The simple song and dance values in folkloric music have been taken up by American, British, Russian, French, and Spanish composers, with or without percussive underpinning. Thus, Virgil Thomson, in his suite taken from music he wrote for the documentary film, *The Plow that Broke the Plains,* uses the traditional hymn tune *Old Hundred* in one movement and the Western song *Montana* in another. Pioneer and rural American life has provided a rich source of material for contemporary American composers, ranging upward from the writer of hillbilly songs to the composer of serious and ambitious symphonies. Folk songs and dances make strong and immediate impressions upon the listener; he does not have to search long and painfully to grasp the portent of the music.

Folkloric materials have not always come from rural or primitive sources. The early types of jazz, ragtime, and blues fascinated European composers. Hindemith, Bartók, Křenek, Milhaud, Stravinsky, Honegger, Debussy, and Ravel—all these composers have borrowed rhythmic patterns, instrumentation effects, melodic formulas, and blue harmonies from jazz. Milhaud's very entertaining music to the ballet, *La Création du monde,* takes off on jazz; throughout the piece we hear the characteristic harmonies and sonorities as well as the steady rhythms that mean jazz to us. You will hear, especially, the plaintive tones of the saxophones dominating the orchestral sound. Here is an example from this work, illustrating blue harmony:

Ex. 8–17. Milhaud: *La Création du monde.**

The connection between jazz and serious music runs by no means as a one-way street. More than we generally realize jazz has borrowed harmony and orchestration from late romantic and early twentieth-century music. Stan Kenton's style represents an advanced stage of harmony; Gershwin's music, such as *Rhapsody in Blue* and the Concerto in F, represents probably the most successful effort to employ jazz idioms within a large-scale form. Today, progressive jazz composers, writing for the listener rather than the

* Copyright 1929 by Editions Max Eschig, Paris; used by permission of Associated Music Publishers, Inc., New York.

FIG. 17. Gino Severini: *Dynamic Hieroglyphic of the Bal Tabarin*. 1912. (From the Collection of the Museum of Modern Art, Purchase Fund.)

dancer, have taken many techniques of harmony, texture, and manner from contemporary French composers, particularly Darius Milhaud, who has been mentor to some of the younger composers. There is a vast gulf between the "Roseland" dance orchestra and the chamber-music groups which test and perform the new products of progressive jazz.

PARODY AND SATIRE

Antiromanticism in the early twentieth century gave rise to many compositions that parodied or satirized romantic ideas or procedures, as well as those of still earlier periods. The idealism of the nineteenth century was replaced by a clever cynicism that took relish in making familiar musical ideas seem ludicrous or grotesque. One of the favorite subjects for parody was the waltz, the grandiose dance of the nineteenth century, the symbol of imperial elegance. Ravel's *La Valse* and his *Valses nobles et sentimentales* give the waltz a bittersweet distorted aspect; Schönberg's waltzes in *Pierrot lunaire,* Nos. 2 and 5, carry the process of distortion much farther. We have already mentioned the subject matter of Richard Strauss's music which has an element of bitter satire.

Stravinsky's *L'Histoire du soldat* is perhaps the best example of a parodistic treatment of subject matter. In this piece, Stravinsky parodies the theme of Faust and the Devil, a favorite romantic topic; he also pokes fun at the rags-to-riches idea, which itself is a parody of the redemption wish of romanticism. Folk magic, such as we find in *Der Freischütz* (magic bullets) and *Das Rheingold* (the gold and the Tarnhelm) is treated in a satirical manner in the episodes dealing with the soldier and his violin. Musically, dances current in the early twentieth century are paraphrased, such as ragtime, tango, and waltz. The chorale style of Bach is satirized; also the French can-can (in the Royal March) and the baroque instrumental concerto. At the end, the Devil wins out; nothing is left but the percussion beating away, insistent and inarticulate, the victory of the new primitive over the old decadent civilized world.

NEOROMANTICISM

Although the first quarter of the twentieth century saw a violent reaction against romanticism, it did not by any means cause the romantic idea in music to disappear. In many composers we find a direct continuation of romantic modes of expression. Latter-day romanticism uses the rich textures, the grandly serious manner, and the eloquent declamation of nineteenth-century orchestral music, but carefully adds musical techniques that have been evolved in the twentieth century. The long line and the big design are structural objectives in this style. Jean Sibelius, Sergei Rachmaninov, Howard Hanson, Ernest Bloch, Gustav Holst, and Ralph Vaughan-Williams have written consistently in a romantic vein.

Bloch's *Schelomo,* Hebrew Rhapsody for Violoncello Solo and Orchestra, illustrates this trend in a very distinctive and personal manner. This piece encompasses a wide range of kaleidoscopic moods, deep introspection, intensely emotional declamation, wild abandon, exaltation, prophetic fervor.

The solo cello becomes a hero, just as the soloist in the romantic concerto. The grandeur of the conception, the fullness and richness of the scoring, and the demands made upon both the soloist and orchestra are in line with nineteenth-century traditions. Structurally, this piece also looks to music of the romantic era; it is in sonata form with well-marked thematic contrasts.

Schelomo cannot be mistaken, however, for a purely romantic composition. We find its harmony, with its biting dissonances, its exotic colors and scales, its strange progressions, often far removed from the world of romantic harmony. Moreover, the debt Bloch owes to the music of impressionism is frequently manifest. The chords that support the solo cello at the beginning of the piece bear witness to Bloch's impressionism; and the frequent use of the celesta in prominent places provides additional testimony.

EXPERIMENTS IN NEW KINDS OF SOUND

During the twentieth century some composers have explored new ways of building scales and using instruments, ways which were different from the traditional usages of Western music. Impressionism, with its concern for fresh and evocative sonorities, gave a strong impetus to this trend, as did the knowledge of exotic musical cultures, such as Javanese, Indian, and Chinese. The striking effects of microtones, tones which are smaller than a half step, found in some folk music, also stirred the imagination of modern composers. Below we have listed some of the representative experiments along these lines.

Microtones. An entire school, led by Alois Hába, was built up around the use of quarter tones by all types of performing media. Pianos with two full keyboards, tuned a quarter tone apart, were constructed to play this music. Other composers, such as Bartók and Bloch, have used microtones for incidental effects in music based otherwise upon the traditional chromatic scale.

New instruments and new uses of traditional instruments. Among these may be mentioned Harry Partch's creation of an entire orchestra of new instruments, based largely on variations of older types, such as marimba, plucked string instruments, and percussion instruments. Some of these are tuned to a 43-tone scale. Also there is John Cage's prepared piano, and Henry Cowell's manner of playing the strings of a piano as though they were a harp.

Electronic musical instruments. Since the development of radio and electronics there have been many new instruments created using electronic principles. Most of these have been modifications of the traditional instruments, such as keyboard, string, or wind, and have been intended principally for amplification of tone. The Theremin, an instrument which is played by the performer moving his hands through space near a control rod, is based upon a radio-wave principle. Interesting experiments have been made recently in which the possibilities of the tape recorder for altering and combining sounds were explored.

These experiments are addressed to the fundamental appeal of music, the power of sound to be evocative. Thus they lie close to the wellsprings of musical experience. Their weakness lies in the difficulties of giving them structural scope. They will survive as they become assimilated into and subordinated to the mainstream of musical expression.

NEOCLASSICISM

By the middle of the 1920s, preoccupation with romanticism, either for or against, seemed to have passed its most intense phase. Also, by this time, the era of exploration of specific new musical techniques was drawing to a close. Harmonically, any combination of notes seemed to be usable; melodically, there were few restrictions of contour or range; rhythmically, a whole new field had opened up; texturally, a tremendous catalogue of new sounds had been made available. Structurally, however, the new music had raised perplexing new problems. The minutiae of the early twentieth century, which were striking and distinctive gestures in their own right, did not submit easily to being organized into large-scale coherent forms. Neoclassicism represents an effort to achieve clarity and the big structural design.

Expressive Values

In the strict sense, neoclassicism refers to the trend that appeared in the middle 1920s to use features of the music of the eighteenth century and earlier periods. Balance and clarity were sought for in reaction against the one-sided exaggerations of impressionism, expressionism, and folkloric music. Neoclassicism is characterized by an economy of means; very often a chamber music texture is used. Specific emotional connotations and pictorial values are avoided. There is a sense of purpose, of well-controlled

FIG. 18. Pablo Picasso: *Pierrot and Harlequin, Seated.* 1918–1919. (From the Collection of the Museum of Modern Art, Lillie P. Bliss Collection.)

movement directed solidly to a logical point of arrival. We find strong coherence in the melodic lines and the interplay of motives. Neoclassicism stands apart from the easy drift of impressionism, the tortured spasms of expressionism, or the brutal stamp of folkloric music. Hindemith's Third String Quartet and Stravinsky's Octet exemplify the neoclassicism of the 1920s.

In a larger view, neoclassicism could refer to the aims of the majority of the composers writing during the past two or three decades to bring traditional and contemporary musical values and techniques to terms with each other. Serious efforts have been made to codify musical practice in order to establish some areas of common usage. Whatever expressive objectives the composer might have, whatever special effects he may wish to employ, whatever his harmonic language, he has felt the need to place these factors in balance within a form of some scope. We cannot speak of a neoclassic harmonic style. Indeed, works that are clearly neoclassic can have diametrically opposed harmonic procedures. The harmony may be strikingly dissonant, as in the fugato which opens Hindemith's Third Quartet; or, it might be suavely consonant, and give a clear sense of tonal center, as in the first movement of Randall Thompson's Quartet in D Minor. We can speak of a neoclassic feeling for synthesis and the shaping of form. Neoclassicism is an attitude toward all musical materials; it is not a specific gesture, effect, or sonority value.

Techniques

In their techniques neoclassic composers have borrowed much from eighteenth-century music. Structural units are comparable to phrases and periods; harmonic effects of cadence are made, although not with traditional formulas. There is a lively give-and-take with distinctive, easily handled motives and much use of counterpoint. Contrapuntal lines tend to run smoothly, to rise and fall deliberately, and to spin out like the lines of Bach's music. The scoring is economical and transparent; interest has diminished in sound for sound's sake. Example 8–18, from Hindemith's Third Quartet, illustrates a typical neoclassic passage. Notice here the bass which acts like a basso continuo supporting two solo parts, a typical baroque layout. The interest lies in the steady, controlled, yet free sense of movement that the winding lines create as they work against each other.

Ex. 8–18. Hindemith: Third String Quartet, Op. 22, first movement.*

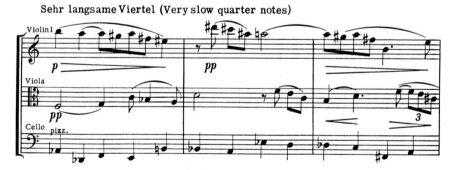

Sehr langsame Viertel (Very slow quarter notes)

* Copyright 1923 by B. Schott's Soehne, Mainz; used by permission of Associated Music Publishers, Inc., New York.

One of the most significant aspects of the neoclassic attitude is the publication of explanatory and didactic works dealing with contemporary techniques. We have already mentioned the systematization of expressionism by means of the tone row. Strikingly enough, this took place just at the time that neoclassicism was making its first appearance in a definite manner. Two other outstanding composers of the present era have concerned themselves with codification: Béla Bartók and Paul Hindemith, both of them neoclassicists. Bartók, in his *Mikrokosmos,* has written a graded series of piano pieces using many contemporary devices for harmony and rhythm. These pieces are intended for the purposes of teaching piano. Hindemith, in his theoretical work, *The Craft of Musical Composition,* has made a notable contribution toward a harmonic system in which traditional and contemporary values can be reconciled and evaluated in relation to each other. In his idea of the *two-voice framework* he has proposed a norm for texture; in his idea of *harmonic fluctuation* he has provided a harmonic scheme for organizing basic structural units.

Form in Neoclassic Music

As we might expect, neoclassic music uses the forms of earlier periods, the sonata form, the rondo, the concerto grosso, the fugue, the chorale, the variation, the motet, etc. Moreover, some composers have been led to synthesize and coordinate various styles within a given piece, much as the Viennese classic composers did with the many styles available to them in the eighteenth century. Combining different styles in a composition has its pitfalls; if it is not done with skillful timing, the work may sound stylistically inconsistent and the composer will be open to the charge of eclecticism. Yet the values to be achieved by a wide range of expression are very rich; they can give contour and strength to the form.

One of the most successful works along these lines of synthesis, and one which has had a tremendously strong popular appeal is Béla Bartók's Music for String Instruments Percussion and Celesta. We shall look at the structure of this piece in order to see how a neoclassic solution to the problem of form has been achieved.

1. The *first movement* is a fugue, worked out very tightly. The plan of the form is one of the most impressive solutions of the problem in all of modern music. It has no counterpart among the standard forms, yet it is thoroughly logical, and is typical of Bartók's sense for structure. The diagram below shows the outline of the form:

Ex. 8–19. Bartók: Music for String Instruments Percussion and Celesta; diagram: first movement.

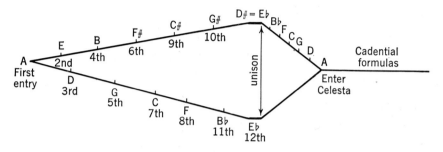

The most remarkable feature of this movement is the effectiveness with which Bartók has succeeded in directing movement forward to strong points of arrival. Notwithstanding the thoroughly dissonant harmony, a sense of progressing tonal centers is present. The entries of the subject explore systematically all the tonal centers of the chromatic scale. When the two streams of harmonic movement reach the point farthest away from the original tonal center, A, they have described a full circle and converge upon the tonal center, D♯–E♭. At this point the polyphonic texture disappears and an intensely powerful unison hammers out the E♭, the tone of arrival and the climax of the form. Reversing the build-up, the music returns to the original tonal center, A in more relaxed fashion. Upon reaching the tonic, final area of arrival in the movement, the music undergoes a striking change in texture. A curtain of sound created by the celesta, heard for the first time, and by shimmering strings introduces an element of textural stability not yet heard in the piece. The entries now begin and end on the tonic, giving the effect of being cadential formulas. There is a striking combination of styles in this movement: the neoclassic aspect is represented by the fugal manner and the tightly knit form; the chromaticism of the late nineteenth and early twentieth centuries saturates the harmonic idiom; at the return, the curtain of celesta and strings is frankly impressionistic.

Bartók's characteristic use of "wedge" shapes is manifest in this movement. In a wedge plan there is a point of departure that represents stability; this is generally the tonal center. The music progresses by stages away from this center, either melodically or structurally, and then returns. The diagram of the form given above shows a typical wedge formation. The subject of the fugue and the cadential formulas at the end of the movement represent this configuration melodically. Notice in Example 8–20*b*, that the two lines moving together create a tone row!

Ex. 8–20. Bartók: Music for String Instruments Percussion and Celesta, first movement.*

a.

b.

2. The *second movement* represents an electrifying contrast to the first. It is principally a dance, based on short, vigorous motives. The harmony, in contrast to the complete chromaticism of the first movement, is basically diatonic, with polytonal elaborations. Much is made of the percussive rhythms of folkloric music. The form is a clearly defined sonata form as follows:

First key area	C	1–19	
Transition		20–68	
Second key area	G	69–185	(Note the broad cadences in G, 180–185)
Development		187–372	
Recapitulation		373–520	
Material of second key area at measure 412			

The key definition in the form is obvious; repetitions and cadences involving the tonal centers leave no doubt as to harmonic points of reference. The principal expressive value is the dance quality. As such then, this movement is quite in the spirit of a Beethoven or a Haydn sonata form. Moreover, the texture and part-writing show the active manipulation of motives and the energetic contrasts that characterize Viennese classic style.

3. In the *third movement* again we have a tremendous contrast. The sound of the xylophone tapping away by itself at the beginning of this movement is one of the most unexpected and weird effects in all music. A bit later the disembodied texture, created by totally different figures in viola, timpani, and xylophone, suggests expressionism, although the improvisatory style of the viola has folkloric associations. The entire movement is concerned with curious effects of sonority, and therefore, recalls impressionism. The form, like the first movement, is a "wedge," this time worked out like a palindrome or mirror structure.

A.	Improvisation	1–19
B.	Lyric melody, first presented, then treated contrapuntally	20–44
C.	Bell-like motive, treated percussively in many variations of texture	45–62
B.	Return of lyric melody	63–75
A.	Return of improvisation	76–83

Bartók, in this movement, has managed to keep the cadential sense very clear. This helps to bind the highly contrasted episodes into a smoothly continuous form. Each succeeding episode seems to come as a point of arrival, a cadential resolution to the movement of the preceding section.

4. The *finale* is a folk dance, an exhilarating summing up of the entire piece. The syncopations and cross rhythms of folk music permeate the entire piece. The form is episodic, with rondolike refrains; contrasts are sharp; the melodic material is well defined, as dance tunes should be. An interesting and amusing detail of style is noted (measures 262–270) where Bartók slips into a typical jazz break by giving a fresh nuance to the syncopations of his refrain theme. Throughout this last movement the sense of tonal center is more clear than in any previous movement. One might say that it is the harmonic area of arrival, then, for the whole composition, a relationship quite proper for a neoclassic concept. Further binding relationships include the restatement of material from previous movements and the contrapuntal treatment of a chromatic, legato subject, not only in the finale but also in movements two and three. This is a direct reference to the first movement.

SUMMARY

In retrospect, the modern period of music exhibits two phases: (1) continuation and intensification of tendencies already well-developed in romantic music; (2) evaluation and codification of musical procedures. The first period extends to about 1920, the second period to the present day. The impulse toward new ways of composing, however, has by no means died out; there are many signs of experiment and search in today's music. It is notable, however, that we find tremendous preoccupation with technique throughout the entire twentieth century. The romantic idea of self-expression, which was largely responsible for the development of individual styles, is no longer the basic motivating force in today's stylistic heterogeneity. Very often, the impression is given that a *modus operandi* is being sought, rather than a *modus vivendi*.

Briefly, we shall close with a summary of the principal features of the styles we have discussed: They are:

1. Impressionism

a. Quality of sound. Interest in special effects of color, pervasive sonorities, exotic values

b. Quality of movement. Steady, moderate, level, without strong drive

c. Expressive values. Pictorialism, mood projection, prismatic effects, pointillism

d. Technical resources. Chromatic chords, modal scales, special effects of sonority

2. Expressionism

a. Quality of sound. Hard, edgy, nonblended, frequently without core

b. Quality of movement. Irregular, angular, explosive, highly tense

c. Expressive values. Suggestive of inner states of tension, crises in the subconscious mind; subject matter sometimes turning to night, darkness, nightmares, unreality; parody

d. Technical resources. Atonality, avoidance of traditional harmonic formulas; continuous spinning out; eventually tone-row technique

3. Folkloric music

a. Quality of sound. Brilliant, striking colors, often harsh in effect, making strong immediate impact

b. Quality of movement. Percussive, motoric; underlying regular beat grouped into varying measures; alternating at times with singsong lyric style

c. Expressive values. Concern with the play of sounds and colors, based on a direct sensory appeal, but addressing itself to the analytic sense by subtle variations and imbalances

d. Technical resources. Rhythms and figures based on folk-music patterns; the sounds of folk music; the melodic materials and scales of folk music; modality, polytonality, atonality; massive effects of orchestration, often to create a percussive quality

4. Parody

Parody, in its distortions, has some affinity with musical expressionism. It is less a style than an attitude. Hence, its resources, its qualities of sound and movement, its expressive values will depend upon the object being parodied.

5. Neoromanticism

The sound, movement, expression, and technical resources of neoromanticism resemble very closely those of the late romantic period, particularly the music of Brahms, Mahler, and Bruckner. The harmony makes use of greater dissonance, atonal or polytonal resources at times, and the scoring is more brilliant or exotic now and then. But the fundamental expressive aim is not materially different from that of sixty or seventy years past.

6. Experiments

    a. Microtones

    b. New instruments and new uses of standard instruments

    c. Electronic instruments

7. Neoclassicism

    a. Qualities of sound. Tendency toward transparency without loss of core; clarity without special search for brilliance; wide range of harmonic usage, from well-defined minor-major sounds to modality, polytonality, and atonality

    b. Qualities of movement. Inclined to be steady, purposeful, with indications of drive to rhythmic and harmonic points of arrival; sense of phrase and period structure quite clear, often with strongly maintained relation of statement and counterstatement

    c. Expressive values. Play of sounds, figures, gestures against each other without special emotional or picturesque connotations; feeling for self-contained, clearly projected design; desire for balance, codification, reconciliation within a large framework

    d. Technical resources. Forms, styles, manners of preceding style periods, handled harmonically with resources developed in the twentieth century; considerable reliance upon contrapuntal procedures; development and working over of motives in the manner of baroque and classic music.

As you listen to a modern work, you will observe that it makes its own synthesis from the materials and resources available. Although modern music may seem very different from music of the past, the difference lies not so much in basic musical values and impulses as in the manner in which these are embodied. Modern music, as we come to know it, appears less unique and strange. Rather, it represents lasting musical and aesthetic values in its own way. The impressive, the charming, the pathetic, the dramatic, the clear, the obscure—all these we find in music being written today. Today's musical audience is coming to know this music with increasing sympathy and discrimination.

SUGGESTED LISTENING PROJECTS

1. Stravinsky, *Les Noces* (The Wedding). Vox PL–8630

Listen for: Contrast between percussive, dancelike effects and lyric, song-like passages; contrast between voice and percussion instruments; subtle play of fluctuating meters; short, unequal phrases; clusters of chords superimposed upon each other for special sonority effects; contrast of final section with remainder of piece.

2. Bartók, Quartet No. 5, first movement. Col. ML–4280

Listen for: Percussive treatment of strings, contrasting with a liquid flow of short motives; intensive development of all material; tendency to return to basic thematic material again and again in a very clear manner; clear effects of arrival, often signaled by the unison passage heard first at the beginning; setting of a tonal center by repetition of opening tone; use of the dynamic curve; dancelike material.

3. Hindemith, *Mathis der Maler* (Matthias the Painter), first movement. Col. ML–4816

Listen for: Traditional handling of textures and phrase structure; well-defined tonal centers, without use of traditional dominant-tonic cadences; clear organization of sonata form by key shifts and thematic contrast; easily grasped development of motives; frequent use of unusual, dissonant harmonic combinations and angular melodic progressions to lend a contemporary flavor; rather long melodic lines.

4. Berg, *Wozzeck,* Act I, scene 3, Military music and Marie's Lullaby. Col. SL–118

Listen for: Mixture of highly dissonant, unstable harmony with many touches of traditional triad harmony; richness of sonorities; touches of impressionistic color; focus given to the unstable harmony by the military rhythms and figures; *Sprechstimme* contrasted with very graceful vocal lines in Marie's lullaby; balanced, clearly articulated phrase structure in the lullaby; Wagnerian touches in the use of rising sequences and the dynamic curve; the generally direct, vigorous emotional impact of the music.

5. Copland, Symphony No. 3, second movement. Mer. 50018

Listen for: Characteristic antiphonal, concertato treatment of instruments and groups of instruments; diatonic style of the themes; brevity of the motive, making it suitable for development; layering of textures rather than blending; contrasts of color between brass, wind, and strings, often emphasized by unison passages or brilliant registers; dancelike character of piece, contrasted with songlike manner of trio.

Chapter *9.* Retrospect

THE STYLE trends we have described in this book apply not so much to individual compositions as they do to musical ideas that were "in the air" at any given time. For example, Renaissance music was generally concerned with smoothly flowing consonant effects; baroque music frequently dealt with the systematic working over of a few distinctive motives; classic music played period structure and long-range harmonic contrast against each other; romantic music looked for special, intense, and personal types of expression; modern music is exploring and codifying at the same time, particularly in matters of sonority and rhythm.

When you approach a musical composition, it will help to know what kind of music it represents, what style it embodies; on the other hand, do not stop once you are satisfied that a piece is in one style or another; you should guard against the danger of pigeonholing a composition stylistically. To know a piece well, and thus, to receive a full satisfaction from the musical experience it can provide calls for several hearings, perhaps many, and for your own personal evaluation.

As a means of proceeding in this direction and of tying together the information and ideas you have acquired from this book, you can apply the following criteria to a piece of music:

1. General qualities of sound, movement, and arrival
2. More specific characteristics of melody, rhythm, texture and harmony
3. The relation of the items in 1 and 2 to various types of musical style and manner
4. Some observations about the form of the piece, i.e., well-defined sections, continuous flow, development, relationship of statement and counterstatement; the form type, such as two-part, sonata, fugue, concerto, variation, etc.
5. The relation of all the above to the expressive values and purpose of the piece

This approach will help us to recognize the distinction between what is *general* in a piece, coming from the style and the era, and what is *distinctive* and *unique* to the composer himself. Marenzio's chromaticism, Handel's vigorous open-air quality, Beethoven's tremendous cadential drives, Wagner's ability to construct a broadly arched dynamic curve, Bartók's effective synthesis: these can be understood only through a recognition of the respective positions of the composer and his era with regard to the final musical result.

Each composer, and indeed, each listener selects that which is meaningful to him and shapes it into a musical composition or a musical experience. There is actually no end to the process of musical synthesis, only a richer, deeper, more satisfying experience, as musical knowledge and the power to know increase. Musical relationships and the affective power of music reveal more and more with each hearing of a great work. In the last analysis, the musical experience is a personal relationship between composer, performer, and listener. Its target is the affectable feeling of the listener. To this end all the techniques, forms, symbols, and constructs of music are inevitably directed. This book has tried to show in what ways the listener can interpret musical data in their affective functions. It is hoped that the ideas contained herein will have enough vitality and meaning to be useful long after the listener-reader has set this book aside.

Recommended Readings

Abraham, Gerald, *A Hundred Years of Music,* Gerald Duckworth & Co., London, 1949.

A survey of romantic and early modern music. Many valuable observations on style and aesthetics.

Apel, Willi, *Harvard Dictionary of Music,* Harvard University Press, Cambridge, Mass., 1944.

Compact one-volume dictionary giving information on musical terms and music history. Good bibliographies. No biographical material.

Baker's Biographical Dictionary of Musicians, G. Schirmer, Inc., New York, 1940.

Compact one-volume dictionary providing biographical material. Complement to the Apel dictionary. Good bibliographical references.

Bauer, Marion, *Twentieth Century Music,* G. P. Putnam's Sons, New York, 1947.

A survey of twentieth-century techniques of composition, especially harmony, to about 1946. Written in a straightforward, relatively nontechnical style.

Bekker, Paul, *The Story of the Orchestra,* W. W. Norton & Company, Inc., New York, 1936.

The history of the modern orchestra from the eighteenth century to the twentieth.

Bukofzer, Manfred, *Music in the Baroque Era,* W. W. Norton & Company, Inc., New York, 1947.

An excellent history of music from 1600 to 1750. Styles, forms, aesthetics, and sociology are linked together in an informative and interesting manner.

Chase, Gilbert, *America's Music,* McGraw-Hill Book Company, Inc., New York, 1955.

A comprehensive study of American music to the present day. A valuable reference.

Einstein, Alfred, *Mozart, His Character, His Work,* W. W. Norton & Company, Inc., New York, 1945.

Although a biography, the best work in the English language dealing with eighteenth-century classic music. The eighteenth-century scene is set forth in rather full detail.

Einstein, Alfred, *Music in the Romantic Era,* W. W. Norton & Company, Inc., New York, 1947.

Survey of the principal trends and concepts of nineteenth-century music. Much speculation on style and aesthetics.

Forsyth, Cecil, *Orchestration,* The Macmillan Company, New York, 1936 (rev. ed.).

A comprehensive study of orchestral instruments, both past and present. Valuable reference.

Grove's Dictionary of Music and Musicians, St. Martin's Press, Inc., New York, 1955.

The most comprehensive dictionary of music in the English language. Extended treatment of most topics, both technical and biographical.

Lang, Paul Henry, *Music in Western Civilization,* W. W. Norton & Company, Inc., New York, 1941.

A monumental work, encompassing the relation of music to art, philosophy, literature, religion, and politics from Greek times to the end of the nineteenth century. Well-written, full of challenging ideas.

Reese, Gustave, *Music in the Middle Ages,* W. W. Norton & Company, Inc., New York, 1940; and *Music in the Renaissance* (Norton), 1954.

Two comprehensive studies of music covering the period from Greek music to 1600. A great deal of specific information. Recommended for students engaged in research in these periods.

Tovey, Donald Francis, *Essays in Musical Analysis,* Oxford University Press, London, 1935–1939; and musical articles from the *Encyclopaedia Britannica,* Oxford University Press, London, 1944.

Beautifully written articles on specific compositions and musical topics, containing many original and fresh insights on musical style and form. Tovey was one of the soundest musical analysts of our century.

Biographies (arranged chronologically by composer)

Schrade, Leo, *Monteverdi, Creator of Modern Music,* W. W. Norton & Company, Inc., New York, 1950.

Westrup, J. A., *Purcell,* J. M. Dent & Sons, Ltd., London, 1938.

David, H. T., and Mendel, A. J., *The Bach Reader,* W. W. Norton & Company, Inc., New York, 1945.

Spitta, P., *Johann Sebastian Bach,* Novello, London, 1899 (the monumental work on Bach).

Flower, Newman, *George Frideric Handel,* Charles Scribner's Sons, New York, 1948.

Kirkpatrick, Ralph, *Domenico Scarlatti,* Princeton University Press, Princeton, N.J., 1953.

Einstein, Alfred, *Gluck,* E. P. Dutton & Co., Inc., New York, 1936.

Geiringer, Karl, *Haydn, a Creative Life in Music,* W. W. Norton & Company, Inc., New York, 1946.

Einstein, Alfred, *Mozart, His Character, His Work,* W. W. Norton & Company, Inc., New York, 1945.

Thayer, Alexander, *Beethoven,* The Beethoven Association, New York, 1921 (a monumental work on Beethoven's life).

Burk, John, *The Life and Work of Beethoven,* Random House, Inc., New York, 1943.

Tovey, Donald F., *Beethoven,* Oxford University Press, London, 1945.

Flower, Newman, *Schubert, the Man and His Circle,* Frederick A. Stokes Company, Philadelphia, 1928.

Barzun, Jacques, *Berlioz and the Romantic Century,* Little, Brown & Company, Boston, 1950.

Weinstock, Herbert, *Chopin, the Man and His Music,* Alfred A. Knopf, Inc., New York, 1949.

Chissell, Joan, *Schumann,* J. M. Dent & Sons, Ltd., London, 1948.

Newman, Ernest, *The Man Liszt,* Charles Scribner's Sons, New York, 1935.

Newman, Ernest, *Wagner as a Man and Artist,* Alfred A. Knopf, Inc., New York, 1924.

Toye, F., *Giuseppe Verdi: His Life and Works,* William Heinemann, Ltd., London, 1931.

Geiringer, Karl, *Brahms, His Life and Work,* Houghton Mifflin Company, Boston, 1936.

Calvocoressi, M. D., *Musorgsky,* J. M. Dent & Sons, Ltd., London, 1946.

Vallas, L., *Claude Debussy: His Life and Works,* Oxford University Press, London, 1933.

Demuth, N., *Ravel,* J. M. Dent & Sons, Ltd., London, 1947.

Stevens, H., *The Life and Music of Béla Bartók,* Oxford University Press, New York, 1953.

White, E. W., *Stravinsky, a Critical Survey,* Philosophical Library, Inc., New York, 1948.

List of Composers

Bach, Johann Christian   1735–1782   b. Leipzig
The youngest son of Johann Sebastian Bach. Composer of orchestral works, chamber music, operas. Very successful in London. He influenced Mozart greatly, particularly with reference to the use of the Italian galant style.

Bach, Johann Sebastian   1685–1750   b. Eisenach
Bach's music represents the final culmination of the baroque style and a synthesis of many different idioms. He wrote in many media and forms, and though he wrote no opera, employed operatic techniques in his cantatas, passions, and other choral works. Served at Weimar, Cöthen, and Leipzig. Greatest master of the harmonically oriented counterpoint of the late Baroque period. Among his important works are the Mass in B minor, the *Well-Tempered Clavier, The Art of the Fugue,* and the six *Brandenburg* Concertos.

Bach, Karl Philipp Emanuel   1714–1788   b. Weimar
Son of Johann Sebastian Bach. Identified with the *Empfindsamkeit* manner. A brilliant keyboard performer at the court of Frederick the Great. Exerted considerable influence upon Mozart and Haydn. Solo works for keyboard, concertos, orchestral works.

Barber, Samuel   1910–   b. West Chester
American composer of orchestral and chamber music. His works, based largely upon traditional forms and harmonic procedures, are frequently performed in America and Europe.

Bartók, Béla   1881–1945   b. Nagyszentmiklós
Hungarian composer in the forefront of the folkloric trend of the twentieth century. Bartók, moreover, had an extremely eloquent and distinctive personal style which influenced many composers. Important works include six string quartets, Concerto for Orchestra, operas, orchestral works, teaching pieces (*Mikrokosmos*).

Beethoven, Ludwig van   1770–1827   b. Bonn
The culmination of the classic style and an important link to nineteenth-century romanticism. He exerted a profound influence upon musical structure and expression, establishing the idea of the "monumental" symphony and in-

tensifying expression much beyond the scope of his predecessors. He wrote nine symphonies, of which the Third, the *Eroica,* is a landmark in the history of music. Seventeen string quartets, thirty-two piano sonatas, opera *Fidelio,* five piano concertos, much other chamber music.

Bellini, Vincenzo   1801–1835   b. Catania, Sicily
Opera composer noted especially for the attractiveness of his melodic style. Chief works are *Norma, I Puritani, La Sonnambula.*

Berg, Alban   1885–1935   b. Vienna
Together with von Webern and Schönberg, Berg represents the grand triumvirate of twelve-tone music in the first half of the twentieth century. Pupil of Schönberg. His music tends to be more directly grasped and more openly dramatic than that of his two colleagues. His opera *Wozzeck* is one of the monuments of the modern lyric stage.

Berlioz, Louis Hector   1803–1869   b. near Grenoble
French composer whose treatment of the orchestra was highly original and imaginative; his textures and phrase structure foreshadowed modern techniques of orchestration and composition. Important works include the *Symphonie fantastique,* the symphony, *Harold in Italy,* the operas *Benvenuto Cellini* and *The Trojans,* a Requiem Mass, the dramatic symphony, *Romeo and Juliet,* and the secular oratorio, *The Damnation of Faust.*

Bizet, Georges   1838–1875   b. Paris
Opera composer whose work, *Carmen,* is one of the most popular of the entire operatic repertoire. *Carmen* represents the new realistic lyric drama, with emphasis upon sharp dramatic impact, fresh and striking color, and winning melody.

Bloch, Ernest   1880–   b. Geneva
Composer of Jewish origin, now resident in the United States. His music combines various aspects of impressionism, folkloric style, and romanticism, held together by a firm neoclassic command of structure and of polyphonic procedures. Important works include *Schelomo* (rhapsody for violoncello and orchestra) a Violin Concerto, Quintet for Piano and Strings, two Concerti Grossi, a Sacred Service, chamber music of various types.

Borodin, Aleksandr   1833–1887   b. St. Petersburg
A member of the group that worked for the establishment of a Russian national school. His music uses many materials based on folk idioms; some compositions are descriptive of Russian or Asiatic scenes, as the opera, *Prince Igor,* and the symphonic sketch, *On the Steppes of Central Asia.* The Symphony No. 2 in B minor is a well-known concert item.

Brahms, Johannes   1833–1897   b. Hamburg
Principal representative of the classic tradition in nineteenth-century music. Brahms' music, particularly his symphonies, concertos, chamber music, and choral works, has the grand manner and the broad scope associated with large-scale music of the classic era. His songs and small keyboard pieces reflect

romantic moods very characteristically. Brahms' style, particularly his rhythms, textures, and broad melodies, was frequently imitated by later composers.

Britten, Benjamin   1913–   b. Lowestoft, Suffolk
English composer noted especially for his operas, which include *Peter Grimes, Albert Herring, The Rape of Lucrece, Gloriana, The Turn of the Screw*. Britten has developed a very direct, easily grasped style, drawn from many traditional sources and eminently suited for dramatic purposes.

Bruckner, Anton   1824–1896   b. Upper Austria
Austrian composer noted especially for his nine symphonies and for sacred music. Bruckner transferred the techniques and the manner of Wagner to orchestral music.

Buxtehude, Dietrich   1637–1707   b. Hälsingborg
Composer of the North German school, and organist who contributed to the evolution of the suite, the fugue, and German sacred music. He influenced Johann Sebastian Bach greatly.

Byrd, William   1540–1623
Important Tudor composer, versatile in all forms of English Renaissance music. Works include Masses, motets, anthems, madrigals, chamber music, and keyboard music.

Caccini, Giulio   c. 1546–1618   b. Rome
Italian composer who was one of the principal exponents of the new monodic style, in which he wrote madrigals and operas. His *Euridice* is the first opera presented in a public theater. He also wrote a book of madrigals called *Nuove musiche*, in which new techniques of vocal performance are described.

Carissimi, Giacomo   1605–1674   b. near Rome
Roman composer noted chiefly for his oratorios. An exponent of the *stile rappresentativo*. His oratorios include *Jephthe, The Judgment of Solomon, Jonah, Balthazar*.

Cherubini, Luigi   1760–1842   b. Florence
Italian composer of operas and instrumental music. Cherubini was admired by Beethoven, upon whom he had considerable influence. He was also an important musical theorist, and as his music shows, a skillful contrapuntalist.

Chopin, Frédéric   1810–1849   b. near Warsaw
Polish composer; one of the most important figures of the early romantic period. Almost exclusively a composer for piano, Chopin worked out an individual style which explored the sonority resources of his instrument. Works include two Concertos for Piano, four Scherzi, Fantasies, Ballades, Preludes, Études, Valses, Polonaises, Mazurkas, etc.

Copland, Aaron   1900–   b. Brooklyn
One of the most widely performed American composers. Copland has developed a highly distinctive personal style, based in part upon folk-dance rhythms and American folk melodies. His music turns to subjects of popular interest,

such as the orchestral works, *El Salón Mexico, An Outdoor Overture,* the ballets, *Appalachian Spring* and *Billy the Kid.*

Corelli, Arcangelo   1653–1713   b. near Imola
Italian composer and violinist. Important in the development of late baroque chamber and orchestral music. Sonatas and concertos comprise his chief works. Teacher of many eighteenth-century violinists.

Couperin, François   1668–1733   b. Paris
French composer at the court of Louis XIV. Brilliant clavecinist, evolving a distinctive manner of ornamentation. Compositions for organ, clavecin, choral works, chamber music, orchestral works. His keyboard style, explained in his *L'Art de toucher le clavecin,* influenced Johann Sebastian Bach.

Cowell, Henry   1897–   b. Menlo Park
American composer notable for experiments in sonority and for works in many forms, including symphonies, chamber music, choral music, stage music. Cowell has been interested also in Oriental musical systems and has introduced Oriental elements into his concert music. He teaches at Columbia University, has written books on music and much musical criticism.

Dallapiccola, Luigi   1904–   b. Pisino
Italian composer; works include the opera, *Il Prigionero,* chamber music, orchestral works, etc. Writes in the twelve-tone system, adapting it to Italianate style.

Debussy, Claude   1862–1918   b. St. Germain-en-Laye
French composer; the principal figure in musical impressionism. Important works include the opera *Pelléas et Mélisande,* which, in its subtle nuances and calculated understatement, represented a strong reaction against Wagner's emphasis and violence. Debussy wrote many songs, preludes and other works for piano, orchestral works including the nocturnes, *La Mer* and *Iberia,* and some chamber music.

Delius, Frederick   1862–1934   b. Bradford
English composer; one of the foremost exponents of impressionism. Important works include the opera, *A Village Romeo and Juliet,* orchestral rhapsody, *Brigg Fair,* the orchestral variations with chorus, *Appalachia,* many descriptive works for orchestra, operas, concertos, choral works, etc.

Deprès, Josquin   c. 1450–1521   b. Hainaut
Represents the first complete embodiment of Renaissance style, and very likely the finest. His music combines mastery of Netherlands counterpoint (imitation, canon) with a clarity of structure and sureness of harmonic procedure (feeling for cadential action) derived probably from Italian music. He wrote Masses, motets, chansons, some instrumental works.

D'Indy, Vincent   1851–1931   b. Paris
Noted French composer and music educator. Cofounder of the Schola Cantorum. His music is oriented toward the past, using traditional forms and styles

of expression. D'Indy, an important theorist, wrote a *Cours de composition*

Donizetti, Gaetano   1797–1848   b. Bergamo

Italian opera composer. Wrote over sixty operas, including *Don Pasquale, The Daughter of the Regiment, The Elixir of Love, Lucrezia Borgia,* and one of the greatest favorites in the entire operatic repertoire, *Lucia di Lammermoor.* Donizetti's music is distinguished by an extremely elegant, ingratiating melodic style.

Dufay, Guillaume   c. 1400–1474

Netherlandish composer, representing the period during which the Renaissance style was evolved. Strong influence upon the generation which followed him. Sacred and secular works which show the tendency toward triadic consonant sonorities.

Dunstable, John   c. 1370–1453   b. Bedfordshire

English composer; one of the most important figures in the change of style from Ars nova to Renaissance. Spent a number of years in France.

Dvorak, Anton   1841–1904   b. Muhlhausen

Bohemian composer, whose strong interest in folk subjects is shown in such works as his *From the New World* Symphony, the Slavonic Dances, the American Quartet. Brilliant orchestrator with a vivacious imaginative style of composition. His Second Symphony, little known, is one of the finest works of its kind after Beethoven.

Elgar, Sir Edward   1857–1934   b. Broadheath

English composer; Master of the King's Musick. One of the principal representatives of English romanticism, largely influenced by Brahms. Works include oratorios, cantatas, symphonies, chamber music. His Enigma Variations for orchestra, and the oratorio, *The Dream of Gerontius,* are among his most celebrated works.

Falla, Manuel de   1876–1949   b. Cadiz

Spanish composer, particularly important for his use of Spanish idioms and subjects. Works include the ballets, *Love, the Magician, The Three Cornered Hat, Nights in the Gardens of Spain.*

Fauré, Gabriel   1845–1924   b. Pamiers

French composer, notable for his retention of classic structural and developmental principles, within which he evolved many striking harmonic, melodic, and expressive nuances. Teacher and strong influence upon the present generation of French composers. Operas, ballets, orchestral works, chamber music, choral works, of which the Requiem is perhaps best known. Director of the Conservatoire de Musique in Paris.

Franck, César   1822–1890   b. Liége

Belgian composer and organist. Symbolized reaction against operatic domination of French music; strong influence on later composers, such as D'Indy, Chausson, Ropartz, etc. Works include the famous Symphony in D minor, chamber music, organ, and choral music. Franck was constantly trying to reconcile the rich harmonic language of the late nineteenth century with traditional principles of structure.

Frescobaldi, Girolamo   1583–1643   b. Ferrara
Italian organist and composer who was important in the evolution of a distinctive seventeenth-century keyboard style. Organist of St. Peter's in Rome. Fantasias, ricercare, toccatas, canzone, capriccios, and other types of keyboard music.

Gabrieli, Andrea   c. 1510–1586   b. Venice
Composer and organist, especially important in the evolution of an idiomatic instrumental style in the sixteenth century. Many works in various media.

Gabrieli, Giovanni   1557–1612   b. Venice
Nephew of Andrea Gabrieli. One of the foremost figures in the evolution of the concertato style, and hence of modern instrumental music. A forerunner of baroque music; teacher of Schütz. Works for divided chorus and for combinations of voices and instruments, including *Sacrae Symphoniae*.

Gershwin, George   1898–1937   b. Brooklyn
Foremost American representative of the popular style, equally successful in straight song and dance forms, or in larger forms which develop and extend jazz material. Works include opera *Porgy and Bess, Rhapsody in Blue,* Concerto in F for piano, *An American in Paris,* and numerous highly successful and long popular musical comedies, such as *Strike up the Band, Lady, Be Good, Let 'em Eat Cake,* etc.

Gesualdo, Carlo   c. 1560–1613   b. Naples
Composer of madrigals, distinctive for their unusual chromatic style, highly affective manner of expression, marked by strong contrasts.

Gluck, Christoph Willibald von   1714–1787   b. Erasbach
German composer noted especially for his "reform" of opera, in which he substituted a simpler style for the more ornate Italian manner, giving more immediate and direct expression to the dramatic content. His "reform" operas include *Orfeo ed Euridice, Paris and Helen, Iphigenia in Tauris, Iphigenia in Aulis, Armide,* and *Alceste.* Gluck also wrote operas in the Italian style.

Gounod, Charles François   1818–1893   b. Paris
French composer whose opera, *Faust,* is one of the most frequently performed works in the operatic repertoire. In addition to other operas, Gounod wrote many sacred works.

Gregory I   (Pope from 590–604)
Supposedly the Pope responsible for the coordination and systematization of plain song. His role has not been fully established historically; there is evidence pro and con.

Grieg, Edvard   1843–1907   b. Bergen
Norwegian composer, influential in the establishment of a national school. In his harmonic innovations, his handling of sonority and color, Grieg foreshadows some of the techniques of impressionism. Works include incidental

music for Ibsen's drama, *Peer Gynt,* Concerto for Piano in A minor, chamber music, many songs and small works in lyric vein.

Griffes, Charles T.   1884–1920   b. Elmira
American composer, with leanings toward the impressionist style. Works include *Roman Sketches* for piano (including the well-known sketch, *The White Peacock*), the symphonic poem, *The Pleasure Dome of Kubla Khan,* songs, chamber music. His music shows some Oriental influences.

Handel, Georg Friedrich   1685–1759   b. Halle
German composer who represents, with Johann Sebastian Bach, the culmination of the late Baroque period. Much of his life was spent in England, where he wrote many operas, oratorios (*The Messiah*), concertos, chamber music. His style tended toward the grand, with unexcelled rhythmic vigor and a bold melodic manner.

Hanson, Howard   1896–   b. Wahoo, Nebraska
American composer. Director of the Eastman School of Music. Principally known for symphonic works and the opera *Merry Mount.*

Harris, Roy   1898–   b. Lincoln, Oklahoma
American composer whose works have drawn often from American folk culture and history for subject matter and style. Many orchestral works and compositions in other media.

Haydn, Franz Joseph   1732–1809   b. Rohrau
Austrian composer; the oldest of the Viennese classic group (*see* Mozart and Beethoven). More than any other, Haydn was responsible for the structural and technical principles underlying the mature classic forms. Wrote 104 symphonies, 88 quartets, oratorios, including *The Seasons* and *The Creation,* keyboard music, choral music, operas. Many years in service with the Esterházy house; later, in London, Haydn composed some of his greatest works.

Hindemith, Paul   1895–   b. near Frankfurt
German composer noted for his classic tendencies, as exemplified in the use of traditional forms, consistent contrapuntal texture, key-controlled structure. Works in many media and forms; his symphony *Mathis der Maler* (from the opera of the same name) is a classic of the modern period. An exponent of "music for practical use," written to accommodate the limitations of amateur performers. Very influential on younger composers.

Hoffmann, E. T. A.   1776–1822   b. Königsberg
German writer and musician noted for his enthusiastic support of the romantic movement.

Holst, Gustav   1874–1934   b. Cheltenham
English composer of orchestral, dramatic, chamber, and choral music. His orchestral suite, *The Planets,* is his most noted work.

Honegger, Arthur   1892–1955   b. Le Havre
Swiss composer, generally linked with the postimpressionist French composers. Wide range of style in his music, from the futuristic sketch, *Pacific 231* (im-

pression of a locomotive) to *Pastorale d'été* (a delicate nature study). Very successful with stage and dramatic music, especially his oratorio, *King David*, and his music for Claudel's mystery play, *Joan of Arc at the Stake.*

Ibert, Jacques   1890–   b. Paris
Contemporary French composer of operas (including *Angélique, The King of Ivetot*), attractive instrumental works, and considerable music for the motion pictures.

Ives, Charles   1874–1954   b. Danbury
One of the most individual figures of the twentieth century. Within a style basically romantic, Ives experimented with harmonies, textures, sonorities, rhythms, anticipating many of the procedures of modern music. Many orchestral works, chamber music, keyboard, and theater music.

Jacobi, Frederick   1891–1952   b. San Francisco
American composer of chamber and orchestral works. His music leans to romantic idioms, exhibiting a fresh melodic manner. Works include *Hagiographa* for piano and string quartet, concertos for violin, for piano, and for cello, *A Sabbath Evening Service,* and the opera, *The Prodigal Son.*

Jannequin, Clément   c. 1485– ?
French composer; the first important representative of sixteenth-century French music; writer of many chansons, some of them extended pictorial representations of scenes or events; also motets and other sacred music.

Kodály, Zoltán   1882–   b. Kecskemét
With Bartók, Kodály represents best the modern Hungarian school. Like Bartók, his interest in Hungarian folk music is profound and has influenced his style. His work covers many media; the *Háry János* suite for orchestra, from the opera of the same name, is well known. His style, in addition to folk-music elements, exhibits features of impressionism, romanticism, and contemporary harmonic practices of atonality and polytonality.

Korngold, Erich   1897–   b. Brno
Austrian composer, now resident in the United States. Recently Korngold has written considerable film music. One of his most noted works is the opera, *The Dead City.*

Křenek, Ernst   1900–   b. Vienna
One of the more noted representatives of twelve-tone music, of the generation following Schönberg. Also interested in jazz as a stylistic resource, as well as other contemporary techniques. His opera *Jonny spielt auf* displays jazz elements; his opera *Karl V* is in the tone-row technique. Křenek has also written small pieces to demonstrate the applicability of tone-row techniques to simple lyric expression.

Landino, Francesco   1325–1397   b. Florence
The principal representative of Italian Ars nova music. Known for his secular music, madrigals, cacce, ballate. Organist of the Church of Lorenzo. In contrast

to the rhythmic compexities of French Ars nova, Landino's music displays typical Italian cantilena qualities.

Lassus, Orlandus   c. 1530?–1594   b. Hainaut

One of the greatest composers of the late Renaissance, a Netherlandish composer who represents, with Palestrina, the culmination of the Roman sacred style. Lassus also wrote in the French chanson style, German songs, and Italian madrigals. He thus epitomizes the ideal of the cosmopolitan culture of the Renaissance.

Leoninus   (twelfth century)

The earlier of the two composers (*see* Perotinus) who represent the Notre Dame school of composition. He was important in establishing the use of rhythmic modes in melismatic organum.

Liszt, Franz   1811–1886   b. near Ödenburg

Hungarian composer and pianist who was a prototype of the transcendental virtuoso of the romantic period. His brilliant declamatory style of composition and performance, his harmonic innovations, his flamboyant expression had a profound effect upon musical style during his life and afterward. He established a single-movement form with many episodes, called the *symphonic poem,* which suited the many changes of mood and feeling in his music. The most famous of these is *Les Préludes.* Also wrote *Hungarian Rhapsodies,* brilliant piano works, *Faust* Symphony. Influenced Richard Wagner and Richard Strauss.

Lully, Jean Baptiste   1632–1687   b. Florence

Italian composer who became the virtual dictator of French music at the court of Louis XIV. Established a style of opera, including recitative, and a style of orchestral performance that prevailed in France for almost a century. Lully was responsible also for the establishment of the French overture as an important instrumental form.

MacDowell, Edward   1861–1908   b. New York City

One of the earliest American composers to receive international recognition. His music includes large-scale compositions modeled after European patterns, such as his concertos for piano. He has also written charming characteristic smaller pieces, such as the *Indian Suite* for orchestra and *Woodland Sketches* for piano.

Machaut, Guillaume de   c. 1300–1377   b. Machaut

The most noted representative of French fourteenth-century music. Composer of secular songs, motets, and the first polyphonic setting of the Mass by a single composer.

Mahler, Gustav   1860–1911   b. Kalisz

Bohemian composer noted chiefly for his broadly scaled symphonies and for songs with orchestral accompaniment. Conductor of the Metropolitan Opera and New York Philharmonic Society. His style has many facets, a grandiose manner recalling Beethoven and Wagner, a poignant lyricism (perhaps his most convincing vein) in the manner of the Viennese song composers, and a starkness, expressed in clashing dissonances and strange textures, foreshadowing expressionism. Both the lyricism and the expressionist tendencies are manifest in one of his last works, *The Song of the Earth,* a song cycle with orchestra.

Marenzio, Luca   1560–1599   b. Coccaglio
Italian madrigalist, one of the finest composers in the genre. His works show the tendencies toward chromaticism that foreshadow baroque harmonic and expressive style.

Mason, Daniel Gregory   1873–1953   b. Brookline
American composer, educator, and writer on music. Works include symphonies and chamber music.

Massenet, Jules   1842–1912   b. Montaud
French composer of operas, the best known being *Manon* and *Hérodiade.* His music is characterized by an ingratiating melodic style. Professor at the Conservatoire.

Mendelssohn-Bartholdy, Felix   1809–1847   b. Hamburg
German composer whose elegant style, crystal-clear structural layouts, easy manner, and exquisite melodies have made his music a concert favorite. Well-known works include the *Scotch* and *Italian* Symphonies (Nos. 3 and 4), the violin concerto, music for Shakespeare's *A Midsummer Night's Dream, Hebrides* Overture, *Songs Without Words* for piano. Mendelssohn was largely responsible for the revival of interest in Bach during the nineteenth century.

Menotti, Gian-Carlo   1911–   b. Cadigliano
Highly successful composer of operas including *The Medium, The Telephone, The Old Maid and the Thief, Amahl and the Night Visitors, The Consul,* etc.

Meyerbeer, Giacomo   1791–1864   b. Berlin
Opera composer born in Germany but noted as the founder of French grand opera in Paris in the 1830s. His works include *Robert the Devil, The Huguenots, The Prophet,* and *The African.*

Milhaud, Darius   1892–   b. Aix-en-Provence
French composer, a member of the post-Debussy group known as *The Six.* A prolific writer in a wide variety of forms and idioms, from dissonant polytonality to traditional major-minor and modal harmony. His work is characterized by clarity of design and elegance of melodic manner. Works include much chamber music, theater music, operas *David, Medea, Christopher Columbus,* and orchestral music.

Monteverdi, Claudio   1567–1643   b. Cremona
Italian composer; one of the first and among the greatest composers of the Baroque era. Established opera on a firm footing after the experiments of the Camerata. Pioneer and extremely successful exponent of the new use of dissonance for expressive purposes. Works include operas *Orfeo, The Return of Ulysses, The Coronation of Poppea,* many madrigals, and sacred works.

Moore, Douglas   1893–   b. Cutchogue, N.Y.

American composer of operas, symphonic works, and chamber music. Chairman of the department of music, Columbia University. His works include the operas *White Wings, The Devil and Daniel Webster, The Ballad of Baby Doe.* Orchestral music includes *The Pageant of P. T. Barnum, Village Music, A Farm Journal.* Moore's style is clear and straightforward, with strong emphasis upon frank, appealing melody; idioms of traditional American songs and dances appear frequently in his music.

Morley, Thomas   1557–1603

Important Elizabethan composer of madrigals and keyboard music. Organist at St. Paul's Cathedral. Author of the first theoretical treatise on music published in England, *A Plaine and Easie Introduction to Practicall Musicke.*

Moussorgsky, Modest   1839–1881   b. Pskov

One of the foremost representatives of the Russian nationalist movement. Rejecting Western techniques of building form, he used characteristic folk rhythms and melodies, combining them with a sense of brilliant color and dramatic effect. The opera *Boris Godunov* is his masterpiece. *Pictures at an Exhibition* for piano, later orchestrated by Ravel, is a piquant group of sketches. He had strong influence upon the impressionists.

Mozart, Wolfgang Amadeus   1756–1791   b. Salzburg

One of the great triumvirate of the Viennese classic era (with Haydn and Beethoven). One of the most astonishing geniuses in the history of music. He represents the full flowering of the eighteenth century in music. He combined dramatic, popular, and learned styles, contributed to the broadening of classic structure, established the modern piano concerto, coordinated buffa and seria styles in opera, expanded the expressive role of harmony in all media. His style is based upon an Italianate, operatic melodic manner strengthened and expanded by a sure sense for counterpoint and harmonic action. Operas *Don Giovanni, The Magic Flute, The Marriage of Figaro, Così fan tutte,* etc., symphonies, concertos, chamber music, choral music, etc.

Offenbach, Jacques   1819–1880   b. Cologne

Famous French composer of burlesque opera and *opéra comique. Tales of Hoffmann* is his masterpiece; also wrote *Orpheus in the Underworld, La Belle Héléne, The Grand Duchess of Gerolstein,* etc. His music is characterized by vivacious dance rhythms, captivating melodies, and a general effervescence of manner.

Okeghem, Jean d'   c. 1420–1495   b. Flanders

Netherlandish composer, spanning the generation between Dufay and Deprès. Important in establishing imitative counterpoint as a basic technical feature of Renaissance music. Sacred style characterized by long, weaving melodic lines, retaining something of the mystic quality of medieval, Gothic music. This is in contrast to the "rational," clearly organized treatment of short motives by

Okeghem's pupil Deprès. Sacred and secular works, some instrumental music. Master of the Chapel Royal in France.

Paganini, Niccoló   1782–1840   b. Genoa
Supposedly the greatest violin virtuoso in music history. The counterpart of Franz Liszt, with whom he is responsible for establishing the idea of the super-human performer. His violin compositions, concertos, and studies make fantastic demands upon the technique of the performer.

Palestrina, Giovanni Pierluigi da   1524–1594   b. Palestrina
The epitome of the Roman sacred school of polyphony. Palestrina's music has served as model for contrapuntal composition for more than three hundred years. Style characterized by smoothness of movement, gently rounded melodic contours, carefully used dissonances, richness and sweetness of sonority. Masses, motets, psalms, hymns, and other sacred music, some madrigals in a quasi-sacred style.

Pergolesi, Giovanni Battista   1710–1736   b. Jesi
Italian composer chiefly famous for his opera buffa, *La Serva padrona,* which took Europe by storm in the mid-eighteenth century, and which served as a model for succeeding composers in that genre. Also wrote chamber music, serious operas, choral music.

Peri, Jacopo   1561–1633   b. Florence
A member of the Florentine Camerata and composer of the first opera (*Dafne*) set in the *stile rappresentativo.*

Perotinus   (twelfth and thirteenth centuries)
The later of the two important composers of the Notre Dame school (*see* Leoninus). Noted for the full realization of modal rhythmic procedure (in all voices) and for some organa in four parts.

Piston, Walter   1894–   b. Rockland, Me.
American composer of orchestral and chamber music. Style combines contemporary scoring, rhythmic patterns, and harmonic devices with a classic clarity of structure and purpose. Professor of music at Harvard University. Piston has also written a number of books on music.

Poulenc, Francis   1899–   b. Paris
French composer of the postimpressionist era. Music is attractive and witty.

Prokofiev, Sergei   1891–1953   b. Sonzovka
Outstanding modern Russian composer, with works in many different media. Operas (*Love of Three Oranges* frequently performed), symphonies, concertos, chamber music, choral music, including *Alexander Nevsky,* a cantata, *Peter and the Wolf,* an immensely successful fairytale for narrator and orchestra. His style has much melodic appeal; his music addresses itself directly to the audience.

Puccini, Giacomo   1858–1924   b. Lucca
Principal representative of the Italian verismo school of opera. *La Bohême, Tosca, Madame Butterfly* are standard items in the repertoires of most opera

houses. Style distinguished by broad, somewhat sentimental melodies, rich orchestration, with a colorful harmonic support that has many unusual touches.
Has influenced much present-day music, including semipopular and theater
music.

Purcell, Henry   c. 1659–1695   b. London
   The principal representative of English baroque music. His opera *Dido and
Aeneas* is one of the masterpieces of dramatic composition. Chamber music,
choral music, incidental music for the stage.

Rachmaninov, Sergei   1873–1943   b. Onega
   Russian composer and pianist. Concertos, symphonies, orchestral music, piano
works, operas. His music continues the romantic tradition represented earlier by
Tchaikovsky.

Rameau, Jean Philippe   1683–1764   b. Dijon
   Important French composer and theorist. Wrote operas in the tradition of
Lully, extending harmonic and melodic scope, also orchestration. Author of
epoch-making treatises on harmony, the foundation of harmonic theory to the
present day.

Ravel, Maurice   1875–1937   b. Ciboure
   French composer, with Debussy, the principal representative of French impressionism. In addition, Ravel displays a neoclassic vein with emphasis upon well-
developed melodic lines. Works include the orchestral works, *Boléro, La Valse,
Rapsodie espagnole, Daphnis et Chloé, Ma mère l'oye* Suite, the opera *L'Heure
espagnole,* and many chamber, keyboard, vocal works.

Rimsky-Korsakov, Nicholas   1844–1908   b. Tichvin
   Russian composer noted for his skill in orchestration and for his brilliant col-
orful style of composition. Works include the orchestral pieces *Scheherazade,
Capriccio espagnol, Russian Easter* Overture, symphonies, operas, chamber music.
He turned frequently to Oriental subjects and idioms for his material. Strong
influence on the young Stravinsky. Professor at the St. Petersburg Conservatory.

Rossini, Gioachino   1792–1868   b. Pesaro
   Italian opera composer, noted especially for *The Barber of Seville,* the last
great work in the eighteenth-century opera-buffa tradition. Other operas include
the grand opera, *William Tell, Semiramide, Cinderella, Tancred,* etc. Overtures
to Rossini's operas are popular concert items although most of the operas have
rarely been performed recently.

Saint-Saëns, Charles Camille   1835–1921   b. Paris
   Eminent French composer, pianist, and conductor. His opera *Samson and De-
lilah,* symphonic poems *Danse macabre, The Spinning Wheel of Omphale,* and
his concertos for violin, piano, and cello are frequently heard.

Scarlatti, Alessandro   1659–1725   b. Palermo
   One of the pioneers of the Neapolitan opera; important in the evolution of
the *da capo* aria, the accompanied recitative, and the sinfonia preceding the

opera. Composer of much chamber and choral music. Maestro of the royal chapel at Naples.

Scarlatti, Domenico   1685–1757   b. Naples

Son of Alessandro Scarlatti. Important as a harpsichordist and composer. Wrote hundreds of pieces for his instrument, working out many innovations of figuration, sonority, and harmony, leading to the modern keyboard style. Preferred the galant manner although he wrote considerable amounts of contrapuntal music.

Schönberg, Arnold   1874–1951   b. Vienna

Leading figure of the twelve-tone school, which he established in the 1920s. Works show an evolution from Wagnerian and Brahmsian romanticism through expressionism, to a wide range of form and expression in the twelve-tone technique. Began his career in Vienna; in 1936 became professor of music at the University of California at Los Angeles. Works include *Pierrot lunaire,* a chamber work for voice and instruments, the sextet *Transfigured Night,* four string quartets, opera *Moses and Aaron,* many chamber and keyboard works.

Schubert, Franz   1797–1828   b. Lichtenthal

Austrian composer; one of the leading figures of early romanticism. His lyric style was embodied in hundreds of exquisite songs, and was also evident in his orchestral and chamber music. Regarded as the founder of the German *lied* style. Eight symphonies, of which the great C major ranks among the finest in symphonic literature; considerable chamber music, including *Death and the Maiden* string quartet, *Trout* quintet, choral music.

Schumann, Robert   1810–1856   b. Zwickau

Important German romantic composer, pianist, and writer on music. Best in smaller forms, songs and short piano pieces such as *Carnaval, Kreisleriana, Scenes from Childhood.* Four symphonies, concertos for piano, violin, cello, chamber music. Schumann's style contains a wealth of harmonic detail and innovation, interesting rhythmic imbalances within regular period structure. Editor and cofounder of *Neue Zeitschrift für Musik.*

Schütz, Heinrich   1585–1672   b. Köstritz

German composer; the link between the earliest Italian baroque style of Giovanni Gabrieli and the late German baroque. Responsible for much of the systematization of procedures in German sacred music of the seventeenth century. Many sacred and secular works. Music director to the Elector of Saxony.

Scriabin, Alexander   1872–1915   b. Moscow

Russian composer notable for his efforts to create a new chordal basis for harmony, constructing chords by fourths instead of thirds. This procedure is exemplified in his symphonic poem *Prometheus.* He also tried to coordinate color and sound in performance, prescribing colors to be projected on a screen while music was being performed. In general, his works have a late romantic flavor, his keyboard music showing the influence of Chopin.

Sessions, Roger   1896—   b. Brooklyn

Influential American composer, linked stylistically to advanced trends. His manner is serious, introspective, and broadly scaled. Symphonies, operas, chamber music. Professor of music at Princeton University; formerly at the University of California.

Shostakovitch, Dmitri   1906—   b. St. Petersburg

Russian composer, one of the leading symphonic composers of the present day. Uses traditional forms and manners of expression with freshness and imagination. Symphonies, operas, chamber music.

Sibelius, Jean   1865—   b. Tavastehus

Finnish composer; one of the leading symphonic composers of the early modern period. Rather conservative and traditional in his procedures; works are conceived on a grand scale and in serious vein. Principal works are for orchestra, including eight symphonies, many tone poems, and smaller works. Some chamber and vocal music.

Smetana, Friedrich   1824–1884   b. Leitomischl

Important as a figure in the Bohemian national school. His opera, *The Bartered Bride,* is his most notable work. He is known also for the set of six orchestral pieces entitled *My Country,* of which *The Moldau* (descriptive of the river Moldau) is familiar to concert audiences everywhere. Smetana's music has a strong flavor of Slavonic song and dance.

Strauss, Johann, Jr.   1825–1899   b. Vienna

The Waltz King. Strauss epitomizes the musical spirit of nineteenth-century Vienna with his incomparable waltz melodies, the brilliant scoring of his music, and his rhythmic élan. Among his world-famous waltzes are *The Beautiful Blue Danube, Tales from the Vienna Woods, Roses from the South, The Artist's Life, Wine, Women, and Song,* and many others. His operetta, *Die Fledermaus,* is a masterpiece of its kind.

Strauss, Richard   1864–1949   b. Munich

German composer of the late romantic and early modern period, noted first for his tone poems including *Don Juan, Till Eulenspiegel, Death and Transfiguration,* etc.; later for his operas, including *Elektra, Salome, Der Rosenkavalier.* Also wrote many songs, some chamber music. Strauss followed the path laid out by Wagner and Liszt, adding melodic and harmonic elements distinctly Italian in flavor.

Stravinsky, Igor   1882—   b. Oranienbaum

Russian composer; one of the most important figures of the contemporary era. Early works in folkloric style, such as the ballets *Petrouchka, The Firebird, The Rite of Spring,* the cantata *The Wedding;* later works in neoclassic vein, such as the Symphony of Psalms, Octet, opera *The Rake's Progress.* Works in many media. Stravinsky's rhythmic and textural innovations represent a major contribution to twentieth-century musical techniques.

Sullivan, Sir Arthur   1842–1900   b. London
The musical half of the English team, Gilbert and Sullivan, which produced the comic operas *Trial by Jury, Iolanthe, The Mikado, The Yeomen of the Guard, H.M.S. Pinafore,* etc. Notable for their fine melodies and delightful patter songs.

Tchaikovsky, Pëtr Ilich   1840–1893   b. Kamsko-Votinsk
Russian composer whose works are among the most popular and frequently performed in all concert literature. Although his works are a little loose in structure, the brilliance of his orchestration, the excellence of his melodies, his sureness of effect, and his vivid imagination have made his music a favorite everywhere. He is unexcelled as a composer for ballet, e.g., *Sleeping Beauty, Swan Lake, Nutcracker.* Of six symphonies, the last three are well known, also his concertos for violin and for piano, the opera *Pique Dame,* the overture-fantasy *Romeo and Juliet.*

Thompson, Randall   1899–   b. New York
American composer of choral, symphonic, and chamber music. Professor of music and chairman of the department at Harvard University.

Thomson, Virgil   1896–   b. Kansas City
American composer and former music critic of the *New York Herald Tribune.* Noted for his opera, *Four Saints in Three Acts* (texts by Gertrude Stein). Music for motion pictures (*Plow that Broke the Plains,* etc.). Thomson's style has a strong flavor of traditional American songs and dances.

Vaughan-Williams, Ralph   1872–   b. Gloucestershire
One of the most distinguished modern English composers. Symphonies, operas, chamber music, choral music. Strong interest in English folk song, the style of which appears frequently in his music.

Verdi, Giuseppe   1813–1901   b. Le Roncole
The master of nineteenth-century Italian opera; continued and developed the tradition of eighteenth-century opera. The dramatic power, the stageworthiness, the keen psychological insight, the well-delineated melody, and the effective scoring of Verdi's operas mark him as supreme in the genre. His last works, *Otello* and *Falstaff,* show a modification of the set number plan toward a more continuous flow of music and action. *La Traviata, Il Trovatore, Rigoletto,* and *Aida* are probably his most popular works.

Villa-Lobos, Heitor   1881–   b. Rio de Janeiro
Prolific Brazilian composer. Over 1300 works. Strong element of Brazilian folk music in his style.

Vivaldi, Antonio   c. 1675–1741   b. Venice
Important late baroque composer, notable for his brilliant concertos, of which there are hundreds extant. His works served as models for the concertos of Johann Sebastian Bach. (Bach transcribed a number of Vivaldi's concertos.)

Wagner, Richard   1813–1883   b. Leipzig

Tremendously influential and important German composer; creator of the music drama, an operatic form different in many respects from the other opera types of Wagner's era. Wagner established stylistic trends in harmony, scoring, and expressive content that have their repercussions to the present day. Works include *Lohengrin, Tannhäuser, The Flying Dutchman, Tristan und Isolde,* the *Ring* Cycle, *Parsifal, The Mastersingers of Nurenberg.* Wrote his own librettos; evolved his own theories of art. Subject of countless books, studies, articles.

Walton, William   1902–   b. Oldham

English composer of opera (*Troilus and Cressida*), symphonic works (*Portsmouth Point* Overture), choral works (*Belshazzar's Feast*).

Weber, Karl Maria von   1786–1826   b. Oldenburg

Early romantic German composer; wrote the first German opera, *Der Freischütz,* distinguished by folk elements such as pastoral locale, German folk music, traditional story. Other works include operas (*Oberon, Euryanthe*) concertos, chamber music, *Invitation to the Dance.* Weber's style is brilliant, facile, with a boldness and dramatic impact suggestive of Beethoven's music.

Webern, Anton von   1883–1945   b. Vienna

The most advanced of the three Viennese tone-row masters. (*See* Berg, Schönberg) Webern wrote in a highly condensed, cryptic style, with sparing use of sonority resources. Orchestral, vocal, chamber music. Webern's manner has found many adherents among younger tone-row composers.

Weelkes, Thomas   d. 1623

English madrigal composer, one of the most accomplished in the genre.

Wolf, Hugo   1860–1903   b. Windischgräz

Austrian composer, noted chiefly for his superb songs, many of which were set to the poems of Edward Mörike.

Principal Compositions

1. Bach, J. S., *Brandenburg* Concerto No. 2 in F major, first movement
2. Bach, J. S., *Crucifixus* and *Et Resurrexit* from B-minor Mass
3. Bartók, Béla, Ostinato from *Mikrokosmos*
4. Bartók, Béla, Music for String Instruments Percussion and Celesta
5. Beethoven, Ludwig van, Symphony No. 3 in E-flat major
6. Beethoven, Ludwig van, Symphony No. 5 in C minor
7. Berlioz, Hector, *Symphonie fantastique*
8. Brahms, Johannes, Symphony No. 1 in C minor, first movement
9. Chopin, Frédéric, Preludes
10. Debussy, Claude, Preludes for Piano
11. Deprès, Josquin, *Ave Maria*
12. *Drink to Me Only with Thine Eyes*
13. Gabrieli, Giovanni, *In ecclesiis*
14. Handel, Georg Friedrich, Concerto Grosso in C major
15. Haydn, Joseph, Symphony No. 103 in E-flat major
16. *Laus Deo Patri* (plain song)
17. Liszt, Franz, Sonata for Piano in B minor
18. Lassus, Orlandus, *Tristis est anima mea*
19. Mozart, W. A., *Don Giovanni,* Act I. Introduction
20. Mozart, W. A., *Jupiter* Symphony, first movement
21. Mozart, W. A., *Prague* Symphony
22. Mozart, W. A., Quintet in E-flat major
23. Schönberg, Arnold, *Pierrot lunaire*
24. Schönberg, Arnold, Fourth String Quartet
25. Schubert, Franz, *The Erlking*

26. Schubert, Franz, *Die Schöne Müllerin*
27. Schumann, Robert, *Carnaval*
28. Schütz, Heinrich, sacred cantata, *O Herr Hilf*
29. Stravinsky, Igor, *Le Sacre du printemps*
30. Verdi, Giuseppe, Ritorna vincitor from *Aida*
31. *Victimae paschali laudes* (plain song)
32. *Vidimus stellam* (plain song)
33. Wagner, Richard, Prelude and excerpts from Act I of *Tristan und Isolde*
34. Weelkes, Thomas, *As Vesta Was from Latmos Hill Descending*

Glossary of Terms

Note: The glossary contains terms which are in common use today in music. It also gives brief explanations of special phrases and terms used in this book, such as "key area," "point of arrival," etc. See Chapter 2 for tempo definitions.

a capella: Literally, "for the chapel"; hence without accompaniment. Applied to choral singing without instruments.

accelerando: Becoming faster in tempo.

accidental: A sign which alters the pitch of a tone. (*See* natural, sharp, flat)

ad libitum: "At will." Indicates a style of performance in which strict metric regularity is abandoned for a freer quality of movement. Applies also to a voice or part which may be included or omitted at will.

Alberti bass: A simple accompaniment for the left hand of a keyboard instrument, consisting of simple chord figurations in a narrow range. The Alberti bass was named after Domenico Alberti. Such an accompaniment gives evidence of the simpler amateur style of music that became prevalent during the eighteenth century.

allemande: A dance of moderate pace, German in origin, in duple meter and rather heavy quality of movement.

alto: Voices of upper middle register are called *alto voices.* This applies to singers, violas, horns, clarinets, and other instruments.

anthem: Originally, a sacred choral composition with English words from the scriptures: now applied to sacred or solemn compositions for chorus.

antiphonal: Pertaining to performance with alternating groups.

arco: Literally, "arch" or "bow": applied, in string performance, to playing with the bow.

aria: A composition for solo singer and accompaniment, generally of considerable length, with rather elaborate musical techniques of performance. As a rule, arias are found in dramatic works, such as operas, oratorios, and cantatas, although many independent arias have been written, notably by Mozart.

armonia perfetta: In later Renaissance and Baroque times, the major triad.

Ars nova: Music of the fourteenth century, French and Italian: called *Ars nova* because of the innovations in rhythm that elaborated and finally broke down the older system of modal rhythm prevalent in the thirteenth century.

a tempo: An indication for the performer to resume the original pace after slowing down or speeding up.

atonal: Pertaining to, or characterized by harmony which gives no indication of tonal center nor of procedures which will define tonal centers: applied to such contemporary music which uses other than traditional chord forms and procedures.

augmented triad: a three-note chord, consisting of an augmented fifth and a major third above the lowermost note.

authentic cadence: The strongest harmonic effect of arrival. It involves dominant with 5 in bass moving to tonic, and usually 7 moving to 8 in uppermost voice.

band: A large instrumental ensemble using no strings (except occasionally double-bass).

bass: Usually designates the lowermost voice of an ensemble, if the range of that voice lies in the bass (F) clef: applied to human voices, and the lowermost representatives of instrumental families, cello, and string bass, bassoon (and double bassoon), bass trombone, and tuba. Sometimes the very lowest voices are designated as *contrabass*.

basso continuo: In baroque music, the bass part, which is present and active throughout a piece; a *continuing bass*. In this part were written the figures which determined the full harmony; this harmony was filled in by the upper register of the continuo instrument, either a keyboard instrument or lute. Supporting the continuo line, we generally find a low string instrument or a bassoon.

beat: A pulse or stroke, which, in a series, helps establish the quality of movement, involving pace and accent.

blues: Originally, an important type of early American folk song and folk music, characterized by certain chromatic inflections in melody and harmony: the *blue notes* or chords. It has become a part of modern American jazz.

bourrée: A popular dance of the seventeenth and eighteenth centuries, in quick duple time with a short upbeat. Bourrée style is frequently used in symphonies, chamber music, etc., of the classic era.

brass instruments: A family of instruments, constructed of metal, producing their tones by lip-vibration against a metal mouthpiece. The family includes cornets, trumpets, French horns, trombones, and tubas. The bugle is also a brass instrument.

caccia: Literally "hunt." A canonic piece of the fourteenth century, whose text describes a hunt, a pastoral scene, a market place, or a fishing scene. The music often has touches of realistic imitation of the text.

cadence: A pause, or stopping point, usually applied to a harmonic progression.

cadential formula: A harmonic phrase which proceeds through the cycle of departure-movement-arrival, as represented by:

1   2
Tonic harmony — subdominant harmony
3   4
Leading-tone harmony — tonic

caesura: A point of arrival; a resting point: variable in its action, comparable to the comma, semicolon, or period of a sentence.

Camerata: A group of amateurs and musicians who were influential in evolving the new style in Florence around 1600. (*See* monody, stile rappresentativo, seconda prattica)

canon: A strict or literal imitation by one voice of a preceding voice, at a given interval and a given time.

cantata: Literally, a "sung piece." A composition, sacred or secular, for soloists and/or chorus, and instruments, containing a number of individual pieces, solos, choruses, recitatives, sinfonias. An important type of baroque music.

cantus firmus: Literally, "fixed song." The melody, liturgical or otherwise, used as a framework upon which a composition was built.

canzona francese: In Renaissance music, the instrumental paraphrase of the French chanson. The canzona is an ancestor of most of the instrumental forms of the seventeenth and eighteenth centuries.

cembalo: German and Italian name for the harpsichord.

chaconne: A dance of the Baroque era in moderately slow triple time, used characteristically as the pattern for a series of variations. The fixed element might be a melodic line, a harmonic progression, or a recurrent bass line. Similar to the passacaglia (the distinctions have not yet been clarified).

chords: A vertical combination of tones; also refers to figurations made up of familiar combinations, such as triads and seventh chords.

chord of tension: Generally, a chord which contains some element of instability, such as a tritone, second, seventh, augmented sixth, ninth, etc. These intervals all call for resolution.

chorale: Hymn tune of the German Protestant Church.

chorale prelude: An organ piece, based upon a chorale tune, and performed as a prelude or introduction to the singing of the chorale tune itself by a Protestant congregation. The chorale prelude became an important vehicle for improvisation and elaboration in baroque music of Germany.

chromatic: Referring to the presence of alterations in the harmony or melody. (*See* natural, sharp, flat, chromatic scale)

chromatic scale: The scale which uses all twelve chromatic tones, as for example, from D through to C♯.

clavier: Any keyboard instrument.

clef: A sign placed upon a staff to locate the position of tones. Originally these signs were letters, G above middle C, middle C, and F below middle C. The clefs presently in use are treble (G on second line), alto (C on middle line), tenor (C on fourth line), bass (F on fourth line).

coda: Literally, "tailpiece." A section added to the structure of a movement to provide a satisfactory summing up and conclusion.

color: The special quality or qualities inherent in tones produced by various instruments and voices, singly or together: qualified by such terms as *brilliant, rich, muffled, dark, reedy, transparent, edgy,* etc.

commedia dell'arte: The improvised comedy of Renaissance and Baroque times, a forerunner of opera buffa.

concertato: A style in which the participating voices or instruments 'compete' with each other in an active give-and-take: applied to early seventeenth-century vocal music with instruments.

concerto: A large-scale composition for solo instrument and orchestra; concertos generally have three movements.

In baroque music, an instrumental composition for an ensemble with interspersed solo passages, employing a characteristic brilliant figuration and driving rhythmic manner.

conjunct interval: A melodic interval that gives the impression of moving by step. The largest conjunct interval is the major second; anything smaller, minor second, microtone, gives a conjunct impression. Anything larger, minor third or more, gives the impression of movement by leap.

consonant: A relative term, generally equated with harmonic stability or euphony: applied to harmonic intervals. Standards of consonance have varied during the history of Western music.

contrast: The effect achieved when two musical elements are placed in a bold or significant juxtaposition with each other. Contrast may be direct and immediate, as between two different melodic motives, or it may be long-range, as between two important keys, or two different movements. The tension and the dramatic effects of contrast contribute importantly to musical structure.

counterpoint: The placing of distinctive musical lines against each other simultaneously.

courante: A moderately quick dance in triple time, employing momentary shifts of accent: French in origin.

crescendo: Increase in strength or loudness of sound.

da capo aria: The standard form for the Italian opera aria of the Baroque era; it consisted of a principal section, a contrasting middle section, and a return to the principal section. *Da capo* means "to the head (or beginning)" once more.

decelerando: Becoming slower in tempo.

deceptive cadence: A cadence in which the expected chord of resolution is displaced by some other harmony, leaving the ear not quite satisfied, requiring further cadential action.

development: Working over of melodic material by:
1. Breaking it up into its motives
2. Reforming motives into new phrases
3. Changing the shape of motives
4. Directing the underlying harmony into shifting key patterns

These procedures are usually found in the section following the exposition of a sonata form, although they are constantly used in almost any large-scale composition.

diatonic scale: A scale of seven different tones, containing five whole steps and two half steps arranged so that the half steps are placed a fourth or fifth apart. The effect of a diatonic scale is one of evenness and balance.

diminished triad: A three-note chord consisting of a diminished fifth and a minor third above the lowermost note.

discant: Polyphonic music of the thirteenth century in which modal rhythm governs; the term also refers to counterpoint, generally, and as well, to the uppermost voice in a polyphonic setting; it also refers to a melody sung above a cantus firmus.

disjunct interval: An interval (melodic) larger than a second.

dissonance: A relative term, generally equated with harmonic instability, or sometimes with *disagreeable* or *unpleasant*: applied to harmonic intervals. Standards of consonance have varied during the history of Western music. (*See also* consonant)

divertimento: A work similar in character to the eighteenth-century serenade.

doctrine of the affections: An aesthetic theory of the seventeenth and eighteenth centuries in which certain musical figures were considered proper for various expressive and rhetorical purposes.

dominant: The fifth degree of a scale or key; the triad, seventh, or ninth chord built upon the dominant degree.

downbeat: An accented tone, usually found at the beginning of a measure, or upon a normally stressed beat.

duet, duo: A composition for two performers.

duplum: A part above the tenor in Ars antiqua music.

dynamic curve: A means of organizing a large section of music by constant increase in strength of sound, or the converse, a constant decrease: found particularly in nineteenth-century music.

dynamics: That branch of musical science relating to the strength of sound. Dynamic signs include:

pp	pianissimo	very soft
p	piano	soft
mp	mezzopiano	moderately soft
mf	mezzoforte	moderately loud
f	forte	loud
ff	fortissimo	very loud
sf	sforzando	sudden, short, strong accent

episode: A section in a fugue, rondo, and sometimes a sonata, in which the principal thematic material or the principal key is absent.

estampie: An important dance and song form of later medieval times. Its form builds up by a series of repeated phrases or sections.

étude: Literally, "a study." A short piece, developing one particular type of figuration, designed for pedagogical purposes. In the nineteenth century études were sometimes written for concert performance.

exposition: Statement of subject matter, as in the opening section of a sonata form or the entries of a fugue.

expressionism: An early twentieth-century school of composition concerned with expression of strongly subjective feelings, particularly with reflecting subconscious tensions and drives. Dissonances, angular melodies, irregular rhythms, sparse texture are characteristic of this style.

fanfare: A flourish upon the notes of the major triad, usually performed by brass instruments, but occasionally scored for drums in addition, as well as for full orchestra or band. Lately the term has been extended to include short pieces which serve the purpose or emulate the manner of a fanfare.

fantasia: A work of improvisatory character, usually for keyboard (piano, organ, harpsichord). Fantasias generally include brilliant virtuoso passages, sharp contrasts of manner, interesting harmonic explorations.

faux-bourdon: A technique of early fifteenth-century music in which the voices move parallel to each other at the intervals of thirds and sixths.

feet: Metric units applied to poetry and taken over in medieval times by music. (*See* Chapter 2)

figured bass: *See* continuo.

finale: Last movement of a sonata, symphony, quartet, or other multi-movement work: also applied to the final section of an operatic act.

flat: A sign (♭) which lowers by a semitone any note before which it is placed.

folkloric music: Music of a style that took shape during the latter part of the nineteenth century, in Eastern European countries, particularly. It is concerned with simple folk melodic material, vigorous rhythms, and striking, brilliant textures and colors, and is represented in the twentieth century principally by Stravinsky and Bartók.

free imitation: Imitation in which the succeeding voices are not strict in their restatement of the material presented by preceding voices.

free organum: Organum in which the added voices move in different directions from the cantus firmus, although in very much the same rhythmic pattern.

French overture: The instrumental number which preceded operas and ballets in French seventeenth- and eighteenth-century music. The French overture consisted of a slow opening section, using dotted rhythms, projecting an air of grand ceremony, followed by a quick imitative section.

fugue: Literally, "flight"; hence a composition in which voices follow or chase each other. Strictly speaking, fugue is a process in which a given theme or subject is presented and worked over in contrapuntal imitation by two or more voices or parts. This process lent its name to pieces so composed.

galant style: The light, popular, elegant style that appeared in the eighteenth century. It emphasized simple textures, ingratiating melody, song and dance idioms, and was opposed to the learned style.

gigue: A quick dance in triple meter, often treated imitatively. English in origin.

give-and-take: A texture that is basically homophonic, but which shows many aspects of contrapuntal treatment; the melodies are shared between the component voices; incidental imitations enter and disappear; the accompaniment figures have distinct melodic interest. This type of texture is one of the important features of the classic style.

grace note: A short note, ornamenting a principal note which follows it. Grace notes are not counted in the metrical notation of a measure.

half cadence: A harmonic pause upon the dominant, equivalent to a comma or semicolon in language.

harmonic series: When a tone is sounded, the vibrating body (string, reed, pipe, membrane) vibrates, in addition to its full length, in successively smaller fractions. Each of these fractions produces a faint tone auxiliary to the principal or fundamental tone. The combination of all these tones is called the *harmonic series*. For example, C has the following series:

$$C \quad c \quad g \quad c \quad e \quad g$$
$$1 \quad \tfrac{1}{2} \quad \tfrac{1}{3} \quad \tfrac{1}{4} \quad \tfrac{1}{5} \quad \tfrac{1}{6} \quad \text{etc.}$$

The tones above the fundamental are called *overtones*. The prominence of certain overtones has much to do with the specific tone color of a voice or instrument.

harmonic tension: Instability in harmony, especially when a resolution is forthcoming or implied.

harmony: The element of music which deals with the relationships tones can form with each other to give a sense of position, stability and instability, and specific sonority value, aside from melodic, rhythmic, or textural considerations.

homophonic: Pertaining to music in which one principal melodic idea is stated at a given time.

imitation: The taking up of the subject or melody by successive voices in turn: said of polyphonic music.

impressionism: The musical style represented principally by Debussy and Ravel, in which subtle textures and colors were used to suggest impressions of the physical world, such as the play of light, air, water, leaves, or to depict exotic, nostalgic, and sentimental ideas.

incidental music: Music intended for performance during the course of a play or other dramatic presentation. Such music may accompany dramatic action, be performed for dances or songs, or it may signal entrances and exits.

instability: A quality in rhythm and harmony which indicates movement, imbalance, action, dissonance. (*See* stability)

intermezzo: An interlude piece; name also given to certain pieces of light or lyric character; also light entertainments given between the acts of serious Renaissance and baroque theatrical performances.

interval: Distance between two tones. Intervals are named according to the staff degrees they encompass. Thus a second covers two degrees, a third, three, etc. Intervals are further qualified according to their exact size. Following are the dimensions:

minor second	½ step
major second	1 step
augmented second	1½ steps
diminished third	2 half steps
minor third	1½ steps
major third	2 steps
diminished fourth	1 step, 2 half steps
perfect fourth	2½ steps
augmented fourth	3 steps
diminished fifth	2 steps, 2 half steps

perfect fifth	$3\frac{1}{2}$ steps
augmented fifth	4 steps
minor sixth	3 steps, 2 half steps
major sixth	$4\frac{1}{2}$ steps
diminished seventh	3 steps, 3 half steps
minor seventh	4 steps, 2 half steps
major seventh	$5\frac{1}{2}$ steps
octave	5 steps, 2 half steps

intonation: Tuning of a voice or instrument with regard to accuracy of pitch; the opening phrase of a plain song; in Renaissance music, an instrumental piece used as a prelude to liturgical singing and called *intonation* because it sets the tone of the song to follow.

introduction: An opening section, preceding the body of a movement, usually in slower tempo than the main part. Handled in style and harmony so as to build up an expectation for the section to come. Found in overtures, symphonies, and some chamber music. The introduction is an optional section. The first movement of a suite or the opening of an opera may sometimes be called *introduction.*

inversion: In harmony, placing the root, or root *and* third of a chord in the upper voices, and thereby causing the third or fifth of a chord to become the lowermost tone.

In polyphony, reversing the direction of the intervals in a subject.

key: A tonal center, generally one defined by cadential (leading-tone) action; the system of tones governed by a given tonal center, such as C major, F minor, etc. The key sense in Western music is said to have become fully developed in the late seventeenth century when cadential formulas were first used in great strength and numbers, saturating the harmony.

key area: A section of a composition principally or entirely in one key: applied to sonata form.

leading tone: Ordinarily, the seventh degree of the major scale, or the seventh degree (raised) of the minor scale. A leading tone, being part of the tension element of a cadential formula, *leads* to its tonic. The term is also applied to any tone which has a leading function in harmony.

learned style: In later eighteenth-century music, contrapuntal composition.

leger line: Line added below or above a staff in order to notate tones lying outside the staff.

leitmotif: A significant motive, melodic, rhythmic, or harmonic, assigned to some idea, person, or situation, and introduced when the corresponding literary or dramatic situation requires. Prevalent in nineteenth-century music, especially in Wagner.

libretto: The text or book of an opera or oratorio.

lied: German for song.

liturgical: Pertaining to Church rites and services.

madrigal: A secular choral composition of the Renaissance.

major scale: A scale in which the order of whole steps and half steps is: 1 1 ½ 1 1 1 ½.

marcato: Literally, "marked": said of a vigorous style of performance.

march: A piece in more or less rapid tempo, steady duple meter, with incisive rhythmic patterns and regular period structure.

mastersinger: The fifteenth- and sixteenth-century continuation of the minnesingers. In contrast to their aristocratic forebears, mastersingers were middle-class townsmen and artisans. (German: *Meistersinger*)

mazurka: Polish dance in quick triple time, with strong accents on beats 2 or 3.

measure: A group of beats marked off on a musical score by a vertical line.

measured organum: Organum in which the upper voice or voices, and sometimes the cantus firmus, move in the measured system of the rhythmic modes, in patterns of long and short tones.

melismatic organum: Organum in which the added ˚voice moves in melismas (elaborate melodic turns) while the cantus firmus moves in slow notes.

melismatic style: In plain song, a melody that has elaborate melodic turns upon one syllable is in melismatic style.

melodic interval: The distance between two tones sounded successively.

melodic motive: A melodic fragment, two notes in length or longer, which gives a distinct impression of manner or style.

melody: A series of tones which moves forward to delineate and complete a meaningful musical shape.

mensural notation: A system of notation expressing specific relative values for tones, comparable to present-day notation. Evolved in Ars nova music.

meter: Grouping of beats into small, recurrent units. *Simple duple* meter involves two beats; *simple triple* involves three beats; *compound duple* involves four or six beats subdivided into two subgroups of two or three each; *compound triple* involves triple division, the subgroups containing two or three beats each.

microtone: An interval smaller than the smallest conventional interval, i.e., the half step. A number of composers have used microtones for melodic ornamentation; others have experimented systematically with musical composition that employs microtones consistently.

middle C: The note C in the midpoint of the piano keyboard.

minnesinger: German counterpart of the troubadour.

minor scale: Scale characterized by the minor third between 1 and 3. The *natural minor scale* has the following order of steps and half steps: 1 ½ 1 1 ½ 1 1. In order to make the minor scale effective cadentially, the seventh degree was made a leading tone with the following order: 1 ½ 1 1 ½ 1½ ½. This *harmonic minor scale* had to be adjusted to eliminate the awkward melodic interval between 6 and 7. Therefore, in the *melodic minor scale* the order is as follows: 1 ½ 1 1 1 1 ½.

minor triad: A three-note chord, consisting of a perfect fifth and a minor third above the lowermost tone.

minuet: A dance of French origin, in triple meter, with a moderately quick yet elegant and graceful quality of movement. The minuet was the most popular dance of the eighteenth century.

mode: A scalewise arrangement of tones in whole steps and/or half steps, from which a phrase, period, or composition may draw its material. Modes differ in their whole-step and half-step arrangements and thus offer different color effects.

modulation: A formal shift of tonal center, usually confirmed by an authentic cadence in the new key. Also, a change of key.

monody: Single-line music; specifically, the music for solo singer and chordal accompaniment in recitative style developed around 1600 as a reaction to the highly developed polyphony of the Renaissance.

motet: In Renaissance music, a sacred choral composition using a Latin text other than that of the Mass, and performed in Catholic services. In medieval music, a composition of measured organum in which one or more of the upper voices has words (*mots*); hence the term *motet*.

musette: A rather simple dance or songlike piece in which a melody is accompanied by a long-held tone in the lower register.

music drama: Term used by Wagner to distinguish his works from other nineteenth-century operas, and to emphasize their dramatic aspect.

natural sign: A sign (♮) which cancels the raising or lowering effect of a previous sharp or flat.

neoclassic music: Music of the twentieth century having a tendency to organize contemporary idioms along the lines of eighteenth-century music, with clear contrapuntal relationships, well-defined phrase structure, transparent texture, and often, strongly projected cadences and keys.

neoromanticism: The retention, in twentieth-century music, of certain broadly expressive, eloquent attitudes of romanticism, together with the rich texture and harmony associated with romantic music.

neumatic style: A plain-song style in which several notes are sung to one syllable.

obbligato: Literally, "obliged." A part or voice necessary to the full realization of the composition. (*See* ad libitum) At present, the term has just the opposite meaning, indicating an ornamental part accompanying the principal melody (as a violin or flute supporting a singer).

octave: An interval consisting of five whole steps and two half steps. The most consonant interval in music, since the two notes sound as upper and lower duplicates of each other.

opera: A drama, performed with scenery and action, sung throughout, and accompanied by some instrumental group. Some eighteenth- and nineteenth-century comic operas have occasional spoken dialogue.

opera buffa: Comic opera, taking rise toward the end of the seventeenth century and becoming a major dramatic form in the eighteenth. Opera buffa used a much greater variety of styles and forms than did opera seria, and was responsible for the ensemble techniques of composition that characterized classic and romantic opera. Buffa subject matter was concerned with the tug-of-war between upper- and lower-class eighteenth-century society.

opera seria: The principal operatic type of the later Baroque period. Opera seria was principally composed of elaborate arias interspersed with recitatives. The subject matter was mythological or historical and always dealt with noble personages.

opus: Literally, "work." A composition or group of compositions designated usually with numbers, thus giving the chronological position of the work within the output of a single composer.

oratorio: A dramatic representation of a religious or thoughtful subject or story, using many of the techniques of opera: usually performed without staging or costumes, although this was not always the case in the Baroque period, nor is it invariably true today.

orchestra: A large group of instrumental performers, including string instruments.

organum: The earliest polyphony, consisting of the cantus firmus, a plain song, and the organal, or added voices. (*See* free, melismatic, and measured organum)

ornamentation: The art of adding figures to a given musical text, a process which was already in operation during plain-song times and which still is valid today.

outer voices: In seventeenth-, eighteenth-, and nineteenth-century music, the outer voices are usually the most important in the entire texture. They provide a framework for the sound, and they control the forward progress of the music.

pace: The speed at which music moves.

parallel organum: Organum in which the added voice moves parallel to the cantus firmus at the interval of the fifth, fourth, or octave.

parody Mass: In Renaissance music, a Mass elaborated from a smaller composition, such as a chanson, motet, or madrigal.

passacaglia: *See* chaconne.

pavane: A slow, stately, dignified dance of the Renaissance, usually in duple meter. Often paired with a faster dance, the galliard.

pedal: A foot-operated mechanism; the pedal keyboard of the organ; *pedal-point* refers to a sustained tone held while other voices move, the passage generally extending for several measures.

percussion instruments: Instruments whose tone is produced by striking a membrane, wood block, or bar of metal. Percussion instruments include the kettledrums, snare drums, bass drum, xylophone, chimes, tambourine, cymbals, etc.

perfect fifth: An interval encompassing five scale degrees, containing three whole steps and one half step. The perfect fifth is one of the strongest embodiments of harmonic stability.

period: A section of music, generally consisting of two or more phrases, ending with a full or conclusive point of arrival, and containing a rather fully expressed musical idea.

phase of movement: A musical statement whose progress forward is marked off and controlled by points of departure and arrival. Phases of musical movement are variable in length.

phrase: A fairly short section of music with a well-defined point of arrival, containing clearly formed ideas, yet lacking something in form or sense to be complete.

pictorialism: The linking of distinctive musical ideas to specific pictorial or literary effects; the musical idea suggests by its design the nonmusical concept.

pitch: The level of musical sound, based on the number of vibrations given out by any specified tone.

pizzicato: An indication for string performers to pluck the strings with the fingers.

plagal cadence: A cadence in which the subdominant precedes the tonic. This is a very restful sort of cadence and is heard in the amen phrase at the end of many sacred compositions.

plain song: Medieval church song.

point of arrival: The point at which a phase of movement reaches an end or is marked off from the succeeding phase. This may be a caesura or a cadence; it may arrest movement partially or completely.

point of departure: A statement, gesture, idea, or impulse which provides the opening momentum for a phase of musical movement. This may be a sound quality, a rhythm, a motive, or a general expressive quality.

polka: A Bohemian dance, quick, in duple time, very popular in the nineteenth century.

polonaise: A Polish dance in moderate tempo, triple meter.

polyphonic: Pertaining to music which employs counterpoint.

prelude: An introductory piece; a short study.

prima prattica: In the early seventeenth century, the style of composition practiced in Roman polyphony of the Renaissance.

quartet: A group of four performers; a composition for four performers.

quintet: A group of five performers; a composition for five performers.

recitative: Musical declamation which reflects the movement and accent of speech, rather than that of regular musical rhythm.

recitative accompagnato: A vocal declamation accompanied by distinctive, short figures in the orchestra. Accompagnato leans toward the expressive, songlike manner of aria, in contrast to the matter-of-fact narrative of recitative secco, although like secco, accompagnato has no set phrase structure nor any standardized harmonic plan.

recitative secco: A kind of recitative in which the voice declaims over the sustained chords of an accompanying keyboard instrument. Generally, the voice declaims rather quickly, without much expressive nuance.

register: Section of the range of an instrument or voice with a characteristic color. In organ performance, a set of pipes governed by one stop.

remembrance motive: A distinctive motive or passage associated with some situation in an opera and recalled when the situation itself reappears or is recalled. Used frequently by Verdi.

repetition: Restatement of any musical effect, melody, rhythm, harmony, texture, phrase, period, etc. Repetition may be literal or varied. In any case, repetition may be taken as counterstatement.

resolution: In counterpoint and harmony, the settling of dissonance or tension by conducting the dissonant tones to tones which are consonant.

retrograde: Backward; in polyphony, a subject is made to run *retrograde* when its tones are reversed in order, that is, instead of 1, 2, 3, 4, we have 4, 3, 2, 1.

rhapsody: An improvisatory piece, along the lines of a fantasia; structurally, often written as a series of episodes.

rhythm: The element which generates, measures, organizes, and controls musical time.

ricercar: In Renaissance music, the instrumental counterpart or paraphrase of a motet.

ripieno: Literally, filling up: applied to full orchestra, as distinguished from the soloists, particularly in the concerto grosso.

ritardando: Becoming slower in tempo.

rococo: An eighteenth-century style, applied to art as well as music, designating a highly ornate type of embellishment.

rondo form: A form based upon the recurrence of a principal theme or subject; a refrain, following episodes as in: A B A C A D A

root position: A chord position in which the lowermost note is the fundamental root or generator. (*See* harmonic series) In practice this works out so that the root is the lower note of the perfect fifth of the triad. In chords which have no perfect fifth, the root is considered to be the bottom note when the chord is arranged in thirds.

round: A simple type of imitation, in which a number of voices, beginning at different points, sing the same melody over and over again.

```
1 2 3 4 1 2 3 4
4 1 2 3 4 1 2 3
3 4 1 2 3 4 1 2
2 3 4 1 2 3 4 1
```

All voices begin with 1.

rubato: Literally, "robbed." A manner of performance in which time values are stolen from some tones in order to give greater stress or expressive accent to others.

sarabande: A rather slow dance in triple time, generally with an accent of length upon the second beat of the measure. Spanish in origin.

satire (and parody): In the late nineteenth and early twentieth centuries, the distortion and ridiculing of familiar or traditional ideas and musical idioms. This was often done with a strong flavor of bitterness or irony.

scale: A stepwise series of tones, usually denoting a rising line. Scales are qualified according to the arrangement of whole steps and half steps. (*See* major scale, minor scale, mode, whole-tone scale, chromatic scale, diatonic scale)

scherzo: A quick dancelike composition, which all but supplanted the minuet in the nineteenth-century symphony.

seconda prattica: In the early seventeenth century, the seconda prattica referred to the new manner of treating dissonances, and the generally more intensely expressive style linked to opera.

semitone: A half step; the smallest interval commonly used in Western music.

Sensibility: Sensitivity of emotion and taste: applied to a late eighteenth-century manner, concerned with intimate, capricious, sentimental expression; it was closely allied to lyric poetry of its time.

sequence: Restatement of a motive or phrase upon several successively higher or lower levels; a way of giving a larger contour to a group of motives or phrases.

serenade: Music for evening, generally light and entertaining in character. The term is also applied to sets of instrumental pieces in the eighteenth century, performed for open-air events and consisting partly of marches and dances, partly of more extended movements.

sextet: A group of six performers; a composition for six performers.

sharp: A sign (♯) which raises by a semitone any note before which it is placed.

signature: The group of sharps or flats and the meter indication of a composition; both are found at the beginning of the piece; the key signature (sharps or flats) is placed at the left of each staff system throughout the piece.

sinfonia: The instrumental number which preceded the curtain in Italian operas of the seventeenth and eighteenth centuries. Instrumental episodes in choral or dramatic works are also called *sinfonias.*

Singspiel: German comic opera, with spoken dialogue.

solo: A single instrument or voice; a passage performed by a single instrument or voice.

sonata da camera: An instrumental form of the Baroque era consisting of a number of movements, three or more, in varied styles and tempos; the majority of these movements were specifically labeled as dances. As the term *camera* indicates, these works were performed for domestic entertainment.

sonata da chiesa: An instrumental form of the Baroque era, consisting of three or four movements alternating in tempo between slow and fast, and performed, as the term *chiesa* indicates, in the church.

sonata form: The most important instrumental form of the eighteenth and nineteenth centuries: laid out as a long-range harmonic plan, presenting area of the home key, then area of the contrasting key, followed by harmonic exploration, and finally return to and confirmation of the home key. The first two key areas are usually represented by distinctive themes; the exploratory section is principally concerned with development of thematic material. The final section emphasizes the harmonic reconciliation of the form by presenting the important thematic material all in the home key.

soprano: Literally, "above." The highest women's voice; also the highest instrument of a family, such as the soprano saxophone.

sostenuto: Sustained.

Sprechgesang: A type of singing, half-declaimed, half-sung, evolved by Wagner to mirror the accents and expressive nuances of his dramatic texts.

stability: In rhythm and harmony, rest, balance, arrival, consonance. Stability is a quality which is not absolute but is relative to what is taking place. For instance, one might say, "This chord is somewhat unstable but it acts as a point of arrival for the preceding very unstable chord. Therefore, the second chord seems relatively stable."

staccato: Performed in a markedly detached manner.

staff: The system of five lines upon which music is notated.

stile rappresentativo: The declamatory style of the early seventeenth century, intended to *represent* the direct mood or expression of the poetry.

Storm and Stress: Turmoil; violence: applied to a late eighteenth-century manner, dedicated to impetuous, personal, violent expression; it took its cue from early romantic drama and literature. German *Sturm und Drang.*

string instruments: A family of instruments constructed of a sounding box over which strings are stretched. The tone is produced by drawing a bow across the strings or by plucking. The modern orchestral strings are violins, violas, cellos, string basses.

subject: A distinctive melodic statement, generally in a large composition, which will be treated in some fashion after it has been presented.

suite: A group of four or more dances, evolved in the late Baroque period. The standard dances were: allemande, courante, sarabande, and gigue. Other dances were included at the composer's option. The term is also applied to a group of pieces dealing with the same general idea.

superius: The soprano, treble, or uppermost voice in a polyphonic setting.

suspension: Holding over; an effect achieved when one or more voices are held over as one chord moves to another. These voices are *suspended,* and create dissonances, which are then directed or resolved into the proper tones of the second chord.

syllabic style: A style in vocal music in which each syllable of the text has a single note. This applies particularly to one style of plain song.

symphonic poem: A one-movement form with a number of episodes, suitable for epic, heroic, dramatic, and other types of program music: evolved by Franz Liszt.

symphony: The most important orchestral form of the late eighteenth and nineteenth centuries. A three- or four-movement work, each movement broadly scaled; the first movement is always in sonata form.

syncopation: Shift of accent or length from the normal position occupied by a point of arrival; it creates imbalance and intensifies movement.

tactus: The unit of time in Renaissance music.

temperament: The act of modifying or tempering: applied to the tuning of instruments (especially keyboard) to adjust for minor discrepancies which arise when the ratios of the harmonic series are used.

tempo: Synonym for *pace.* (*See* Chapter 2 for various tempo designations)

tenor: Originally, a *held* voice, the voice which held the cantus firmus in early polyphonic music; later, a low middle range of voice or instrument, such as a male tenor voice, a cello, a bassoon, or a tenor trombone.

terrace dynamics: An arrangement of tutti and solo in baroque music that alternates loud and soft phrases or periods. The term *terrace* describes the sharp rise and fall between levels or terraces of loud and soft which makes the contrast.

tessitura: The general working range of a vocal part in a song or aria.

texture: "Action of the component voices or parts."

thematic transformation: The technique of altering the character of a theme without destroying its basic shape or identity: frequently used in romantic music as a means of creating a coherence in the form of a large work.

theme: A distinctive melodic statement, usually part of a large-scale movement.

three-part structure: Ternary form, the important feature of which is some sort of contrasting episode setting off two statements of the principal idea, phrase, period, or larger section. A B A.

through-composed: Term applied to songs in which each stanza is set more or less differently: opposed to *strophic* in which each stanza is sung to the same music.

toccata: Literally, "touched": applied to a study for a keyboard or possibly a string instrument involving brilliant scale and arpeggio passages, often with a bold, exploratory harmonic plan.

tonal center: A tone which is given prominence in a phrase, period, or larger section acting as a point of reference, arrival, or stability. This prominence can be given by melodic, rhythmic, or most strongly, by harmonic means.

tone poem: *See* symphonic poem.

tone row: A distinctive pattern using all twelve tones of the chromatic scale without repetition; this pattern forms the source material for an entire movement or composition.

tonic: The tonal center, the principal note of a key or mode.

treble: A voice or instrument performing in a high range, such as a treble viol. The high range itself, as applied particularly to choral composition.

tremolo: In strings, the rapid repetition of the same note. The term has also been used to designate a rapid alternation between two notes.

triad: A chord of three tones, reducible to a fifth divided by a third.

trill: An ornamental figure consisting of the rapid alternation of a principal note with the note directly above.

trio: A composition for three instruments. The second part of a minuet, called *trio* because originally it was often performed by three instruments. A group of three performers.

trio sonata: A standard layout for baroque music, in which two actively melodic voices move above a figured bass. Actually, there were four performers: the two solo instruments, a keyboard or lute performer who played the bass and completed the harmony, and a bass instrument to reinforce the bass.

tritone: The augmented fourth, involving three whole steps, as F to B. The term is also applied to inversion of the augumented fourth, i.e., the diminished fifth, since both have a similar function of creating harmonic tension so as to indicate a tonal center.

trope: An insertion or addition to an established text or formula; particularly an addition to the authorized text of the Mass.

troubadours: Poet-musicians, generally of noble birth, who were active in southern France and northern Italy from the eleventh to the thirteenth centuries.

trouvères: Northern French counterparts of the troubadours.

tutti: The full ensemble; a passage performed by the full ensemble. *Tutti* is distinguished from or opposed to *solo* or *concertino*.

two-part structure (binary form): A form consisting of two complementary sections. The cadence or the point of arrival of the first part usually gives an impression of being incomplete or of requiring further action; the point of arrival or cadence of the second part acts as a completion of the form.

unison: A combination created when two or more voices sound the same tone.

upbeat: A note or group of notes preceding an accented tone. The upbeat usually is found immediately preceding the measure line (or bar line).

variation: The alteration or elaboration of one or more features of a subject or theme. Also compositions in which the procedure of variation is the principal means of carrying the structure forward.

vibrato: A rapid and very small change of pitch in string-instrument and in vocal performance. Properly handled, in moderation, vibrato can add richness and expressive nuance to given tones.

whole-tone scale: A scale which uses only whole-steps, such as C D E F♯ G♯ B♭ C. The exotic effect inherent in this scale was exploited in late romantic and early twentieth-century music.

wood-wind instruments: A family of instruments, constructed of a keyed tube of wood (or metal) and producing the sound by the vibration of a reed (or double-reed) in the mouthpiece (with the exception of the flute). In addition to flutes, the family includes clarinets, oboes, bassoons.

Index

EVOLUTION OF VOCAL MUSIC

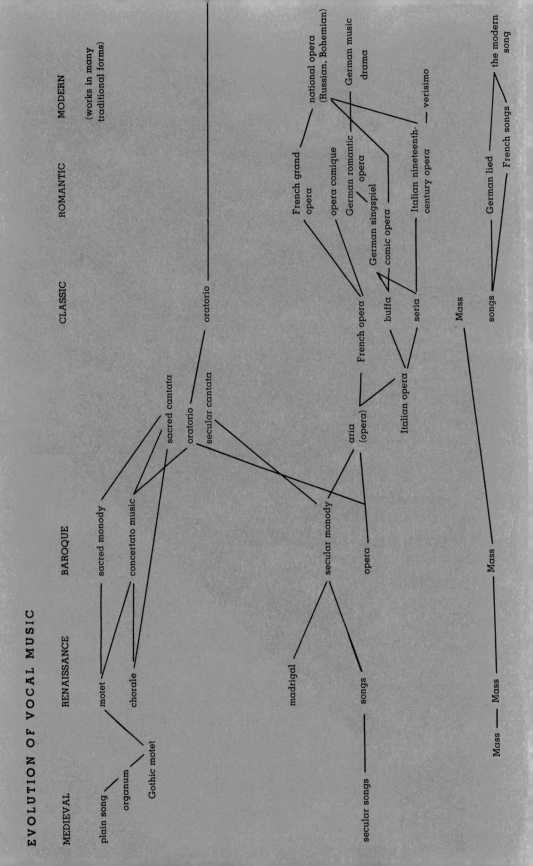

MEDIEVAL	RENAISSANCE	BAROQUE	CLASSIC	ROMANTIC	MODERN

MODERN
(works in many traditional forms)

national opera (Russian, Bohemian)
German music drama
verisimo
the modern song

French grand opera
opera comique
German romantic opera
German singspiel
comic opera
Italian nineteenth-century opera
German lied
French songs

oratorio

sacred cantata
oratorio
secular cantata

French opera
buffa
seria
Mass
songs

sacred monody
concertato music

aria (opera)
Italian opera

motet
chorale

secular monody
opera

Mass

plain song
organum
Gothic motet

madrigal
songs

secular songs

Mass — Mass — Mass